Transcripts:	Susan Cook
Project Editor:	Loyneta Rhorer
Text Design:	Michelle Foote
Cover Design:	Bruce Thompson

For information about the videotapes designed to accompany this book, write or call:

The Educational Video Group
291 Southwind Way
Greenwood, Indiana 46142
(317) 888-6581

To Showalter Fountain, the
Commons, the Gables, and
Nick's English Hut

PREFACE

This collection of speeches and critical essays is designed for classes in contemporary public address, political communication, persuasion, speech criticism, speechwriting, and any other class in which speech texts will be useful. To facilitate comparison and analysis, each chapter in this book highlights speeches which share a common purpose. Obviously, the instructor of the individual class may wish to use an alternative format such as thematic, or chronological.

Political activity entails certain recurring tasks which evoke speeches that share common characteristics. In a democratic society, a primary purpose of political activity is the winning of elections. Two types of speeches predominate at this stage of political communication. Campaign speeches must influence an electorate increasingly characterized by independent voters who do not identify strongly with either party. Rally speeches attempt to motivate already committed supporters to active involvement in a campaign.

At times during a campaign or during a career a prominent figure will face an attack on his or her character. Although speeches of prosecution and defense more properly belong to legal speaking, public figures frequently find themselves in the court of public opinion where accusations of immoral or illegal activity must be answered to the satisfaction of the general public. At times this metaphorical court becomes an actual trial before a Congressional investigating committee in which testimony is compelled by subpoena and the possibility of impeachment for criminal activity arises.

Once elected, the office holder faces the difficult task of governing. The issues that seemed so simple during the campaign now become far more complicated as the search for consensus among various interest groups comes to the fore. Legislative speeches weigh the means and ends of public policy. Designed to influence public opinion they are common to this stage of political communication.

Political activity is not without its ceremonial aspects as political figures perform the rituals that remind the public of its heritage and its commitment to certain fundamental values. The manipulation of political symbols is an important function of political communication. Certain ceremonial occasions such as inauguration day or the eulogizing of an important public figure unite the speaker and the audience in the celebration of the basic values of the society and promote a vision of the better life that is the promise of political action.

This work includes chapters devoted to all of these rhetorical purposes and, contains both transcripts of speeches and critical examinations of those efforts. Obviously, not all of the speakers included herein are elected officials but they all are or have been influentially involved in issues of public affairs. The editors concede that many outstanding speeches have necessarily been omitted. The selection process included the evaluation of speeches for their appropriateness as models of each purpose, the desire for contrasting styles and the historic significance of both the speaker and the speech. Visual footage of all the speeches is contained in the *Great Speeches* video series which has been produced as a component of this project. The transcripts were constructed from the video footage of the actual presentation. The author/editors of this book believe that it is unique in its ability to afford the student of public discourse an opportunity to practice "speech criticism." Other books which include "texts" of speeches draw their content either from press releases or periodicals which allow the speaker to alter the text prior to publication. With these texts the student can at best practice only literary criticism. Frankly, after comparing our transcripts with those speech texts, we have frequently been surprised how dissimilar they are. Offering these *exact* transcripts has been a difficult undertaking but we hope the serious student of public address will benefit from the effort. Speakers rarely say what they planned to say or even what they wanted to say.

Several of the transcripts are followed by critical analyses, most of which were written exclusively for *Great Speeches*. Only a few of the speeches have received this critical treatment, leaving most for the reader's self-evaluation.

Part I of the book includes a chapter on the various critical theories employed by scholars to evaluate speeches. Students of public address and rhetorical theory will find this discussion useful in their consideration of the speeches provided in the text and on the videotapes.

This project has evolved over a period of years and the authors wish to thank the rhetorical scholars who have contributed to the book and the many others who have suggested content material. We extend a special thanks to Mac Cripe of Butler University who shared our dream and contributed his experience and talents to the development of this text/video project.

TABLE OF CONTENTS

PART I:
AN INTRODUCTION

CHAPTER 1:

Critical Perspectives: A Brief Introduction

Lloyd E. Rohler

If human nature is any guide, the criticism of public speaking began in the long forgotten past when the first man gave the first speech to an audience of our primitive ancestors. The first speech may have been greeted with grunts of approval or possibly a shower of sticks and stones to express the antagonism of the audience to the speaker's plans. It seems natural that man as the only animal endowed with conscientiousness should sort out and evaluate the possibilities available to him. Since speech is the primary means of communicating ideas, the criticism of public speaking has an important role in the proper functioning of society that goes beyond the mere granting of approval or disapproval. Criticism of the public dialogue in a democratic society is vital to improving the understanding of the many complex issues on which the public must pass judgment. This book is designed to contribute to that process by providing a brief survey of the major critical methods, and texts of important contemporary speeches for reading and analysis and several critical essays to serve as guides in helping the reader to develop a critical perspective. The *Great Speeches* series of videotapes that accompany this book are an important part of the critical process that technology has made available to the student.

Public speaking is an art form based on natural ability, study of the basic principles of rhetoric, and extensive practice. By definition, an art is the systematic application of knowledge by a creative individual to produce a certain result or effect. The public speaker uses his skill and inspiration to affect the audience in some way. In common with such other arts as painting or composing, speechmaking does not have a mechanical process that guarantees to produce a successful work. A knowledgeable and experienced speaker with a pleasing voice and an imposing presence may still fail to inspire an audience. Certainly part of the fascination surrounding a major political speech derives from the possibility that even the most carefully crafted effort by an important public figure will fail.

Understanding the reasons for the success of some speeches and the failure of others is essential to improving the theory, the teaching, and the practice of public speaking. Rhetoricians have been concerned with this problem since the study of speech began in Ancient Greece in the Fifth Century B.C. Plato and Aristotle established the basis for a systematic inquiry by identifying the elements in the speech situation and by providing a critical analysis of the techniques taught by the Sophists, the travelling teachers who originated the teaching of public speaking.

THE CLASSICAL CRITICAL SYSTEM

Classical rhetoricians identified four elements in the speech situation that interact: the speaker, the speech, the audience, and the occasion. Each element contributes to the overall effectiveness of the speech in its own right, but the interaction of the elements can be crucial to the success or failure of the speech.

The personal characteristics of the speaker as projected through his delivery and self-presentation to the audience are vital to the success or failure of the speech. Great speakers are able to convey to the audience a sense of the person behind the message—a meaning that resides not in the mere text but in the life of the speaker himself.

The audience brings to the speech situation its own expectations, experiences, and values. Often the audience's emotions have been aroused before the speaker begins. Sometimes the audience has had the experience of listening to the speaker before. The audience is aware of certain stylistic preferences or idiosyncratic behaviors and anticipates them. When achieved, the symbolic union of the speaker and the audience at a moment in time is the unique characteristic of public speech.

The speaker has a text (message) to deliver. In some cases the speaker actually wrote the speech. More commonly, the basic text was written by others and the speaker edited it to conform to his personal style. Whether he wrote the entire text or merely parts of it, the speech text is the speaker's responsibility. He will have to answer for the accuracy of its details, the truth of its charges, and the meaning of its message. What the speaker says is important. The reasons he gives to justify policies or actions will be scrutinized by others. Often a speech that is delivered to a favorable audience will be read much more critically by another. Confronted by multiple audiences and critical interpretations by the news media, a contemporary speaker must weigh the relative importance of each to his goal as a speaker and address each, according to his priorities, in the text of his address.

Lastly, the occasion will influence the speaker's reception, the text of the speech, and the audience's expectations. A ceremonial occasion such as Inauguration Day with its high drama of state and its rich tradition of solemn ceremony will heighten the patriotic feelings of the audience and make it more receptive to the speech of the newly elected President. Similarly, the solemnity of the occasion will influence the text of the speech and the demeanor of the speaker.

Although as critics we often focus attention on one or more of these elements in the speech situation to explain the success or failure of a speech, we must not forget that the speech situation is dynamic. All of these elements interact and contribute something to the total success or failure of the speech.

For convenience in teaching rhetoric to their pupils, classical rhetoricians divided the subject into five parts: invention, arrangement, style, delivery, and memory. Each division is an important component in the process of composing and presenting a speech. In the discussion that follows, references are made to speeches collected in this text, which are available for viewing on the *Great Speeches* videotapes.

Invention refers to the speaker's use of the resources at his disposal. These involve the three forms of proof: *ethos*, the speaker's reputation or personal credibility; *logos*, the rational arguments and evidence that the speaker gives to support his claims; and *pathos*, the psychological or emotional appeals that the speaker makes to the audience. Speakers rarely use one of these forms of proof to the exclusion of the others. The forms of proof are usually combined for total effect. For example, when Martin Luther King claimed that black Americans felt like exiles in their own land, he used his own credibility as a black American who grew up under a segregated school system, combined with specific examples or evidence of segregation in public accommodations and emotional appeals such as patriotic and religious symbols to reinforce his conclusion that segregation was "a shameful condition."

When, as critics, we examine a speaker's invention, we are concerned with his analysis of the situation and his use of the entire range of available proofs to create a speech to influence an audience. Each speaker chooses those proofs that he feels will most effectively accomplish his objectives. This reveals to the critic the speaker's view of himself and his evaluation of the critical abilities of the audience. For example, emotional appeals without any rational proof may produce a dramatic audience response but have a relatively short-lived impact. Critics quickly note a speaker's overreliance on such appeals and question his objectives and sincerity. Similarly, a critic recognizing MacArthur's exclusive reliance on his *ethos* as a means of proof in his "Farewell Address" might question the wisdom of this choice and consider what alternatives were available to him. To a great extent a speaker's use of invention is a key indication of his character, his objectives, and his attitude toward his audience.

Arrangement refers to the order of the ideas in the speech. Critics generally divide arrangement into two categories: the general strategy that the speaker uses in adapting his ideas to the audience and the more specific organization pattern. Effective speeches have a psychologically compelling order that effectively moves the audience from acceptance of one idea to another. Often great emphasis is placed on the introduction to secure goodwill and to conciliate any negative feelings that the audience might have toward the speaker's position. A good example of this strategy is Senator Edward Kennedy's speech to a convocation at Liberty Baptist College in which his introduction compliments the Reverend Jerry Falwell for his generous introduction, uses humor to lessen tension and to secure goodwill, and calls for a fair hearing of divergent views such as his own. Once audience goodwill has been secured, Kennedy then advances from general principles to specific applications to move the audience toward his position.

Often ceremonial speeches follow the sequence of past, present, and future; recalling glorious actions in the past, singling out important aspects of the present, and predicting great accomplishments in the future. This is the pattern of Martin Luther King's "I Have A Dream" Speech (videotape Volume I). He locates the promise of freedom in the sacred writing of the Founding Fathers and the Emancipation Proclamation, notes the failure of the present to make real those promises, and dreams of the glorious day in the future when the promises will come true. Franklin Roosevelt, in his Declaration of War Address, follows a similar sequence when he recounts the terrible events of "Yesterday, December 7, 1941," describes the difficulties immediately confronting the American people, and predicts the great victory that lies ahead for the United States and its allies.

The specific organization pattern used by the speaker contributes clarity to the speech. It aids the audience in following the arguments and it indicates the relationship among ideas. Through subordination, it reveals the ideas the speaker considers most important. Organization patterns may vary widely from speech to speech depending on purpose and length. All speeches have an introduction, a body and a conclusion. Many include a section anticipating counter attacks and answering them. Ceremonial speeches usually follow the past, present, and future sequence.

A speaker's style is his signature. In combination with delivery, it reveals his sense of who he is and what he is about. The speakers's choice of words involves matters of taste and reveals a sensitivity to what is appropriate to the situation, and to the audience. It is also an index to his knowledge of his culture as it has been transmitted through the language and the literature. A speaker's style is not uniform, but must be adapted to the situation and to the needs of the audience. The classical rhetoricians recognized three levels of style—plain, middle, and grand—which correspond to the three purposes of the speaker—to instruct, to delight, and to move or persuade. The plain or natural style is conversational and appropriate to conveying information. The middle style is more metaphorical or philosophical and corresponds to pleasing or delighting an audience. The grand style is vigorous, abundant, or profuse, and is used to persuade. The three levels of style may be used in one speech or a single style may be relied upon exclusively. When a professor speaks to a civic club about a recent trip he and his class made to England, he may use both the plain and middle styles. If the same speaker gives a commencement address, he might rely on the grand style. John Kennedy's Inaugural Address is in the grand style. The word choice, the sentence structure, and the abounding use of metaphors aim for an overwhelming effect on the audience. In contrast, General MacArthur's speech is predominately in the plain style as he informs his audience of the situation in the Pacific.

Delivery may be divided into two parts, physical action and voice, although obviously both combine to make a strong impression on the audience. The use of physical action to convey meaning is the most difficult skill for beginning speakers to develop, and has posed problems for teachers of public speaking as well. There are two approaches to the teaching of gestures; natural and artificial. The natural approach relies on the emotional involvement of the speaker in the speech situation to motivate physical activity. If a speaker feels strongly about his message, he will be carried along by his emotions and physically display his concern. The artificial school believes that this may occur for experienced speakers, but beginning speakers will need rehearsal and conscious effort. The speakers on the accompanying tapes predominantly follow the advice of the natural school with only Hitler subscribing to the artificial school and consciously rehearsing his gestures.

Before the development of newsreels, motion pictures, and television, a speaker needed broad gestures to project vitality and convey emphasis and meaning to large crowds that could only view the speaker from a distance. With television close-up pictures, a mass audience of millions of individuals can easily see facial expressions involving small movements of the eyes. As a consequence broad sweeping movements of the arms are not only unnecessary but appear exaggerated. Obviously a speaker's style is greatly influenced by the media of the era. Adolf Hitler was most effective when he appeared in person before mass rallies. Franklin Roosevelt brought his intimate "Fireside Chats" into living rooms throughout the country on radio. John Kennedy effectively utilized the visual dimension of television to project the image of a vigorous young leader with his boyish grin, confident gaze, and quick wit.

Memory is the last division of classical rhetoric and the most neglected today. In an age of teleprompters, speakers need not take the time to memorize their speeches. Elaborate systems of mnemonic devices such as the Ancients used are passé. But memory meant more to the Ancients than the ability to recite a text. It included familiarity with the commonplaces—those lines from poetry, sacred hymns, popular songs, nonsense rhymes, and fables that encompassed the collective wisdom and experience of the culture. In ancient Greece and Rome, books were expensive and rare. The education of the young included memorization of long passages of epic poetry, stories of the gods, and exploits of the heroic warriors and leaders of the past. Today's educational system rarely asks the student to memorize even a line from the great literature of our past. What we have lost is well illustrated on the videotape of Martin Luther King's speech. The entire "I have a dream" sequence was not a part of King's written text. He completely extemporized the lines—finding them in his memory. He took lines from previous speeches, verses from the Bible, stanzas from patriotic songs and Negro spirituals to make a moving and memorable conclusion. In doing so, he illustrated for the contemporary student the value of memory, i.e., having a storehouse of commonplaces that can be called upon when necessary.

The Greek and Roman rhetoricians noticed that rhetorical forms used by speakers in recurring situations shared certain characteristics. Legal speeches addressed the issues of justice or injustice and primarily used the tactics of accusation and defense. Epideictic or ceremonial speeches focused on honor and dishonor and utilized praise or blame. Political or deliberative speeches primarily addressed the advantages or disadvantages of policy choices and used encouragement or warnings to move the audience. These genres or types represent only a speech's general tendency; rarely will a speech be a pure example of one type. Identifying the genre of a speech will help to clarify the speaker's duties and aid in evaluating how well he utilized the persuasiveness of form to satisfy audience expectations.

NEO-ARISTOTELIAN CRITICAL SYSTEM

Aristotle considered rhetoric, the art of persuasion, distinct and poetic, which is the realm of imaginative literature. Following Aristotle's lead, Herbert Wichelns wrote an influential essay in 1925, "Literary Criticism of Oratory," which initiated a critical movement that profoundly influenced the scholarly criticism of public speeches in America. Wichelns distinguished a public speech and its criticism from a literary work and its criticism by the differing purposes of the two discourses. A literary work such as a poem is an autonomous work that is complete in and of itself. In contrast, a speech always addresses an audience and is designed to achieve some specific purpose. The very term "public address" which is used as a synonym for a speech implies an audience which is "addressed" or spoken to by an individual. Frequently in contemporary literature, the sense that the work has any relationship to an audience or to the real world is completely lacking. Many literary works are entirely self-referential. The "world" of the poem or novel or play is self-contained as it unravels or turns back upon itself. The complexity of the language and the opaqueness of the work to an uninitiated reader unfamiliar with the latest critical exegesis serve as a barrier to understanding. In contrast, a speech must be accessible to its audience and the speaker desires to achieve certain effects with his presentation. The speech is not a literary artifact to be admired for its beauty and technique nor mined for meaning at leisure but a vital attempt to influence the audience to accept the speaker's view.

The emphasis upon the effect of the speech means that neo-Aristotelian criticism of speeches has been inescapably influenced by the temporal nature of public speaking. There is no escaping the truism that a public speech is a product of the time, and that nothing is so old as yesterday's news. Speeches that once stimulated the imagination of an audience, that moved the conscience, that touched the very soul of every person present, when read today may bring boredom and a stifled yawn. To compensate for this difficulty, many critics focus on factors external to the speech itself in an attempt to situate the speech in its time and place. To do so requires adopting the methods of the historian to recreate the events that influenced the composition and delivery of the speech. The critic often uses biography to understand the role that the speaker plays in the historical drama and to understand the speaker's personal contribution to the speech situation. At times the critic uses the methods of the sociologist to understand the forces that move an issue to the forefront of the society or to study the speech as one event and the speaker as one actor in a complex social movement for change. In adopting these methods, the critic imaginatively recreates the situation that inspired the speech to gain a greater understanding of the constraints that the speaker faced and the strategy that the speaker used to overcome them. Such a recreation requires both a description of the actual events and an interpretation of them. The critic must know what happened but mere description is not enough. The critic must confront the more important and more difficult question of "Why did it happen?" To successfully answer this requires interpretation of the facts. It requires an imaginative act in which the critic weighs the relative importance of the factors involved, identifies the constraints operating on the speaker, and provides an explanation that satisfactorily deals with the known facts.

The classical system outlined above focused on the construction of a persuasive message for a particular audience. It assumed that certain recurring rhetorical forms succeed because they correspond to the way individual members of the audience decide upon the "Truth." The selection of proofs, and their arrangement in a certain format compels the audience to accept the claims of the speaker because the total effect of the message is satisfying. Given the assumptions of the system, audience response became the major criterion for evaluating the success or failure of a speech. A successful speech satisfies the requirements of the situation and gains audience approval. The system did not limit the critic's role to measuring the amount of applause or gauging the public mood. The critic evaluated the speech against an ideal standard. Did the speaker utilize all the available proofs to achieve the maximum impact on the audience? The speech may have gained the approval of some members of the audience but not others. The critic might decide that a different strategy would have made the speech far more successful.

The development of the mass media and the multiplication of audiences has modified this criterion for the contemporary critic. Often speeches are staged before a friendly audience but really designed to influence those listening or viewing the speech far removed from the speaker in space and time. Given this situation, the critic must clearly specify the nature of the speaker's "true" audience and the speaker's effectiveness with that audience. Is the speech to be judged by the reactions of the immediate audience or the delayed effect it has on the opinion leaders of the society? Is the critic concerned with the long-term effect of the speech on public opinion as reflected in actual public policy choice?

Some of these effects are easier to determine than others. We can count the number of times the immediate audience interrupted the speech with applause and we can see visible reactions of agreement or disagreement on films made of the event. The delayed reaction of public opinion leaders can be followed in the editorial columns of the newspapers and journals of opinion in the days following the speech. Sometimes public opinion polls are available to document swings in the public mood following a major speech by a leading political figure. Over an extended period of time, the critic may find recurring references in interviews, speeches, public documents, autobiographical accounts, and scholarly studies to a major speech as the catalyst of change. Even then the critic must be aware of the many factors that influence public opinion and the many pressures that shape policy making and not overestimate the influence of a single speech.

Another way to assess the effectiveness of a speech is to focus on the effect it had on the speaker's overall objectives. The critic can try to understand the speaker's motivation for giving the speech and assess how completely it achieved his purpose. If the speaker gave the speech to gain the nomination for a political office, did the speech help or hinder in the effort? The critic must realize that a speaker may have several goals in mind for a speech and that failure to achieve the primary goal may not make the speech a total failure. A well received speech in a losing cause may be counted a partial success if it brings recognition and marks the speaker as a rising star. John Kennedy's nominating speech for Adlai Stevenson in the 1956 Democratic Convention did not gain him the vice presidential nomination that he sought, but it immensely increased his credibility as a candidate when he began his quest for the 1960 presidential nomination. How the speech influenced the speaker's reputation may be assessed by examining political commentary and public opinion polls.

If the critic is examining delayed effects he may note whether the speech affected the ability of the speaker to act in ways that hindered his career. Sometimes speakers become the victim of their own words. Richard Nixon found that speeches on the growing political scandal in his administration not only failed to gain him public support but limited his freedom of action. Sometimes speakers make predictions or issue warnings that later events prove false. The series of speeches that Charles Lindbergh made against American intervention in Europe prior to the Japanese attack on Pearl Harbor greatly diminished his heroic status.

Several examples of this form of classical criticism appear in this text. One excellent example is Nicholas Cripe's evaluation of John Kennedy's Inaugural Address showing how the blend of the speaker, the occasion and the speech combine to create a memorable moment in American history.

SYMBOLIC INTERACTION OR DRAMATISM AS A CRITICAL SYSTEM

The revived Aristotelian system reigned supreme in academic speech circles and dominated criticism for almost thirty years. In the 1960's dissatisfaction with the dominant methodology began to surface and criticism began to resemble the pluralistic society of which is was a part. Many new approaches competed for the allegiance of the practicing critic. Perhaps no other approach won as many adherents or seemed as influential as the symbolic interactionist or dramatistic method based on the writings and practice of Kenneth Burke.

Dramatistic criticism begins with the premise that man is the symbol creating and using animal. Communication creates a symbolic world through the ability of human beings to make and use symbols. The human condition is an alienated existence in which each person finds himself alone in the world. Man has the ability to transcend this condition through symbolic identification with others. The function of rhetoric is to produce union by inducing cooperation through symbols. It does so through the process of consubstantiality: the sharing of substance symbolically which overcomes the division at the base of the human condition.

Symbols are not limited to messages or even words. Anything can take on symbolic import if it is capable of producing identification. For example, objects such as possessions that identify a person as a member of a group or class or with a particular life style has symbolic meaning, as do hairstyles, clothes, and pets. Membership in various groups, organizations, or institutions such as colleges and universities creates identification with others. Participation in certain communal activities such as watching the Super Bowl or the World Series or attending a rock concert or peace demonstration also functions symbolically to bring people together and to overcome division. The rhetorical critic using this method must be sensitive to the entire range of symbolic meanings in a rhetorical situation.

In addition to identification and consubstantiality, other key terms in this critical method include hierarchy, guilt, purification, and redemption. Hierarchy refers to the structure of the social order. Our technological society is structured along the lines of a pyramid with many people at the base and relatively few people at the top. The further up the pyramid an individual climbs, the more privileges he enjoys. At the same time, a belief system based on the democratic values of equality makes him feel guilty about all those who are left behind. Exercising privilege or status creates a tension in the mind between man's ability to conceptualize a perfect society in which all men would share in the good life and the nagging realization that the world is imperfect and filled with suffering. In an attempt to rid himself of guilt, man undergoes purification rituals that often involve finding scapegoats that can be blamed for the imperfect world and, thus, relieve man of his burden. Frequently, the scapegoat is an outsider of a different religion or race or nationality whose very difference makes the transference of guilt easier. Once the rite of purification has been performed the individual feels redeemed or made acceptable again and able to function in the hierarchy until the burden of guilt becomes again overbearing and the process repeats itself.

The best illustration of this process is Burke's own analysis of Nazi rhetoric that inflamed Germany in the 1930's. Following the defeat in World War I, Germany paid a heavy price in the loss of the traditional government headed by the Kaiser, the seizure of territories by the allies and the imposition of huge reparations or payments for the destruction caused by the war. Following a brief postwar posterity, Germany suffered a ruinous inflation and then the devastation created by the worldwide depression of the 1930's. Many Germans facing starvation and suffering during these grim years, felt guilt for the suffering of their families and friends, and sought a means of salvation. Adolf Hitler and his party provided the means of purification and redemption through scapegoating the Jews. By joining the Nazi party or voting for Hitler, the desperate German people achieved unity with a vision of the greatness of the past and a dream of better days ahead. Their guilt for the postwar failures, could be transferred to the Jews and, redeemed at last, they would seek salvation through Hitler and his leadership.

The strength of this analysis is the focus on unconscious processes that are released through the manipulation of symbolic means. Rather than focus on an individual speech, Burke does not ignore Hitler's messages. In fact, his discussion of the Nazis focuses on Hitler's writings, especially *Mine Kampf.* However, the message is examined not for the kinds of proofs that it contains or the content *per se*, but as a means of transmitting a symbolic inducement to cooperate with others in advancing the Nazi cause.

Burke's system is usually referred to as dramatistic criticism because he borrowed the vocabulary of the theatre to identify the various perspectives that the critic could take in analyzing a rhetorical situation. The five elements of the pentad are: agent, act, agency, scene, and purpose. These terms correspond to the traditional questions of the journalist: who (the agent) did what (the act), how (the agency), where (the scene) and why (the purpose)? The pentad is useful is reminding the rhetorical critic that a rhetorical situation is not a unitary action but a blend of many elements. In using the pentad, the critic may focus on one or many perspectives or try to establish the relative weight of one term to another. For example, in some situations the scene may exert more influence than the agent as when a priest delivers a homily in a magnificent cathedral. In other situations, the agent may be more significant than the purpose as when a glamorous celebrity such as Robert Redford makes a personal appearance at a shopping center. By focusing on the dominant term in the pentad, the critic can gain a clearer understanding of the symbolic transaction and by exploring the relationship of the dominant term to the others, the critic can discover the multiple meanings of the event.

As an example of symbolic interaction, this author's essay evaluating John Kennedy's address to the Houston Ministerial Association provides an example of how Kennedy's speech symbolically called for the "American Dream" to achieve, his persuasive goals. By accepting Kennedy's arguments the audience can validate the American values of toleration and fair play.

STYLISTIC OR LINGUISTIC CRITICISM

Aristotle separated rhetoric from poetic, investigated each subject and wrote seminal work in each field. Even in Aristotle's time, the distinction between rhetoric and poetic began to break down under the influence of Isocrates who wrote essays in the form of speeches that were never intended to be delivered in the conventional sense. The convergence of rhetoric and poetic in our time has been fostered by advances in the fields of semantics and linguistics which focus on the word as a symbol of meaning. Obviously both rhetoric and poetic depend on words to convey meaning. Methods for analyzing the meaning of metaphors or images in a poem should also be effective in discovering the meaning of metaphors in a public speech.

Both I.A. Richards and Richard Weaver have demonstrated the value of close analysis of language and style in criticizing speeches. Unlike their predecessors in the Renaissance who saw language as ornamentation and delighted in classifying every possible scheme and trope, Richards and Weaver view language choice as central to meaning and not a mere decoration to give variety to discourse. Key concepts in this approach include the qualities of language such as abstraction and ambiguity, the choices implied by grammatical structure and the characteristic use of figures of speech, especially metaphor. Although this approach is primarily intrinsic or internal criticism, in skillful hands it can reveal much about the speaker and the times. For example, a study of the characteristic metaphors employed by a speaker may reveal a mechanistic view of the universe or a mercantile bent. Weaver has even suggested that the characteristic form of argument can reveal basic philosophical differences in the worldview of a conservative and a liberal. David Henry's critical essay on Mario Cuomo's keynote address is an excellent example of the strength of this critical analysis. Henry identifies "family" as the key metaphorical term in Cuomo's speech and demonstrates how effectively he used this metaphor to frame his argument that the Democrats not the Republicans can best advance the family ideals that are the basis of the middle class.

GENRE CRITICISM

Both stylistic criticism and genre criticism share a concern for underlying forms, and a tendency to examine a speech from a formalistic perspective that emphasizes basic principles and patterns of discourse. Genre comes from the French word meaning form or pattern and genre critics are interested in analyzing groups of speeches or closely related units of discourse to discover common characteristics of style, structure or situational response. For example, by examining several eulogies from diverse time periods such as Ancient Greece and Rome, Medieval Europe, Victorian England, and the contemporary United States, the critic may uncover recurring patterns of organization, of forms, of proof or variations on a common metaphor. If eulogies from such diverse societies and time periods share a common form, then the critic has discovered something that is permanent and enduring over time. This may lead to stronger and more powerful theories about human communication, and it is certainly helpful in teaching students to write speeches by identifying effective formats.

Roger Cook in his essay on Robert Kennedy's eulogy of Martin Luther King, Jr., illustrates the value of genre analysis by showing that Kennedy's extemporaneous speech gained its power not only from the overwhelming emotion experienced by both the speaker and audience but also from the psychological satisfaction provided by the underlying structure of the speech. Similarly, Richard Katula's analysis of Nixon's resignation draws upon the work of two contemporary critics of the genre of apology to explain that speech's failure as a result of Nixon's unwillingness to meet the demands of the form and own up to his personal responsibility for the collapse of his administration.

FANTASY THEME ANALYSIS

This critical method shares the constructivist perspective that social reality is mutually constructed through communication, and derives from an insight of small group research. Frequently small groups will cooperate to develop a group fantasy— a shared understanding or explanation of some difficulty that the group is experiencing or some dream that they have of the future. For example, a group of high school students who form a band may interrupt a practice session to fantasize that some day the band will be discovered and they will make hit record after hit record. Obviously, this fantasy will probably be limited to the band and a small group of friends. Other fantasies may chain out from the original small groups and come to dominate the consciousness of larger and larger social groups. Perhaps this was the very process by which small groups of black Americans began to dream of ending segregation and attaining equality. As the fantasy chained out into larger and larger groups through such mechanisms as the black church and black social groups, white Americans began to share the fantasy. As it was transmitted to larger and larger audiences through communication contexts such as public speeches, demonstrations, and marches, it became a rhetorical vision and found its most profound expression in Martin Luther King's March on Washington Speech. When the fantasy moves from small groups to a larger audience through rhetorical transactions, it is gradually molded and shaped into a full scale rhetorical vision. The rhetorical critic may focus on the individual rhetorical vision or adopt the method of the genre critic and investigate recurring scenarios in an effort to understand the process of constructing heroes and villains. This method focuses attention on interaction between the audience and the message. Critics may be more concerned with the motivation of the audience and how the audience uses the information provided by the speaker. Although most of the criticism that uses this method attempts to identify fantasy themes that worked, it is possible to use the insights from this analysis and identify speeches that failed to develop a fantasy theme that could move the audience to concerted action. Robert Denton uses a variation on this method suggested by Rod Hart to analyze the values underlying President Carter's Energy Address. Denton's analysis suggests that one reason for the failure of the speech is that it did not promote the chaining necessary for group fantasies and thus was not able to sustain a rhetorical vision necessary for effective political action.

BECOMING AN EFFECTIVE CRITIC

It is impossible in this short space to discuss the various critical systems or methodologies in great detail. This essay is designed to be suggestive: to stimulate your interest in criticism and to get you started thinking about the various ways to evaluate a speech. Some interesting approaches are not formulized as critical schools but combine insights into the way technology has influenced the nature of the speaker-audience relationship with rhetorical analysis of the speech itself. The essay by Solomon and Stewart on Jesse Jackson is illustrative of this type of analysis. Since the videotapes contain speeches dating back to Roosevelt's First Inaugural given in 1933, through Nixon's "Checkers" speech in 1952, and George Bush's speeches on the Gulf War, the instructor may wish to devote class time to a discussion of the way that television has effected public speaking. Students may want to elect this topic for a written assignment.

The following bibliography contains some of the most influential articles and books on criticism, and should provide direction for further study.

BOOKS

James R. Andrews, *The Practice of Rhetorical Criticism*, 2nd ed. (New York and London: Longman, 1990).

Edwin Black, *Rhetorical Criticism: A Study in Method* (New York: Macmillan, 1965, rptd. Madison: University of Wisconsin Press, 1978).

Bernard L. Brock, Robert L. Scott and James W. Chesebro, eds., *Methods of Rhetorical Criticism: A Twentieth Century Perspective*, 3rd. ed. (Detroit: Wayne State University Press, 1989).

Karlyn Kohrs Campbell and Kathleen Hall Jamieson, eds., *Form and Genre: Shaping Rhetorical Action* (Falls Church, VA: Speech Communication Association, 1978).

Sonja K. Foss, *Rhetorical Criticism* (Prospect Hts., IL: Waveland Press, Inc., 1989).

Roderick P. Hart, *Modern Rhetorical Criticism* (Glenview: Scott, Foresman, 1990).

Anthony Hilbruner, *Critical Dimensions: The Art of Public Address Criticism* (New York: Random House, 1966).

Marie Hochmuth Nichols, *Rhetoric and Criticism* (Baton Rouge: Louisiana State university, 1963).

Lester Thonssenl and A. Craig Baird, *Speech Criticism* (New York: Ronald Press, 1976).

ARTICLES

Neo Aristotelian Criticism

Herbert W. Wichelns, "The Literary Criticism of Oratory," in *Studies in Rhetoric and Public*

Speaking in Honor of James Albert Winans, by pupils and colleagues. The Century Company, 1925. Reprinted in *Methods of Rhetorical Criticism: A Twentieth Century Perspective,* by Bernard L. Brock and Robert L. Scott. 2nd ed. (Detroit: Wayne State University Press, 1980), pp. 40-72.

Historical Criticism
W. Charles Redding, "Extrinsic and Intrinsic Criticism," *Western Speech* 21 (1957), pp. 96-102.

Burkean Criticism
Kenneth Burke, "The Rhetoric of Hitler's 'Battle,'" in *The Philosophy of Literary Form: Studies in Symbolic Action,* 3rd ed. (University of California Press, 1973).

Marie Hochmuth, "Kenneth Burke and the 'New Rhetoric,'" *Quarterly Journal of Speech* 38 (1952), pp. 133-44.

L. Virginia Holland, "Kenneth Burke's Dramatistic Approach in Speech Criticism," *Quarterly Journal of Speech* 41 (1955), pp. 352-58.

Fantasy Theme and Rhetorical Vision Criticism
Ernest G. Bormann, "Fantasy and Rhetorical Vision: The Rhetorical Criticism of Social Reality," *Quarterly Journal of Speech* 58 (1972), pp. 396-407.

Stylistic Criticism
Hermann G. Stelzner, "War Message, December 8, 1941: An Approach to Language," *Speech Monographs* 33 (1966), pp. 419-37.

Metaphoric Criticism
Michael Osborn, "Archetypal Metaphor in Rhetoric: The light-Dark Family," *Quarterly Journal of Speech* 53 (1967), pp. 115-26.

Generic Criticism
Thomas Clark, "An Analysis of Recurrent Features of Contemporary American Radical, Liberal, and Conservative Political Discourse," *Southern Speech Communication Journal* 44 (1979), pp. 399-422.

B. L. Ware and Wil A. Linkugel, "They Spoke in Defense of Themselves: On the Generic Criticism of Apologia," *Quarterly Journal of Speech* 59 (1973), pp. 273-83.

Ghostwriters
Lois J. Einhorn, "The Ghosts Unmasked: A Review of Literature on Speechwriting," *Communication Quarterly* 30 (1981), pp. 41-47.

PART II: DELIBERATIVE SPEECHES

CHAPTER 2:

Campaign Speeches

Prior to influencing policy or the machinery of government and prerequisite to most other forms of political communication, a politician must seek office. The campaign speech, old as the democracies of ancient Greece and Rome, provides a vehicle for political office seekers to solicit and solidify support. They do so by depicting themselves within the broad boundaries of popular ideology and tradition. In contrast, they characterize their opponents' positions as alien to this acceptable belief system.

We first offer a speech by Harry Truman from his historic "Whistle Stop" campaign. This hard hitting address at Dexter, Iowa was crafted by his advisors to initiate the attack on the Republicans and their candidate, Thomas Dewey. John Kennedy's speech to the Greater Houston Ministerial Association marked the first time in his campaign that he directly confronted the religious issue by demonstrating the un-American nature of those who would oppose him on religious grounds. Lloyd Rohler examines why this memorable speech may have been the turning point in Kennedy's presidential campaign. Using repetition to generate audience participation in his speech, Hubert Humphrey accepted his party's Vice Presidential Nomination and skillfully portrayed his Republican opposition as representing only the fringe of American thought. Geraldine Ferraro, accepting her party's Vice Presidential nomination, used the American "play by the rules" maxim to attack a popular opponent. Ronald Reagan's 1980 Acceptance Speech masterfully incorporated patriotism and tradition to broaden his appeal.

WHISTLE STOP SPEECH, DEXTER, IOWA

Harry S Truman

National Plowing Match, Dexter, Iowa, September 18, 1948 (Transcribed from the video, GREAT SPEECHES, VOLUME VIII–additional material drawn from various sources)

Mr. Chairman and all the good farmers who are responsible for this wonderful demonstration.

It does my heart good to see the green fields of this Nation once more. They are a wonderful sight. The record-breaking harvests you have been getting in recent years have been a blessing. Millions of people have been saved from starvation by the food you have produced. The whole world has reason to be everlastingly grateful to the farmers of the United States.

In a very real sense, the abundant harvests of this country are helping to save the world from Communism. Communism thrives on human misery. And the crops you are producing are driving back the tide of misery in many lands. Your farms are a vital element in America's foreign policy. Keep that in mind. That's a vital importance to you and to the world.

And while I'm on that subject—I know that the war talk which is so prevalent today is causing all of you deep concern. It is plain enough that we are facing a very disturbing international situation. I should like every American to realize that this country is making every possible effort to preserve the peace. In this critical situation, my motto has been: "Keep your temper and stand firm." We have kept our tempers. We have stood firm. And we have been reasonable and straightforward at all times. It is the policy of this Government to continue working for peace with every instrument at our command. At the same time, we have been rapidly building up our strength. The peace of the world and the prestige of the United States require that the Nation be strong and vigilant.

{But that is not the main point I wish to cover today. In addition to the issue of peace, there is another important reason why this is a critical period for America. I am talking about our economic future—your economic future.

Will this Nation succeed in keeping its prosperity? Will it preserve its high standards of living next year, and the year after, and the year after that? I know of only one way to get assured prosperity. That is by cooperation among agriculture, labor, and business, large and small. When these groups work together in a common cause, this country can achieve miracles. We saw that during the war. We saw it before the war. By common effort, in the last fifteen years, every group in the Nation steadily increased its income.}* Our people rose from despair to the highest living standards in the history of the world. So long as the farmer, the worker and the businessman pull together in the national interest, this country has everything to hope for.

But it is terribly dangerous to let any one group get too much power in the Government. We cannot afford to let one group shape the Nation's policies in its own interest, at the expense of the others. That is what happened in the 1920's, under the big business rule of the Republicans. Those were the days when big corporations had things their own way. The policies that Wall Street big business wanted were the policies that the Republicans adopted. Agriculture, labor, and small business played second fiddle, while big business called the tune.

{Those were the days of Republican high tariffs—tariffs that penalized the American farmer by making him pay high prices for manufactured goods, while he was receiving low prices for his crops.}

You remember the results of that Wall Street Republican policy. You remember the big boom and the great crash of 1929. You remember that in 1932 the position of the farmer had become so desperate that there was actual violence in many farming communities. You remember that insurance companies and banks took over much of the land of small independent farmers. 223,000 farmers lost their farms. That was a painful lesson. It should not be forgotten for one moment.

{Since then, the farmer has come a long way. The agricultural program of the Democratic Administration in sixteen years has enabled farmers to attain decent standards of living. Interest rates on farm credit have been sharply brought down. Farm mortgage indebtedness has been reduced by more than 50 per cent. Farm mortgage foreclosures have almost disappeared.

All this was done under and by Democratic Administrations.

Today the world needs more food than ever before.} There is every reason for the American farmer to expect a long period of good prices—if he continues to get a fair deal. His great danger is that he may be voted out of a fair deal, and into a Republican deal. The Wall Street reactionaries are not satisfied with being rich. They want to increase their power and their privileges, regardless of what happens to the other fellow. They are gluttons of privilege. These gluttons of privilege are now putting up fabulous sums of the money to elect a Republican administration.

Why do you think they are doing that? For the love of the Republican candidates? Or do you think it is because they expect a Republican administration to carry out their will, as it did in the days of Harding, Coolidge and Hoover? I think we know the answer. I think we know that Wall Street expects its money this year to elect a Republican administration that will listen to the gluttons of privilege first, and to serve priv [sic] the people not at all.

Republican reactionaries want an Administration that will assure privilege for big business, regardless of what may happen to the rest of the Nation. The Republican strategy is to divide the farmer and the industrial worker—to get them to squabbling with each other—so that big business can grasp the balance of power and take the country over, lock, stock and barrel.

To gain this end, they will stop at nothing. On the one hand, the Republicans are telling industrial workers that the high cost of food in the cities is due to this Government's farm policy. On the other hand, the Republicans are telling the farmers that the high cost of manufactured goods on the farm is due to this Government's labor policy. That's plain hokum. It's an old political trick. "If you can't convince 'em, confuse 'em." But this time it won't work.

The farmer and the worker know that their troubles have been coming from another source. Those gluttons of privilege remember one plain fact. Never once during the great crises of the past fifty years have the Wall Street Republican Administrations lifted a finger to help the farmer. Wait a minute, wait a minute—they did once. They gave you a Farm Board. That was their great contribution.

How well you must remember the depression of the 1930's. The Republicans gave you that greatest of all depressions—as I said before when hogs went down to three cents, and corn was so cheap that you burned it up.

All through this country the American farmer and the worker have been the victims of boom and bust cycles—with accent on the bust especially for the farmers and the workers. And they have suffered alike in these misfortunes. I wonder how many times you have to be hit on the head before you find out who's hitting you? It's about time that the people of America realized what the Republicans have been doing to them.

{Why is it that the farmer and the worker and the small businessman suffer under Republican administrations and gain under Democratic administrations? I'll tell you why. It is a result of a basic difference in attitude between the Democratic and the Republican parties.}

The Democratic party represents the people. It is pledged to work for agriculture. It is pledged to work for labor. It is pledged to work for the small businessman and the white-collar worker.

The Democratic party puts human rights and human welfare first.

But the attitude of the Republican gluttons of privilege is very different. The big-money Republican looks on agriculture and labor merely as expense items in his business venture. He tries to push their share of the national income down as low as possible and increase his own profits. And he looks upon the Government as a tool to accomplish this purpose.

{These Republican gluttons of privilege are cold men. They are cunning men. And it is their constant aim to put the Government of the United States under the control of men like themselves. They want a return of the Wall Street economic dictatorship.}

You had a sample of what a Republican administration would mean to you. Two years ago, in the Congressional elections, many Americans decided that they would not bother to vote. Others thought they'd like to have a change. And they brought into power a Republican Congress—that notorious "do nothing" 80th Republican Congress.

Let us look at the change—the results of that change. This Republican Congress has already stuck a pitchfork in the farmer's back. They've already done their best to keep the price supports from working. Many growers have sold wheat this summer at less than the support price because they could not find proper storage.

When the Democratic Administration had to face this problem in the past, the Government set up grain bins all over the wheat and corn belts to provide storage. Now the farmers need such bins again. But when the Republican Congress rewrote the charter of the Commodity Credit Corporation this year, there were certain lobbyists in Washington representing the speculative grain trade—your old friends.

These big-business lobbyists and speculators persuaded the Congress not to provide the storage bins for the farmers. They tied the hands of the Administration. They are preventing us from setting up storage bins that you will need in order to get the support price for your grain. When the farmers have to sell their wheat and corn below the support price because they have no place to store it, they can thank this same Republican 80th Congress that gave the speculative grain trade a rake-off at your expense.

But the Republican reactionaries are not satisfied with that. Now they are attacking the whole structure of price supports for farm products. This attack comes at a time when many farm prices are dropping and the price support program is of the greatest importance to the farmer.

The Democratic Party originated the farm support program. We built the price support plan out of hard experience. We built it for the benefit of the entire Nation— not only for the farmer, but for the consumer as well. Republican spokesmen are now complaining that my Administration is trying to keep farm prices up. They have given themselves away. They have given you a plain hint of what they have in store for you if they come into power. They are obviously ready to let the bottom drop out of farm prices.

{The purpose of price support is to prevent farm prices from falling to ruinously low levels. Every consumer should realize that these supports apply only when farm prices have dropped below parity. The Government is not now supporting the price on major food items such as meats, dairy products, and poultry. The Government has just begun to support the price of wheat, which has dropped from around three dollars a bushel to about two dollars. This support price has nothing to do with the price the consumer is paying for his bread.

When wheat prices were going up, the price of bread rose steadily. It went up from 10 cents a loaf to 11 cents—to 12 cents—to 13 cents—to 14 cents. Now wheat prices have fallen a dollar a bushel. But the price of bread has not come down one cent.

There you have the policy of reactionary big business. Pay as little as you can to the farmer, and charge the consumer all he can bear. That is a fair sample of what the Republican reaction has meant to you in the past two years—to you, and to every consumer, in cities and on farms alike.

When the Republicans claim that wheat price supports are to blame for the high price of bread, they are trying to stir up the city consumer against the farmer by downright dishonesty. The truth of the matter is that by encouraging the record production of the last few years, the support program has actually kept consumer prices down. Those who are wilfully trying to discredit the price support system don't want farmers to be prosperous. They believe in low prices for farmers, cheap wages for labor, and high profits for big corporations.

These are the facts the people need to know. I am going to keep hammering away at the facts until the whole country rings with the truth about these gluttons of privilege. The record of the Republican 80th Congress is one long attack on the welfare of the farmer.

Under the Democratic Administrations since 1933, the Government sponsored the great soil conservation program that helped to lay the foundations for the present prosperity of the American farmer. But the Republican 80th Congress, under the false mask of economy, cut and threatened to kill the soil conservation program. You people here know best the importance of soil conservation to American agriculture. You know what the reactionary attack on soil conservation will cost the farmer if we let the Republicans have their own way.

At every point the Republican 80th Congress did what the speculative grain lobby wanted it to do. They killed the International Wheat Agreement, which would have assured American wheat growers a large export market for five years at fair prices. They started a move to put a death-tax on farm cooperatives. They ruled out the grain bins that help make the ever-normal granary effective. They have invited a depression by refusing to curb inflation. And now they are attacking the farm support program.

The Wall Street Republicans are not worrying about whether you like it or not. Their political wiseacres have assured them that the farmer has fallen back into his old habit of voting Republican, whatever happens. The Republicans are saying, "Don't worry about the farm vote. It's in the bag." So long as you had a good year once in a while, you would be satisfied. So they thought. So they think today.

You and I know they're making a big mistake. From what I have seen, the farmers of this country have their eyes open. You're not going to be fooled again by the slick propaganda of Wall Street.}

In only two years, with only the Congress under their control, the Republicans were able to weaken the position—your position gravely. Well, imagine what would happen if they were to get both the Congress and the Presidency for four years. What they have taken away from you thus far would be only an appetizer for the economic tapeworm of big business.

Your best protection is to elect a Democratic Congress and a President that will play fair with the farmer—an Administration that will reinforce soil conservation, provide adequate storage facilities for grain, encourage production, and help the farmer make enough on his crop to meet the cost of living, and have something left over.

I don't need to tell you how long it takes to get a good crop, and how big the dangers are. You can work a year, plowing and cultivating, and then at the last minute, a sudden drought or flood can wipe you out. You all know how terrible these disasters of nature can be.

Now you are faced with the danger of another kind of disaster—a man-made disaster bearing the Republican trademark. For sixteen years the Democrats have been working on a crop of prosperity for the farmer. We have been plowing and seeding, and cultivating the soil of the American economy in order to get a crop of prosperity that you have been enjoying for the past several years. The question is: Are you going to let another Republican blight wipe out that prosperity?

I have reminded you of the evils wrought by Republican Administration in recent times. But my purpose has not been merely to bring up the past. I am trying to point the way to a healthy future. The Democratic Party is looking forward, not back. We are planning to aid the farmers of America meet their pressing problems and avoid catastrophe.

Today farmers are faced with the threat that markets will fail to keep up with their production. The reactionary Republican answer is to let prices crash to the bottom. But the Democratic Party has a constructive way of preventing such a collapse. We are reaching out to develop world markets that will absorb production above America's own needs. Scientific research is discovering more and new uses for farm products. We know that the world can absorb the farmers' output, if the right creations [*sic*] conditions are created, and we are working to insure continued prosperity for American agriculture.

The Democratic Party is fighting the farmer's battle. We believe that farmers are entitled to share equally with other people in our national income. We believe that a prosperous and productive agriculture is essential to our national welfare.

But the Democratic Party does not stand in defense of the farmer alone. It stands for the people of the United States—the farmer, the industrial workers, and the white-collar worker. Our intentions are made clear by our deeds. In this Twentieth Century, every great step forward has come during Democratic administrations of the National Government. Every movement backward has come under Republican auspices, and it is the people who have paid dearly for these reactionary moves. Too much is now at stake—here and throughout the world—to take the wrong path now.

There is one way to stop the forces of reaction. Get every vote out on Election Day, and make it count. You can't afford to waste your votes this year. I'm not asking you just to vote for me. Vote for yourselves! Vote for your farms! Vote for the standard of living that you've won under a Democratic Administration! Get out there on Election Day and vote for your future!

*EDITOR'S NOTE:

The transcripts throughout this text are verbatim from the video footage of the speeches as they appear in the videotape series, "Great Speeches." On occasion these video presentations are incomplete. On these occasions we have, where we thought it important, provided text of the omitted portions of the speech in brackets. These portions come from various reliable sources.

ADDRESS TO THE GREATER HOUSTON MINISTERIAL ASSOCIATION

John Fitzgerald Kennedy

Houston, Texas, September 12, 1960 (Transcribed from the video, GREAT SPEECHES, VOLUME IV)

Reverend Mesa, Reverend Rock, I am grateful for your generous invitation to state my views.

While the so-called religious issue is necessarily and properly the chief topic here tonight, I want to emphasize from the outset that I believe that we have far more critical issues in the 1960 campaign: the spread of Communist influence, until it now festers only ninety miles from the coast of Florida—the humiliating treatment of our President and Vice President by those who no longer respect our power—the hungry children I saw in West Virginia, the old people who cannot pay their doctor's bills, the families forced to give up their farms—an America with too many slums, with too few schools, and too late to the moon and outer space.

These are the real issues which should decide this campaign. And they are not religious issues—for war and hunger and ignorance and despair know no religious barrier.

But because I am a Catholic, and no Catholic has ever been elected President, the real issues in this campaign have been obscured—perhaps deliberately in some quarters less responsible than this. So it is apparently necessary for me to state once again—not what kind of church I believe in, for that should be important only to me, but what kind of America I believe in.

I believe in an America where the separation of church and state is absolute—where no Catholic prelate would tell the President (should he be Catholic) how to act and no Protestant minister would tell his parishioners for whom to vote—where no church or church school is granted any public funds or political preference—and where no man is denied public office merely because his religion differs from the President who might appoint him or the people who might elect him.

I believe in an America that is officially neither Catholic, Protestant nor Jewish—where no public official either request or accept [sic] instructions on public policy from the Pope, the National Council of Churches or any other ecclesiastical source—where no religious body seeks to impose its will directly or indirectly upon the general populace or the public acts of its officials—and where religious liberty is so indivisible that an act against one church is treated as an act against all.

For, while this year it may be a Catholic against whom the finger of suspicion is pointed, in other years it has been, and may someday be again, a Jew—or a Quaker—or a Unitarian—or a Baptist. It was Virginia's harassment of Baptist preachers, for example, that led to Jefferson's statute of religious freedom. Today, I may be the victim—but tomorrow it may be you—until the whole fabric of our harmonious society is ripped apart at a time of great national peril.

Finally, I believe in an America where religious intolerance will someday end—where all men and all churches are treated as equals—where every man has the same right to

23

attend or not to attend the church of his choice—where there is no Catholic vote, no anti-Catholic vote, no block voting of any kind—and where Catholics, Protestants and Jews, at both the lay and the pastoral levels, will refrain from those attitudes of disdain and division which have so often marred their works in the past, and promote instead the American ideal of brotherhood.

That is the kind of America in which I believe. And it represents the kind of Presidency in which I believe—a great office that must be neither humbled by making it the instrument of any religious group, nor tarnished by arbitrarily withholding it, its occupancy from the members of any one religious group. I believe in a President whose views on religion are his own private affair, neither imposed upon him by the nation or imposed by the nation upon him as a condition to holding that office.

I would not look with favor upon a President working to subvert the First Amendment's guarantees of religious liberty (nor would our system of checks and balances permit him to do so.) And neither do I look with favor upon those who would work to subvert Article VI of the Constitution by requiring a religious test—even by indirection—for if they disagree with that safeguard, they should be openly working to repeal it.

I want a chief executive whose public acts are responsible to all and obligated to none—who can attend any ceremony, service or dinner his office may appropriately require him to fulfill—and whose fulfillment of his Presidential office is not limited or conditioned by any religious oath, ritual or obligation.

This is the kind of America I believe in—and this is the kind of America I fought for in the South Pacific and the kind my brother died for in Europe. No one suggested then that we might have a "divided loyalty," that we did "not believe in liberty" or that we belonged to a disloyal group that threatened I quote "the freedom for which our forefathers died."

And in fact this is the kind of America for which our forefathers did die when they fled here to escape religious test oaths, that denied office to members of less favored churches, when they fought for the Constitution, the Bill of Rights, the Virginia Statute of Religious Freedom—and when they fought at the shrine I visited today—the Alamo. For side by side with Bowie and Crockett died Fuentes and McCafferty and Bailey and Bedillio and Carey—but no one knows whether they were Catholics or not. For there was no religious test there.

I ask you tonight to follow in that tradition, to judge me on the basis of fourteen years in the Congress—on my declared stands against an ambassador to the Vatican, against unconstitutional aid to parochial schools, and against any boycott of the public schools (which I attended myself)—and instead of doing this do not judge me on the basis of these pamphlets and publications we have all seen that carefully select quotations out of context from the statements of Catholic Church leaders, usually in other countries, frequently in other centuries and rarely relevant to any situation here—and always omitting, of course, the statement of the American bishops in 1948 which strongly endorsed church-state separation, and which more nearly reflects the views of almost every American Catholic.

I do not consider these other quotations binding upon my public acts—why should you? But let me say, with respect to other countries, that I am wholly opposed to the state being used by any religious group, Catholic or Protestant, to compel, prohibit or prosecute the free exercise of any other religion. And that goes for any persecution at any time, by anyone, in any country.

And I hope that you and I condemn with equal fervor those nations which deny their Presidency to Protestants and those which deny it to Catholics. And rather than cite the misdeeds of those who differ, I would also cite the record of the Catholic Church in such nations as France and Ireland—and the independence of such statesmen as de Gaulle and Adenauer.

But let me stress again that these are my views—for, contrary to common newspaper usage, I am not the Catholic candidate for President. I am the Democratic party's candidate for President who happens also to be a Catholic.

I do not speak for my church on public matters—and the church does not speak for me.

Whatever issue may come before me as President, if I should be elected—on birth control, divorce, censorship, gambling, or any other subject—I will make my decision in accordance with these views, in accordance with what my conscience tells me to be in the national interest, and without regard to outside religious pressure or dictates. And no power or threat of punishment could cause me to decide otherwise.

But if the time should ever come—and I do not concede any conflict to be remotely possible—when my office would require me to either violate my conscience, or violate the national interest, then I would resign the office, and I hope any other conscientious public servant would do likewise.

But I do not intend to apologize for these views to my critics of either Catholic or Protestant faith, nor do I intend to disavow either my views or my church in order to win this election. If I should lose on the real issues, I shall return to my seat in the Senate satisfied that I tried my best and was fairly judged.

But if this election is decided on the basis that 40 million Americans lost their chance of being President on the day they were baptized, then it is the whole nation that will be the loser in the eyes of Catholics and non-Catholics around the world, in the eyes of history, and in the eyes of our own people.

But if, on the other hand, I should win this election, then I shall devote every effort of mind and spirit to fulfilling the oath of the Presidency—practically identical, I might add, with the oath I have taken for fourteen years in the Congress. For, without reservation, I can, and I quote "solemnly swear that I will faithfully execute the office of President of the United States and will to the best of my ability preserve, protect and defend the Constitution, so help me God."

NOTE: A question and answer session follows this speech on the videotape, GREAT SPEECHES, VOLUME IV.

"I AM NOT THE CATHOLIC CANDIDATE FOR PRESIDENT"

JFK'S Houston Ministerial Association Speech

I am the Democratic party's candidate for President who happens also to be a Catholic.

CRITIC: Lloyd E. Rohler

In 1928 Al Smith, the first Catholic to run for President, was soundly defeated in a vicious campaign dominated by charges of a Catholic conspiracy to subvert religious freedom, lurid tales of sexual misconduct in monasteries and cross burnings by the Ku Klux Klan.[1] The memories of that campaign haunted the leaders of the Democratic Party and the campaign staff of John F. Kennedy in 1960. Although in the intervening 32 years the country had changed profoundly, the "religious issue," as it was known in the short hand of journalism, would not go away. Partly to demonstrate that he could win votes from Protestant voters, John Kennedy entered all the primary elections in 1960. His convincing win over Hubert H. Humphrey in the West Virginia primary in 1960 seemed to show that religion was not going to be the dominating factor in the 1960 election. After all, West Virginia was 97% Protestant and dominated largely by Evangelical and Fundamentalist groups. If Kennedy could win in West Virginia in spite of his religion, so the reasoning went, he could win anywhere. Unfortunately, human behavior is rarely governed by logic, and shortly after the Democratic Convention nominated Kennedy for President, his campaign confronted a resilient anti-Catholic and anti-Kennedy campaign that eventually distributed over "three hundred different anti-Catholic tracts...to more than twenty million homes." On September 7, when a new organization, the Conference of Citizens for Religious Freedom, with the popular preacher and religious columnist Dr. Norman Vincent Peale as its spokesman, challenged Senator Kennedy to repudiate those teachings of the Catholic Church which supposedly threatened religious liberty in the United States, Kennedy's advisors knew that a major response was needed. When the Houston Ministerial Association offered an invitation to Kennedy to discuss the religious issue, he reluctantly accepted.[2]

Thus, at 8:55 p.m. on Monday, September 12, 1960, John F. Kennedy, dressed in a conservative black suit and white shirt, entered the ballroom of the Rice Hotel and sat down beside the chairman of the Greater Houston Ministerial Association to await the moment when a network of twenty television stations across Texas would begin their broadcast of his speech. The huge room held over 600 people including members of the national press who came to Houston to report this major event in the Presidential campaign. In his hands Kennedy held the speech that he and Ted Sorensen had written over the weekend and on the plane flying from Los Angeles to El Paso. Although hurriedly written amidst the confusion of the political campaign, the speech is a carefully crafted statement that reflects the excellent staff work that made John Kennedy an effective speaker. For example, the morning of the speech, while preparing to campaign throughout the state, Kennedy suggested to Sorensen that some reference to the number of Catholics killed defending the Alamo be included in the speech. Sorensen telephoned Mike Feldman, a Kennedy staffer in Washington, D.C., at 4:00 a.m. Texas time with the request. Within a few hours, Feldman had called several scholars around the country, mobilized the staff at the Library of Congress and turned up a list of names that suggested possible Irish-American backgrounds. That morning Sorensen, himself, read the draft over the telephone to Reverend John Courtney Murray, S. J., an authority on church-state relations. On the plane to Houston, James Winn, Kennedy's campaign aide on religious issues, and John Cogley, a former editor of the religious periodical *Commonweal,* gave the draft a final review.[3]

Although this speech has been analyzed as an example of the genre of apologia, it can more easily be seen as an example of an effective campaign speech designed to turn the tables on the opposition.[4] Kennedy's strategy is clear: first, to minimize the importance of religion as an issue in the campaign; second, to seize the high ground by taking such a strong stand on the separation of church and state that no one could accuse him of trying to hide behind vague words or duck any sensitive issues; and lastly, to isolate the bigots and the hatemongers from those who might have legitimate concerns by showing that their intolerance was outside the American tradition of fair play, tolerance and respect for differences of belief. Sorensen's speech is carefully crafted to achieve all these aims. It combines forthright statements on church-state issues, careful answers to questions raised by critics and appeals based on fundamental American values.

Kennedy begins with a compliment to the audience and immediately emphasizes that more pressing issues should determine the outcome of the election. Kennedy than states the thesis of his speech and in doing so subtly divides the question into private and public realms: "So it is apparently necessary for me to state once again—not what kind of church I believe in, for that should be important only to me, but what kind of America I believe in." In doing so, he places himself firmly in the American tradition. By explicitly forbidding an "establishment" of religion, the Constitution grants to all Americans freedom to regard religion as a private matter of conscience not enforced upon them by the power of the state. In framing the area for discussion this way, Kennedy properly rules out of bounds questions about his private religious beliefs. He will only discuss how those beliefs might effect the public performance of his duties as President, if he should be elected.

In the next section of the speech, Kennedy describes his views on church and state and affirms his belief in a total separation of church and state that should satisfy even his most extreme critics. In this section of the speech Sorensen's characteristic use of contrasting phrases and balanced clauses works effectively as an argumentative strategy—Kennedy expresses first a phrase that embodies the beliefs of the audience followed adroitly by a second phrase expressing a similar position that they may not agree with that, nonetheless, logically follows from the first. For example, in paragraph five Kennedy says: "I believe in an America…where no Catholic prelate would tell the President…how to act and no Protestant minister would tell his parishioners for whom to vote." In paragraph nine Kennedy says: "And it represents the kind of Presidency in which I believe—a great office that must be neither humbled by making it the instrument of any religious group, nor tarnished by arbitrarily withholding it, its occupancy from the members of any religious group." And in the following paragraph, he says: "I would not look with favor upon a President working to subvert the First Amendment's guarantees of religious liberty.… And neither do I look with favor upon those who would work to subvert Article IV of the Constitution by requiring a religious test—even by indirection...."

Kennedy concludes this section with a personal appeal that makes the arguments emotionally compelling:

> This is the kind of America I believe in—and this is the kind of America I fought for in the South Pacific and the kind my brother died for in Europe. No one suggested then that we might have a "divided loyalty," that we did "not believe in liberty" or that we belonged to a disloyal group that threatened "the freedoms for which our forefathers died."

He follows this with a reference to the Alamo identifying with the Texas audience (his immediate one) that again makes the point:

> Side by side with Bowie and Crockett died Fuentes and McCafferty and Bailey and Bedillio and Carey—but no one knows whether they were Catholics or not. For there was no religious test there.

This is an excellent example of indirect evidence. Kennedy can't prove that those men were Catholics, but no one else can disprove the implication that they were. And this is precisely the point of the illustration. No one cares because "there was no religious test there."

Kennedy makes a transition from the Alamo to his own record of fourteen years in Congress, urging his audience to follow in the frontier tradition of judging a man on the basis of his actions; and he reiterates his public record on issues affecting the separation of church and state: "my declared stands against an ambassador to the Vatican, against unconstitutional aid to parochial schools, and against any boycott of the public schools (which I attended myself)." The unstated premise behind this argument is that Kennedy opposes many positions supported by the Catholic Church, and having done so for the fourteen years he has been in public office can be trusted to continue to do so. He then repudiates the malicious propaganda spread by hate groups labeling them, "carefully select[ed] quotations [taken] out of context from the statements of Catholic Church leaders, usually in other countries, frequently in other centuries, and rarely relevant to any situation here." He challenges the audience: "I do not consider these other quotations binding upon my public acts—why should you?" And to make the point as clear as possible, he states the obvious: "contrary to common newspaper usage, I am not the Catholic candidate for President. I am the Democratic party's candidate for President who happens also to be a Catholic."

The conclusion of the speech incorporates appeals to fairness, toleration and patriotism with a strong restatement of his position. He underlines his commitment to the separation of church and state by listing issues involving public morality that he would decide on the basis of "the national interest, and without regard to outside religious pressure or dictate." He dramatically vows to "resign" if any conflict should arise that would cause him to do otherwise. The last paragraph is the most effective part of the entire speech as Kennedy, standing before his critics, rehearses his taking of the Presidential oath of office. He allows them to visualize the possibility that this man who has been carefully and patiently explaining his views could become President.

The applause for Kennedy was louder and longer after the speech than when he was first introduced. Sorensen wrote a powerful speech, and Kennedy presented it in a competent manner. Because additions were being made to the text during the day of the speech, Kennedy did not have time to become thoroughly familiar with it. Thus his having to read the manuscript limited the effectiveness of his delivery. It was only in the question and answer session that he became animated, using gestures and bodily posture to convey his interest and concern. The question period increased the effect of a dramatic confrontation as Kennedy patiently and calmly answered the hostile and often demeaning questions. David Halberstam notes that this "effect" which worked so well in Kennedy's favor was entirely unanticipated by his ministerial inquisitors: "the ministers posing the questions not only were highly emotional but laboring under the impression that Kennedy had never dealt with these issues before. The Houston audience was—a prop." [5]

The members of the Houston Ministerial Association who crowded the hall did, indeed, provide the backdrop for Kennedy's performance. Conventional wisdom says that a speaker should stage a speech before a friendly audience to demonstrate enthusiastic support. In this case, Kennedy staged his speech before a largely hostile audience to demonstrate his courage in facing his critics. Had he spoken the same words before a predominately Catholic audience, the effect on the mass mediated audience would not have been the same. Kennedy gained sympathy for his willingness to endure hostile questions that at times bordered on personal insults. The contrasting image of the cool, calm and courteous candidate and the many smug, condescending and rude questioners heightened the drama.

Kennedy's speech symbolically enacted the triumph of the American Dream in its most basic formulation for his audience. The American Dream is the affirmation that the United States is *the* land of opportunity where any child regardless of background can take advantage of the immense opportunities offered by this society and become a success. Although this success is frequently defined in economic terms ("become a millionaire"), achieving high political office is part of the dream too. Many American politicians have portrayed themselves as fulfilling this aspect of the Dream by going from the log cabin to the White House. Using the terminology of Kenneth Burke, we can view the attack on Kennedy for his religious beliefs as an attack on the hierarchy of values supporting the American Dream.[1] Values of toleration, fair play and respect for individual differences of religious belief were in danger of being undermined and thus polluted by the opposite values of hatred, fear and suspicion. In order to redeem the American Dream, Kennedy placed the blame for the pollution on unnamed others, "less responsible than this" audience, who have deliberately spread their message of hate. Thus, Kennedy gave his listeners an opportunity to atone for their own secret fears by blaming them on others. Atonement makes possible redemption through supporting Kennedy, and thus salvation in an America which has reaffirmed its commitment to toleration, fair play and respect for individual difference of belief.

Kennedy's speech functions symbolically to allow those members of the audience who usually vote Democratic but who have doubts about voting for a Catholic to release the guilt they feel for betraying the basic values of the American Dream. They can purge themselves of guilt and feel proud of themselves in doing so. After all, a vote for Kennedy is a vote for "the freedoms for which our forefathers died." And Catholic voters who had been voting Republican when Eisenhower headed the ticket can now come back to the Democratic Party confident that their votes will help elect a symbol of religious toleration and affirm that they, too, share in the American Dream.

This speech is also a good example of the multiple audiences created by the mass media. Although Sorensen wrote the speech for Kennedy's appearance before the Houston ministers, he knew that the potential audience numbered far more than the 600 people crowded in the ballroom. A twenty-station network carried the speech "live" throughout Texas, and the presence of the national media guaranteed that the networks would run portions on their news broadcasts. So, too, would stories be carried in the national press. The New York *Times* printed the complete text of both the speech and the question and answer session.[6] *US News & World Report* reprinted most of the text, and various other newspapers and journals through their reports and commentary circulated the basic ideas throughout the nation.[7]

Once they realized the impact of the speech, the Kennedy campaign workers distributed hundreds of copies of the video nationwide. The speech was edited for both one- and five-minute political spots, and the entire exchange was edited by Leonard Reinsch, Kennedy's media adviser, "to comply with the requirements of half-hour political programming on television.... The program created so much excitement that some stations responded to viewer's requests by repeating the program without charge."[8]

Kathleen Jamieson examined the Kennedy campaign's media expenditures and concluded that "more total time was purchased to rebroadcast Kennedy's September 12 performance in Houston than any other single piece of campaign propaganda."[9] She further concludes that while the one- and five-minute segments were aired in the last two weeks before the election primarily in states in which Protestant concern about his religion was vocal, "the half hour program...was aired disproportionally...in the fourteen states...that could be swung into the Democratic column by Catholic voters."[10] The Kennedy campaign showed great sensitivity in deciding when to schedule the showing of the spots. Sorensen reports that they were "carefully selected with an eye to what programs would be displaced, thus displeasing their fans and what programs would compete for an audience. Five minute "spot" presentations were also strategically placed at the end of popular shows."[11]

EVALUATION OF THE SPEECH

Kathleen Hall Jamieson in her study of presidential campaign advertising devotes over nine pages to the Houston Ministerial Association speech and calls it "the most eloquent speech he made either as a candidate or president."[12] Sorensen who wrote the speech is more modest in his claims, saying it "did make some converts to his candidacy...and impressed all who watched it then and later."[13] Sam Rayburn, a Texan who was the Speaker of the House and a commanding force in the Democratic Party, remarked, "As we say in my part of Texas, he ate 'em blood raw."[14] Teddy White noted that "he had addressed a sullen, almost hostile audience when he began...[and] won the applause of many and the personal sympathies of more; the meeting had closed in respect and friendship."[15] The New York *Times* reported a sampling of comments by ministers present that predictably ranged from the negative ("I don't believe it lessened the intensity of the issue") to the positive ("I personally am completely satisfied with his answers").[16] John W. Turnbull, a Protestant minister who observed the meeting for *The Reporter* magazine wrote that many ministers felt "embarrassment" because the meeting had "many of the earmarks of an inquisition, and we always thought we were against inquisitions."[17]

The long term effect of the speech is difficult to isolate from the many factors that influenced the outcome of the campaign. Theodore White, whose book, *The Making of the President 1960*, redefined the genre of campaign reporting, believes that it did make a difference:

> The Kennedy victory is a triumph of many facets—a triumph first of American tolerance and of the enlightened leadership of contemporary Protestant churchmen, a triumph next of the planning of the man who became President, a triumph finally of the American spirit which is unafraid.[18]

Jamieson believes that the use of the tape of the speech in heavily Catholic areas solidified Kennedy's support in the industrial states and helped him in the electoral college. She cites a study which shows that Kennedy's religion cost him 16.5 percent of the Democratic vote in the heavily Protestant South but gained him 1.6 percent in the more heavily populated states in the Northeast which helped him in the electoral vote.[19] The difficulty of generalizing about the motivations of voters and the role that chance events can play in an electoral campaign is well illustrated by the experience of Martin Luther King, Sr., father of the civil rights leader. A Baptist minister who shared the concerns of many other Southerners about Kennedy's religion, King originally endorsed Richard Nixon's candidacy. Senator Kennedy's telephone call to Mrs. King offering help in arranging for her husband's release from jail following his arrest at a sit-in in Atlanta and Robert Kennedy's plea with the presiding judge to set bail caused King, Sr. to reverse course and change his endorsement saying, "Because this man was willing to wipe the tears from my daughter-in-law's eyes, I've got a suitcase of votes, and I'm going to take them to Mr. Kennedy and dump them in his lap."[20] Black voters in Illinois, many of them Baptists, supported Kennedy as a result of King's endorsement, giving him the narrow margin of victory for that state's crucial electoral votes. It is difficult for us now to understand the strong feelings that the religious issue aroused in voters in 1960, but John Kennedy's speech stands as an eloquent testament to the basic American values of toleration, fair play and respect for individual differences.

NOTES

1. Alan Lichtman *Prejudice and the Old Politics. The Presidential Election of 1928* (Chapel Hill: UNC Press, 1979), p. 58.
2. Theodore Sorensen, *Kennedy* (New York: Harper & Row, 1965), pp. 188-194. This is the most authoritative source. Sorensen wrote the speech and was present at the meeting.
3. *Ibid.*, p. 189-190.
4. David Henry, "Senator John F. Kennedy Encounters the Religious Question: 'I am not the Catholic Candidate for President'" in *Oratorical Encounters, Selected Studies and Sources of Twentieth-Century Political Accusations and Apologies*, Edited by Halford Ross Ryan, (Westport, Conn.: Greenwood Press, 1988), pp. 153-174.
5. David Haberstam, *The Powers That Be* (New York: Knopf, 1979), pp. 325-26.
6. New York *Times*, September 13, 1960, p. 22
7. *U.S. News & World Report*, September 26, 1960, p. 74-78.
8. J. Leonard Reinsch, *Getting Elected: From Radio and Roosevelt to Television and Reagan* (New York: Hippocrene Books, 1988), p. 131.

9. Kathleen Hall Jamieson, *Packaging the Presidency,* 2nd Edition (New York: Oxford University Press, 1992), p. 136.
10. *Ibid.,* p. 134.
11. Sorensen, p. 195.
12. Jamieson, p. 130.
13. Sorensen, p. 192-193.
14. *Ibid.,* p. 193.
15. Theodore H. White, *The Making of the President 1960* (New York: Anthenum House, Inc., 1961), p. 298.
16. New York *Times,* September 14, 1960 p 1, 32.
17. "The Clergy Faces Mr. Kennedy," *The Reporter,* October 13,1960.
18. White, p. 400.
19. Jamieson, p. 135.
20. White, p. 363.

VICE PRESIDENTIAL ACCEPTANCE SPEECH

Hubert H. Humphrey

Democratic National Convention, Atlantic City, New Jersey, August 27, 1964
(Transcribed from the video, GREAT SPEECHES, VOLUME IV)

Mr. Chairman, Mr. President, my fellow Democrats, my fellow Americans, I proudly and humbly accept your nomination.

Will we ever be able to forget this unbelievable, this moving, this beautiful, this wonderful evening? What a challenge to every person in this land to live up to the goals, and the ideals of those who have gone before us and have chartered the course of our action!

I was deeply moved last night. I received a singular tribute from a friend and a great President—a tribute that I shall never forget. And I pray to Almighty God that I shall have the strength and the wisdom to measure up to the confidence and the trust that has been placed in me. And please let me say, thank you, thank you, my fellow Democrats.

I believe that it [sic] that I know President Johnson as well as any man. So let me tell you about him. I have known for 16 years his courage, his wisdom, his tact, and his persuasion, his judgment, and his leadership. But I shall never forget those hours and those days of tragedy and crisis last November that we once again relived tonight when a dear and wonderful friend and a great President was taken from us and another stepped forward without a falter, without a moment of hesitation or a moment of doubt. I was among those that he called to his side. He asked us—we the people, Republicans and Democrats alike, Americans all—for our help. And I say thank God that John Fitzgerald Kennedy was the patriot that he was, that he had the foresight that day in Los Angeles to provide for his country. And thank God for this country and for the peace of the world that President Kennedy had the wisdom to choose a Lyndon Johnson as his Vice President.

I'm sure you remember these words: "Let us continue." Those simple and direct words of President Johnson reached the hearts of our people. Those words rallied them, lifted them, and unified them. In this world disaster is ever but a step away. There is no margin for error. The leader of the free world, the leader of American democracy, holds in his hands the destinies not only of his own people but holds in his hands the destinies of all mankind. Yes, yes, the President of the United States must be a man of calm and deep assurance who knows his country and who knows his people. Above all, he must be a man of clear mind and of sound judgment and a man who can lead, a man who can decide, a man of purpose and conviction, and Lyndon Johnson is that man.

He is a man with the instincts of the teacher who would rather persuade than to compel, who would rather unite than divide. President Johnson is respectful of the traditions of the Presidency and he understands the compelling need for restraint in the use of the greatest power ever assembled by man. In President Johnson's hands our people know that our power is for justice. In his hands our people know that our power is for peace, and in his hands our people know that our power is for freedom. President

Johnson has helped to make the Democratic party the only truly national party and this very convention demonstrates our strong and our abiding unity and brotherhood.

And what a contrast, what a contrast with the shambles at the COW Palace in San Francisco! What a contrast with that incredible spectacle of bitterness, of hostility, of personal attack! The American people have seen the contrast. The American people do have a clear choice, and I predict their choice will be Lyndon Johnson in November.

Ralph Waldo Emerson once spoke of the two parties which divide the states: the party of hope, my fellow Democrats, and the party of memory. They renew their rivalry, he said, from generation to generation. This contest between the party of hope and the party of memory lies at the very heart of this coming campaign.

During the last few weeks shrill voices have tried to lay claim to the great spirit of the American past, but they long for a past that never was. In their recklessness, in their radicalism they distort the American conservative tradition. Yes, those who have kidnapped the Republican Party have made it this year not a party of memory and sentiment but one of stridency, of unrestrained passion of extreme and radical language.

And by contrast which is clear to all under the leadership of President Lyndon Johnson, the Democratic Party stands today as the champion of great causes, as the party of purpose of conviction, as the party of national unity, and as the party of hope for all of mankind.

Now, let me document my case. Above all the contrast between the Democratic leadership and that of the Goldwater party is sharp and decisive on the question of peace and security. For 25 years, my fellow Americans, both parties have held the conviction that politics should stop at the water's edge, that we must be united in the face of our enemies, and we must be united in support of our allies and our friends. And I say here tonight to every American, to every friend of freedom, woe to that party or that spokesman that turns its back upon bipartisan foreign policy. Woe to those who are willing to divide this nation and beware of those who cast false doubts upon our great strength.

What great problems there are to solve—problems to control the awesome power of nuclear [sic] of the nuclear age, to strengthen the grand alliance with Europe, to continue the task of building a strong and prosperous and united hemisphere under the Alliance for Progress; to assist our friends in Asia and Africa in preserving their freedom and promoting their progress, and to defend and extend freedom throughout the world. Now, my fellow Americans, these urgent problems demand reasoned solutions not empty slogans. Childlike answers cannot solve man-sized problems. These problems demand leadership that is prudent, restrained, responsible; they require a President who knows that Rome was not built in a day, but who also knows that the great edifice of Western civilization can be brought down in ruins in one hour.

The American Presidency is not a place for a man who is impetuous at one moment and indecisive the next. Nor is it a place for one who is violently for something one day and violently opposed to it on the next. Nor is it a [sic] an office where statements on matters of major policy are so confusing and so contradictory that neither friend nor foe knows where he stands. And my...and my fellow Americans, it is of the highest importance that both friend and foe know that the...that the American President means what he says and says what he means.

The temporary spokesman of the Republican Party—yes the temporary Republican spokesman is not only out of tune with the great majority of his countrymen he is even out of step with his own party. In the last 3 1/2 years most Democrats and Republicans have agreed on the great decisions our nation has made, but not the Republican spokesman, not Senator Goldwater. He's been facing backward against the mainstream of American history.

Most Democrats and most Republicans in the United States Senate, for example, voted for the nuclear test-ban treaty but not the temporary Republican spokesman.

Most…most Democrats and Republicans in the Senate voted for an $11.5 billion tax cut for American citizens and American business, but not Senator Goldwater.

Most Democrats and Republicans in the Senate—in fact four fifths of the members of his own party—voted for the Civil Rights Act, but not Senator Goldwater!

Most Democrats and Republicans in the Senate voted for the establishment of a United States Arms Control and Disarmament Agency that seeks to slow down the nuclear arms race among the nations, but not the temporary Republican spokesman!

Most Democrats and most Republicans in the Senate voted last year for an expanded medical-education program, but not Senator Goldwater!

Most…most Democrats and most Republicans in the Senate voted for education legislation, but not Senator Goldwater!

Most Democrats and most Republicans in the Senate voted for the National Defense Education Act, but not the temporary…Goldwater!

And, my fellow Americans most Democrats and most Republicans in the Senate voted to help the United Nations in its peacekeeping functions when it was in financial difficulty, but not Senator Goldwater!

Yes, yes, my fellow Americans, it is a fact that the temporary Republican spokesman is not in the mainstream of his party. In fact, he has not even touched the shore. Now I believe, I believe in the two party system, but there must be two responsible parties. And there must be men who are equipped to lead a great nation as the standard bearers of the two parties. It is imperative that the leadership of the great parties move within the mainstream of American thought and philosophy.

I pledge to this convention, I pledge to our great President, to all the American people, my complete devotion to this task to prove once again that the Democratic party deserves America's affections and that we are indeed the party of hope for the American people. So tonight let us here and now pledge that the campaign that we will wage will be worthy of our great President Johnson. And, my fellow Americans, let us hereby resolve and pledge tonight that that campaign will be worthy of the memory of the late and beloved President John Fitzgerald Kennedy.

While others may appeal to passions and prejudice, and appeal to fear and bitterness, we of the Democratic Party call upon all Americans to join us in making our country a land of opportunity for our young, a home of security and dignity for our elderly, and a place of compassion and care for our afflicted. I say to those responsible and forward-looking Republicans who put our country above their party—and there are thousands of them—we welcome you to the banner of Lyndon Baines Johnson. We welcome your support.

Yes, yes, we…we extend the hand of fellowship. We ask you to join us tonight for this President, my fellow Americans, is the President of all of the American people. He…he is the President in the great American tradition—for labor and for business: no class conflict; for the farm family that will receive the unending attention and care of this President and for the city worker; for North and for the South; for East and for the West—this is our President!

President Lyndon Johnson represents—in fact he is the embodiment—of the spirit of national unity, the embodiment of national purpose, the man in whose hands we place our lives, our fortunes and our sacred honor. I am proud to be the friend of this great President, and I am very proud that he has asked this convention to select me as his running mate.

And I ask you, my fellow Americans, I ask you to walk with us, to work with us, to march forward with us to help President Johnson build the great society for America of the future.

Yes, let us continue. Let us fellow Democrats and fellow Americans, let us go forward. Let us take those giant steps forward to which the President has called us—to end the shame of poverty, to end the injustice and prejudice and the denial of opportunity, to build the great society and to secure the freedom of man and the peace of the world.

We can do no less. And to this tonight, let us resolve to pledge our every effort. Thank you.

VICE PRESIDENTIAL ACCEPTANCE SPEECH

Geraldine Ferraro

Democratic National Convention, San Francisco, California, July 19, 1984
(Transcribed from the video, GREAT SPEECHES, VOLUME III)

Ladies and gentlemen of the convention, my name is Geraldine Ferraro. I stand before you to proclaim tonight: America is the land where dreams can come true for all of us. As I stand before the American people and think of the honor this great convention has bestowed upon me, I recall the words of Dr. Martin Luther King, Jr., who made America stronger by making America more free. He said: "Occasionally in life there are moments which cannot be completely explained by words. Their meaning can only be articulated by the inaudible language of the heart." Tonight is such a moment for me. My heart is filled with pride. My fellow citizens, I proudly accept your nomination for Vice President of the United States. And...and...and...and I am proud to run with a man who will be one of the great presidents of this century, Walter F. Mondale.

Tonight, the daughter of a woman whose highest goal was a future for her children, talks to our nation's oldest party about a future for us all. Tonight, the daughter of working Americans tells all Americans that the future is within our reach if we're willing to reach for it. Tonight, the daughter of an immigrant from Italy has been chosen...has been chosen to run for President *[sic]* in the new land my father came to love.

Our faith that we can shape a better future is what the American dream is all about. The promise of our country is that the rules are fair. If you work hard and play by the rules, you can earn your share of America's blessings. Those are the beliefs I learned from my parents. And those are the values I taught my students as a teacher in the public schools of New York City. At night I went to law school. I became an assistant district attorney, and I put my share of criminals behind bars. I believe: If you obey the law, you should be protected. But if you break the law, you must pay for your crime. When I first ran for Congress, all the political experts said a Democrat could not win my home district in Queens. I put my faith in the people and the values that we shared. Together, we proved the political experts wrong. In this campaign, Fritz Mondale and I have put our faith in the people. And we are going to prove the experts wrong again. We are going to win. We are going to win, because Americans across this country believe in the same basic dream.

Last week, I visited Elmore, Minnesota, the small town—yeah, Elmore—the small town where Fritz Mondale was raised. And soon Fritz and Joan will visit our family in Queens. Nine hundred people live in Elmore. In Queens there are 2000 people on one block. You would think we'd *[sic]* be different, but we're not. Children walk to school in Elmore past grain elevators; in Queens they pass by subway stops. But, no matter where they live, their future depends on education, and their parents are willing to do their part to make those schools as good as they can be. In Elmore, there are family farms; in Queens, small businesses. But the men and women who run them all take pride in supporting their families through hard work and initiative. On the Fourth of July in Elmore, they hang flags out on Main Street; in Queens, they fly them over Grand Avenue. But all of us love our country, and stand ready to defend the freedom that it represents.

Americans want to live by the same set of rules. But under this administration, the rules are rigged against too many of our people. It isn't right that every year, the share of taxes paid by individual citizens is going up, while the share paid by large corporations is getting smaller and smaller. The rules say: Everyone in our society should contribute their fair share.

It isn't right that this year Ronald Reagan will hand the American people a bill for interest on the national debt larger than the entire cost of the federal government under John F. Kennedy. Our parents left us a growing economy. The rules say: We must not leave our kids a mountain of debt.

It isn't right that a woman should get paid 59 cents on the dollar for the same work as a man. If you play by the rules, you deserve a fair day's pay for a fair day's work.

It isn't right that if trends continue—by the year 2000 nearly all of the poor people in America will be women and children. The rules...the rules of a decent society say, when you distribute sacrifice in times of austerity, you don't put women and children first.

It isn't right that young people today fear they won't get the Social Security they paid for, and that older Americans fear they will lose what they have already learned *[sic]*. Social Security is a contract between the last generation and the next, and the rules say: You don't break contracts. We are going to keep faith with older Americans. We hammered out a fair compromise in the Congress to save Social Security. Every group sacrificed to keep the system sound. It is time Ronald Reagan stopped scaring our senior citizens.

It isn't right that young couples question whether to bring children into a world of 50,000 nuclear warheads. That isn't the vision for which Americans have struggled for more that two centuries. And our future doesn't have to be that way.

Change is in the air, just as surely as when John Kennedy beckoned America to a new frontier; when Sally Ride rocketed into space and when Rev. Jesse Jackson ran for the office of President of the United States. By choosing a woman to run for our nation's second highest office, you send a powerful signal to all Americans. There are no doors we cannot unlock. We will place no limits on achievement. If we can do this, we can do anything. Tonight, we reclaim our dream. We're going to make the rules of American life work fairly for all Americans again.

To an administration that would have us debate all over again whether the Voting Rights Act should be renewed and whether segregated schools should be tax exempt, we say, Mr. President: Those debates are over. On the issue of civil rights, voting rights, and affirmative action for minorities, we must not go backwards. We must—and we will—move forward to open the doors of opportunity.

To those who understand that our country cannot prosper unless we draw on the talents of all Americans, we say: We will pass the Equal Rights Amendment. The issue is not what America can do for women, but what women can do for America.

To the...to the Americans who will lead our country into the Twenty-First Century, we say: We will not have a Supreme Court that turns the clock back to the Nineteenth Century. To those...to those concerned about the strength of American family values, as I am, I say: We are going to restore those values—love, caring, partnership—by including, and not excluding, those whose beliefs differ from our own. Because our own faith is strong, we will fight to preserve the freedom of faith for others.

To those working Americans who fear that banks, utilities, and large special interests have a lock on the White House, we say: Join us; let's elect a people's president; and let's have government by and for the American people again.

To an administration that would savage student loans and education at the dawn of a new technological age, we say: You fit the classic definition of a cynic; you know the price of everything, but the value of nothing.

To our students and their parents, we say: We will insist on the highest standards of excellence because the jobs of the future require skilled minds.

To young Americans who may be called to our country's service, we say: We know your generation will proudly answer our country's call, as each generation before you. This past year, we remembered the bravery and sacrifice of Americans at Normandy. And we finally paid tribute—as we should have done years ago—to that unknown soldier who represents all the brave young Americans who died in Vietnam. Let no one doubt we will defend America's security and the cause of freedom around the world. But we want a president who tells us what America is fighting for, not just what we are fighting against. We want a president who will defend human rights—not just where it is convenient, but wherever freedom is at risk—from Chile to Afghanistan, from Poland to South Africa.

To those who have watched this administration's confusion in the Middle East, as it has tilted first toward one and then another of Israel's long-time enemies and wonder, "Will America stand by her friends and sister democracy?" We say: America knows who her friends are in the Middle East and around the world. America will stand with Israel always.

Finally...finally, we want a president who will keep America strong, but use that strength to keep America and the world at peace. A nuclear freeze is not a slogan—it is a tool for survival in the nuclear age. If we leave our children nothing else, let us leave them this Earth as we found it—whole and green and full of life. I know in my heart that Walter Mondale will be that president.

A wise man once said, "Every one of us is given the gift of life, and what a strange gift it is. If it is preserved jealously and selfishly, it impoverishes and saddens. But if it is spent for others, it enriches and beautifies." My fellow Americans, we can debate policies and programs. But in the end what separates the two parties in this election campaign is whether we use the gift of life for others or only ourselves.

Tonight, my husband, John, and our three children are in this hall with me. To my daughters, Donna and Laura, and my son, John, Jr., I say: My mother did not break faith with me and I will not break faith with you. To all the children of America I say: The generation before ours kept faith with us, and like them, we will pass on to you a stronger, more just America.

Thank you.

PRESIDENTIAL ACCEPTANCE SPEECH

Ronald Reagan

Republican National Convention, Detroit, Michigan, July 17, 1980
(Transcribed from the video, GREAT SPEECHES, VOLUME IV)

You're singing...you're singing our song. Well, the first thrill tonight was to find myself for the first time in a long time in a movie on prime time.

But this, as you can imagine, is the second big thrill.

Mr. Chairman, Mr. Vice President-to-be, this convention, my fellow citizens of this great nation: With a deep awareness of the responsibility conferred by your trust, I accept your nomination for the Presidency of the United States. I...I do so with deep gratitude. And I think also I might interject on behalf of all of us our thanks to Detroit and the people of Michigan and of this city for the warm hospitality we've enjoyed.

And I thank you for your wholehearted response to my recommendation regard [sic] to George Bush as the candidate for Vice President.

I'm very proud of our party tonight. This convention has shown to all America a party united, with positive programs for solving the nation's problems; a party ready to build a new consensus with all those across the land who share a community of values embodied in these words: family, work, neighborhood, peace and freedom.

Now I know that we've had...we've had a quarrel or two but of [sic] only as to the method of attaining a goal. There was no argument here about the goal. As President, I will establish a liaison with the 50 governors to encourage them to eliminate, wherever it exists, discrimination against women. I will...I will monitor federal laws to insure their implementation and to add statutes if they are needed.

More than...More than anything else, I want my candidacy to unify our country; to renew the American spirit and sense of purpose. I want to carry our message to every American, regardless of party affiliation, who is a member of this community of shared values.

Never before in our history have Americans been called upon to face three grave threats to our very existence, any one of which could destroy us. We face a disintegrating economy, a weakened defense and an energy policy based on the sharing of scarcity.

The major issue of this campaign is the direct political, personal, and moral responsibility of Democratic Party leadership—in the White House and in the Congress—for this unprecedented calamity which has befallen us. They tell us they've done the most that could humanly be done. They say that the United States has had its day in the sun, that our nation has passed its zenith. They expect you to tell your children that the American people no longer have the will to cope with their problems; that the future will be one of sacrifice and few opportunities.

My fellow citizens, I utterly reject that view. The American people...the American people, the most generous on earth, who created a highest standard of living, are not going to accept the notion that we can only make a better world for others by moving backward ourselves. And those who believe we can have no business leading this nation.

I will not stand by and watch this great country destroy itself under mediocre leadership that drifts from one crisis to the next, eroding our national will and purpose. We have come together here because the American people deserve better from those to whom they entrust our nation's highest offices, and we stand united...we stand united in our resolve to do something about it.

We need a rebirth of the American tradition of leadership at every level of government and in private life as well. The United States of America is unique in world history because it has a genius for leaders—many leaders—on many levels.

But back in 1976, Mr. Carter said, "Trust me." And a lot of people did. And now, many of those people are out of work. Many have seen their savings eaten away by inflation. Many others on fixed incomes, especially the elderly, have watched helplessly as the cruel tax of inflation wasted away their purchasing power. And, today, a great many who trusted Mr. Carter wonder if we can survive the Carter policies of national defense.

"Trust me" government asks that we concentrate our hopes and dreams on one man; that we trust him to do what's best for us. Well, my view of government places trust not in one person or one party, but in those values that transcend persons and parties. The trust is where it belongs—in the people. The responsibility to live up to that trust is where it belongs, in their elected leaders. That kind of relationship, between the people and their elected leaders, is a special kind of compact.

Three-hundred-and-sixty years ago, in 1620, a group of families dared to cross a mighty ocean to build a future for themselves in a new world. When they arrived at Plymouth, Massachusetts, they formed what they called a "compact," an agreement among themselves to build a community and abide by its laws.

This single act—the voluntary binding together of free people to live under the law—set the pattern for what was to come.

A century and a half later, the descendants of those people pledged their lives, their fortunes and their sacred honor to found this nation. Some forfeited their fortunes and their lives; none sacrificed honor.

Four score and seven years later, Abraham Lincoln called upon the people of all America to renew their dedication and their commitment to a government of, for and by the people.

Isn't it once again time to renew our compact of freedom; to pledge to each other...to pledge to each other all that is best in our lives; all that gives meaning to them—for the sake of this, our beloved and blessed land?

Together, let us make this a new beginning. Let us make a commitment to care for the needy; to teach our children the virtues handed down to us by our families; to have the courage to defend those values and virtues and the willingness to sacrifice for them.

Let us pledge to restore, in our time, the American spirit of voluntary service, of cooperation, of private and community initiative; a spirit that flows like a deep and mighty river through the history of our nation.

As your nominee, I pledge to you to restore to the federal government the capacity to do the people's work without dominating their lives. I pledge to you...I pledge to you a government that will not only work well but wisely, its ability to act tempered by prudence, and its willingness to do good balanced by the knowledge that government is never more dangerous than when our desire to have it help us blinds us to its great power to harm us.

You know...you know, the first...the first Republican president once said, "While the people retain their virtue and their vigilance, no administration by any extreme of wickedness or folly can seriously injure the government in the short space of four years."

If Mr. Lincoln could see what's happened in these last three and a half years, he might hedge a little on that statement. But...but with the virtues that are our legacy as a free people and with the vigilance that sustains liberty, we still have time to use our renewed compact to overcome the injuries that have been done to America these past three and a half years.

First, we must overcome something the present administration has cooked up: a new and altogether indigestible economic stew, one part inflation, one part high unemployment, one part recession, one part run-away taxes, one part deficit spending seasoned with an energy crisis. It's an economic stew that has turned the national stomach.

Ours are not problems of abstract economic theory. These are problems of flesh and blood; problems that cause pain and destroy the moral fiber of real people who should not suffer the further indignity of being told by the government that it is all somehow their fault. We do not have inflation because—as Mr. Carter says—we've lived too well.

The head of a government which has utterly refused to live within its means and which has, in the last few days, told us that this coming year's deficit will be $60 billion, dares to point the finger of blame at business and labor, both of which have been engaged in a losing struggle just trying to stay even.

High taxes, we are told, are somehow good for us, as if, when government spends our money it isn't inflationary, but when we spend it, it is.

Those...those who preside over the worst energy shortage in our history tell us to use less, so that we'll run out of oil, gasoline and natural gas a little more slowly. Well, now, conservation is desirable, of course, but we...we mustn't waste energy. But conservation is not the sole answer to our energy needs.

America must get to work producing more energy. The Republican program for solving economic problems is based on growth and productivity.

Large amounts of oil and natural gas lay beneath our land and off our shores, untouched because the present administration seems to believe the American people would rather see more regulation, more taxes and more controls than more energy.

Coal offers a great potential. So does nuclear energy produced under rigorous safety standards. It could supply electricity for thousands of industry [sic] and millions of jobs and homes. It must not be thwarted by a tiny minority opposed to economic growth which often finds friendly ears in regulatory agencies for its obstructionist campaigns.

Now make no mistake. We will not permit the safety of our people or our environmental heritage to be jeopardized, but we are going to reaffirm that the economic prosperity of our people is a fundamental part of our environment.

Our problems...our problems are both acute and chronic, yet all we hear from those in positions of leadership are the same tired proposals for more government tinkering, more meddling and more control—all of which led us to this sorry state in the first place.

Can anyone look at the record of this administration and say, "Well done"? Can anyone compare the state of our economy when the Carter administration took office with where we are today and say, "Keep up the good work"? Can anyone look at our reduced standing in the world today and say, "Let's have four more years of this"?

I believe the American people are going to answer these questions, as you've answered them, in the first week in November and their answer will be, "No—we've had enough." And then...and then it will be up to us—beginning next January 20—to offer an administration and congressional leadership of competence and more than a little courage.

We must have the clarity of vision to see the difference between what is essential and what is merely desirable; and then the courage to bring our government back under control.

It is...it is essential...it is essential that we maintain both the forward momentum of economic growth and the strength of the safety net between those in our society who need help. We also believe it is essential that the integrity of all aspects of Social Security be preserved.

Beyond...beyond these essentials, I believe it is clear our federal government is overgrown and overweight. Indeed, it is time our government should go on a diet. Therefore, my first act as chief executive will be to impose an immediate and thorough freeze on federal hiring. Then...then, we are going to enlist the very best minds from business, labor and whatever...whatever quarter to conduct a detailed review of every department, bureau and agency that lives by federal appropriation.

And we are going to enlist the help and ideas of many dedicated and hard-working government employees at all levels who want a more efficient government just as much as the rest of us do. I...I know that many of them are demoralized by the confusion and waste they confront in their work as a result of failed and failing policies.

Our instructions to the groups we enlist will be simple and direct. We will remind them that government programs exist at the sufferance of the American taxpayer and are paid for with money earned by working men and women and programs that represent a waste of their money—a theft from their pocketbooks—must have that waste eliminated or that program must go. It must go by executive order where possible, by congressional action where necessary.

Everything that can be run more effectively by state and local government we shall turn over to state and local government, along...along with the funding sources to pay for it. We are going to put an end to the money merry-go-round where our money becomes Washington's money, to be spent by states and cities exactly the way the federal bureaucrats tell us it has to be spent.

I will not accept the excuse that the federal government has grown so big and powerful that it is beyond the control of any President, any administration or Congress. We are going to put an end to the notion that the American taxpayer exists to fund the federal government. The federal government...the federal government exists to serve the American people. On January 20, we are going to reestablish that truth.

Also on that date we are going to initiate action to get substantial relief for our taxpaying citizens and action to put people back to work. {None of this will be based on any new form of monetary tinkering or fiscal sleight-of-hand. We will simply apply to government the common sense that we all use in our daily lives.

Work and family are at the center of our lives, the foundation of our dignity as a free people. When we deprive people of what they have earned, or take} away their jobs, we destroy their dignity and undermine their families. We can't support families unless there are jobs; and we can't have jobs unless the people have both money to invest and the faith to invest it.

These...these are concepts that stem from an economic system that for more than 200 years has helped us master a continent, create a previously undreamed-of-prosperity for our people and has fed millions of others around the globe and that system will continue to serve us in the future if our government will stop ignoring the basic values on which it was built and stop betraying the trust and good will of the American workers who keep it were *[sic]* going.

The American people are carrying the heaviest peacetime tax burden in our nation's history—and it will grow even heavier, under present law, next January. We are taxing ourselves into economic exhaustion and stagnation, crushing our ability and incentive to save, invest and produce. This must stop. We must halt this fiscal self-destruction and restore sanity to our economic system.

I've long advocated a 30 percent reduction in income tax rates over a period of three years. This phased tax reduction...this phased tax reduction would begin with a 10 percent "down payment" tax cut in 1981, which the Republicans in Congress and I have already proposed.

A phased reduction of tax rates would go a long way toward easing the heavy burden on the American people. But we shouldn't stop there.

Within the context of economic conditions and appropriate budget priorities during each fiscal year of my Presidency, I would strive to go further. This would include improvement in business depreciation taxes so we can stimulate investment in order to get plants and equipment replaced, put more Americans back to work and put our nation back on the road to being competitive in world commerce. We will also work to reduce the cost of government as a percentage of our gross national product.

The...the first task of national leadership is to set realistic and honest priorities in our policies and our budget, and I pledge that my administration will do that.

When I talk of tax cuts, I am reminded that every major tax cut in this century has strengthened the economy, generated renewed productivity and ended up yielding new revenues for the government by creating new investment, new jobs and more commerce among our people.

The present administration...the present administration has been forced by us Republicans to play follow-the-leader with regard to a tax cut. But in this election year we must take with the proverbial "grain of salt" any tax cut proposed by those who have already given us the greatest single tax increase in our nation's history.

When those...when those in leadership give us tax increases and tell us we must also do with less, have they thought about those who've always had less—especially the minorities? This is like telling them that just as they step on that first rung of the ladder of opportunity, the ladder is being pulled out from under them. That may be the Democratic leadership's message to the minorities, but it won't be our message. Ours...ours will be: We have to move ahead, but we're not going to leave anyone behind.

Thanks to the economic policies of the Democratic Party, millions of Americans find themselves out of work. Millions more have never even had a fair chance to learn new skills, hold a decent job or secure for themselves and their families a prosper [sic] a share in the prosperity of this nation.

It's time to put America back to work, to make our cities and towns...make our cities and towns resound with the confident voices of men and women of all races, nationalities and faiths bringing home to their families a paycheck they can cash for honest money.

For those without skills, we'll find a way to help them get new skills.

For those without job opportunities we'll stimulate new opportunities, particularly in the inner cities where they live.

For those who've abandoned hope, we'll restore hope and we'll welcome them into a great national crusade to make America great again.

When we move from domestic affairs, and cast our eyes abroad, we see an equally sorry chapter in the record of the present administration:

—A Soviet combat brigade trains in Cuba, just 90 miles from our shores.

—A Soviet army of invasion occupies Afghanistan, further threatening our vital interest in the Middle East.

—America's defense strength is at its lowest ebb in a generation, while the Soviet Union is vastly outspending us in both strategic and conventional arms.

—Our European allies, looking nervously at the growing menace from the East, turn to us for leadership and fail to find it.

—And incredibly, more than 50, as you've been told from this platform so eloquently already, more than 50 of our fellow Americans have been held captive for over eight years—eight months—by a dictatorial foreign power that holds us up to ridicule before the world.

Adversaries large and small test our will and seek to confound our resolve, but we are given weakness when we need strength; vacillation when the times demand firmness.

The Carter Administration lives in a world of make-believe. Every day, drawing up a response to that day's problems, troubles, regardless of what happened yesterday and what'll happen tomorrow.

But you and I live in a real world, where disasters are overtaking our nation without any real response from Washington.

This is make-believe, self-deceit and, above all, transparent hypocrisy.

For example, Mr. Carter...Mr. Carter says he supports the volunteer Army, but he lets military pay and benefits slip so low that many of our enlisted personnel are actually eligible for food stamps. Re-enlistment rates drop and, just recently, after he fought all week against a proposed pay increase for our men and women in the military, he then helicoptered out to the carrier the U.S.S. Nimitz, which was returning from long months of duty in the Indian Ocean, and told the crew of that ship that he advocated better pay for them and their comrades. Where does he really stand, now that he's back on shore?

Well, I'll tell you where I stand. I do not favor a peacetime draft or registration, but...but I do favor pay and benefit levels that will attract and keep highly motivated men and women in our volunteer forces and...and back them up with an active reserve trained and ready for instant call in case of emergency.

You know, there may be a sailor at the helm of the ship of state, but the ship has no rudder. Critical...critical decisions are made at times almost in comic fashion, but who can laugh?

Who was not embarrassed when the administration handed a major propaganda victory in the United Nations to the enemies of Israel, our staunch Middle East ally for three decades, and then claimed that the American vote was a "mistake," the result of a "failure of communication" between the President, his Secretary of State and his U.N. Ambassador?

Who does not feel a growing sense of unease as our allies, facing repeated instances of an amateurish and con...and confused administration, reluctantly conclude that America is unwilling or unable to fulfill its obligations as leader of the free world?

Who does not feel rising alarm when the question in any discussion of foreign policy is no longer, "Should we do something?" but "Do we have the capacity to do anything?"

The ad...the administration which has brought us to this state is seeking your endorsement for four more years of weakness, indecision, mediocrity and incompetence. No. No American should vote until he or she has asked: Is the United States stronger and more respected now then it was three-and-a-half years ago? Is the world safer, a safer place in which to live?

It is the…it is the responsibility of the President of the United States, in working for peace, to insure that the safety of our people cannot successfully be threatened by a hostile foreign power. As President, fulfilling that responsibility will be my No. 1 priority.

We're not a warlike people. Quite the opposite. We always seek to live in peace. We resort to force infrequently and with great reluctance—and only after we've determined that it's absolutely necessary. We are awed—and rightly so—by the forces of destruction at loose in the world in this nuclear era.

But neither can we be naïve or foolish. Four times in my lifetime America has gone to war, bleeding the lives of its young men into the sands of island beachheads, the fields of Europe and the jungles and rice paddies of Asia. We know only too well that war comes not when the forces of freedom are strong, it is when they are weak that tyrants are tempted.

We simply cannot learn these lessons the hard way again without risking our destruction.

Of all…of all the objectives we seek, first and foremost is the establishment of lasting world peace. We must always stand ready to negotiate in good faith, ready to pursue any reasonable avenue that holds forth the promise of lessening tensions and furthering the prospects of peace. But let our friends and those who may wish us ill take note: The United States has an obligation to its citizens and to the people of the world never to let those who would destroy freedom dictate the future course of life on this planet. I would regard…I would regard my election as proof that we have renewed our resolve to preserve world peace and freedom. That this nation will once again be strong enough to do that.

Now this evening…this evening marks the last step, save one, of a campaign that has taken Nancy and me from one end of this great nation to the other, over many months and thousands and thousands of miles. There are those who question the way we choose a president, who say that our process imposes difficult and exhausting burdens on those who seek the office. I have not found it so.

It is…it is…it's impossible to capture in words the splendor of this vast continent which God has granted as our portion of His creation. There are no words to express the extraordinary strength and character of this breed of people we call American.

Everywhere…everywhere we've met thousands of Democrats, Independents and Republicans from all economic conditions, all walks of life bound together in that community of shared values of family, work, neighborhood, peace and freedom. They're concerned, yes, they're not frightened. They're disturbed, but not dismayed. They are the kind of men and women Tom Paine had in mind when he wrote, during the darkest days of the American Revolution, "We have it in our power to begin the world over again."

Nearly…nearly 150 years after Tom Paine wrote those words, an American President told the generation of the Great Depression that it had a "rendezvous with destiny." I believe this generation of Americans today also has a rendezvous with destiny.

Tonight…tonight, let us dedicate ourselves to renewing the American compact. I ask you not simply to "trust me," but to trust your values—our values—and to hold me responsible for living up to them. I ask you to trust that American spirit which knows no ethnic, religious, social, political, regional or economic boundaries; the spirit that burned with zeal in the hearts of millions of immigrants from every corner of the earth who came here in search of freedom.

Some say that spirit no longer exists. But I've seen it—I've felt it—all across this land, in the big cities, the small towns and in rural America. It's still there, ready to blaze into life if you and I are willing to do what has to be done; we...we have to do the practical things, the down-to-earth things, such as creating policies that will stimulate our economy, increase productivity and put America back to work.

The time is now to limit federal spending; to insist on a stable monetary reform and to free ourselves from imported oil.

The time...the time is now to resolve that the basis of a firm and principled foreign policy is one that takes the world as it is and seeks to change it by leadership and example; not by harangue, harassment or wishful thinking.

The time now *[sic]* is now...the time is now to say that we shall seek new friendships and expand others and improve others, but we shall not do so by breaking our word or casting aside old friends and allies.

And the time is now to redeem promises once made to the American people by another candidate, in another time and another place. He said: For three long years I have been going up and down this country preaching that government—federal, state and local—costs too much. I shall not stop that preaching. As an immediate program of action, we must abolish useful *[sic]* useless offices. We must eliminate unnecessary functions of government. We must consolidate subdivisions of government and, like the private citizen, give up luxuries which we can no longer afford. And then he said: "I propose to you my friends, and through you, that government of all kinds, big and little, be made solvent and that the example be set by the President of the United States and his Cabinet." End of quote. That was *[sic]* Franklin Delano Roosevelt's words as he accepted the Democratic nomination for President in 1932.

The time...the time is now, my fellow Americans, to recapture our destiny, to take it into our own hands. And to do this will take away *[sic]* many of us...will take many of us working together. I ask you tonight, all over this land, to volunteer your help in this cause so that we can carry our message throughout the land.

Isn't it time that we, the people, carry out those unkept promises? That we pledge to each other and to all America on this July day 48 years later, that now we intend to do just that.

I have...I have thought of something that's not a part of my speech and worried over whether I should do it. Can we doubt that only a Divine Providence placed this land, this island of freedom, here as a refuge for all those people in the world who yearn to breathe free: Jews and Christians enduring persecution behind the Iron Curtain; the boat people of Southeast Asia, of Cuba and of Haiti; the victims of drought and famine in Africa, the freedom fighters in Afghanistan, and our own countrymen held in savage captivity?

I'll confess that I've been a little afraid to suggest what I'm going to suggest. I'm more afraid not to. Can we begin our crusade joined together in a moment of silent prayer?

God Bless America.

Thank you.

CHAPTER 3:
Rally Speeches: Political

Closely related to the campaign speech, the political rally speech primarily seeks to intensify the support and commitment of a friendly audience. The speaker praises the audience for past support but petitions for redoubled efforts to secure the rewards of a victorious future.

We begin with a speech by Adolf Hitler to the 1934 Nazi Party Congress held in Nuremberg. In their critical analysis of the speech, Lloyd Rohler and Justin Gustainis explore the multitude of devices used by this master demagogue to consolidate his power. From 1967, we include an anti-Vietnam war address by Stokeley Carmichael who, by the end of his speech, has his audience chanting, "Hell no, we ain't going." Barbara Jordan's 1976 Democratic Keynote Address philosophically outlined the principles which she sees as the underlying strength of the party. Mario Cuomo demonstrated the rhetorical power of the metaphor to stir and unite a divided Democratic Party. In his critical examination of Cuomo's 1984 Keynote Address David Henry explores the usefulness of the metaphor as an argumentative tool. Jesse Jackson's Rainbow Coalition Speech consoled his political supporters after a "temporary" setback then enlisted their continued efforts toward a more promising tomorrow. In their essay, Martha Solomon and Paul Stewart view Jackson's speech as an important media event. We then follow with Jackson's encore at the 1988 Democratic Convention. Our final entry (from the same convention) is by Ann Richards whose humor made this one of the most memorable keynotes in recent years.

CLOSING ADDRESS TO THE NAZI PARTY CONGRESS

Adolf Hitler

Nuremberg, Germany, September 14, 1934 (Transcribed from the video, GREAT SPEECHES, VOLUME I)

The Sixth Party Rally is coming to an end. What millions of Germans outside our ranks may simply have rated as an imposing display of political power was infinitely more for hundreds of thousands of fighters; the great personal, political and spiritual meeting of the old fighters and battle comrades. And perhaps, in spite of the spectacular forcefulness of this imposing review of the armies of the Party, many among them were wistfully thinking back to the days when it was difficult to be a National Socialist. For when our Party comprised just seven people, it already formulated two principles: it wanted to be a truly ideological party; it wanted, uncompromisingly, sole and absolute power in Germany.

We, as a party, had to remain a minority, because we mobilized the most valuable elements of fight and sacrifice in the nation, and they are never a majority but always a minority. And since the best racial component of the German nation, proudly self-assured, courageously, and daringly, demanded leadership of the Reich and the people, the people followed its leadership in ever greater numbers and subordinated themselves to it.

The German people are happily aware that the eternal flight of appearances has now been replaced by one stable pole, which sensing and knowing that it represented the very best German blood, rose to the leadership of the nation and is determined to keep this leadership, and exercise it, and never give it up again. There will always be only one segment of a people who will be really active fighters, and more is demanded of them than of the millions of other people. For them it is not enough to simply say, "I believe;" they take an oath, "I shall fight."

The party will for all times be the leadership reservoir of the German people, unchangeable in its teachings, hard as steel in its organization, pliable and adaptable in its tactics, and in its total appearance the manifestation of the spirit of the nation. Again it must be that all decent Germans become National Socialists. Only the best National Socialists become party members.

Formerly, our opponents saw to it that through prohibition and persecution our movement was periodically purged of the light chaff.that began to settle in it. Now we must practice selectiveness ourselves and expel what has proved to be rotten and therefore not of our kind. It is our wish and intent that this state and this Reich shall endure through the millennia ahead. We can rejoice in the knowledge that the future belongs totally to us.

Where the older generations might still waver, the youth is sworn to us and given to us, body and soul. Only if we realize in the Party the ultimate essence and idea of National Socialism, through the joint effort of all of us, will it forever and indestructibly be a possession of the German people and the German nation. Then the splendid and glorious army of the old and proud armed services of our nation will be joined by the no less tradition-bound leadership of the Party and together these two establishments will form and firm the German people and carry on their shoulders the German state and German Reich.

At this hour, tens of thousands of party comrades are beginning to leave town. While some are still reminiscing, others are getting ready for the next roll call, and always people will come and go, and always they will be gripped anew, gladdened, and inspired, for the idea and the Movement are expressions of the life of our people and therefore, symbols of eternity.

Long live the National Socialist Movement.

Long live Germany!

RUDOLF HESS:

The party is Hitler! Hitler is Germany as Germany is Hitler!

THE PARTY IS HITLER

Expel what has proved to be rotten and therefore not of our kind.

CRITICS: Lloyd E. Rohler and J. Justin Gustainis

Fifty years after his death, Adolf Hitler continues to exert a perverse fascination for our culture as the evil figure of the Twentieth Century. The daring of his ambition and the monstrosity of his imagination created untold human suffering and profoundly changed the political map of Europe and ultimately the world. Though far removed from Quintilian's ideal of the orator as the good man speaking well, Hitler's forceful delivery of emotional speeches to audiences conditioned by spectacular displays of military and patriotic symbols played a major role in his rise to power.

This essay examines Hitler's speech on the closing night of the Sixth Party Congress at Nuremberg on September 14, 1934. The purpose of the essay is to demonstrate the usefulness of the classical system in evaluating the speech of a man who rejected the concept of rational argument that is the very basis of classical rhetoric. This essay will demonstrate that the application of the classical categories can reveal the reasons for the overwhelming emotional response by the audiences as well as the ultimate weakness in Hitler's method of persuasion.

THE SPEAKER

Adolf Hitler was born in the Austrian town of Braunau on April 20, 1889, the son of a customs officer of the Austro-Hungarian Empire who would prove to be a domineering father. A mediocre student, young Hitler left high school at the age of sixteen without a diploma. Inclined to become an artist, Hitler spent his late adolescence in dreamy idleness. Refused admission to the Academy of Fine Arts in Vienna at the age of 18, disappointed and alienated, Hitler drifted and absorbed the ideas that would dominate his life: anti-Semitism, nationalism, celebration of the will, and the cult of violence. When Germany went to war in 1914, Hitler in a burst of patriotism enlisted in the German army. Serving in the front lines during the next few years, he was twice wounded and five times decorated for bravery. Temporarily blinded by a mustard gas attack in October of 1918, Hitler recuperated in the hospital when the armistice was declared. He remained in the army for several years after the war serving as a political instructor. As part of his duties, he monitored political organizations. While attending a meeting of the German Workers Party, he spoke so forcefully that he was invited to join. His talents were recognized and he soon took charge of recruiting new members. Thanks to his organizational skills and his inspired oratory, party membership grew rapidly and so did Hitler's influence. Within a year, he became the party leader.

By 1923, some 50,000 dues paying members of the party made Hitler a force in German politics. Impressed by Mussolini's successful "March on Rome," Hitler attempted to take advantage of unsettled conditions in Bavaria to lead a "March on Berlin." The "Beer Hall Putsch," as the activities of November 8 and 9, 1923, are called, resulted in the death of several party members and in Hitler and his deputies being arrested and tried for treason. Hitler used his oratorical skills to turn the trial into a propaganda forum for the party and win the minimum sentence possible for himself. While in prison, he wrote the first volume of Mein Kampf, his autobiography. Released after serving only nine months of a five year term, Hitler returned to Munich to rebuild the party. The next years were not very successful, as the post-war prosperity robbed the party of much of its appeal, but the good times were soon to end. The worldwide effects of the Great Depression improved Nazi prospects. Between 1928 and 1930, the party gained enough votes to go from 12 seats in the Reichstag to 107 and become the second largest political party in Germany. This increased political power led to increased respectability and financial support. In Germany, in 1930, no party had a parliamentary majority, and attempts to form one floundered on political polarization between the left and the right. In the absence of a parliamentary majority, the Weimar Constitution empowered the President to use emergency powers to appoint a Chancellor who could rule by decree. President von Hindenburg used this expedient to form a centrist government, but agitation by the Nazi Party led to the calling of new elections in 1932 to remedy the situation. The new elections resulted in a stunning victory for Hitler and the Nazi Party as their representation in the Reichstag grew to 230 seats making them the largest party in parliament. Although still lacking a majority of the votes, a new government would have to include them, and Hitler refused to join any government that did not give him the post of Chancellor. He calculated (correctly) that as Chancellor he would have the opportunity to manipulate the President, Field Marshal von Hindenburg, into issuing a decree giving him emergency powers. Aided by conservative nationalist politicians who thought that they could manipulate him, Hitler assumed office on January 30, 1933, and immediately set to work to subvert the legal institutions of Germany and to gather all power into his hands. In the wake of the mysterious burning of the Reichstag Building on the night of February 27, 1933, which the Nazi propagandists blamed on the communists, Hitler persuaded von Hindenburg to sign an emergency decree suspending indefinitely all the basic rights guaranteed in the constitution. A month later Hitler forced through the Reichstag an "Enabling Act" which gave him the power to enact legislation without parliamentary approval and to deviate from the constitution whenever he deemed it necessary. These two actions ended constitutional government in Germany and formed the basis for Hitler's dictatorship. Hitler moved quickly to use the emergency powers to destroy any independent power base that might challenge him and to bring all institutions in German society under the control of the Nazi Party. In the summer of 1934, in a bid to gain support of the Army, Hitler brought the paramilitary units of the Party, the Storm Troopers of the SA, under tighter control in a bloody purge. The death of von Hindenburg in August, 1934, allowed Hitler, a foreign born, poorly educated, ex-corporal, to assume the title of Head of State and Commander-in-Chief of the Armed Forces of Germany. This is the man who addressed the Party faithful at Nuremberg on September 14, 1934, and received their adulation as "Führer."[1]

OCCASION

The use of spectacle to arouse the emotions of the audience was not unknown in Ancient Greece or Rome. When Pericles gave the funeral oration for Greek soldiers killed in battle, he stood on the sacred ground surrounded by trophies of war and armed soldiers. Mark Antony's funeral oration for Julius Caesar depended for effect on the bloody evidence of the Assassination. However, no ancient rhetorical theorist could imagine the spectacle that an industrialized country in the Twentieth Century would be able to arrange. Classical theorists placed great emphasis upon the speech as an instrument of persuasion; Hitler demonstrated the importance of staging and spectacle to arouse the emotions of the audience and to heighten the effect of the speech.

The party rallies held in Nuremberg in September of each year were a good example of the use of spectacle by the Nazis and of the careful attention to detail that went into their production. The purpose of the rallies was to demonstrate to both Germany and the World the power and unity of the new German Reich. Party organizations and sections such as Hitler Youth, the SA, the SS, and party cadres from local bosses to regional directors, all got an opportunity to meet together, hear party directives, and parade before Hitler. Almost 500,000 persons from all over Germany would be brought to Nuremberg during the eight days in September to be indoctrinated in the new policies of the party and then sent back to their communities to spread the new line to others.[2]

Nuremberg, an ancient medieval town with Gothic cathedrals and gable roofed old houses, served as the setting for these rallies and symbolically united the old Germany with the new. Hitler always stayed at the Deutscher Hof where he frequently appeared on the balcony overlooking the moat in front of the hotel to receive the adulation of the crowd. His every appearance was carefully orchestrated for full dramatic effect. When he appeared at the opening meeting of the Party Congress at Luitpold Hall on the outskirts of the city, the vast auditorium was a sea of Nazi banners. A band that had been playing marching songs suddenly stopped. The crowd quieted, the band struck up the Bandenweiler March, and Hitler, Goring, Goebbels, Hess, and Himmler strode down the center aisle while 30,000 people stood at attention hands raised in the Nazi salute. Hitler mounted the floodlit stage and took his place surrounded by hundreds of party officials. Draped on the wall behind him was the sacred standard carried in the streets of Munich during the attempted "putsch." It was stained with the blood of martyrs, and before Hitler spoke, Hess read the name of each martyr. Members of the audience wept.[3]

Nuremberg provided an ideal setting for the vast open air pageants staged at night and so beloved by Hitler. One evening over 200,000 party faithful crowded into the open air stadium. Over 20,000 flags unfurled to the night breeze and were illuminated by long search lights that stabbed the night. After the chanting, singing, and playing of patriotic music, Hitler entered the stadium to a deafening roar. Standing in the back of the car, he acknowledged the salutes of the crowd. The pageantry of the occasion swept the crowd into an emotional crescendo that reached hysteria when Hitler began to speak. Later over 15,000 party faithful marched in a torchlight parade through the streets of Nuremberg while Hitler reviewed them.[4]

The theme of the 1934 Party Congress, "The Party Day of Unity," assumed great importance for both leadership and rank and file members of the Nazi party that year. Three months earlier, in June, Hitler ordered a bloody purge of the party in which thousands were arrested and shot without trial including many long time associates from the early days in Munich. Hitler worried that the brown-shirted Storm Troopers or SA led by Ernst Roehm posed a threat to his leadership. The SA leadership recalled the days when the Party was the National Socialist Party and resented Hitler's growing alliance with German industrialists. Hitler in turn realized that the boozing, brawling SA, whose members were mostly drawn from the lower classes, threatened the vital support of the Army whose leadership reflected the conservative values of the upper class. As Hamilton Burden wrote in his study of the Nuremberg rallies, "The leaders of the army...regarded the SA as an association of hoodlums and street brawlers. Although Hitler felt indebted to the SA for having stood by him in the years of crisis, he was dependent on the Army to keep him in power."[5]

Thus, toward the end of June, Hitler acted. At his order, Roehm and the rest of the SA leadership were arrested by the SS (the "elite guard" units, which comprised the military arm of the party) and executed without trial. A figurehead, Viktor Lutze, was installed in Roehm's place and instructed to keep the SA in line. The 1934 party rally was to be the first real test of how well he had succeeded.

THE SPEECH

The classical rhetorical system reflects a rational worldview. The members of the audience are rational persons capable of making decisions among competing policies, ideas, or claims, through an analysis of the proofs or evidence offered. Although Classical theory recognizes that emotion and personal influence often play a role in the decision making process, it emphasizes that the speaker must provide rational arguments to satisfy the critical mind of the listener. The classical system strives for a balanced effect—an effective speech should satisfy the demand of the audience for good reasons that are emotionally compelling and given by a believable speaker. Using this system to evaluate Hitler's speech, we can identify his major strategy. Hitler relied on emotional proof and personal force to the total exclusion of rational argument. He theorized that the masses possessed essentially "feminine" characteristics and had an "emotional longing" for domination by a "ruthless and fanatical" speaker.[6] Acting on this assumption, his speeches were not designed to persuade by rational argument but to move audiences by "divining the hidden passions, resentments, and longings in their minds."[7] A speech by Hitler conveyed "an extraordinary impression of force, the immediacy of passion, the intensity of hatred, fury and menace."[8] Often working himself into a rage, he "appeared to lose all control of himself...screamed at the top of his voice, spitting out a stream of abuse, (and) waving his arms wildly."[9] He told the audience what it wanted to hear: "the great universal obvious hopes: that Germany should once again become what it had been, that the economy should function, that the farmer...the townsman, the worker, the employer...should forget their differences and become one in...the love for Germany."[10] His speeches became melodramas of the fight between good and evil moving from the perilous state of the present to a glorious triumph over Germany's enemies. And always, He—Adolf Hitler—Der Führer, was the embodiment of the will of the people, the representative of the State, and the sole defender of the nation. The speech on the videotape, Great Speeches, Volume I, given to the closing session of the Party Congress at Nuremberg, September 14, 1934, is a good example of this technique. Evil is represented by the past—the old generation that grew up with the poisonous party politics of the corrupt parliamentary system. Unfortunately, some of those doubters found their way into the Party where their prejudices undermined its unity. Their "alien spirit" confused the "brain and heart" of the German people. Through vigilant actions of the party, those people have been weeded out of its ranks. This is the basic script of a melodrama—evil appeared, but good struggled with it and triumphed thanks to the leadership of Adolf Hitler. This is all nonsense, of course. It is Hitler's justification for ordering a bloody purge that left many of his old comrades dead—men who had been with him from the beginning in Munich and who now seemed a threat to his new respectability as Chancellor, and an irritant to his smooth dealings with the real source of power, the German Army. The purpose of the speech is to demonstrate to the German people and to the world that the Nazi Party is united behind Hitler's leadership. The speech will also provide an indirect justification for the recent purge that will suffice for loyal party members. Hitler does this in a very traditional way. He secures the good will of the audience by complimenting them as the elite of the German nation. He refers to them as "the best racial component of the nation," and later he says that "only the best National Socialists become party members." What does it mean to be part of the elite? For Hitler, it means three things: to be strong, to be pure, and to be young. Hitler's notion of strength is made clear when he refers to "the spectacular forcefulness of this imposing review of the armies of the party" and later when he says that the party members "will form and firm the German people and carry on their shoulders the German state and the German Reich." Purity means that the party members hold to their right ideas, "truly ideological," and possess "the very best German blood" in contrast to the Jews whose "unclean blood" polluted Germany. Hitler explicitly says that the party is aimed at the young, "Where the older generation might still waver, the youth is sworn to us and given to us, body and soul."

According to Hitler's address, this elitism of the party is achieved in two ways: by a selective recruitment and by weeding out undesirable elements. Hitler brings up the selectivity issue in several parts of the speech. Early in the speech, he reminds them of the legendary "days when it was difficult to be a National Socialist...when our party comprised just seven people." Shortly thereafter, he claims "we mobilize the most valuable elements of fight and sacrifice in the nation, and they are never a majority but always a minority." And, still later, he proclaims that "...only the best National Socialists become party members."

The issue of purging certain deviant elements from the party is mentioned only once, but it is a clear reference to the housecleaning by bullets which the SA underwent a few months earlier. Hitler points out that, in the early days, the party was spared this task as political oppression eliminated weaker elements from the party; but "Now we must practice selectiveness ourselves and expel what has proved to be rotten and therefore not of our kind."

Thus, Hitler's message is essentially one of congratulation. The party members are congratulated for being part of a strong, young, and pure elite, which owes its status to the fact that it is a minority that is periodically purged of undesirables.

The delivery of the first part of the speech is restrained, almost matter-of-fact. In his speeches Hitler liked to build slowly toward a crescendo of passion whipping himself and his audience into hysteria. His voice was harsh and conveyed an extraordinary impression of force. The sound of the voice alone communicated an intensity of hatred, fury, and menace regardless of what he said. Hitler had an extraordinary talent for self-dramatization and for role playing. He could easily switch from one mood to another and be absolutely convincing. His gestures reflected his changing mood. At the beginning of the speech they are restrained. When he builds to an important point, they become vigorous and even threatening. He slashes the air with his hand or pounds the podium with his fist.

Whenever Hitler refers to "us" (meaning the Party), he touches himself or hits himself on the chest. This occurs every time he used words like "we" or "us." Also, when he uses the word "leadership" he again touches himself. The message is clear. Hitler is the party; Hitler is the leader. The party has no leadership, no existence without him. The assembled party members have no existence without him.

EVALUATION

As the videotape clearly indicates, this speech was a rousing success with the immediate audience. Afterward, when Hitler's sycophant, Rudolf Hess, shouted out the phrases, "Hitler is the Party! The Party is Hitler!" and "Hitler is Germany! Germany is Hitler!" the crowd roared its approval. Hitler achieved his goals: he got the adulation of the crowd and he got the demonstration of Party unity.

The Nazi leaders were greatly impressed with their ability to organize party rallies that produced mass hysteria. So impressed were they that Hitler personally chose Leni Riefenstahl to produce a feature length film of the Sixth Party Congress for use in propaganda efforts abroad. Hitler assumed that other audiences particularly those outside of Germany would be equally enthusiastic about the Nazi message. In this he was wrong. The audiences were impressed by the spectacle but shocked at the scenes of otherwise sensible people losing themselves in an emotional frenzy of adulation for a despotic dictator. In this case a message effective for a friendly audience was evaluated differently by an audience that retained its rational faculties. The film had a boomerang effect. It helped to solidify opposition to Hitler and his methods in the democratic states of Europe and in the United States. When people saw the irrational forces unleashed by the maniacal figure of Hitler, it made them understand the threat the Nazis posed to the values of Western Civilization. As the classical system postulates, man is a reasoning being. In the short run, his emotions may make him act foolishly; but to be effective over time, a persuasive message must include good reasons that can be critically evaluated by the audience. Hitler gambled that the irrational fears and hatreds of the audience magnified by spectacular displays of powerful symbols would be sufficient to overcome the rationality of the human mind. He and his audience paid a terrible price for that gamble when Allied troops marched into Berlin in April, 1945.

J. Justin Gustainis, Ph.D., is an assistant professor of speech at the State University of New York College—Plattsburgh.

NOTES

1. Allan Bullock, *Hitler: A Study in Tyranny* (New York: Harper and Row, 1962).
2. Hamilton T. Burden, *The Nuremberg Party Rallies, 1923-1939* (New York: Praeger, 1967), Chapter 1.
3. William L. Shirer, *Berlin Diary: The Journal of a Foreign Correspondent 1934-1941* (New York: Alfred A. Knopf, Inc., 1941), pp. 16-21, 23.
4. *Ibid.*
5. Burden.
6. Adolf Hitler, *Mein Kampf*, trans. Ralph Manheim (Boston: Houghton Mifflin Co., 1943), pp. 337-338.

7. Bullock, pp. 372 ff.

8. *Ibid.*

9. *Ibid.*

10. Ernst Nolte, *Three Faces of Fascism: Action Francaise, Italian Fascism, National Socialism,* trans. Lelia Vennewitz (New York: Holt, Rinehart and Winston, Inc., 1966), pp. 292-293.

"WE AIN'T GOING"

Stokeley Carmichael

Tougaloo College, Tougaloo, Mississippi, April 11, 1967 (Transcribed from excerpts on the video, GREAT SPEECHES, VOLUME VIII)

(Tapping on microphones) I'm trying to figure out which one belongs to the CIA. SNCC...it was once one of the only places we could run to for safety when we started to work in Mississippi in 1961 and '62; so that it's sort of like coming home when we come back to Tougaloo.

Now I want you to, before I begin, to take a look at all the press men before you. You will notice that not one of them are [sic] black. And they are going to have the nerve, tomorrow, to call me a racist. Do you hear me? But we understand how the honkies are—they don't recognize their own racism.

I understand that I'm following the "Great White Father," Bobby Kennedy. I understand last night he told you a couple of things. Now I want to put some of them in perspective for you. When he said the world belongs to you, that comes from a great black man by the name of Frederick Douglas. He said the world belongs to you! Secondly, I understand that Bobby urged us to stand up and speak out against injustice. Well we could tell him that we don't need anybody to tell us to stand up any more. Not only are we going to stand up, we are going to right the wrongs of our people in this generation.

Our generation has the memories of the unpunished murders of Schwainey, Goodley (names spelled as mispronounced by the speaker) and of Medgar Evers. There are going to be no more unpunished murders! No more.

They've been telling you that the kids in Nashville started a riot. Number one, you ought to recognize it is not a riot, it is a rebellion. A rebellion. And number two, you ought to be proud of your black brothers and sisters at Fisk, because a honkey cop touched one of them and they told him, "You've got to touch all of us!" All of us!"

We just have to recognize as we move in this year, that we have to let them know that the days of a honkey cop running in our neighborhood, beating us up and running out are over...over...over.

Now we want to talk about several things tonight. We want to theoretically speak about the theories and the basic assumptions from which the Student Nonviolent Coordinating Committee proceeds. Which will be theories about self-condemnation, denial of one's freedom, the importance of definitions in the world today, and violence. And then we want to move in and speak about those pragmatically in terms of shame that black people feel for themselves, the education system that is completely racist in this society and that is geared against us. We want to talk about developing a concept of "peoplehood" for black people in this country and around the world which is desperately needed. We want to develop that and instill in our people the right to fight back against anybody who messes with us.

Now then we want to talk about the theories of self-condemnation. The existentialist philosophers, Camus and Sartre, notably raise the question about self-condemnation.

They want to know whether or not it is possible for a man to condemn himself. They never answer the question. The revolutionary philosopher, Franz Fanon, answers the question. He said it's impossible. You ought to know Fanon, he's a beautiful black brother. Now let us give...I...we don't think self-condemnation is possible in SNCC—we just don't think it is possible and there are several examples for us, in our generation.

For example, the Nazis after World War II when they had the Nuremberg trials; the Nazis they arrested—if they condemned themselves, they had to inflict punishment upon themselves. An example is that any of the Nazis whom they arrested who lived...who allowed themselves to live...said that they killed Jews who were inferior; they weren't human beings. So they didn't kill human beings, or they said that they didn't know what was happening in Germany at the time the Jews were being killed, or, more sophisticatedly and as more people in America today say, they were just following law and order.

Now the Nazis who admitted that they killed human beings have to commit suicide. They had to commit suicide. The only ones that were able to live were the ones who rationalized away their own guilt. Now that's very important. An immediate example for those of us here in Mississippi would be Mashoba County, Philadelphia, Mississippi where a honkey by the name of Raney and eight other honkies decided to kill...the honkies decided that they had the right to kill three human beings.

Now the entire county of Mashoba is incapable of indicting Raney and his honkies for what they did because they elected Raney to do precisely what he did—to kill anybody who tried to change the status quo. So that it is crystal clear that self-condemnation is, in fact, impossible.

White America cannot do it. If she did she would have to commit suicide. That may not be such a bad idea. So since she cannot condemn herself, it is for us, Black people upon whom she has perpetrated those crimes, to condemn her and to go on for ourselves. We must stop seeking to imitate white society. We must create for ourselves to save our very humanity. Alright?

Now the second very important point—we want to make a differentiation between giving one one's freedom and denying one one's freedom. In this country you would think that white people are gods—that they had the right to give us our freedom. And so what we had to do was to beg them or to act the way they want us to act before they gave us our freedom. You ought to make it crystal clear in your mind that all men are born free but that they are enslaved by other people. That is to say that white America is denying us our freedom. So she can't give it to us. Her job is to stop denying us of our freedom. In other words she ought to become more civilized. You ought to understand that (unintelligible).

They have defined us as Negroes. No where else in the world is there such a word. When we went to Puerto Rico we delivered our speech in Spanish and we tried to find a word that equals Negro in Spanish. There is no such word. The nearest word is "*Negro*" which means "black." There is no such word in German. There is no such word in Swahili. There is no such word in France. The only word is "Negro" and they have named us "Negro" and put with it the adjectives that they have: lazy, stupid, apathetic, loves watermelon, has good rhythm. And when we say that we are black the honkies got a nerve to tell us, "You're not black."

But now there is something, there's something much more insidious about definitions and that is what white America has been able to do is to try to make us react to their definitions of our very terms. Let me give another example. We remember in 1954 when Dr. King and the other great black leaders would say, "We want to integrate." In the minds of black people across this country we meant good housing, good schools, good jobs, better neighborhoods and a good way of life. That was crystal clear in our minds. But as soon as they were on TV or in public area, when they said the word, "integration," some dumb honkey was going to jump up and say, "You want to marry my daughter don't you?

Now, instead...instead of our black leaders...instead of our black leaders having the strength to tell the honkey later, they begin to react to his definition. They would say, "Oh, oh, no, no we don't want to marry your daughter. We don't want to be your brother-in-law, we just want to be your brother. Uh, we don't want to sleep in your bedroom, we just want to make (unintelligible)...." So that what white America was able to do was to have us react to her definition of our term and we never got anywhere because we were playing her game.

Now in SNCC when they ask us that question about whether or not we want to marry their daughters we tell them, "Your daughter, your sister, your mama."

The white woman is not the queen of the world. She's not the Virgin May. She's not.... We tell them so they won't forget, "She's not the Virgin May. She can be made like any other woman. Let's move on. Let's move on."

We have got to see ourselves as a group. We must see ourselves as a community wherever we are and we must let them know that infringement on one is infringement on all...all. Because if we let the honkies know that every time they touch one of us they got to face all of us, they won't touch any of us.

But in order to develop a concept of neighborhood you must know who you are and where you came from, yeah. Do you know that when we asked college students on black college campuses, "Where you from?" "Jackson." "Where [sic] your mother from?" "Jackson." "Where your [sic] grandmother from?" "Jackson." "Where your [sic] great grandmother from?" "Nuh, uh." She is from Africa! Did you hear what I said? She is from Africa and if you don't know how she got here I will tell you. White folks stole her and brought her here...from Africa. But you are ashamed of Africa because you don't know anything but what the honkies tell you about Africa. Yeah.

They start off their civilization with Greece. Yeah. Did they ever tell you that the first university in the world was the University of Timbuktu in Africa? Africa.

Now then finally we want to talk about this thing called "violence" that everybody is so afraid about. Here you are talking about how you afraid of violence and the honkey is drafting you out of school to go fight in Vietnam...to go fight in Vietnam. There you going to set in front of your television set and listen to LBJ tell you that, "Violence never accomplishes anything my fellow Americans." And you're going to set there agreeing with him that violence never accomplishes anything while he's bombing the hell out of North Vietnam.

Don't you see the real problem with violence is that we have never been violent. We have been too nonviolent...too nonviolent...too nonviolent, yeah. The problem isn't that we are violent. The problem is that every time they come into our neighborhood, beat our ass and go back out, we set there and talk about it in a whisper. And today we're telling them hard in their mind, if you touch us with your hand we're going to break your arm...break your arm...break your arm.

So when they come to teach you about nonviolence, tell them you don't need it. Tell them we have been nonviolent. We don't bomb churches. We don't shoot people. We don't lynch people. We don't beat them and throw them in jail. Tell the honkies who are violent to be nonviolent.

We are distressed when they yell, "Burn, baby, burn," because they taught us how to burn. They burned all our churches down to the ground. And nobody in this society ever sought to stop them when they burned our church down but when we retaliate everybody is upset.

Don't you worry about it because we're not going to take it any more. In Lawrence County, Alabama last month, they burned two churches to the ground—they were black churches. A week later a white church was burned to the ground...the ground. Either we will all worship inside or we will all worship outside.

Now let us forget about the issue of violence. This is the most violent society there is. You can't turn on your television set without five minutes getting entertainment of shoot 'em up, killing up and jujitsu chop 'em up.

Now then we want to talk pragmatically about black people and particularly about you black students here at Tougaloo. Now what this country has done she's—white America—is that she's told a number of lies about us which she believes. Now that's bad. But what is pathetic is that a number of us believe those lies ourselves...ourselves. And now what we have to do...what we have to do today is to begin to "un-brainwash" ourselves about those lies about ourselves. Let us give some examples.

White Western society told us that she was civilized and she was coming to civilize us. So she came to Africa and our first act of contact with civilization: the honkies made us slaves. And now there we were believing that that was civilization. There we were just running around, swinging on the vine beating our (unintelligible) drum not messing with anybody...not messing with anybody. And here comes this honkey who's going to civilize us and makes us slaves. Obviously they don't know now and then never did know what civilization is all about...is all about.

But be that as it may, White America has always said in her history that she came to do so many good things—to help everybody else. They're getting ready to help Latin America right now in parts of (unintelligible). (Aside) I'm going to do it.

They came to Africa to make us civilized. They came to Africa to tell us about Jesus Christ. We were in Africa; they were in Europe. They had the Bible; we had the land. They came to be missionaries. When they left, they had the land; we still had the Bible. Jesus Christ says it is more honorable to suffer than to inflict suffering. Yeah.

When you are called to serve, you have a choice. Either you say no and face the possibility of going to jail or you become a hired killer. You inflict suffering on somebody. It is more honorable to suffer. You should join "The Greatest," Mohammed Ali and tell them, "Hell no, I ain't going."

But now for the black youth it is a particular reason why we shouldn't go to the war in Vietnam. Our problem has been as black people we have always been concerned about White America; never about us. And what we've always thought is that White America equal the same interest as us. That is not true. We must now be concerned with us. Let me give you some examples.

We always want to prove what good Americans we are. The very first man to die for the War of Independence in this country was a black man named Crispus Attucks...Crispus Attucks. Because here he was dying for white folk freedom and million *[sic]* of his brothers were enslaved in the very country. Ah, but we wanted to prove what great Americans we were. We begged the white folk to let us fight for the War of Independence. But they said no. So we organized ourselves into bands of armies, training ourselves with our barefoot, to prove to the white folk what great Americans we were. "Please let us fight, white folk." And finally they came and inspected our troops and said, "Good, nigger, you can fight." And they had us fighting the Indians—like fools. We should have teamed up with the Indians and attack the white folk.

But we went out there and we shed our blood...our blood...for the freedom of this country. And when it was over they gave us some medals, a piece of paper and tapped us on the head and told us, "Good niggers." But we weren't satisfied. We were going to prove to this country what great Americans we were.

You will notice...you will notice that your teachers don't know anything about you. How can they teach you? How can they teach you? How can they teach you? Because the move in this country today is to destroy the black colleges and the black ideology. Tougaloo College used to have a black ideology and then you became a brown baby. Yes, yes, and you've got all these young nice white liberal people who never heard of Frederick Douglas teaching you...teaching you. You ought to go to Brown and teach them who never heard of Abraham Lincoln.

Did you read...did you read? You see if you were reading Malcolm X speech *[sic]* and the *Autobiography of Malcolm X,* when you hear his name you would jump to your feet. But you don't read it. You don't read it. What you read is what white folk tell you about Malcolm X. He hated people and you don't want to read him and you live in a world filled with white people who hate you. And you read about...you read about people who are filled with hate telling you that a black man hated white folk and you don't want to read him and you read a white man full of hate against you. You ought to read the primary source for yourself that's what you're in school for.

You have got to know the truth about yourself. The world is moving around us. Every student group around the world is moving for their liberation except us. We're sitting like bumps on a log waiting for white people to come and help us, help us.

You ought to recognize what's going on in that Vietnamese War. Here they taking you, training you to be a soldier, making you shine your shoes until three o'clock in the morning, going 8,000 miles to shoot a man and he ain't never called you a nigger. Yeah.

Now we are not only opposed the war in Vietnam, we're opposed to compulsory conscription. We are against the draft. Now we're against the draft for anybody—black or white.

Now we recognize that when we say, "Hell no," they will say that we should go to jail. Don't be afraid. It is much better to be confined in jail knowing that you have not killed anybody than to be walking outside a murderer...a murderer...a murderer. We must save our humanity—we must. If this country wants to bomb the rest of the world, let them. We will tell them the war in Vietnam is for the birds—Lynda Bird, Lady Bird, Lucy Bird—the birds, the birds, the birds.

(Crowd begins chant, "Hell no, we ain't going" and Carmichael joins in on the, "We ain't going." Chant lasts ten minutes.)

We will tell them. We will tell them that this generation is out of breath. We will face them wherever they come; any time they come. Black power!

KEYNOTE ADDRESS

Barbara Jordan

Democratic National Convention, New York City, July 12, 1976 (Transcribed from the video, GREAT SPEECHES, VOLUME IV)

Thank you ladies and gentlemen for a very warm reception. It was one hundred and forty-four years ago that members of the Democratic Party first met in convention to select a Presidential candidate. Since that time, Democrats have continued to convene once every four years and draft a party platform and nominate a Presidential candidate, and our meeting this week is a continuation of that tradition. But there is something different about tonight. There is something special about tonight. What is different? What is special? I, Barbara Jordan, am a keynote speaker. A lot of years passed since 1832, and during that time it would have been most unusual for any national political party to ask a Barbara Jordan to deliver a keynote address, but tonight here I am. And I feel...I feel that notwithstanding the past that my presence here is one additional bit of evidence that the American Dream need not forever be deferred.

Now...now that I have this grand distinction what in the world am I supposed to say? I could easily spend this time praising the accomplishments of this party and attacking the Republicans but I don't choose to do that. I could list the many problems which Americans have. I could list the problems which cause people to feel cynical, angry, frustrated: problems which include lack of integrity in government; the feeling that the individual no longer counts; the reality of material and spiritual poverty; the feeling that the grand American experiment is failing or has failed. I could recite these problems and then I could sit down and offer no solutions. But I don't choose to do that either. The citizens of America expect more. They deserve and they want more than a recital of problems.

We are a people in a quandary about the present. We are a people in search of our future. We are a people in search of a national community. We are a people trying not only to solve the problems of the present—unemployment, inflation—but we are attempting on a larger-scale to fulfill the promise of America. We are attempting to fulfill our national purpose; to create and sustain a society in which all of us are equal.

Throughout...throughout our history, when people have looked for new ways to solve their problems, and to uphold the principles of this nation, many times they have turned to political parties. They have often turned to the Democratic Party. What is it, what is it about the Democratic Party that makes it the instrument the people use when they search for ways to shape their future? Well I believe the answer to that question lies in our concept of governing. Our concept of governing is derived from our view of people. It is a concept deeply rooted in a set of beliefs firmly etched in the national conscience of all of us. Now what are these beliefs?

First, we believe in equality for all and privileges for none. This is a belief...this is a belief that each American regardless of background has equal standing in the public forum—all of us. Because...because we believe this idea so firmly, we are an inclusive rather than an exclusive party. Let everybody come. I think it no accident that most of

63

those immigrating to America in the Nineteenth Century identified with the Democratic Party. We are a heterogeneous party made up of Americans of diverse backgrounds.

We believe that the people are the source of all governmental power; that the authority of the people is to be extended not restricted. This...this can be accomplished only by providing each citizen with every opportunity to participate in the management of the government. They must have that.

We believe...we believe that the government which represents the authority of all the people, not just one interest group, but all the people, has an obligation to actively—underscore actively—seek to remove those obstacles which would block individual achievement—obstacles emanating from race, sex, economic condition. The government must remove them; seek to remove them.

We...we are a party...we are a party of innovation. We do not reject our traditions, but we are willing to adapt to changing circumstances, when change we must. We are willing to suffer the discomfort of change in order to achieve a better future. We have a positive vision of the future founded on the belief that the gap between the promise and reality of America can one day be finally closed. We believe that.

This my friends, is the bedrock of our concept of governing. This is a part of the reason why Americans have turned to the Democratic Party. These are the foundations upon which a national community can be built. Let all understand that these guiding principles cannot be discarded for short-term political gains. They represent what this country is all about. They are indigenous to the American idea and these are principles which are not negotiable.

In other times...in other times, I could stand here and give this kind of exposition on the beliefs of the Democratic Party and that would be enough, but today that is not enough. People want more. That is not sufficient reason for the majority of the people of this country to decide to vote Democratic. We have made mistakes. We realize that. We admit our mistakes. In our haste to do all things for all people, we did not foresee the full consequences of our actions, and when the people raised their voices, we didn't hear. But our deafness was only a temporary condition, and not an irreversible condition. Even as I stand here and admit that we have made mistakes I still believe that as the people of America sit in judgment on each party they will recognize that our mistakes were mistakes of the heart. They'll recognize that.

And now...now we must look to the future. Let us heed the voice of the people and recognize their common sense. If we do not, we not only blaspheme our political heritage, we ignore the common ties that bind all Americans. Many fear the future. Many are distrustful of their leaders, and believe that their voices are never heard. Many seek only to satisfy their private work wants; to satisfy their private interests.

But this is the great danger America faces. That we will cease to be one nation and become instead a collection of interest groups—city against suburb, region against region, individual against individual—each seeking to satisfy private wants. If that happens, who then will speak for America? Who then will speak for the common good? This is the question which must be answered in 1976. Are we to be one people bound together by common spirit sharing in a common endeavor or will we become a divided nation?

For all of its uncertainty, we cannot flee the future. We must not become the new puritans and reject our society. We must address and master the future together. It can be done if we restore the belief that we share a sense of national community; that we share a common national endeavor. It can be done.

There is no executive order; there is no law that can require the American people to form a national community. This we must do as individuals and if we do it as individuals, there is no President of the United States who can veto that decision.

As a first step...as a first step, we must restore our belief in ourselves. We are a generous people so why can't we be generous with each other? We need to take to heart the words spoken by Thomas Jefferson: Let us restore the social intercourse..."Let us restore to social intercourse that harmony and that affection without which liberty and even life are but dreary things." A nation is formed by the willingness of each of us to share in the responsibility for upholding the common good. A government is invigorated when each one of us is willing to participate in shaping the future of this nation.

In this election year we must define the common good and begin again to shape a common future. Let each person do his or her part. If one citizen is unwilling to participate, all of us are going to suffer. For the American idea, though it is shared by all of us, is realized in each one of us.

And now, what are those of us who are elected public officials supposed to do? We call ourselves public servants but I'll tell you this: We as public servants must set an example for the rest of the nation. It is hypocritical for the public official to admonish and exhort the people to uphold the common good if we are derelict in upholding the common good. More is required...more is required of public officials than slogans and handshakes and press releases. More is required. We must hold ourselves strictly accountable. We must provide the people with a vision of the future. If we promise as public officials, we must deliver. If...if we as public officials propose, we must produce. If we say to the American people it is time for you to be sacrificial: sacrifice. If the public official says that we must be the first to give; we must be. And again, if we make mistakes, we must be willing to admit them. We have to do that. What we have to do is strike a balance between the idea that government should do everything and the idea, the belief, that government ought to do nothing. Strike a balance.

Let there be no illusions about the difficulty of forming this kind of a national community. It's tough, difficult, not easy. But a spirit of harmony will survive in America only if each of us remembers that we share a common destiny; if each of us remembers when self-interest and bitterness seem to prevail, that we share a common destiny.

I have confidence that we can form this kind of national community. I have confidence that the Democratic Party can lead the way. I have that confidence. We cannot improve on the system of government handed down to us by the founders of the Republic—there is no way to improve upon that—but what we can do is to find new ways to implement that system and realize our destiny.

Now, I began this speech by commenting to you on the uniqueness of a Barbara Jordan making a keynote address. Well I am going to close my speech by quoting a Republican President and I ask you that as you listen to these words of Abraham Lincoln, relate them to the concept of a national community in which every last one of us participates: "As I would not be a slave, so I would not be a master." This...this...this expresses my idea of democracy. Whatever differs from this, to the extent of the difference, is no democracy.

Thank you.

KEYNOTE ADDRESS

Mario Cuomo

Democratic National Convention, San Francisco, California, July 17, 1984
(Transcribed from the video, GREAT SPEECHES, VOLUME IV)

Please allow me to skip the stories and the poetry and the temptation to deal in nice but vague rhetoric. Let me instead use this valuable opportunity to deal immediately with the questions that should determine this election and that we all know are vital to the American people.

Ten days ago, President Reagan admitted that although some people in this country seem to be doing well nowadays, others were unhappy, even worried, about themselves, their families and their futures. The President said that he didn't understand that fear. He said, "Why, this country is a shining city on a hill." And the President is right. In many ways we are "a shining city on a hill." But the hard truth is that not everyone is sharing in this city's splendor and glory. A shining city is perhaps all the President sees from the portico of the White House and the verandah of his ranch, where everyone seems to be doing well.

But there's another city, there's another part to the shining city, the part where some people can't pay their mortgages and most young people can't afford one, where students can't afford the education they need and middle-class parents watch the dreams they hold for their children evaporate. In this part of the city there are more poor than ever, more families in trouble. More and more people who need help but can't find it. Even worse: There are elderly people who tremble in the basements of the houses there. And there are people who sleep in the city's streets, in the gutter, where the glitter doesn't show. There are ghettos where thousands of young people, without a job or an education, give their lives away to drug dealers every day.

There is despair, Mr. President, in the faces that you don't see, in the places that you don't visit in your shining city. In fact, Mr. President, this is a nation...Mr. President, you ought to know that this nation is more a "Tale of Two Cities" than it is just a "Shining City on a Hill." Maybe...maybe, Mr. President, if you visited some more places; maybe if you went to Appalachia where some people still live in sheds; maybe if you went to Lackawanna where thousands of unemployed steel workers wonder why we subsidize foreign steel; maybe, maybe, Mr. President, if you stopped in at a shelter in Chicago and spoke to the homeless there; maybe, Mr. President, if you asked a woman who had been denied the help she needed to feed her children because you said you needed the money for a tax break for a millionaire or for a missile we couldn't afford to use; maybe, maybe, Mr. President, but I'm afraid not.

Because, the truth is, ladies and gentlemen, that this is how we were warned it would be. President Reagan told us from the very beginning that he believed in a kind of social Darwinism—survival of the fittest. "Government can't do everything," we were told. "So it should settle for taking care of the strong and hope that economic ambition and charity will do the rest. Make the rich richer and what falls from the table will be enough for the middle class and those who are trying desperately to work their way into the middle class." You know the Republicans called it trickle-down when Hoover tried it. Now they call it supply-side, but its the same shining city for those relative few who are lucky enough to live in its good neighborhoods. But for the people who are excluded, for the people who are locked out—all they can do is stare from a distance at that city's glimmering towers.

It's an old story. It's as old as our history. The difference between Democrats and Republicans has always been measured in courage and confidence. The Republicans...the Republicans believe that the wagon train will not make it to the frontier unless some of the old, some of the young, some of the weak are left behind by the side of the trail. The strong, the strong they tell us will inherit the land! We Democrats believe in something else. We Democrats believe that we can make it all the way with the whole family in tact. And we have more than once, ever since Franklin Roosevelt lifted himself from his wheelchair to lift this nation from its knees. Wagon train after wagon train, to new frontiers of education, housing, peace; the whole family aboard; constantly reaching out to extend and enlarge that family; lifting them up into the wagon on the way; Blacks and Hispanics and people of every ethnic group, and Native Americans— all those struggling to build their families and claim some small share of America. For nearly 50 years we carried them all to new levels of comfort and security and dignity, even affluence; and remember this, some of us in this room today are here only because this nation had that kind of confidence. And it would be wrong to forget that.

So, here we are at this convention to remind ourselves where we come from and to claim the future for ourselves and for our children. Today, our great Democratic Party, which has saved this nation from depression, from fascism, from racism, from corruption, is called upon to do it again—this time to save the nation from confusion and division, from the threat of eventual fiscal disaster, and most of all from the fear of a nuclear holocaust—but that's not going to be easy. Mo Udall is exactly right, it won't be easy and in order to succeed, we must answer our opponents polished and appealing rhetoric with a more telling reasonableness and rationality. We must win this case on the merits. We must get the American public to look past the glitter, beyond the showmanship—to the reality, the hard substance of things. And we'll do it, not so much with speeches that sound good as with speeches that are good and sound; not so much with speeches that will bring people to their feet as with speeches that will bring people to their senses. We must make...we must make the American people hear our "Tale of Two Cities." We must convince them that we don't have to settle for two city [sic] cities, that we can have one city, indivisible, shining for all of its people.

Now we will have no chance to do that if what comes out of this convention is a babble of arguing voices. If that's what's heard throughout the campaign—dissident sounds from all sides—we will have no chance to tell our message. To succeed we will have to surrender some small parts of our individual interests, to build a platform that we can all stand on, at once and comfortably. Proudly singing out, we need...we need a platform we can all agree to so that we can sing out the truth for the nation to hear, in chorus, its logic so clear and commanding that no slick Madison Avenue commercial, no amount of geniality, no martial music will be able to muffle the sound of the truth. And we Democrats must unite...we Democrats must unite so that the entire nation can unite, because surely the Republicans won't bring this country together. Their policies divide the nation into the lucky and the left out, into the royalty and the rabble. The Republicans are willing to treat that division as victory. They would cut this nation in half, into those temporarily better off and those worse off than before. And they would call that division recovery. Now we should not...now we should not be embarrassed or dismayed or chagrined if the process of unifying is difficult, even wrenching at times.

Remember that unlike any other party, we embrace men and women of every color, every creed, every orientation, every economic class. In our family are gathered everyone from the abject poor of Essex County in New York to the enlightened affluent of the gold coasts at both ends of the nation. And in between is the heart of our constituency: the middle class, the people not rich enough to be worry-free but not poor enough to be on welfare, the middle class—those people who work for a living because they have to not because some psychiatrist told them it was a convenient way to fill the interval between birth and eternity—white collar and blue collar, young professionals—men and women in small business desperate for the capital and contracts that they need to prove their worth. We speak for the minorities who have not yet entered the mainstream. We speak for ethnics who want to add their culture to the magnificent mosaic that is America. We speak...we speak for women who are indignant that this nation refuses to etch into its governmental commandments the simple rule, "thou shalt not sin against equality," a rule so simple—I was going to say, and I perhaps dare not, but I will; its a commandment so simple it can be spelled in three letters—ERA! We speak...we speak for young people demanding an education and a future. We speak for senior citizens...we speak for senior citizens who are terrorized by the idea that their only security, their Social Security, is being threatened. We speak for millions of reasoning people fighting to preserve our environment from greed and from stupidity.

And we speak for reasonable people who are fighting to preserve our very existence from a macho intransigence that refuses to make intelligent attempts to discuss the possibility of nuclear holocaust with our enemy. They refuse...they refuse because they believe we can pile missiles so high that they will pierce the clouds and the sight of them will frighten our enemies into submission .

Now we're proud of this diversity. As Democrats we're grateful for it, we don't have to manufacture it the way the Republicans will next month in Dallas, by propping up mannequin delegates on the convention floor. But we—while we're proud of this diversity—we pay a price for it. The different people that we represent have different points of view. And sometimes they compete and even debate, and even argue. That's what our primaries were all about.

But now the primaries are over, and it is time when we pick our candidates and our platform here to lock arms and move into this campaign together. If you need any more inspiration to put some small part of your own difference aside to create this consensus then all you need to do is to reflect on what the Republican policy of "divide and cajole" has done to this land since 1980.

Now the President has asked the American people to judge him on whether or not he's fulfilled the promises he made four years ago. I believe as Democrats we ought to accept that challenge and just for a moment let us consider what he has said and what he's done. Inflation...inflation is down since 1980, but not because of the supply-side miracle promised to us by the President. Inflation was reduced the old-fashioned way, with a recession, the worse since 1932. Now how did we...we could have brought inflation down that way. How did he do it: 55,000 bankruptcies, two years of massive unemployment, 200,000 farmers and ranchers forced off the land, more homeless... more homeless than at any time since the Great Depression in 1932, more hungry— in this world of enormous affluence, the United States of America, more hungry, more poor—most of them women—and...and, he paid one other thing, a nearly $200 billion deficit threatening our future.

Now we must make the American people understand this deficit because they don't. The President's deficit is a direct and dramatic repudiation of his promise in 1980 to balance the budget by 1983. How large is it? The deficit is the largest in the history of the universe. It *[sic]* President Carter's last budget had a deficit less than one third of this deficit. It is a deficit that, according to the President's own fiscal advisor, may grow to as much as $300 billion a year, for as far as the eye can see and ladies and gentlemen it is a debt so large that is *[sic]* almost one half of the money we collect from the personal income tax each year goes just to pay the interest. It is a mortgage on our children's future that can be paid only in pain and that could bring this nation to its knees.

Now don't take my word for it, I'm a Democrat. Ask the Republican investment bankers on Wall Street what they think the chances of this recovery being permanent are. You see, if they're not too embarrassed to tell you the truth, they'll say that they're appalled and frightened by the President's deficit. Ask them what they think of our economy, now that it has been driven by the distorted value of the dollar back to its colonial condition: Now we're exporting agricultural products and importing manufactured ones. Ask those Republican investment bankers what they expect the rate of interest to be a year from now. And ask them, if they dare tell you the truth, you'll learn from them what they predict for the inflation rate a year from now because of the deficit.

Now how important is this question of the deficit? Think about it practically: What chance would the Republican candidate have had in 1980 if he had told the American people that he intended to pay for his so-called economic recovery with bankruptcies, unemployment, more homeless, more hungry and the largest Government debt known to human kind? If he had told the voters in 1980 that truth would American voters have signed the loan certificate for him on Election Day? Of course not! That was an election won under false pretenses. It was won with smoke and mirrors and illusions. And that's the kind of recovery we have now as well.

And what about foreign policy? They said that they would make us and the whole world safer. They say they have by creating the largest defense budget in history—one that even they now admit is excessive—by escalating to a frenzy the nuclear arms race, by incendiary rhetoric, by refusing to discuss peace with our enemies, by the loss of 279 young Americans in Lebanon in pursuit of a plan and a policy that no one can find or describe. We give money to Latin American governments that murder nuns, and then we lie about it. We have been less than zealous in support of our only real friend, it seems to me, in the Middle East; the one democracy there, our flesh and blood ally, the State of Israel. Our...our policy...our foreign policy drifts with no real direction, other than an hysterical commitment to an arms race that leads nowhere, if we're lucky, and if we're not, it could lead us into bankruptcy or war.

Of course we must have a strong defense! Of course Democrats are for a strong defense. Of course Democrats believe that there are times that we must stand and fight, and we have. Thousands of us have paid for freedom with our lives, but always, when this country has been at its best, our purposes were clear. Now they're not. Now our allies are as confused as our enemies. Now we have no real commitment to our friends or to our ideals, not to human rights, not to the refuseniks, not to Sakharov, not to Bishop Tutu and the others struggling for freedom in South Africa. We...we have in the last few years spent more than we can afford. We have pounded our chests and made bold speeches, but we lost 279 young Americans in Lebanon and we live behind sandbags in Washington.

How can anyone say that we are safer, stronger or better? That...that is the Republican record. That it's disastrous quality is not more fully understood by the American people I can only attribute to the President's amiability and the failure by some to separate the salesman from the product. But now...now...now it's up to us, now it's up to you and to me to make the case to America. And to remind Americans that if they are not happy with all that the President has done so far, they should consider how much worse it will be if he is left to his radical proclivities for another four years unrestrained...unrestrained: If...if July...if July brings back Anne Gorsuch Burford, what can we expect of December? Where would...where would another four years take us? Where would four years more take us? How much larger will the deficit be? How much deeper the cuts in programs for the struggling middle class and the poor to limit that deficit? How high will the interest rates be? How much more acid rain killing our forests and fouling our lakes? And, ladies and gentlemen, please think of this, the nation must think of this: What kind of Supreme Court will we have? Please, we...we must ask ourselves what kind of Court and country will be fashioned by the man who believes in having government mandate people's religion and morality, the man who believes that trees pollute the environment, the man that believes that...that the laws against discrimination against people go too far, a man who threatens Social Security and Medicaid and help for the disabled? How high will we pile the missiles? How much deeper will the gulf be between us and our enemies? And, ladies and gentlemen, will four years more make meaner the spirit of the American people?

This election will measure the record of the past four years. But more than that, it will answer the question of what kind of people we want to be. We Democrats still have a dream. We still believe in this nation's future. And this is our answer to the question. This is our credo: We believe in only the government we need, but we insist on all the government we need. We believe in a government that is characterized by fairness and reasonableness, a reasonableness that goes beyond labels, that doesn't distort or promise to do things that we know we can't do. We believe in a government strong enough to use words like "love" and "compassion" and smart enough to convert our noblest aspirations into practical realities. We believe in encouraging the talented, but we believe that while survival of the fittest may be a good working description of the process of evolution, a government of humans should elevate itself to a higher order. We [sic] our...our government...our government should be able to rise to the level where it can fill the gaps that are left by chance or by a wisdom we don't fully understand. We would rather have laws written by the patron of this great city, the man called the "world's most sincere Democrat," St. Francis of Assisi, than laws written by Darwin. We believe...we believe, as Democrats, that a society as blessed as ours, the most affluent Democracy in the world's history, one that can spend trillions on instruments of destruction, ought to be able to help the middle class in its struggle, ought to be able to find work for all who can do it, room at the table, shelter for the homeless, care for the elderly and infirm and hope for the destitute. And we proclaim as loudly as we can the utter insanity of nuclear proliferation and the need for a nuclear freeze, if only to affirm the simple truth that peace is better than war because life is better than death. We believe in firm...we believe in firm but fair law and order. We believe proudly in the union movement. We believe...we believe in privacy for people, openness by government. We believe in civil rights and we believe in human rights. We believe in a single...we believe in a single fundamental idea that describes better than most textbooks and any speech that I could write what a proper government should be: the idea of family, mutuality; the sharing of benefits and burdens for the good of all; feeling one another's pain; sharing one another's blessings, reasonably, honestly, fairly without respect to race or sex or geography or political affiliation. We believe we must be the family of America; recognizing that at the heart of the matter we are bound one to another; that the problems of a retired school teacher in Duluth are our problems, that the future of the child...that the future of the child in Buffalo is our future, that the struggle of a disabled man in Boston to survive and live decently is our struggle, that the hunger of a woman in Little Rock is our hunger, that the failure anywhere to provide what reasonably we might, to avoid pain, is our failure.

For fifty years...for fifty years we Democrats created a better future for our children, using traditional Democratic principles as a fixed beacon, giving us direction and purpose, but constantly innovating, adapting to new realities; Roosevelt's alphabet programs; Truman's NATO and the GI Bill of Rights; Kennedy's intelligent tax incentives and the Alliance for Progress; Johnson's civil rights; Carter's human rights and the nearly miraculous Camp David peace accord. Democrats did it...Democrats did it, and Democrats can do it again. We can build a future that deals with our deficit. Remember this, that fifty years of progress under our principles never cost us what the last four years of stagnation have. And we can deal with the deficit intelligently, by shared sacrifice; with all parts of the nation's family contributing, building partnerships with the private sector, providing a sound defense without depriving ourselves of what we need to feed our children and care for our people.

We can have a future that provides for all the young of the present by marrying common sense and compassion. We know we can, because we did it for nearly fifty years before 1980. And we can do it again, if we do not forget...if we do not forget that this entire nation has profited by these progressive principles, that they helped lift up generations to the middle class and higher, that they gave us a chance to work, to go to college, to raise a family, to own a house, to be secure in our old age, and, before that, to reach heights that our own parents would not have dared dream of.

That struggle to live with dignity is the real story of the shining city. And it's a story, ladies and gentlemen, that I didn't read in a book or learn in a classroom. I saw it and lived it, like many of you. I watched a small man with thick calluses on both his hands work 15 and 16 hours a day. I saw him once literally bleed from the bottoms of his feet— a man who came here uneducated, alone, unable to speak the language, who taught me all I needed to know about faith and hard work by the simple eloquence of his example. I learned about our kind of democracy from my father. And I learned about our obligation to each other from him and my mother. They asked only for a chance to work and to make the world better for their children and they...they asked to be protected in those moments when they would not be able to protect themselves. This nation and this nation's government did that for them. And that they were able to build a family and live in dignity and see one of their children go from behind their little grocery store in South Jamaica on the other side of the tracks where he was born, to occupy the highest seat in the greatest state in the greatest nation in the only world we know is an ineffably beautiful tribute to the democratic process. And...and, ladies and gentlemen, on January 20, 1985 it will happen again, only on a much, much grander scale.

We will have a new President of the United States, a Democrat born not to the blood of kings but to the blood of pioneers and immigrants. And we will have America's first woman Vice President, the child of immigrants and she...she...she will open with one magnificent stroke a whole new frontier for the United States. Now it will happen...it will happen; if we make it happen, if you and I make it happen. And I ask you now, ladies and gentlemen, brothers and sisters—for the good of all of us, for the love of this great nation, for the family of America, for the love of God—please make this nation remember how futures are built. Thank you and God bless you.

SITUATION, SPEAKER, METAPHOR

The Rhetorical Dynamics of Mario Cuomo's 1984 Keynote Address

. . . this nation is more a "Tale of Two Cities" than it is a "Shining City on a Hill."

CRITIC: David Henry

(This essay is reprinted by permission of the Southern Speech Communication Association for whom it appeared in the Southern *Speech Communication Journal.*)

Reaction to Mario Cuomo's keynote address at the 1984 Democratic National Convention was almost universally positive. ABC News commentator David Brinkley rated it among the most memorable convention speeches he had ever witnessed.[1] In the opposition camp, Senator Barry Goldwater called it "one of the best speeches I've ever heard,"[2] and President Reagan lamented to his aids the next morning that Cuomo "really was out there kicking my brains out last night."[3] Even conservative columnist George Will allowed that the New York Governor "did what a keynote speaker is supposed to do" by using "grade-A delivery" to convince "the conventioneers that they are the children of light, destined to push back the darkness."[4]

Democratic responses were, predictably, even more enthusiastic. A South Carolina delegate said Cuomo "overwhelmed" her because "he talks from the heart." And a Maryland state legislator echoed her sentiment when commenting that "He's reaching an emotional chord that hasn't been touched since John Kennedy."[5] Press commentary, too, cited Cuomo's Kennedy-like appeal, though the New York *Times'* Howell Raines suggested the ovation Cuomo received was "reminiscent in its fervor of that given Senator Edward M. Kennedy of Massachusetts at the 1980 convention."[6] Hedrick Smith attributed Cuomo's impact to his manner, as "with his eyes welling with tears and a powerful rhythmic delivery, the Governor repeatedly aroused the Democrats to foot-stomping applause and roaring partisan chants."[7] Cuomo's manner dominated the observations of others as well, who labeled his demeanor variously as "like a priest," in "the fashion of a lawyer," and "professorial."[8]

Though noteworthy for what they convey about the speech's immediate impact, such impressions are not in and of themselves particularly valuable to the speech critic. Movement beyond the surface reactions to a textual examination of the speech proves a productive enterprise, however, for what is revealed about its rhetorical dynamics. For though its emotional force, combative tone, and impressive delivery constituted its most oft-praised qualities, close reading discloses a carefully crafted text adapted to a complex oratorical challenge.

The central contention of this essay is that Cuomo's successful strategy for engaging that challenge entailed a unique pattern of interaction among the situation, the speaker's own role in the inventional process, and metaphor as an argumentative technique. The setting posed both generic and immediate difficulties. Mass broadcasting of national conventions since the late 1950's and early 1960's has created multiple audiences to be addressed simultaneously, often resulting in discourse designed not to offend rather than to inspire. Making Cuomo's situation doubly difficult was the immediate circumstance of the summer of 1984: a populace enthralled by incumbent President Ronald Reagan, and relatively content with his policies. Calling on his advisers for assistance in research for assuming the role of speechwriter himself, Cuomo devised a strategy for at once inspiring multiple audiences and articulating his party's philosophy and program. To implement the strategy, Cuomo introduced a root metaphor with which varied audiences could identify, but which at the same time provided an alternative perspective to President Reagan's vision of America as a "Shining City on A Hill."

The resultant effectiveness of Cuomo's keynote address reinforces conceptions of rhetoric as a vital art, the constituents of which ought to be viewed as mutually interdependent elements of a dynamic process.[9] The analysis begins with an articulation of Cuomo's challenge as defined by situational and audience constraints.

SITUATION AND AUDIENCE

The keynote setting itself posed a significant problem. Early critics of such convention addresses concluded that the genre yields easily predictable discourse: praise of the party's philosophy and programs, blame of the opposition, recognition of the occasion's solemn and important nature, and a call for unity as those gathered move toward the fall elections.[10] More recently, the unique demands faced by individual speakers have begun to draw deserved critical attention.[11] By and large, though, the keynote is typically viewed in terms of its ritualistic or ceremonial role in the convention context,[12] and expectations of memorable eloquence are rare.

Some observers attribute this circumstance to the mass media's increasing pervasiveness in American politics since the 1950's In a probing assessment of Daniel Evans' address to the 1968 Republican convention, for instance, Craig Smith argued that the multiple audiences created by the television era accounted for Evans' lackluster presentation. Smith argued that Evans designed his speech to please (or to avoid offending) three audiences—convention delegates, voters in his home state of Washington, and the television public—and in the process he "failed to excite or to hold [the] interest" of any.[13] Effective adaptation to the multiple audience is possible, Smith surmised, "only if potential issue positions held by various audiences are examined."[14]

The keynote setting's influence on Cuomo's argumentative strategy thus coincides with Lloyd Bitzer's contention that the situation is the "source and ground of rhetorical activity." Particularly relevant here are Bitzer's corollary claims that the situation invites not just any response, but requires a "fitting response," and if that is true then the "situation must somehow prescribe the response which fits."[15] Bitzer extended the theme of a fitting rhetoric in a later essay. Not only must one meet situational constraints, he maintained, but "the discourse created by a public speaker and judged by a public audience will be accredited to the extent that it completely engages or articulates the knowledge and interests of the public."[16] That knowledge and interest consist in shared "personal facts" deemed important by both speaker and audience. Though rhetorical audiences differ from publics in that the former have the capacity for the immediate modification of situational exigencies, that power is derived only insofar as audiences are representative of the larger public.[17] The relationship between rhetoric and the public is one of mutual interdependence, for rhetoric creates as well as exploits public knowledge. Publics change and are continually evolving. "Principles, values, and truths thought to be already accredited," Bitzer asserts, "may be discredited and either abandoned or revised in the course of struggle; and a public...may posit new values and truths which win approval because they are believed to be manifestly right or fit."[18]

Cuomo's formidable task, therefore, was to shape a message comprised of personal facts amenable to the diverse audiences produced by the merging of situational and public factors.[19] The immediate audience of convention delegates and observers formed one obvious target. The setting clearly allowed for the recitation of traditional keynote *topoi:* celebration of the party's past, denigration of the opposition, and a call for unity as the fall election overtook the nomination process in importance. A series of controversies the weekend prior to the convention, however, created divisions within the party which required careful attention in framing a call for unity. Walter Mondale's poorly conceived and ill-timed attempt to replace party chairman Charles Manatt with Bert Lance, for example, was rebuffed by a well-executed defense by Manatt and his supporters. Mondale's subsequent, awkward retreat from his original proposal renewed doubts about his leadership instincts and rekindled hope among his competitors— particularly Gary Hart—who saw Mondale's performance as a possible wedge for re-opening the contest for the party's nomination.[20]

The prominence of a second audience further complicated the inventional process. Middle class voters, in Cuomo's view the historic heart of the Democratic Party, formed the other key target. Ronald Reagan's ability to draw them away four years earlier had solidified his initial election, and by July of 1984 they were central celebrants in the "new patriotism" sweeping the nation. In contrast to the distrust of government and suspicion of national leaders typical of the post-Vietnam War/post-Watergate era, by mid-1983 polls showed that nearly 50% of the people described themselves as "very patriotic" and supportive of the government; a repeat survey six months later pushed the percentages even higher.[21] The celebration of American pride culminated with the patriotic fervor generated by the Olympic games held in Los Angeles in midsummer. Efforts to move voters to reject the in-party amidst such revelry necessitated careful conceptualization and execution, especially when coupled with another factor: the incumbent's amiability. Though polls through the spring and early summer indicated mixed reviews for Reagan administration programs, they also reflected a continuation of the president's personal popularity.

The trick, then, would be to cast a message appealing at once to two audiences, both of which required special treatment. An increasingly content middle America, generally supportive of the president, would not likely react favorably to a scathing denunciation of the *status quo.* Simultaneously, assembled Democrats both expected anti-administration commentary and needed a theme around which a party in disarray could rally.

CUOMO AND THE PROCESS OF RHETORICAL INVENTION

Cuomo's response to these conditions differed markedly from Daniel Evans' approach to like circumstances sixteen years earlier. Cuomo sought not to ground his address in issues equally inoffensive—and concurrently equally uninspiring—to all listeners. Instead, he rooted his arguments in the values, traditions, and personal facts common not only to his audiences but to his preparation for his role in the keynote drama as well.

That role is defined significantly by Cuomo's central participation in the invention of his discourse. In contrast to the dominant practice in contemporary politics of hiring a speechwriting staff, Cuomo writes his own speeches, while his aides serve as rhetorical advisers in the message preparation process.[22] Cuomo drafted the convention address in one five-hour session two weeks before the convention,[23] after having studied his advisers' lengthy briefs on the content, style, and attention-getting devices used in every keynote since 1900.[24] Re-writing followed discussions with his staff, and he declined offers from professional writers and journalists who "write much better than I do," he said, because "I've never felt comfortable reading someone else's words."[25]

Cuomo's personal involvement in the development of his speech texts is a logical extension of both his formal training and his devotion to reading and writing in the years to follow. His education began at St. John's preparatory school, where he also completed college and law school. Study of law resulted in a commitment to close analysis and judicious reasoning in the development of written and oral arguments later in his career. What distinguished Cuomo from his peers in law, however, was his penchant for the literary. His prose rose above that typical of the dry legal brief, as he intertwined allusions to literature, philosophical texts, and religious tracts with the facts of the given case or issue.

Cuomo continued to read widely once he entered politics, for he believed that extensive reading was essential to writing and speaking well.[26] Thus, quotations from John Donne, the Bible, or John Dos Pasos were common in his public speeches as well as in his discussions with advisers and journalists once he entered politics.[27] What differentiated Cuomo from other speakers fond of a "great quotations" approach to oratory, though, was his dedication to sorting out and exploring their historical or social context and the philosophy which underlay them.

His *Diaries*, for instance, served not only as an almost daily log of the campaign events en route to his election as Governor in 1982, but allowed for and perhaps stimulated the articulation of a philosophy which undergirded the policy proposals advanced in the campaign. The resulting philosophy emphasized guidance from religion, respect for the laws of society, and above all, devotion to and promotion of family as the vehicle for achieving the good.[28] In the first event at which all four aspirants for governor appeared together, Cuomo distinguished his philosophy from the divisive approaches of his opponents by advancing the unity theme. At the State Farm Bureau's policy conference in July, he contended that, "This state must think of itself as a family."[29] Voters agreed, and in his inaugural address Governor Cuomo blended the themes of family and ethnic roots with promises to "lift people out of wheelchairs" and find work for the unemployed.[30]

When preparing for the keynote two years later, then, Cuomo sought to focus attention on a message he had been working out over the course of his adult life. He downplayed his oratorical skills by claiming the speech would not "be a tub-thumper, but rather a methodical attempt to deal with the issues. I'm not good at bringing people to their feet. I'm going to try to bring people to their senses."[31] He intended to do so by advancing a political philosophy he termed alternatively "progressive pragmatism," a devotion to "traditional Democratic principles," and "a family kind of politics." The central tenet of the philosophy, and consequently of the speech's root theme, "is reasonableness. Not an addiction to ideology or pat phrases, but an intelligent application of general principles to specific situations."[32]

Cuomo deemed the enunciation of such principles the fitting response to the situation he encountered in the summer of 1984. Moreover, his experiences as his own chief speechwriter and the architect of a political philosophy on which those speeches were based prepared him to meet the keynote challenge which had so often puzzled his recent predecessors. He chose to advance his case metaphorically, thus permitting at once a close examination of the issues he considered critical to the nation and the articulation of a vision of America amenable to his multiple audiences.

METAPHOR AS ARGUMENT

Consideration of metaphor's non-ornamental capacities provides an essential foundation for understanding its functions in Cuomo's keynote. That metaphor serves more than embellishment or semiotic purposes has been demonstrated by scholarship in interaction theory and adapted in speech communication studies illustrating the significant interplay between metaphor and topical invention, wherein metaphor "frames rhetorical situations" while "topics order the elements within the frame."[33] Figures which frame situations support George Lakoff and Mark Johnson's theses that metaphor is "primarily a matter of thought and action and only derivatively a matter of language," instrumental to the creation of reality (especially "social realities"), and advantageous to people in power who "get to impose their metaphors."[34] The power to create a new order by imposing a metaphor which "redescribes reality," Paul Ricoeur argues, is contingent on first "creating rifts in an old order."[35] And the creation of dissonance is promoted when the similarities selected for a metaphorical frame are experiential rather than objective similarities. As Lakoff and Johnson point out, objectivists may be correct to suggest that "things in the world" constrain our conceptual systems, but that matters only if the "things" are experienced.[36] Metaphor's capacity to displace one "reality" with another by focusing on experiential themes is instructive in relation to Cuomo's use of the trope.

Cuomo's ultimate objective was to promote a vision of the American body politic as a "family." Movement toward that goal proceeded through three phases. First, consonant with the dictates of Ricoeur's theory of metaphor, Cuomo aimed to raise doubts about the accuracy of a favored Reagan figure, that of America as a "shining city on a hill."[37] Once that perception was altered, he moved to the articulation of the American family alternative. And finally, Cuomo offered his own family's experience as an embodiment of the metaphor's accurate reflection of the American reality.

Since the creation of a new perception of reality is enhanced by an initial denigration of an old conception, he began his appeal with a revision of a favorite Reagan metaphor. *[Editorial note: reader should see third and fourth paragraph of preceding transcript.]*

Cuomo built the remainder of his anti-administration appeal on the foundation of the two-cities theme, as he proceeded through a series of paired consequences he described as inevitable results of Reagan programs. Republican policies, he argued, "divide the nation: into the lucky and the left-out, the royalty and the rabble. The Republicans are willing to treat that division as victory. They would cut this nation in half, into those temporarily better off and those worse off than before, and call it recovery." The Democrats' task, he continued, was to work for the election of a "new President of the United States, a Democrat born not to the blood of kings but to the blood of immigrants and pioneers." Success of the challengers' venture in *1984*, Cuomo maintained, was contingent on supplanting one vision of the nation with another.

The objective, he intoned, was first to "make the American people hear our 'tale of two cities,'" and then to "convince them that we don't have to settle for two cities, that we can have one city, indivisible, shining for all its people." The metaphorical framing of his theme, further delineated below, allowed Cuomo to describe figuratively the objectionable consequences of the president's policies without alienating an increasingly patriotic electorate overwhelmingly enamored of the incumbent. At the same time, by raising doubts about the opposition's ideas he fulfilled one ritualistic function of the keynote speaker.

Praise of the Democratic Party, an equally important ritual, stemmed from the subsequent introduction of the family metaphor. The trope addressed the concerns of both the immediate convention observers and the "middle America" target audience. The figure of the family served two functions for partisans. At one level, Cuomo's enunciation of party achievements differentiated what he termed realistic, principled Democrats from their Republican counterparts. Cuomo contended, for instance, that whereas GOP policies preclude the "wagon train" of American progress from reaching the "frontier unless some of our old, some of our young, and some of our weak are left behind," Democrats believe that "we can make it all the way with the whole family intact." That "we have," he continued, is attested to by "wagon train after wagon train" of success, ever since Franklin Roosevelt "lifted himself from his wheelchair to lift this nation from its knees." Democrats led the way, in Cuomo's view, to,

> new frontiers of education, housing, peace. The whole family aboard. Constantly reaching out to extend and enlarge that family. Lifting them up into the wagon on the way. Blacks and Hispanics, people of every ethnic group, and Native Americans—all those struggling to build their families and claim some small share of America.

In addition to distinguishing Democrats from Republicans, Cuomo used the family metaphor at a second level: to make a virtue of the divisive and potentially counterproductive atmosphere produced by the series of controversies the weekend prior to the convention. Rather than ignoring the aborted attempt to replace Charles Manatt with Bert Lance or attempting to downplay ensuing dissension, Cuomo cast controversy as a telling trait of the party's strength. Not only is the Democratic Party comprised of varied, sometimes contrary "family" members, he argued, "[w]e're proud of it.... But we pay a price for it. The different people we represent have many points of view. Sometimes they compete and then we have debates, even arguments. That's what our primaries were." As in a family dispute, however, unity must follow for "now that the primaries are over,...it is time to lock arms and move into this campaign together." While the family metaphor thus helped to promote party unity, it was in turn vital in Cuomo's appeal to "middle America."

For the principles which underlay Cuomo's description of the party surely meshed with the personal facts influential in this target audience's thinking: family, mutual support, equality, and progress. Cuomo made explicit the link between such values and the ideals of the middle class when, late in the speech, he extended the family theme from the past and present to the future. "We can have a future that provides for all the young of the present," he asserted in a subtly worded play on the guiding family metaphor, "by marrying common sense and compassion." Success will depend, he suggested, on continued recognition of the importance of the party's "progressive principles. That they helped lift up generations to the middle class and higher: gave us a chance to work, go to college, to raise a family, to own a house, to be secure in our old age, and before that to reach heights that our own parents would not have dared dream of."

Though it is unlikely that many members of the larger public would take issue with the desirability of the middle class family ideals he described, Cuomo clearly believed that his perspective of the American "city" and "family" differed sharply from that of citizens who consistently expressed favor with President Reagan's performance. Consequently, he endeavored to revise the dominant perception of the country's status. Cuomo spoke of policies guided by a philosophy which dictated that government "can't do everything," so it should settle for taking care of "the strong and hope that economic ambition and charity will do the rest. Make the rich richer and what falls from the table will be enough for the middle class and those trying to make it into the middle class." Left to their own survival skills in a nation governed by such a philosophy are the "retired school teacher in Duluth," the "child in Buffalo," the "disabled man in Boston," and the hungry in Little Rock. An alternative, Cuomo maintained, was the Democratic principle of mutuality, which undergirded a government committed to the "good of us all, for the love of this great nation, for the American family, for the love of God."

What distinguished his pronouncement of this litany of stock political god-terms was Cuomo's personalization of them, for the ideas were not merely lines in a speech but convictions produced of a lifetime. Thus, when he moved into his peroration Cuomo reinforced the metaphorical base of his message. In so doing he offered his own experience as a warrant for a shift in the focus of public attention, away from a now tarnished "shining city on a hill" and toward recognition of a strong future via the "American family." The philosophy of mutuality which had moved Democrats to protect the retired, the young, the disabled, and the hungry, he claimed, "is the real story of the shining city. It's a story I didn't read in a book, or learn in a classroom. I saw it, and I lived it. Like many of you." Then Mario Cuomo's family became the symbol of the American story. *[Editor's note: reader should see next to last paragraph of preceding transcript.]*

That Cuomo was able to employ such powerful imagery in advancing the case for the "family of America" was anticipated by one of his advisers who observed during the 1982 gubernatorial campaign that the "reason Mario Cuomo will be a very important national figure is that he can talk to his roots and represent them. And his roots are the very people who are abandoning the Democratic Party: the working class, the sons and daughters of immigrants."[38] That Cuomo's approach appealed to his dual audience is a critical precept of the theory of public knowledge advanced by Bitzer, who describes "the spokesman" as one who "engages the public's fund of knowledge; his speeches echo its terms and maxims; he honors its heroes, rehearses its traditions, performs it rituals; he represents the public both to itself and to others."[39] With the choice of the family metaphor, Cuomo not only offered an alternative to the dominant Reagan trope, but provided through his own experience a case for the efficacy of the alternative.

CONCLUSION

Veteran campaign analysts Jack Germond and Jules Witcover attempted to put the emotional impact of Mario Cuomo's speech on the immediate audience in perspective when they commented that while the keynote "thrilled the assembled party activists," it "was another question how it played out in the country, in the living rooms of the greatly expanded middle class...where Reagan's 'feel good' ads and speeches were effective soothing syrup."[40] Other assessments were less reserved. As Bruce Gronbeck wrote in estimating the speech's appeal in one heartland state, for instance, Cuomo "expressed perfectly Iowans' vision of family and good Samaritanism."[41] His family theme, *The New Republic* contended, tapped in the nation a conception of America the electorate could easily understand and might even "prefer to Ronald Reagan's vision of atomized, relentlessly competing individuals."[42] That thought occurred to the president's advisers as well. Reagan administration and re-election officials recognized the potential power of Cuomo's message to middle America and reacted quickly to counter his appeal to blue-collar workers and ethnic groups by scheduling campaign trips for both the president and vice president.[43]

Clearly, Cuomo's rhetorical strategy met the situational and audience challenges posed by the keynote setting. By first raising doubts about the accuracy of Ronald Reagan's vision of America as a "shining city on a hill," Cuomo was able to unite his diverse listeners around the shared values and experiences common to both target audiences. He did so by packaging his theme of progressive pragmatism or traditional Democratic principles in the metaphorical container of the family, thereby offering an appealing alternative to the president's preferred but allegedly misleading trope.

Convention speakers faced with similar demands thus might be well advised to give due attention to the potential of figurative language as a powerful force for framing complex issues and engaging multiple audiences. Metaphor's demonstrated capacity to act in concert with rhetorical invention[44] and to generate reason and argument[45] suggests the prospective value of such endeavors.

David Henry, Ph.D., is professor of Speech Communication at California Polytechnic State University, San Luis Obispo.

NOTES

1. Author's notes of ABC News' coverage of the convention, 16 July 1984.
2. Quoted in Patt Morrison, "Goldwater Gives Ringing 'Last Hurrah'," Los Angeles *Times* 23 August 1984: I, 10.
3. Cited in Jack Germond and Jules Witcover, *Wake Us When It's Over* (New York: Macmillan, 1985) 429.
4. George Will, "Cuomo: A Shadow Over the Campaign," Los Angeles *Times* 18 July 1984: II, 7.
5. Quoted in Lou Cannon and Helen Dewar, "Governor Cuomo Rouses Dispirited Delegates," Washington *Post* 17 July 1984: A1.
6. Howell Raines, "Democrat Calls on Party to Unify and Seek Out 'Family of America'," New York *Times* 17 July 1984: A17.
7. Hedrick Smith, "Cuomo Would Attack Record, Not Reagan," New York *Times* 17 July 1984: A15.
8. John J. Goldman, "Cuomo Charles 'Social Darwinism' Under Reagan," Los Angeles *Times* 17 July 1984: I, 14; and "Drama and Passion Galore," *Time* 30 July 1984: 24-25.

9. An excellent case for rhetoric's dynamic, interactive nature is made by Michael C. Leff in "Topical Invention and Metaphoric Interaction," *Southern Speech Communication Journal* 48 (1983): 214-229.

10. Examples of early studies include Edwin A. Miles, "The Keynote Speech at National Nominating Conventions," *Quarterly Journal of Speech* 46 (1960): 26-31; E. Neal Clausen, "John Sharp Williams: Pace-setter for Democratic Keynotes;' *Southern Speech Journal* 31 (1965): 1-9; and Carl Allen Pitt, "Judd's Keynote Speech: A Congruous Configuration of Communication," *Southern Speech Journal* 33 (1968): 278-288.

11. Wayne N. Thompson's critiques of Barbara Jordan's 1976 speech, for instance, deserve attention: "Barbara Jordan's Keynote Address: Fulfilling Dual and Conflicting Purposes," *Central States Speech Journal* 39 (1979): 272-277; and "Barbara Jordan's Keynote Address: The Juxtaposition of Contradictory Values," *Southern Speech Communication Journal* 44 (1979): 223-232.

12. Thomas B. Farrell's treatment of the 1976 Democratic and Republican Keynote speeches in relation to both conventions' ritualistic dimensions is exemplary: "Political Conventions as Legitimation Rituals," *Communication Monographs* 45 (1978): 293-296 and 298-299.

13. Craig R. Smith, "The Republican Keynote Address of 1968: Adaptive Rhetoric for the Multiple Audience," *Western Speech* 39 (1975): 33-34.

14. Smith, "The Republican Keynote Address of 1968" 39.

15. Lloyd Bitzer, "The Rhetorical Situation," *Contemporary Theories of Rhetoric*, ed. Richard L. Johannesen (1968, repr: New York: Harper and Row, 1971) 386 and 389-90.

16. Lloyd F. Bitzer, "Rhetoric and Public Knowledge," *Rhetoric, Philosophy, and Literature*, ed. Don M. Burks (West Lafayette, IN: Purdue University Press, 1978) 76.

17. Bitzer, "Rhetoric and Public Knowledge" 73 and 76-77.

18. Bitzer, "Rhetoric and Public Knowledge" 90. For another view of the public's dependence on a "competent rhetoric," see: Gerard A. Hauser and Carole Blair, "Rhetorical Antecedents to the Public," *Pre/Text* 3 (1982): 143-145.

19. For a discussion of three types of audiences which emerge from the interaction of Bitzer's notions of situation and public, consult: Michael C. Leff and Margaret Organ Procario, "Rhetorical Theory in Speech Communication," *Speech Communication in the 20th Century*, ed. Thomas W. Benson (Carbondale: Southern Illinois University Press, 1985) 20-21.

20. The Lance-Manatt fiasco is recounted clearly by Germond and Witcover in *Wake Us When It's Over* 381-399.

21. R. W. Apple, Jr., "The New Patriotism," *San Francisco Sunday Examiner Chronicle*, 12 February 1984: "This World" section, 7-8; Richard E. Meyer, "Patriotism: An Ebb and Flow Fervor," *Los Angeles Times* 18 March 1984: I, 1 and 22-23.

22 For an overview of Cuomo's rhetorical practices, see: David Henry, "Mario Cuomo," *American Orators of the Twentieth Century: Critical Studies and Sources*, ed. Bernard K. Duffy and Halford R. Ryan (Westport, CT: Greenwood Press, 1987) 81-85. Though the tasks of speechwriters and rhetorical advisers may often converge, perhaps the critical consideration for determining reliance on outside authors is the orator's role in the preparation process. Cuomo drafts, edits, re-writes, and polishes his own speeches, which provides the foundation for his claim that he does not employ a speechwriting staff.

23. Mary A. Tragale, Executive Assistant to Governor Cuomo, letter to the author, 7 May 1985.

24. John J. Goldman, "Cuomo Well-Prepared for Keynote," *Los Angeles Times* 16 July 1984: I, 6.

25. Cited in David Fink, "Oratory in an Age of Ineloquence," *USA Today* 20 July 1984: 2D

26. Henry, "Mario Cuomo" 82.

27. E. J. Dionne, "Cuomo: The Old Liberalism,' *New York Times Magazine 31* October 1982: 92.

28. *Diaries of Mario M. Cuomo: The Campaign for Governor* (New York: Random House, 1984) 7-15.

29. Quoted in Maurice Carroll, "Four Running for Governor Meet for First Skirmish;' New York *Times* 17 July 1982: 23. Cuomo first articulated his view of the "body politic as a family" in 1981. See: "What Makes Mario Run?," *Newsweek* 24 March 1986: 28.

30. Cited in Michael Oreskes, "Rising Voice in Democratic Ranks," New York *Times* 17 July 1984: A17.

31. Frank Lynn, "Cuomo Puts Final Touches on Keynote Address," New York *Times* 16 July 1984: A14.

32. The "reasonableness" notion recurs in Cuomo's discourse. This definition is provided in his *Diaries* 15.

33. Leff, "Topical Invention and Metaphoric Interaction: 218 and 223. Also instructive are: Michael Osborn, "Archetypal Metaphor in Rhetoric: The Light-Dark Family," *Quarterly Journal of Speech* 53 (1967): 115-126; Michael Osborn, "The Evolution of the Archetypal Sea in Rhetoric and Poetic," *Quarterly Journal of Speech* 63 (1977): 347-363; and William J. Jordan, "Toward a Psychological Theory of Metaphor," *Western Speech* 35 (1971): 169175.

34. George Lakoff and Mark Johnson, *Metaphors We Live By* (Chicago: University of Chicago Press, 1980) 153, 156, and 157.

35. Paul Ricoeur, *The Rule of Metaphor,* trans. by Robert Czerny (1975; Toronto: University of Toronto Press, 1977) 22.

36. Lakoff and Johnson, *Metaphors We Live By* 154.

37. William F. Lewis makes passing reference to the wisdom of Cuomo's tack in his assessment of Ronald Reagan's reliance on, and success with, the narrative form in his presidential discourse. In effect, the analysis of metaphor in Cuomo's keynote that follows reinforces Lewis' thesis as it pertains to how Reagan's rhetoric has re-defined the nature of political "debate." See: "Telling America's Story: Narrative Form and the Reagan Presidency," *Quarterly Journal of Speech* 73 (1987) 280-302. The allusion to Cuomo's keynote speech is at 289.

38. Meyer S. Frucher, quoted by Dionne, "Cuomo: The Old Liberalism" 84-85.

39. Bitzer, "Rhetoric and Public Knowledge" 74.

40. Germond and Witcover, *Wake Us When It's Over* 405.

41. Bruce E. Gronbeck, "The Presidential Campaign Dramas of 1984," *Presidential Studies Quarterly* 15 (1985) 386.

42. "Come to Order," *The New Republic* 30 July 1984 11.

43. James Gerstenzang explains the speech's significance in the alteration of Reagan-Bush campaign schedules in "Reagan, Bush to Hit the Road," Los Angeles *Times* 19 July 1984: I, 6.

44. Leff's "Topical Invention and Metaphoric Interaction" is illustrative.

45. Consider, for example, Ernesto Grassi's delineation of the concept of *ingenium* in *Rhetoric as Philosophy* (University Park: The Pennsylvania State University Press, 1980) 91-94 and *passim.*

THE RAINBOW COALITION

Jesse Jackson

Democratic National Convention, San Francisco, California, July 17, 1984
(Transcribed from the video, GREAT SPEECHES, VOLUME III)

Tonight we come together bound by our faith in a mighty God, with genuine respect and love for our country, and inheriting the legacy of a great party—the Democratic Party—which is the best hope for redirecting our nation on a more humane, just and peaceful course.

This is not a perfect party. We are not a perfect people. Yet, we are called to a perfect mission: our mission, to feed the hungry, to clothe the naked, to house the homeless, to teach the illiterate, to provide jobs for the jobless, and to choose the human race over the nuclear race. We are gathered here this week to nominate a candidate and adopt a platform which will expand, unify, direct and inspire our party and the nation to fulfill this mission.

My constituency is the desperate, the damned, the disinherited, the disrespected, and the despised. They are restless and seek relief. They've voted in record numbers. They have invested the faith, hope and trust that they have in us. The Democratic Party must send them a signal that we care. I pledge my best not to let them down. There is the call of conscience: redemption, expansion, healing and unity. Leadership must heed the call of conscience, redemption, expansion, healing and unity, for they are the key to achieving our mission.

Time is neutral and does not change things. With courage and initiative leaders change things. No generation can choose the age or circumstance in which it is born, but through leadership it can choose to make the age in which it is born an age of enlightenment—an age of jobs, and peace, and justice. Only leadership—that intangible combination of gifts, discipline, information, circumstance, courage, timing, will and divine inspiration—can lead us out of the crisis in which we find ourselves. Leadership can mitigate the misery of our nation. Leadership can part the waters and lead our nation in the direction of the Promised Land. Leadership can lift the boats stuck at the bottom.

I have had the rare opportunity to watch seven men, and then two, pour out their souls, offer their service and heel [sic] heed the call of duty to direct the course of our nation. There is a proper season for everything. There is a time to sow and a time to reap. There is a time to compete, and a time to cooperate. I ask for your vote on the first ballot as a vote for a new direction for this party and this nation; a vote of conviction, a vote of conscience. But I will be proud to support the nominee of this convention for the President of the United States of America. Thank you.

I have…I have watched the leadership of our party develop and grow. My respect for both Mr. Mondale and Mr. Hart is great. I have watched them struggle with the crosswinds and cross-fires of being public servants, and I believe that they will both continue to try to serve us faithfully. I am elated by the knowledge that for the first time in our history a woman, Geraldine Ferraro, will be recommended to share our ticket.

Throughout this campaign, I have tried to offer leadership to the Democratic Party and the nation. If in my high moments, I have done some good, offered some service, shed some light, healed some wounds, rekindled some hope or stirred someone from apathy and indifference, or in any way along the way helped somebody, then this campaign has not been in vain. For friends who loved and cared for me, and for a God who spared me, and for a family who understood, I am eternally grateful.

If in my low moments, in word, deed or attitude, through some error of temper, taste or tone, I have caused anyone discomfort, created pain, or revived someone's fears, that was not my truest self. If there were occasions when my grape turned into a raisin and my joy bell lost its resonance, please forgive me. Charge it to my head and not to my heart. I am...my head is so limited in its finitude; my heart which is boundless in its love for the human family. I am not a perfect servant. I am a public servant doing my best against the odds. As I develop and serve, be patient. God is not finished with me yet.

This campaign has taught me much: that leaders must be tough enough to fight, tender enough to cry, human enough to make mistakes, humble enough to admit them, strong enough to absorb the pain, and resilient enough to bounce back and keep on moving. For leaders, the pain is often intense. But you must smile through your tears and keep moving with the faith that there is a brighter side somewhere.

I went to see Hubert Humphrey three days before he died. He had just called Richard Nixon from his dying bed, and many people wondered why. And, I asked him. He said, "Jesse, from this vantage point, the sun setting in my life, all of the speeches, the political conventions, the crowds and the great fights are behind me now. At a time like this you are forced to deal with your irreducible essence, forced to grapple with that which is really important to you. And what I have concluded about life," Hubert Humphrey said, "when all is said and done, we must forgive each other, and redeem each other, and move on."

Our party is emerging from one of its most hard-fought battles for the Democratic Party's presidential nomination in our history. But our healthy competition should make us better, not bitter. We must use...we must use the insight, wisdom and experience of the late Hubert Humphrey as a balm for the wounds in our party, this nation and the world. We must forgive each other, redeem each other, regroup and move on.

Our flag is red, white and blue, but our nation is rainbow—red, yellow, brown, black and white—we're all precious in God's sight. America...America is not like a blanket—one piece of unbroken cloth, the same color, the same texture, the same size. America is more like a quilt—many patches, many pieces, many colors, many sizes, all woven and held together by a common thread. The white, the Hispanic, the black, the Arab, the Jew, the woman, the Native American, the small farmer, the businessperson, the environmentalist, the peace activist, the young, the old, the lesbian, the gay and the disabled make up the American quilt. Even in our fractured state, all of us count and fit somewhere. We have proven that we can survive without each other, but we have not proven that we can win and make progress without each other. We must come together.

From Fannie Lee Hamer in Atlantic City in 1964 to the Rainbow Coalition in San Francisco today; from the Atlantic to the Pacific, we have experienced pain but progress as we ended American apartheid laws; we got public accommodations; we secured voting rights; we obtained open housing; as young people got the right to vote; we lost Malcolm, Martin, Medgar, Bobby, John and Viola.

The team that got us here must be expanded, not abandoned. Twenty years ago, tears welled up in our eyes as the bodies of Schwerner, Goodman and Chaney were dredged from the depths of a river in Mississippi. Twenty years later, our communities, black and Jewish, are in anguish, anger and pain. Feelings have been hurt on both sides. There is a crisis in communications. Confusion is in the air. We cannot afford to lose our way. We may agree to agree, or agree to disagree on issues; we must bring back civility to these tensions.

We are co-partners in a long and rich religious history—the Judeo-Christian traditions. Many blacks and Jews have a shared passion for social justice at home and peace abroad. We must seek a revival of the spirit, inspired by a new vision and new possibilities. We must return to higher ground. We are bound by Moses and Jesus, but also connected with Islam and Mohammed. These three great religions—Judaism, Christianity and Islam—were all born in the revered and holy city of Jerusalem. We are bound by Dr. Martin Luther King, Jr. and Rabbi Abraham Heschel, crying out from their graves for us to reach common ground. We are bound by shared blood and shared sacrifices. We are much too intelligent; much too bound by our Judeo-Christian heritage; much too victimized by racism, sexism, militarism and anti-Semitism; much too threatened as historical scapegoats to go on divided one from another. We must turn from finger-pointing to clasped hands. We must share our burdens and our joys with each other once again. We must turn to each other and not on each other and choose higher ground.

Twenty years later…twenty years later, we cannot be satisfied by just restoring the old coalition. Old wine skins must make room for new wine. We must heal and expand. The Rainbow Coalition is making room for Arab-Americans. They too know the pain and hurt of racial and religious rejection. They must not continue to be made pariahs. The Rainbow Coalition is making room for Hispanic-Americans who this very night are living under the threat of the Simpson-Mazzoli bill, and farm workers from Ohio who are fighting the Campbell Soup Company with a boycott to achieve legitimate workers rights.

The Rainbow is making room for the Native Americans, the most exploited people of all, a people with the greatest moral claim amongst us. We support them as they seek the restoration of their ancient land and claim amongst us. We support them as they seek the restoration of land and water rights, as they seek to preserve their ancestral homelands and the beauty of a land that was once all theirs. They can never receive a fair share for all they have given us, but they must finally have a fair chance to develop their great resources and to preserve their people and their culture.

The Rainbow Coalition includes Asian-Americans, now being killed in our streets—scapegoats for the failures of corporate, industrial and economic policies. The Rainbow is making room for the young Americans. Twenty years ago, our young people were dying in a war for which they could not even vote. But 20 years later, Young America has the power to stop a war in Central America and the responsibility to vote in great numbers. Young America must be politically active in 1984. The choice is war or peace. We must make room for Young America.

The Rainbow includes disabled veterans. The color scheme fits in the Rainbow. The disabled have their handicap revealed and their genius concealed; while the able-bodied have their genius revealed and their disability concealed. But ultimately we must judge people by their values and their contribution. Don't leave anybody out. I would rather have Roosevelt in a wheelchair than Reagan on a horse.

The Rainbow is making room for small farmers. They have suffered tremendously under the Reagan regime. They will either receive 90 percent parity or 100 percent charity. We must address their concerns and make room for them. The Rainbow includes lesbians and gays. No American citizen ought be denied equal protection under the law.

We must be unusually committed and caring as we expand our family to include new members. All of us must be tolerant and understanding as the fears and anxieties of the rejected and of the party leadership express themselves in many different ways. Too often what we call hate—as if it were some deeply rooted philosophy or strategy—is simply ignorance, anxiety, paranoia, fear and insecurity. To be strong leaders, we must be long-suffering as we seek to right the wrongs of our party and our nation. We must expand our party, heal our party and unify our party. That is our mission in 1984.

We are often reminded that we live in a great nation—and we do. But it can be greater still. The Rainbow is mandating a new definition of greatness. We must not measure greatness from the mansion down, but the manger up. Jesus said that we should not be judged by the bark we wear but by the fruit that we bear. Jesus said that we must measure greatness by how we treat the least of these.

President Reagan says the nation is in recovery. Those 90,000 corporations that made a profit last year but paid no federal taxes are recovering. The 37,000 military contractors who have benefited from Reagan's more than doubling the military budget in peacetime, surely they are recovering. The big corporations and rich individuals who received the bulk of the three-year, multibillion tax cut from Mr. Reagan are recovering. But no such recovery is under way for the least of these. Rising tides don't lift all boats, particularly those stuck at the bottom.

For the boats stuck at the bottom there is a misery index. This administration has made life more miserable for the poor. Its attitude has been contemptuous. Its policies and programs have been cruel and unfair to working people. They must be held accountable in November for increasing infant mortality among the poor. In Detroit, one of the great cities of the Western world, babies are dying at the same rate as Honduras, the most underdeveloped nation in our hemisphere.

This administration must be held accountable for policies that contribute to the growing poverty in America. There are now 34 million people in poverty, 15 percent of our nation. Twenty-three million are white, 11 million black, Hispanic, Asian and others. Mostly women and children. By the end of this year, there will be 41 million people in poverty. We cannot stand idly by. We must fight for change, now.

Under this regime we look at Social Security. The 1981 budget cuts included nine permanent Social Security benefit cuts totaling $20 billion over five years. Small businesses have suffered under Reagan tax cuts. Only 18 percent of total business tax cuts went to them—82 percent to big business. Health care under Mr. Reagan has been sharply cut. Education under Mr. Reagan has been cut 25 percent. Under Mr. Reagan there are now 9.7 million female-head families. They represent 16 percent of all families, half of all of them are poor. Seventy percent of all poor children live in a house headed by a woman, where there is no man. Under Mr. Reagan, the administration has cleaned up only 6 of 546 priority toxic waste dumps. Farmers' real net income was only about half its level in 1979.

Many say that the race in November will be decided in the South. President Reagan is depending on the conservative South to return him to office. But the South, I tell you, is unnaturally conservative. The South is the poorest region in our nation and, therefore, with the least to conserve. In his appeal to the South, Mr. Reagan is trying to substitute flags and prayer cloths for food, and clothing, and education, health care and housing. But Mr. Reagan will ask us to pray, and I believe in prayer—I've come this way by the power of prayer. But, we must watch false prophecy.

He cuts energy assistance to the poor, cuts breakfast programs from children, cuts lunch programs from children, cuts job training from children and then say [*sic*] to an empty table, "let us pray." {Apparently he is not familiar with the structure of a prayer. You thank the Lord for the food that you are about to receive, not the food that just left.}

I think that we should pray. But don't pray for the food that left, pray for the man that took the food to leave. We need a change. We need a change in November. Under Mr. Reagan, the misery index has risen for the poor, but the danger index has risen for everybody. Under this administration we've lost the lives of our boys in Central America, in Honduras, in Grenada, in Lebanon. A nuclear standoff in Europe. Under this administration, one-third of our children believe they will die in a nuclear war. The danger index is increasing in this world. With all the talk about defense against Russia, the Russian submarines are closer and their missiles are more accurate. We live in a world tonight more miserable and a world more dangerous.

While Reaganomics and Reaganism is talked about often, so often we miss the real meaning. Reaganism is a spirit. Reaganomics represents the real economic facts of life. In 1980, Mr. George Bush, a man with reasonable access to Mr. Reagan, did an analysis of Mr. Reagan's economic plan. Mr. George Bush concluded that Reagan's plan was "voodoo economics." He was right. Third-party candidate John Anderson said that the combination of military spending, tax cuts and a balanced budget by '84 could be accomplished with blue smoke and mirrors. They were both right.

Mr. Reagan talks about a dynamic recovery. There is some measure of recovery, three and half years later. Unemployment has inched just below where it was when he took office in 1981. But there are still 8.1 million people officially unemployed, 11 million working only part-time. Inflation has come down, but let's analyze for a moment who has paid the price for this superficial economic recovery.

Mr. Reagan curbed inflation by cutting consumer demand. He cut consumer demand with conscious and callous fiscal and monetary policies. He used the federal budget to deliberately induce unemployment and curb social spending. He then waged and supported tight monetary policies of the Federal Reserve Board to deliberately drive up interest rates—again to conserve to concurb [*sic*] consumer demand created through borrowing.

Unemployment reached 10.7 percent; we experienced skyrocketing interest rates; our dollar inflated abroad; there were record bank failures; record farm foreclosures; record business bankruptcies; record budget deficits; record trade deficits. Mr. Reagan brought inflation down by destabilizing our economy and disrupting family life.

He promised…he promised in 1980 a balanced budget, but instead we now have a record $200 billion budget deficit. Under Mr. Reagan, the cumulative budget deficit for his four years is more than the sum total of deficits from George Washington to Jimmy Carter combined. I tell you, we need a change.

How is he paying for these short-term jobs? Reagan's economic recovery is being financed by deficit spending—$200 billion a year. Military spending, a major cause of this deficit, is projected over the next five years to be nearly $2 trillion, and will cost about $40,000 for every taxpaying family.

When the government borrows $200 billion annually to finance the deficit, this encourages the private sector to make its money off of interest rates as opposed to development and economic growth. Even money abroad—we don't have enough money domestically to finance the debt, so we are now borrowing money abroad, from foreign banks, government and financial institutions—$40 billion in 1983; $70 to $80 billion in 1984 (40 percent of our total); over $100 billion (50 percent of our total) in 1985.

By 1989, it is projected that 50 percent of all individual income taxes will be going just to pay for interest on that debt. The U.S. used to be the largest exporter of capital, but under Mr. Reagan we will quite likely become the largest debtor nation. About two weeks ago, on July 4, we celebrated our Declaration of Independence. Yet every day, supply-side economics is making our nation more economically dependent and less economically free. Five to six percent of our gross national product is now being eaten up with President Reagan's budget deficits.

To depend on foreign military powers to protect our national security would be foolish, making us dependent and less secure. Yet Reaganomics had us increasingly dependent on foreign economic sources. This consumer-led but deficit-financial recovery is unbalanced and artificial.

We have a challenge as Democrats: support a way out. Democracy guarantees opportunity, not success. Democracy guarantees the right to participate, not a license for either the majority or a minority to dominate. The victory for the rainbow coalition in the platform debates today was not whether we won or lost; but that we raised the right issues. We could...we could afford to lose the vote; issues are non-negotiable. We cannot afford to avoid raising the right questions. Our self respect and our moral integrity were at stake. Our heads are perhaps bloodied but not bowed. Our back is straight. We can go home and face our people. Our vision is clear. When we think, on this journey from slave ship to championship, we've gone from the planks of the boardwalk in Atlantic City in 1964 to fighting to have the right planks in the platform in San Francisco in '84. There is a deep and abiding sense of joy in our souls, in spite of the tears in our eyes. Though there are missing planks, there is a solid foundation upon which to build. Our party can win. But we must provide hope which will inspire people to struggle and achieve; provide a plan to show the way out of our dilemma, and then lead the way.

In 1984, my heart is made to feel glad because I know there is a way out. Justice. The requirement for rebuilding America is justice. The linchpin of progressive politics in our nation will not come from the North; they in fact will come from the South. That is why I argue over and over again—we look from Virginia, 'round to Texas, there is only one black congressperson out of 115. Nineteen years later, we're locked out of the Congress, the Senate and the governor's mansion. What does this large black vote mean? Why do I fight to end second primaries and fight gerrymandering and annexation and at large? Why do we fight over that? Because I tell you, you cannot hold someone in the ditch unless you linger there with them...unless you linger there. You want a change in this nation, you enforce that Voting Rights Act—we'll get 12 to 20 black, Hispanic, female and progressive congresspersons from the South. We can save the cotton, but we've got to fight the boll weevils—we've got to make a judgment. We've got to make a judgment.

It's not enough to hope ERA will pass; how can we pass ERA? If blacks vote in great numbers, progressive whites win. It's the only way progressive whites win. If blacks vote in great numbers, Hispanics win. If blacks, Hispanics and progressive whites vote, women win. When women win, children win. When women and children win, workers win. We must all come up together. We must come up together.

I tell you, with all of our joy and excitement, we must not save the world and lose our souls; we should never short-circuit enforcement of the Voting Rights Act at every level. One of us rise, all of us will rise. Justice is the way out. Peace is a way out. We should not act as if nuclear weaponry is negotiable and debatable. In this world in which we live, we dropped the bomb on Japan and felt guilty. But in 1984, other folks also got bombs. This time, if we drop the bomb, six minutes later, we, too, will be destroyed. It's not about dropping the bomb on somebody; it's about dropping the bomb on everybody. We must choose developed minds over guided missiles, and think it out and not fight it out. It's time for a change.

Our foreign policy must be characterized by mutual respect, not by gunboat diplomacy, big stick diplomacy and threats. Our nation at its best feeds the hungry. Our nation at its worst...at its worst will mine the harbors of Nicaragua; at its worst, will try to overthrow that government; at its worst, will cut aid to American education and increase aid to El Salvador; at its worst our nation will have partnership with South Africa. That's a moral disgrace. It's a moral disgrace. It's a moral disgrace.

When we look at Africa, we cannot just focus on apartheid in southern Africa. We must fight for trade with Africa, and not just aid to Africa. We cannot stand idly by and say we will not relate to Nicaragua unless they have elections there and then embrace military regimes in Africa, overthrowing Democratic governments in Nigeria and Liberia and Ghana. We must fight for democracy all around the world, and play the game by one set of rules.

Peace in this world. Our present formula for peace in the Middle East is inadequate; it will not work. There are 22 nations in the Middle East. Our nation must be able to talk and act and influence all of them. We must build upon Camp David and measure human rights by one yardstick and as which we have too many interests and too few friends.

There is a way out. Jobs. Put Americans back to work. When I was a child growing up in Greenville, S.C. the Rev. Sample used to preach every so often a sermon relating to Jesus and said, "If I be lifted up, I'll draw all men unto me." I didn't quite understand what he meant as a child growing up. But I understand a little better now. If you raise up truth, it's magnetic. It has a way of drawing people. With all this confusion in this convention—the bright lights and parties and big fun—we must raise up the simple proposition: if we lift up a program to feed the hungry, they'll come running. If we lift up a program to study war no more, our youth will come running. If we lift up a program to put America back to work, an alternative to welfare and despair, they will come working. If we cut that military budget without cutting our defense, and use that money to rebuild bridges and put steelworkers back to work, and use that money, and provide jobs for our cities, and use that money to build schools and train teachers and educate our children, and build hospitals and train doctors and train nurses, the whole nation will come running to us.

As...as I leave you now, we vote in this convention and get ready to go back across this nation in a couple of days, in this campaign, I'll try to be faithful to my promise. I'll live in the old barrios, ghettos and in reservations, and housing projects. I have a message for our youth. I challenge them to put hope in their brains, and not dope in their veins. I told them that like Jesus, I, too, was born in a slum, but just because you're born in a slum, does not mean the slum is born in you, and you can rise above it if your mind is made up. I told them in every slum, there are two sides. When I see a broken window, that's the slummy side. Train some youth to become a glazier, that's the sunny side. When I see a missing brick, that's the slummy side. Let that child in the union, and become a brickmason, and build, that's the sunny side. When I see a missing door, that's the slummy side. Train some youth to become a carpenter, that's the sunny side. When I see the vulgar words and hieroglyphics of destitution on the walls, that's the slummy side. Train some youth to become a painter, an artist—that's the sunny side. We need this place looking for the sunny side because there's a brighter side somewhere. I am more convinced than ever that we can win. We'll vault up the rough side of the mountain; we can win. I just want young America to do me one favor. Just one favor.

Exercise the right to dream. You must face reality—that which is. But then dream of the reality that ought to be, that must be. Live beyond the pain of reality with the dream of a bright tomorrow. Use hope and imagination as weapons of survival and progress. Use love to motivate you and obligate you to serve the human family.

Young America, dream. Choose the human race over the nuclear race. Bury the weapons and don't burn the people. Dream...dream of a new value system. Teachers, who teach for life, and not just for a living, teach because they can't help it. Dream of lawyers more concerned about justice than a judgeship. Dream of doctors more concerned about public health than personal wealth. Dream of preachers and priests who will prophecy and not just profiteer. Preach and dream. Our time has come.

Our time has come. Suffering breeds character. Character breeds faith. And in the end, faith will not disappoint.

Our time has come. Our faith, hope and dreams will prevail. Our time has come. Weeping has endured for the night. But, now joy cometh in the morning.

Our time has come. No graves can hold our body down.

Our time has come. No lie can live forever.

Our time has come. We must leave racial battleground and come to economic common ground and moral higher ground. America, our time has come.

We've come from disgrace to Amazing Grace, our time has come.

Give me your tired, give me your poor, your huddled masses who yearn to breathe free and come November, there will be a change because our time has come.

Thank you and God bless you.

BEYOND THE RAINBOW

Jesse Jackson's Speech to the 1984 Democratic National Convention

Our time has come.

CRITICS: Martha A. Solomon and Paul B. Stewart

Jesse Jackson's appearance on the podium of the Democratic National Convention the night of July 17, 1984, represented a personal as well as a political triumph. Born in abject poverty in Greenville, South Carolina, on October 8, 1941, Jackson never knew his father. He grew up in the supportive environment of a small town that encouraged him to become a success. His athletic skills won him a scholarship to the University of Illinois in 1959, but loneliness led him to transfer to North Carolina A & T in Greensboro. Here he found himself on a campus whose students initiated the sit-in movement in the South, desegregated the local Woolworths and provided a model of direct action for thousands of college students.

Following graduation in 1964, Jackson enrolled in Chicago Theological Seminary where he recruited fellow students to travel to Selma to join in the demonstrations that would culminate in the Voting Rights Act of 1965. Jackson's activities in Selma impressed Ralph Abernathy who convinced Martin Luther King to hire him to organize ministers for the Southern Christian Leadership Conference (SCLC) in Chicago. His effectiveness in carrying out this assignment combined with his energy and speaking skills soon won him a coveted place as one of King's top aides. On the day that King was killed, Jackson, ignoring a tacit understanding among King's aides to refuse to speak of the assassination to the press, seized the initiative and made a moving statement that was broadcast nationwide. He further angered his colleagues in the movement by claiming to be the last person to speak to King before the fatal shot rang out and by appearing on the "Today Show" to discuss details of the assassination. His actions established a pattern that would be repeated during the next few years as Jackson capitalized on his celebrity to push himself into the forefront of the civil rights movement. His actions frequently alienated his friends and co-workers, but the resulting publicity seemed to legitimize his tactics and his claim to being the heir to Martin Luther King's following (House 1-17).

From his base in Chicago as head of Operation PUSH (People United to Serve Humanity), a civic action group that combined political agitation with self-help activities such as job training, Jackson used his growing influence to promote greater black participation in the political process through voter registration drives and active competition for political office. He made little secret of his ambition to run for the Presidency during the summer of 1983 and tested the themes that would form his candidacy in a speech at the 20th anniversary celebration of the March on Washington. When he formally announced his candidacy on November 3, 1983, few believed that he would be a serious challenger for the nomination. Many black elected officials expressed little enthusiasm for his candidacy, and the resentment among his early allies in the civil rights movement still lingered. Mayor Coleman Young of Detroit summed up the feelings of many when he said, " Jesse...has no experience...no platform...and no chance. As a politician he's out of his league." (Donnelly 9). Young's assessment proved true. After campaigning through all the primaries, Jackson entered the convention with only 458.5 out of the total of 3850 delegate votes available. This was more than many expected but significantly behind either Mondale or Hart (Current 246).

Even if Jackson were not a viable contender for the candidacy, he could be a principal figure in the coming campaign. Seen by many as the representative of the powerless, he amassed over three million popular votes in the primaries largely as a result of blacks who voted in record numbers positioning him only nineteen percentage points below Mondale's popular vote total (Corrigan 1344). If Mondale were to have a chance to defeat Ronald Reagan, he needed Jackson to attract and deliver the black vote. If Jackson left the convention to run as an independent or gave Mondale anything less than his full support, the Democrats' efforts would have been seriously handicapped.

Coming into the convention, Jackson, an independent figure who used the media and his faithful constituency to accomplish his goals, failed to express unequivocal support for the Party slate. Besides his bid for the presidency, the agenda Jackson brought to San Francisco consisted of several platform proposals, as well as a request for "self-respect" (Corrigan 1348). The platform committee rejected all of the Rainbow Coalition's proposals, because many of them would have alienated moderate voters. But, eager to appease Jackson and his followers, the Party leaders accorded Jackson and his coalition the respect they demanded by issuing him an invitation to address the convention during prime time television. The frustrations his supporters experienced at the convention and his own lack of influence at the convention despite his successes in the primaries gave Jackson cause to be resentful and bitter toward the Party. His response in this difficult situation was unpredictable and the tension increased when, as he prepared to speak, Jackson was introduced as "the next President of the United States" (Coffey and Jackman 20).

Because of the dramatic circumstances leading up to and surrounding Jackson's speech as well as the publicity it received, assessing it rhetorically is difficult. Certainly, Jackson calmed fears that he would refuse to support the Democratic Party and its nominee. At least one critic, Di Mare, has argued that Jackson used the tensions within the party positively to generate a sense of unity by creating "accommodative relations among his audience that allowed for agreement" (224). Moreover, Jackson's support of the party and his work for Mondale apparently did mobilize black voters, although Reagan's overwhelming popularity offset this impact (Barker 243). While not disagreeing with Di Mare's assessments or disputing Jackson's influence with black voters, we believe that the force of the speech lies not entirely in its content nor even in Jackson's style and delivery, both of which were typical for him. Instead, Jackson's speech draws much of its rhetorical power from the performance of a politically symbolic act that media coverage transformed into political spectacle.

STRUCTURE AND ARGUMENT

Jackson's speech blends religious appeals, self-promotion, attacks on the opposition, compliments to the party leadership, appeals to the disaffected, and an apology for his past statements into an intoxicating brew spiked with rhymed slogans and vivid images. He preached a political sermon that ended in a dream of national redemption. When he began, it became obvious that the convention and the national television audience were in for something more than the traditional political speech.

Experiencing a Jackson speech is like a long automobile excursion—you know where it began and where it is supposed to end, but in between it is fraught with detours, and surprises, as well as long familiar stretches. Jackson is the despair of television programmers and commentators as he frequently departs from the prepared text on the teleprompter in front of him and talks beyond the standard television time segments designed for commercial breaks. His "text" is a pastiche of many elements including his prepared text, remembered portions of his standard campaign speech and inspired improvisation. Jackson varies the mood conveyed by the speech playing off the tensions within the audience to create a dramatic spectacle.

The first part of the speech is designed to defuse the tensions within the party created by Jackson's campaign. He acts immediately to reassure worried party leaders that he will endorse the ticket and actively campaign for it. He also apologizes for his comments that alienated a major bloc of Democratic voters. The second section of the speech introduces the metaphor of the rainbow to describe his followers and their agenda. This is immediately followed by the longest segment of the speech—an attack on the Reagan administration for its failure to address the needs of the less fortunate in our society. The last part is an inspirational conclusion in which Jackson exhorts his audience to dream of a future America living up to its promise of justice for all.

In the introduction, Jackson moves from the mundane world of politics to the exalted realm of religion by uniting God, country and party in a "mission, to feed the hungry, to clothe the naked, to house the homeless, to teach the illiterate, to provide jobs for the jobless and to choose the human race over the nuclear race." He uses religious terms to define the tasks of the party: to "heed the call of conscience, redemption, expansion, healing and unity." He echoes the language of the *Bible* in describing the tasks of political leadership to "part the waters and lead our nation in the direction of the Promised Land." Religious language pervades the speech and unifies the diverse themes. "God" sanctifies the "mission" of the "Party" which is to provide "leadership" for the "country" by delivering it from the present crisis into the "Promised Land."

In making these connections, Jackson adroitly stakes his claim as a leader representing the oppressed and simply ignores the work of others to meet the needs of the poor. Jackson enacts his claim to leadership by his passionate delivery of the speech which stands in stark contrast to the cool demeanor of his two rivals for the nomination, Gary Hart and Michael Dukakis. This section accomplishes several purposes: it elevates Jackson from a mere politician (a term of universal scorn) into a leader with a divinely sanctioned mission; secondly, it transforms the political process with its petty deals, compromises and its squabbles over the division of resources into a noble "mission," and lastly, it provides a framework for an apology for his demeaning comments about Jews.

Jackson's apology masterfully transforms his public humiliation into a cause for joy as a sinner is redeemed before the Lord, "I am not a perfect servant... God is not finished with me yet." The transition to the next section contains an emotionally appealing story about Hubert Humphrey that reinforces the point. If Humphrey could forgive Nixon—a partisan foe of the Democrats—then the Democratic leaders can surely forgive Jackson—a fellow Democrat—for his failures.

STYLE AND ARGUMENT

The central theme of the speech is embodied in the metaphor of the rainbow and the supplementary image of the quilt. Although vivid and colorful images in their own right, this highly stylized use of language should not be seen as mere packaging or an attempt to add some spice to the speech. Rather, the metaphors deepen our understanding of the speech by embedding meaning in easily recognized symbols. The rainbow has long functioned as a religious or popular symbol. In the *Old Testament* story of Noah and the Ark, God sent a rainbow as a sign to Noah that the flood was receding, a new day was dawning and it was time to leave the ark. In legend, the Leprechaun hides his gold at the end of the rainbow, and anyone who finds it, may keep it. In popular culture, songs describe the land over the rainbow, and even a popular children's cartoon series, "The Care Bears," takes place in Rainbow Land. The association of the rainbow with new beginnings, with promises, with visions of peace and prosperity is widely held. Jackson will return to this aspect of the rainbow—the vision of a new beginning with promises of great fulfillment—in the conclusion of the speech.

The rainbow with its many hues of colors also signifies for Jackson and his followers what the United States has become and will increasingly become: a multi-racial, multi-ethnic land of diverse cultures. The attraction of the rainbow is that the many colors attain the beauty of the whole yet retain their separate identity. As if searching for another more homey way to express this idea, Jackson adds the supplemental image of the quilt. Unlike a blanket that is all the same color, a quilt is many patches of many different colors that are worked into a harmonious design. A quilt is made from rags, from cast off clothing and from bits and pieces of material that are too small to make a regular article of clothes. Quilts were originally made from necessity by those who could not afford to buy woven blankets.

These metaphors reconfigure our way of seeing or understanding the American experience of diversity. In the past, the favored image to describe the American experience of ethnicity and diversity was the "melting pot" which suggested that peoples of diverse backgrounds became transformed through the process of assimilation into something new—a recognizable or standard type of "American"—shedding their old customs and folkways in the process. This image may have had some validity when immigration was overwhelmingly from Northern Europe, but by the last years of the Twentieth Century as the population became truly multi-cultural, multi-racial and multi-ethnic, the image lost any relevance. By substituting the image of the rainbow for the melting pot, Jackson helps the audience to understand this change in positive and not negative ways. In using the rainbow to represent the multi-cultural society of America, Jackson suggests that out of diversity America will achieve a new unity founded upon respect for differences within a harmonious framework of shared beliefs. Religious values which transcend individual differences and frequently share common sources such as holy books, religious figures or places can provide this framework.

Jackson uses this image of beauty and harmony arising from diversity to underscore his message that the Democratic party and by extension the governing institutions must adapt to the changing composition of the American populace and welcome the participation of many groups who now are outside the process. Although many of the people in these groups are poor, the image of the quilt reminds the audience that useful and beautiful things can be made from common materials rescued from the scrap heap.

He indicates that one way to accomplish this is to identify the common ground that many of the factions share rather than accentuating the differences. He shows his willingness to confront potentially divisive issues by reminding Jews and blacks of their long record of cooperation toward the goal of eliminating racial or religious discrimination. He confronts the potentially divisive issue of Palestinian rights and the Arab-Israeli conflict by reminding the audience that the three religions Judaism, Christianity and Islam all revere Jerusalem as a holy city. And he invokes the names of revered leaders from both sides to implore his audience to turn "from finger-pointing to clasped hands." This is revival preaching at its best, as Jackson implores his audience to forgive, forget and move on to a new land.

The longest section of the speech is the traditional attack on the opposition. In this section, Jackson follows the demands of the genre and the expectations of the delegates seated in the hall and lambasts the Reagan administration for a long catalogue of sins. Since this speech was given in 1984 and conditions as well as statistics have changed, this section has the least interest for us today. It does show that Jackson can perform the rituals expected of any major political figure.

Jackson returns to his revival style in the conclusion imitating one of the most famous passages from Martin Luther King's speeches. In the conclusion, Jackson tries to bring the themes of the speech together in a vision of a transformed America living out the dream of justice and brotherhood. Unfortunately, as a comparison with the King speech will easily demonstrate, Jackson's creativity does not match his vision and his delivery is too strident for television. He is shouting, straining his voice and not projecting the dignity appropriate for a president. However, his use of parallelism, repetition and antithesis combine with the rhymed slogans to make some of the lines memorable and to increase the impact of the speech.

Jackson's signature as a speaker is his use of rhymed slogans often in the form of antithetical ideas to emphasize his message. These are effective because they are short and memorable. In the conclusion, he uses this technique notably in the lines: "put hope in their brains, not dope in their veins," and "choose the human race over the nuclear race." Jackson likes to play on words to involve the audience in his speech, such as, "Dream of preachers and priests who will prophecy and not just profiteer." He combines these rhymed, almost musical sounds with repetition that imitates the structure of the revival sermon with its call and response. At one point Jackson exhorts his audience to "preach and dream" which is precisely what he is doing. He concludes his political sermon by quoting from the widely known lines by Emma Lazarus on the base of the Statue of Liberty which reinforce his plea for diversity and unity within an America that is restored to its rightful place as the beacon of hope for all the world.

JACKSON'S SPEECH AS POLITICAL SPECTACLE

Jackson's style and delivery were colorful, but they alone are not sufficient to account for public reaction to his speech. Jackson has long been known as a powerful orator, and some observers found this speech less effective than others he has delivered. To understand this speech's full impact we must then move beyond the speech itself and look for clues in the context which framed it. In our view, the media coverage of Jackson prior to the convention established his speech as a complex symbolic political spectacle, and the televisual treatment of the address itself intensified this depiction.

In his analysis of "the Jesse Jackson phenomenon," Adolph L. Reed, Jr. argues that Jackson's rise to prominence in 1984 "was fueled by a number of factors," including "his impressive knack for self-promotion and the dispirited and uncertain conditions prevailing within the Afro-American population" (106). But Reed contends that the dynamic relationship between Jackson and his black constituency "was catalyzed by the functional intervention of the mass media" (106). After a detailed examination of the progress of Jackson's campaign, Reed concludes that not only did the media propel Jackson's candidacy, but it also "anointed Jackson's attempt to gain paramountcy as a black spokesperson" (107). Reed believes that the media "focused on Jackson more as a historical figure than as a serious presidential candidate" (108). Although Reed's analysis is critical of the media's role in "fomenting" Jackson's image as the single significant spokesperson for a mythically monolithic black America, he provides evidence that this is precisely what media coverage of Jackson accomplished. In a sense, then, the media's intense coverage of the Jackson campaign could only achieve closure by framing his participation in the convention as a symbolically and historically dramatic event. This effect was, of course, intensified by the Democratic party's leaders' uncertainty about what Jackson would do at the convention and what his followers might do in the election.

The convention itself was a notable political spectacle. As Murray Edelman observes, a convention is a "contrived" setting "unabashedly built up to emphasize a departure from men's daily frame" (96). Such settings or backgrounds, Edelman argues, make "for heightened sensitivity and easier conviction in onlookers." Moreover, as Burke notes, "From the motivational point of view, there is implicit in the quality of a scene the quality of the action that is to take place within it. This would be another way of saying that the act will be consistent with the scene" (3, 6-7). In short, when Jackson mounted the platform at the convention to deliver his Rainbow Coalition address, the delegates and the American viewing public recognized that this was an historical event: Jackson, a black American and a serious candidate for President, in addressing the Democratic Party Convention symbolized the progress of democracy itself.

In a very complete and insightful analysis, Tiemens, Sillars, Alexander and Werling have examined television coverage of Jackson's speech. Although the coverage provided by five different sources (ABC, CBS, NBC, CNN and C-SPAN) differed in many respects, these scholars conclude that while the news sources apparently did not tell "the viewer directly what parts of the speech were most important...they did...give the visual aspects a life of their own apart from the speech itself" because "the visual emphasis was not on what Jackson was saying, but on members of his audience and their dramatic relation to the speaker" (19). In essence, the televisual presentation of Jackson's speech was far from neutral and, indeed, sometimes distorted the physical reality in the Convention Hall. For example, an analysis of crowd shots painted a demographic profile of the convention delegate as a "44-year-old black woman, without a college education, of modest or low income, with an emotional attachment to Jesse Jackson." The typical delegate was in fact "age 44, a college-educated professional with a family income of nearly $44,000, liberal in politics, attending a national party convention for the first time and white. It is slightly better than even money that the person would be a man" (16).

Obviously, the vast majority of Americans who saw the speech viewed it on television or through later media coverage. The speech that Jackson performed on that evening was, in effect, an orchestrated political spectacle conveyed in the mass media. Jackson's actual words on that occasion were less important than the mediated environment in which he delivered them.

Jackson's performance was framed by an invitation which was an important rhetorical act of the Democratic Party: Jackson was invited to speak. Inviting Jackson to speak acknowledged him as a significant player in the Democratic Party. Accepting Jackson's planks would have met Jackson's platform goals, but not his goal of "self-respect." By allowing him to speak, the Democrats acknowledged Jackson and his constituency as significant members of the Party.

Jackson's speech became his opportunity to reciprocate the goodwill of the party leaders who granted him the trust and importance he wanted. His claims, couched in a rhythmic, sermonic style, substantiated the offer and confirmed the trust. The importance of his propositional argument was significant, not because the arguments were convincing, but because of what his act of arguing accomplished. His audience did not need to be convinced of the viability of the Democratic party; they did not need to be reminded of their differences with the Reagan administration; they did not even need to be told what their platform could accomplish. What the Democrats needed to hear was a Jackson willing to support the party platform and its candidates, willing to place himself under the party leadership and willing to pledge his efforts to electing the party's nominees in the general election. By means of performing a speech act consistent with the hopes of the Democratic party, Jackson's address placated fears, merged constituencies and unified the party.[1] The rhetorical moment performed the symbolic act of subordinating Jackson to the party hierarchy but also elevating him in the national consciousness. Jackson's political goals were expressed as consonant with the party's goals and thus allied Jackson and Mondale. Jackson assured the party that he shared their common enemy. With this act accomplished, the differences Jackson accentuates in the speech are not threatening because Jackson speaks from within the social community.

In essence, Jackson's speech achieves its impact as part of a complex political ritual. Within the political spectacle of the Democratic Convention, the invitation to Jackson to address the Party and Jackson's rather formulaic speech work simultaneously both to subordinate himself to party guidance and to elevate him to symbolic leadership. Although Jackson lost the nomination and had virtually no impact on the party platform, the handling of his performance by the mass media made him the "rhetorical star" of the Democratic Convention and assured his continuing political visibility.

---

[1] Austin and Searle have developed the key works in speech act theory which advance the notions of illocutions (in saying something we do something) and perlocutions (the effect of illocutions on auditors). Gaines treats the perlocution as a critical element for the study of rhetoric.

Martha A. Solomon is a professor of Speech Communication at the University of Maryland. Paul B. Stewart is a doctoral student at the University of Maryland.

WORKS CITED

Austin, J.L. *How to do Things with Words,* 2nd edition, ed. J.O. Urmson and Mariana Sbisa,

Harvard Univ. Press: Cambridge 1962.

Barker, Lucius J. & Ronald W. Walters. *Jesse Jackson's 1984 Presidential Campaign: Challenge and Change in American Politics,* University of Illinois: Urbana. 1989.

Burke, Kenneth. *A Grammar of Motives.* Univ. of California Press: Berkeley. 1974.

Coffey, Raymond & Frank Jackman. "Jackson Pledges to Back the ticket" Chicago *Tribune* 18 July 1984, 20.

Corrigan, Richard. "Jackson's Guessing Game—What Does He Want and What Will Mondale Give Him?" *National Journal,* vol. 16 #28. 14 July 1984. 1337-1384.

Current Biography Yearbook 1986. ed. Charles Moritz. H.W. Wilson: New York. 243-47.

Di Mare, Lesley A. "Functionalizing Conflict: Jesse Jackson's Rhetorical Strategy at the 1984 Democratic National Convention." *Western Journal of Speech Communication,* 51 (Spring 1987), 218-26.

Donnelly, Harrison. "The Jackson Mystique: Emotion, Ambition." *Congressional Quarterly,* 7 January 1984, 9-12.

Edelman, Murray. *The Symbolic Uses of Politics.* Univ. of Illinois Press: Urbana. 1977.

Gaines, Robert N. "Doing by Saying: Toward a Theory of Perlocution." *The Quarterly Journal of Speech,* 65 (1979), 207-17.

"Great Speeches." Washington *Post* 18 July 1984, A14.

House, Ernest R. *Jesse Jackson & the Politics of Charisma.* Westview Press: Boulder & London. 1988.

Landess, Thomas H. & Richard M. Quinn. *Jesse Jackson & The Politics of Race.* Jameson Books: Ottawa, Illinois. 1985.

Reed, Adolph L. *The Jesse Jackson Phenomenon: The Crisis of Purpose in Afro-American Politics.* Yale Press: New Haven. 1986.

"Rousing Convention." *Editorials on File,* pub. by *Facts on File.* New York. vol. 15 #14, July 16-31 1984

Searle, John R. *Expression and Meaning: Studies in the Theory of Speech Acts.* 1st ed. 1979. Cambridge Press: Cambridge. 1989.

"Speech Sets Mood for Conciliation." Los Angeles *Times* 18 July 1984, record ed., sec. 1, 5.

Stone, Eddie. *Jesse Jackson.* Holloway House: Los Angeles. 1988.

Tannen, Deborah. *Talking Voices: Repetition, Dialogue, and Imagery in Conversational Discourse.* Cambridge Press: Cambridge. 1989.

Tiemens, Robert K., Malcolm O. Sillars, Dennis C. Alexander & David Werling. "Television Coverage of Jesse Jackson's Speech to the 1984 Democratic National Convention." *Journal of Broadcasting & Electronic Media,* 32 (Winter 1988), 1-22.

COMMON GROUND AND COMMON SENSE

Jesse Jackson

Democratic National Convention, Atlanta, Georgia, July 20, 1988
(Transcribed from the video, GREAT SPEECHES, VOLUME VII)

{Tonight} we pause and give praise and honor to God for being good enough to allow us to be at this place at this time. When I look out at this convention, I see the face of America, red, yellow, brown, black and white, we're all precious in God's sight—the real rainbow coalition. All of us... all of us who are here think that we are seated. But we're really standing on someone's shoulders. Ladies and gentlemen, Mrs. Rosa Parks. The mother of the civil rights movement.

I want to express my deep love and appreciation for the support my family has given me over these past months. They have endured pain, anxiety, threat and fear. But they have been strengthened and made secure by a faith in God, in America and in you. Your love has protected us and made us strong. To my wife, Jackie, the foundation of our family; to our five children whom you met tonight; to my mother, Mrs. Helen Jackson, who is present tonight; and to my grandmother, Mrs. Maltilda Burns; my brother, Chuck, and his family; my mother-in-law, Mrs. Gertrude Brown, who just last month at age 61 graduated from Hampton Institute, a marvelous achievement; I offer my appreciation to Mayor Andrew Young who has provided such gracious hospitality to all of us this week.

And a special salute to President Jimmy Carter. President Carter...President Carter restored honor to the White House after Watergate. He gave many of us a special opportunity to grow. For his kind words, for his unwavering commitment to peace in the world and for the voters that came from his family, every member of his family, led by Billy and Amy, I offer my special thanks to the Carter family.

My right and my privilege to stand here before you has been won...won—in my lifetime—by the blood and the sweat of the innocent. Twenty-four years ago, the late Fanny Lou Hamer and Aaron Henry—who sits here tonight from Mississippi—were locked out onto the streets of Atlantic City, the head of the Mississippi Freedom Democratic Party. But tonight, a black and white delegation from Mississippi is headed by Ed Cole, a black man, from Mississippi, 24 years later.

Many were lost in the struggle for the right to vote. Jimmy Lee Jackson, a young student, gave his life. Viola Luizzo, a white mother from Detroit, called nigger lover, and brains blown out at point blank range. Schwerner, Goodman and Chaney—two Jews and a black—found in a common grave, bodies riddled with bullets in Mississippi. The four darling little girls in the church in Birmingham, Alabama. They died that we might have a right to live. Dr. Martin Luther King, Jr. lies only a few miles from us tonight. Tonight he must feel good as he looks down upon us. We sit here together, a rainbow, a coalition—the sons and daughters of slave masters and the sons and daughters of slaves sitting together around a common table, to decide the direction of our party and our country. His heart would be full tonight.

As a testament to the struggles of those who have gone before; as a legacy to those who have come after; as a tribute to the endurance, the patience, the courage of our forefathers and mothers; as an assurance that their prayers are being answered that their work has not been in vain and hope is eternal; tomorrow night my name will go in nomination for the Presidency of the United States of America.

We meet tonight at the crossroads, a point of decision. Shall we expand, be inclusive, find unity and power or suffer division and impotence? We come to Atlanta, the cradle of the Old South, the crucible of the New South. Tonight there is a sense of celebration because we are moved—fundamentally moved from racial battlegrounds by law to economic common ground. Tomorrow we'll challenge to move to higher ground, common ground.

Think of Jerusalem, the intersection where many trails met, a small village that became the birthplace for three great religions—Judaism, Christianity and Islam. Why was this village so blessed? Because it provided a crossroads for [sic] different people met, different cultures, different civilizations could meet and find common ground. When people come together flowers always flourish. The air is rich with the aroma of a new spring.

Take New York, the dynamic metropolis. What makes New York so special? It's the invitation at the Statue of Liberty "Give me your tired, your poor, your huddled masses who yearn to breathe free. Not restricted to England only, many people, many cultures, many languages with one thing in common, they yearn to breathe free, common ground.

Tonight in Atlanta, for the first time in this century we convene in the South. A state where governors once stood in schoolhouse doors; where Julian Bond was denied his seat in the state legislature because of his conscientious objection to the Vietnam war. A city that through its five black universities has graduated more black students than any city in the world. Atlanta, now a modern intersection of the New South.

Common ground, that's the challenge of our party tonight. Left wing, right wing, progress will not come through boundless liberal...liberal [sic] liberalism, nor static conservatism, but at the critical mass of mutual survival...not at boundless liberalism nor static conservatism, but at the critical mass of mutual survival. It takes two wings to fly whether you're a hawk or a dove, you're just a bird living in the same environment in the same world. The *Bible* teaches that when lions and lambs be down together, none will be afraid and there will be peace in the valley. It sounds impossible. Lions eat lambs. Lambs sensibly flee from lions. Yet even lions and lambs find common ground. Why? Because neither lions nor lambs want the forest to catch on fire. Neither lions nor lambs want acid rain to fall. Neither lions nor lambs can survive nuclear war. If lions and lambs can find common ground surely we can as well as civilized people.

The only time that we win is when we come together. In 1960, John Kennedy, the late John Kennedy, beat Richard Nixon by only 112,000 votes, less than one vote per precinct. He won by the margin of our hope. He brought us together, he reached out. He had the courage to defy his advisors and inquire about Dr. King's jailing in Albany, Georgia. We won by the margin of our hope, inspired by courageous leadership. In 1964, Lyndon Johnson brought both wings together. The thesis, the antithesis and the creative synthesis and together we won. In 1976, Jimmy Carter unified us again and we won. When we do not come together we never win. In 1968, division and despair in July led to our defeat in November. In 1980, rancor in the spring and the summer led to Reagan in the fall. When we divide we cannot win. We must find common ground as a basis for survival and development and change and growth.

Today when we debated, differed, deliberated, agreed to agree, agreed to disagree, when we had the good judgment to argue a case and did not self destruct, George Bush was just a little further away from the White House and a little closer to private life.

Tonight I salute Governor Michael Dukakis, he has run...he has run a well managed and a dignified campaign. No matter how tired or how tried he always resisted the temptation to stoop to demagoguery. I've watched a good mind fast at work and steel nerves guiding his campaign out of the crowded field without appeal to the worst in us. I've watched his perspective grow as his environment has expanded. I've seen his toughness and tenacity close up. Know his commitment to public service. Mike Dukakis' parents were a doctor and a teacher. My parents, a maid, a beautician and a janitor. There's a great gap between Brookline, Massachusetts and Haney Street, the Fieldcrest Village Housing Projects in Greenville, South Carolina. He studied law, I studied theology. There are differences of religion, region and race, differences in experiences and perspectives, but the genius of America is that out of the many we become one. Providence has enabled our paths to intersect. His forebears came to America on immigrant ships. My foreparents *[sic]* came to America on slave ships, but whatever the original ships we're in the same boat tonight. Our ships could pass in the night if we have the false sense of independence or they could collide and crash. We would lose our passengers. We can seek a higher reality and a greater good. Apart we can drift on the broken pieces of Reaganomics, satisfy our baser instincts and exploit the fears of our people. At our highest, we can call upon noble instincts and navigate this vessel to safety.

The greater good is the common good. As Jesus said, "Not my will, but thine be done." It was his way of saying there's a higher good beyond personal comfort or position. The good of our nation is at stake. Its commitment to working men and women, to the poor and the vulnerable, to the many in the world. With so many guided missiles and so much misguided leadership the stakes are exceedingly high. Our choice, full participation in a democratic government or more abandonment and neglect. And so this night, we choose not a false sense of independence, not our capacity to survive and endure. Tonight we choose interdependency and our capacity to act and unite for the greater good.

Common good is finding commitment and new priorities to expansion and inclusion. A commitment to expanded participation in the Democratic party at every level. A commitment to a shared national campaign strategy and involvement at every level. A commitment to new priorities that ensure that hope will be kept alive. A common ground commitment to a legislative agenda for empowerment for the John Connor's bill—universal, on site, same day registration everywhere. A commitment to D.C. statehood and empowerment. D.C. deserves statehood. A commitment to economic set-asides. A commitment to the Dellam's bill for comprehensive sanctions against South Africa. A shared commitment to a common direction, common ground; easier said than done.

Where do you find common ground at the point of challenge? This campaign has shown that politics need not be marketed by politicians, packaged by pollsters and pundits. Politics can be *[sic]* moral arena where people come together to find common ground. We find common ground at the plant gate that closes on workers without notice. We find common ground at the farm auction where a good farmer loses his or her land to bad loans or diminishing markets. Common ground at the school yard where teachers cannot get adequate pay and students cannot get a scholarship and can't make a loan. Common ground at the hospital admitting room where somebody tonight is dying because they cannot afford to go upstairs to a bed that's empty waiting for someone with insurance to get sick. We are a better nation than that. Common ground.

What is leadership if not present help in a time of crisis? And so I met you at the point of challenge: in Jay, Maine where paperworkers were striking for fair wages; in Greenville, Iowa where family farmers struggled for a fair price; in Cleveland, Ohio where working women seek comparable worth; in McFarland, California where the children of Hispanic farm workers may be dying from poisoned land—dying in clusters with cancer; in AIDS hospice in Houston, Texas where the sick support one another, where they've been rejected by their own parents and friends. Common ground.

America is not a blanket woven from one thread, color, one cloth. When I was a child growing up in Greenville, South Carolina and Grandmama could not afford a blanket she didn't complain and we did not freeze. Instead she took pieces of old cloth— patches; wool, silk, gabardine croca sack. Only patches barely good enough to wipe off your shoes with, but they didn't stay that way very long. With sturdy hands and a strong cord she sewed them together into a quilt—a thing of beauty and power and culture.

Now, Democrats, we must build such a quilt. Farmers, you seek fair prices and you are right, but you cannot stand alone. Your patch is not big enough. Workers, you fight for fair wages, you're right, but your patch, labor, is not big enough. Women, you seek comparable worth and pay equity, you're right, but your patch is not big enough. Women, mothers who seek Headstart and day care and pre-natal care on the front side of life rather than jail care and welfare on the back side of life, you're right, but your patch is not big enough. Students, you seek scholarships, you're right, but your patch is not big enough. Blacks and Hispanics, when we fight for civil rights we are right, but our patch is not big enough. Gays and lesbians, when you fight against discrimination and a cure for AIDS, you're right, but your patch is not big enough. Conservatives and progressives, when you fight for what you believe—right wing, left wing, hawk, dove— you're right from your point of view, but your point of view is not enough. But don't despair, be as wise as my grandmama. Pull the patches and the pieces together—bound by a common thread. When we form a great quilt of unity and common ground we'll have the power to bring about health care and housing and jobs and education and hope to our nation.

We the people can win. We stand at the end of a long dark night of reaction. We stand tonight united in the commitment to a new direction. For almost eight years, we've been led by those who view social good coming from private interests, who view public life as a means to increase private wealth. They've been prepared to sacrifice the common good of the many to satisfy the private interest and the wealth of a few. We believe in a government that's a tool of our democracy in service to the public, not an instrument of the aristocracy in search of private wealth. We believe in government with the consent of the governed—of, for and by the people.

We must then emerge into a new day with a new direction. Reaganomics, based on the belief that the rich had too much money...too little money and the poor had too much. That's classic Reaganomics. They believe that the poor had too much money and the rich had too little money so they engaged in reverse Robin Hood—took from the poor, gave the rich, paid for by the middle class. We cannot stand four more years of Reaganomics in any version, in any disguise.

How do I document that case? Seven years later, the richest one percent of our society pays twenty percent less in taxes, the poorest ten percent pay twenty percent more—Reaganomics. Reagan gave the rich and the powerful a multi-billion dollar party. Now the party is over. He expects the people to pay for the damage. I take this principal position, convention, let us not raise taxes on the poor and the middle class, but those who had the party, the rich and the powerful, must pay for the party.

I just want to take common sense to high places. We're spending 150 billion dollars a year defending Europe and Japan 43 years after the war is over. We have more troops in Europe tonight than we had seven years ago. Yet the threat of war is ever more remote. Germany and Japan are now creditor nations. That means they [sic] got a surplus. We are a debtor nation, means we are in debt. Let them share more of the burden of their own defense. Use some of that money to build decent housing. Use some of that money to educate our children. Use some of that money for long-term health care. Use some of that money to wipe out these slums and put America back to work.

I just want to take common sense to high places. If we can bail out Europe and Japan, if we can bail out Continental Bank and Chrysler and Mr. Iacocca make [sic] eight thousand dollars a hour, we can bail out the family farmer.

I just want to make common sense. It does not make sense to close down 650,000 family farms in this country while importing food from abroad, subsidized by the U.S. government. Let's make sense. It does not make sense to be escorting oil tankers up and down the Persian Gulf, paying $2.50 for every $1.00 worth of oil we bring out while oil wells are capped in Texas, Oklahoma and Louisiana. I just want to make sense.

Leadership must meet the moral challenge of its day. What's the moral challenge of our day? We have public accommodations. We have the right to vote. We have open housing. What's the fundamental challenge of our day? It is to end economic violence. Plant closing without notice, economic violence. Even the greedy do not profit long from greed. Economic violence. Most poor people are not lazy. They're not black. They're not brown. They're mostly white and female and young. But whether white, black or brown, a hungry baby's belly turned inside out is the same color. Color it pain. Color it hurt. Color it agony. Most poor people are not on welfare.

Some of them are illiterate and can't read the want-ad sections. And when they can, they can't find a job that matches their address. They work hard every day, I know. I live amongst them. I'm one of them. I know they work. I'm a witness. They catch the early bus. They work every day. They raise other people's children. They work every day. They clean the streets. They work every day. They drive dangerous cabs. They work every day. They change the beds you slept in in these hotels last night and can't get a union contract. They work every day.

No more. They're not lazy. Someone must defend them because it's right, and they cannot speak for themselves. They work in hospitals. I know they do. They wipe the bodies of those who are sick with fever and pain. They empty their bedpans. They clean out their commode. No job is beneath them, and yet when they get sick, they cannot lie in the bed they made up every day. America, that is not right. We are a better nation than that. We are a better nation than that.

We need a real war on drugs. You can't just say no. It's deeper than that. You can't just get a palm reader or an astrologer; it's more profound than that. We're spending $150 billion on drugs a year. We've gone from ignoring it to focusing on the children. Children cannot buy $150 billion worth of drugs a year. A few high profile athletes—athletes are not laundering $150 billion a year—bankers are. I met the children in Watts who unfortunately in their despair, their grapes of hope have become raisins of despair, and they're turning on each other and they're self-destructing—but I stayed with them all night long. I wanted to hear their case. The said, "Jesse Jackson, as you challenge us to say no to drugs, you're right. And to not sell them, you're right. And to not use these guns, you're right." And, by the way, the promise of CETA—they displaced CETA. They did not replace CETA. We have neither jobs nor houses nor services nor training—no way out. Some of us take drugs as anesthesia for our pain. Some take drugs as a way of pleasure—both short-term pleasure and long-term pain. Some sell drugs to make money. It's wrong, we know, but you need to know that we know. We can go and buy the drugs by the boxes at the port. If we can buy the drugs at the port, don't you believe the federal government can stop it if they want to?

They say, "We don't have Saturday night specials any more." They say, "We buy AK-47s and Uzis, the latest lethal weapons. We buy them across the counter on Long Beach Boulevard." You cannot fight a war on drugs unless and until you gonna [sic] to challenge the bankers and the gun sellers and those who grow them. Don't just focus on the children, let's stop drugs at the level of supply and demand. We must end the scourge on the American culture.

Leadership. What difference will we make? Leadership cannot just go along to get along. We must do more than change presidents. We must change direction. Leadership must face the moral challenge of our day. The nuclear war build-up is irrational. Strong leadership cannot desire to look tough, and let that stand in the way of the pursuit of peace. Leadership must reverse the arms race. At least we should pledge no first use. Why? Because first use begats first retaliation, and that's mutual annihilation. That's not a rational way out. No use at all—let's think it out, and not fight it out, because it's an unwinnable fight. Why hold a card that you can never drop? Let's give peace a change.

Leadership—we now have this marvelous opportunity to have a breakthrough with the Soviets. Last year, 200,000 Americans visited the Soviet Union. There's a chance for joint ventures into space, not Star Wars and the war arms escalation, but a space defense initiative. Let's build in space together, and demilitarize the heavens. There's a way out.

America, let us expand. When Mr. Reagan and Mr. Gorbachev met, there was a big meeting. They represented together one-eighth of the human race. Seven-eighths of the human race was locked out of that room. Most people in the world tonight—half are Asian, one-half of them are Chinese. There are 22 nations in the Middle East. There's Europe; 40 million Latin Americans next door to us; the Caribbean; Africa—a half-billion people. Most people in the world today are yellow or brown or black, non-Christian, poor, female, young, and don't speak English—in the real world. This generation must offer leadership to the real world. We're losing ground in Latin America, the Middle East, South Africa, because we're not focusing on the real world, that real world. We must use basic principles, support international law. We stand the most to gain from it. Support human rights; we believe in that. Support self-determination; we'll build on that. Support economic development; you know it's right. Be consistent, and gain our moral authority in the world.

I challenge you tonight, my friends, let's be bigger and better as a nation and as a party. We have basic challenges. Freedom in South Africa—we've already agreed as Democrats to declare South Africa to be a terrorist state. But don't just stop there. Get South Africa out of Angola. Free Namibia. Support the front-line states. We must have a new, humane human rights assistance policy in Africa.

I'm often asked, "Jesse, why do you take on these tough issues? They're not very political. We can't win that way." If an issue is morally right, it will eventually be political. It may be political and never be right. Fannie Lou Hamer didn't have the most votes in Atlantic City, but her principles have outlasted every delegate who voted to lock her out. Rosa Parks did not have the most votes, but she was morally right. Dr. King didn't have the most votes about the Vietnam war, but he was morally right. If we're principled first, our politics will fall in place.

"Jesse, why did you take these big bold initiatives?" A poem by an unknown author went something like this:

We mastered the air, we've conquered the sea,
Annihilated distance and prolonged life,
We were not wise enough to live on this earth
Without war and without hate.
(As for Jesse Jackson,)
I'm tired of sailing my little boat,
Far inside the harbor bar.
I want to go out where the big ships float,
Out on the deep where the great ones are.

And should my frail craft prove too slight,
The waves that sweep those billows o'er.
I'd rather go down in the stirring fight,
Than drown to death in the sheltered shore.

We've got to go out, my friends, where the big boats are.

And then, for our children, young America, hold your head high now. We can win. We must not lose you to drugs and violence, premature pregnancy, suicide, cynicism, pessimism and despair. We can win. Wherever you are tonight, I challenge you to hope and to dream. Don't submerge your dreams. Exercise above all else, even on drugs, dream of the day you're drug-free. Even in the gutter, dream of the day that you'll be up on your feet again. You must never stop dreaming. Face reality, yes. But don't stop with the way things are; dream of things as they ought to be. Dream. Face pain, but love, hope, faith, and dreams will help you rise above the pain. Use hope and imagination as weapons of survival and progress, but you keep on dreaming, young America. Dream of peace. Peace is rational and reasonable. War is irrational [*sic*] in this age and unwinnable.

Dream of teachers who teach for life and not for living. Dream of doctors who are concerned more about public health than private wealth. Dream of lawyers more concerned about justice than a judgeship. Dream of preachers who are concerned more about prophecy than profiteering. Dream on the high road of sound values.

And in America, as we go forth to September, October and November and then beyond, America must never surrender to a high moral challenge. Do not surrender to drugs. The best drug policy is a no first use. Don't surrender with needles and cynicism. Let's have no first use on the one hand, or clinics on the other. Never surrender, young America. Go forward. America must never surrender to malnutrition. We can feed the hungry and clothe the naked. We must never surrender. We must go forward. We must never surrender to illiteracy. Invest in our children. Never surrender; and go forward.

We must never surrender to inequality. Women cannot compromise ERA or comparable worth. Women are making 60 cents on the dollar to what a man makes. Women cannot buy meat cheaper. Women cannot buy bread cheaper. Women cannot buy milk cheaper. Women deserve to get paid for the work that you do. It's right and it's fair.

Don't surrender, my friends. Those who have AIDS tonight, you deserve our compassion. Even with AIDS you must not surrender in your wheelchairs. I see you sitting here tonight in those wheelchairs. I've stayed with you. I've reached out to you across our nation. Don't you give up. I know it's tough sometimes. People look down on you. It took you a little more effort to get here tonight. And no one should look down on you, but sometimes mean people do. The only justification we have for looking down on someone is that we're going to stop and pick them up. But even in your wheelchairs, don't you give up. We cannot forget 50 years ago when our backs were against the wall, Roosevelt was in a wheelchair. I would rather have Roosevelt in a wheelchair than Reagan and Bush on a horse. Don't you surrender and don't you give up. Don't surrender and don't give up.

Why can I challenge you this way? "Jesse Jackson, you don't understand my situation. You be on television. You don't understand. I see you with the big people. You don't...you don't understand my situation." I understand. You see me on TV but you don't know the me that makes me, me. They wonder why does Jesse run, because they see me running for the White House. They don't see the house I'm running from. I have a story. I wasn't always on television. Writers were not always outside my door. When I was born late one afternoon, October 8th, in Greenville, S.C., no writers asked my mother her name. Nobody chose to write down our address. My mama was not supposed to make it. And I was not supposed to make it. You see, I was born to a teenage mother who was born to a teen-age mother.

I understand. I know abandonment and people being mean to you, and saying you're nothing and nobody, and can never be anything. I understand. Jesse Jackson is my third name. I'm adopted. When I had no name, my grandmother gave me her name. My name was Jesse Burns until I was 12. So I wouldn't have a blank space, she gave me a name to hold me over. I understand when nobody knows your name. I understand when you have no name. I understand. I wasn't born in the hospital. Mama didn't have insurance. I was born in the bed at house [sic]. I really do understand. Born in a three-room house, bathroom in the backyard, slop jar by the bed, no hot and cold running water. I understand. Wallpaper used for decoration? No. For a windbreaker. I understand. I'm a working person's person, that's why I understand you whether you're black or white. I understand work. I was not born with a silver spoon in my mouth. I had a shovel programmed for my hand. My mother, a working woman. So many days she went to work early with runs in her stockings. She knew better, but she wore runs in her stockings so that my brother and I could have matching socks and not be laughed at at school. I understand. At 3 o'clock on Thanksgiving Day we couldn't eat turkey because mama was preparing someone else's turkey at 3 o'clock. We had to play football to entertain ourselves and then around 6 o'clock she would get off the Alta Vista bus; and we would bring up the leftovers and eat our turkey—leftovers, the carcass, the cranberries around 8 o'clock at night. I really do understand.

Every one of these funny labels they put on you, those of you who are watching this broadcast tonight in the projects, on the corners, I understand. Call you outcast, low down, you can't make it, you're nothing, you're from nobody, subclass, underclass—when you see Jesse Jackson, when my name goes in nomination, your name goes in nomination. I was born in the slum, but the slum was not born in me. And it wasn't born in you, and you can make it. Wherever you are tonight you can make it. Hold your head high, stick your chest out. You can make it. It gets dark sometimes, but the morning comes. Don't you surrender. Suffering breeds character. Character breeds faith. In the end faith will not disappoint. You must not surrender. You may or may not get there, but just know that you're qualified and you hold on and hold out. We must never surrender. America will get better and better. Keep hope alive. Keep hope alive. Keep hope alive. On tomorrow night and beyond, keep hope alive.

I love you very much. I love you very much.

KEYNOTE ADDRESS

Ann Richards

**Democratic National Convention, Atlanta, Georgia, July 18, 1988
(Transcribed from the video, GREAT SPEECHES, VOLUME VIII)**

Thank you very much.

Good evening, ladies and gentlemen. Buenäs noches mis amïgos. I'm delighted to be here with you this evening because after listening to George Bush all these years I figured you needed to know what a real Texas accent sounds like.

Twelve years ago Barbara Jordan, another Texas woman, Barbara made the Keynote Address to this convention and two women in 160 years is about par for the course. But if you give us a chance, we can perform. After all, Ginger Rogers did everything that Fred Astaire did. She just did it backwards and in high heels.

I want to announce to this nation that in a little more than 100 days the Reagan, Meese, Deaver, Nofzieger, Poindexter, North, Weinberger, White, Vorsex, Lavelle, Stockman, Haig, Bork, Noriega, George Bush will be over.

You know, tonight I feel a little bit like I did when I played basketball in the eighth grade. I thought I looked real cute in my uniform and then I heard a boy yell from the bleachers "Make that basket bird legs." And my greatest fear is that same guy is somewhere out there in the audience tonight and he's gonna cut me down to size. Because where I grew up there really wasn't much tolerance for self importance, people who put on airs.

I was born during the depression in a little community just outside Waco and I grew up listening to Franklin Roosevelt on the radio. Well it was back then that I came to understand the small truths and the hardships that bind neighbors together. Those were real people with real problems and they had real dreams about getting out of the depression.

I can remember summer nights when we'd put down what we called a Baptist pallet and we listened to the grownups talk. I can still hear the sound of the dominoes clicking on the marble slab my daddy had found for a tabletop. I can still hear the laughter of the men telling jokes you weren't suppose to hear, talking about how big that old buck deer was, laughing about mamma putting Clorox in the well when the frog fell in. They talked about war and Washington and what this country needed. They talked straight talk and they came from people who were living their lives as best they could. And that's what we're gonna do tonight. We're gonna tell how the cow ate the cabbage.

I got a letter last week from a young mother in Lorena, Texas and I want to read part of it to you. She writes:

> Our worries go from payday to payday just like millions of others and we have two fairly decent incomes, but I worry how I am going to pay the rising car insurance and food. I pray my kids don't have a growth spurt from August to December, so I don't have to buy new jeans. We buy clothes at the budget stores and we have them fray and fade and stretch in the first wash. We ponder and try to figure out how we're gonna pay for college and braces

and tennis shoes. We don't take vacations and we don't go out to eat. Please don't think me ungrateful. We have jobs and a nice place to live and we're healthy. We're the people you see everyday in the grocery stores and we obey the laws. We pay our taxes. We fly our flags on holidays and we plod along trying to make it better for ourselves and our children and our parents. We aren't vocal anymore. I think maybe we're too tired. I believe that people like us are forgotten in America.

Well, of course you believe you're forgotten, because you have been. This Republican administration treats us as if we were pieces of a puzzle that can't fit together. They've tried to put us into compartments and separate us from each other. Their political theory is divide and conquer. They've suggested time and time again that what is of interest to one group of Americans is not of interest to anyone else. We've been isolated. We've been lumped into that sad phraseology called special interests.

They've told farmers that they were selfish, that they would drive up food prices if they asked the government to intervene on behalf of the family farm. And we watched farms go on the auction block while we bought food from foreign countries. Well, that's wrong.

They told working mothers it's all their fault that families are falling apart because they had to go to work to keep their kids in jeans and tennis shoes and college and they're wrong.

They told American labor they were trying to ruin free enterprise by asking for sixty days notice of plant closings and that's wrong. And they told the auto industry and the steel industry and the timber industry and the oil industry, companies being threatened by foreign products flooding this country, that you're protectionists if you think the government should enforce our trade laws and that is wrong.

When they belittle us for demanding clean air and clean water, for trying to save the oceans and the ozone layer, that's wrong.

No wonder we feel isolated and confused. We want answers and their answer is that something is wrong with you. Well, nothing's wrong with you. Nothing's wrong with you that you can't fix in November.

We've been told, we've been told that the interests of the South and the Southwest are not the same interests as the North and the Northeast. They pit one group against the other. They've divided this country and in our isolation we think government isn't gonna help us and that we're alone in our feelings. We feel forgotten. Well, the fact is that we are not an isolated piece of their puzzle, we are one nation. We are the United States of America.

Now we Democrats believe that America is still the country of fair play. That we can come out of a small town or a poor neighborhood and have the same chance as anyone else and it doesn't matter whether we are black or Hispanic or disabled or women. We believe that America is a country where small business owners must succeed because they are the bedrock, backbone of our economy. We believe that our kids deserve good day care and public schools. We believe our kids deserve public schools where students can learn and teachers can teach. And we want to believe that our parents will have a good retirement and that we will too. We Democrats believe that Social Security is a pact that cannot be broken. We want to believe that we can live out our lives without the terrible fear that an illness is going to bankrupt us and our children. We Democrats believe that America can overcome any problem including the dreaded disease called AIDS. We believe that America is still a country where there is more to life than just a constant struggle for money. And we believe that America must have leaders who show us that our struggles amount to something and contribute to something larger. Leaders who want us to be all that we can be. We want leaders like Jesse Jackson.

Jesse Jackson is a leader and a teacher who can open our hearts and open our minds and stir our very souls. And he has taught us that we are as good as our capacity for caring. Caring about the drug problem, caring about crime, caring about education and caring about each other.

Now, in contrast, the greatest nation of the free world has had a leader for eight straight years that has pretended that he cannot hear our questions over the noise of the helicopter. And we know he doesn't want to answer, but we have a lot of questions. And when we get our questions asked or there is a leak or an investigation the only answer we get is "I don't know" or "I forgot," but you wouldn't accept that answer from your children. I wouldn't. Don't tell me you don't know or you forgot.

We're not going to have the America that we want until we elect leaders who are going to tell the truth, not most days, but every day. Leaders who don't forget what they don't want to remember. And for eight straight years George Bush hasn't displayed the slightest interest in anything we care about. And now that he's after a job that he can't get appointed to he's like Columbus discovering America. He's found child care. He's found education. Poor George, he can't help it. He was born with a silver foot in his mouth.

Well, no wonder, no wonder we can't figure it out, because the leadership of this nation is telling us one thing on TV and doing something entirely different. They tell us, they tell us that they're fighting a war against terrorists. And then we find out that the White House is selling arms to the Ayatollah. They, they tell us that they're fighting a war on drugs and then people come on TV and testify that the CIA and the DEA and the FBI knew they were flying drugs into America all along. And they're negotiating with a dictator who is shovelling cocaine into this country like crazy. I guess that's their Central American strategy.

Now they tell us that employment rates are great and that they're for equal opportunity, but we know it takes two paychecks to make ends meet today when it used to take one. And the opportunity they're so proud of is low wage, dead end jobs. And there is no major city in America where you cannot see homeless men siting in parking lots holding signs that say I will work for food.

Now my friends we really are at a crucial point in American history. Under this administration we have devoted our resources into making this country a military colossus. But we've let our economic lines of defense fall into disrepair. The debt of this nation is greater than it has ever been in our history. We fought a world war on less debt than the Republicans have built up in the last eight years. You know it's kind of like that brother-in-law who drives a flashy new car but he's always borrowing money from you to make the payments.

Well, let's take what they're proudest of, that is their stand on defense. We Democrats are committed to a strong America and quite frankly when our leaders say to us we need a new weapons system our inclination is to say, well, they must be right. But when we pay billions for planes that won't fly, billions for tanks that won't fire and billions for systems that won't work, that old dog won't hunt. And you don't have to be from Waco to know that when the Pentagon makes crooks rich and doesn't make America strong that it's a bum deal.

Now I'm gonna tell you I'm really glad that our young people missed the depression and missed the great big war but I do regret that they missed the leaders that I knew. Leaders who told us when things were tough and that we'd have to sacrifice and that these difficulties might last for awhile. They didn't tell us things were hard for us because we were different or isolated or special interests. They brought us together and they gave us a sense of national purpose. They gave us Social Security and they told us they were setting up a system where we could pay our own money in and when the time came for our retirement we could take the money out. People in the rural areas were told that we deserve to have electric lights and they were gonna harness the energy that was necessary to give us electricity so my grandmama didn't have to carry that old coal oil lamp around. And they told us that they were gonna guarantee when we put our money in the bank that the money was gonna be there and it was gonna be insured. They did not lie to us. And I think one of the saving graces of Democrats is that we are candid. We talk straight talk. We tell people what we think. And that tradition and those values live today in Michael Dukakis from Massachusetts. Michael Dukakis knows that this country is on the edge of a great new era. That we're not afraid of change. That we're for thoughtful, truthful strong leadership. Behind his calm there's an impatience to unify this country and to get on with the future. His instincts are deeply American. They're tough and they're generous and personally, I have to tell you that I have never met a man who had a more remarkable sense about what is really important in life.

And then there's my friend and my teacher for many years, Senator Lloyd Bentsen. And I couldn't be prouder both as a Texan and as a Democrat because Lloyd Bentsen understands America from the barrio to the boardroom. He knows how to bring us together by regions, by economics and by example and he's already beaten George Bush once.

So when it comes right down to it, this election is a contest between those who are satisfied with what they have and those who know we can do better. That's what this election is really all about. It's about the American dream—those who want to keep it for the few and those who know it must be nurtured and passed along.

I'm a grandmother now and I have one nearly perfect granddaughter named Lily. And when I hold that grandbaby I feel the continuity of life that unites us, that binds generation to generation, that ties us with each other. And sometimes I spread that Baptist pallet out on the floor and Lily and I roll a ball back and forth and I think of all the families like mine and like the one in Lorena, Texas, like the ones that nurture children all across America. And as I look at Lily I know that it is within families that we learn both the need to respect individual human dignity and to work together for our common good within our families, within our nation. It is the same. And as I sit there I wonder if she'll ever grasp the changes I've seen in my life, if she'll ever believe that there was a time when blacks could not drink from public water fountains, when Hispanic children were punished for speaking Spanish in the public schools and women couldn't vote.

I think of all the political fights I've fought and all the compromises I've had to accept as part payment. And I think of all the small victories that have added up to national triumphs and all the things that would never have happened and all the people who would have been left behind if we had not reasoned and fought and won those battles together. And I will tell Lily that those triumphs were Democratic party triumphs.

I want so much to tell Lily how far we've come, you and I. And as the ball rolls back and forth I want to tell her how very lucky she is. That for all of our difference we are still the greatest nation on this good earth and our strength lies in the men and women who go to work every day, who struggle to balance their family and their jobs; and who should never ever be forgotten. I just hope that like her grandparents and her great grandparents before that Lily goes on to raise her kids with the promise that echoes in homes all across America. That we can do better and that's what this election is all about. Thank you very much.

CHAPTER 4:
Rally Speeches: National Crisis

Perhaps at no other time during his career does a public figure's success hinge so much on effective speaking as during times of crisis. The speaker confronts the challenge of preparing the audience to endure hardship and to suffer occasional defeat, while simultaneously instilling in them the determination to fight on. His or her style and leadership must convince them that they will, in the end, triumph.

Two masters of the crisis speech were Winston Churchill and Franklin Roosevelt. We include examples of Churchill's wartime speaking with excerpts from his St. James Palace Speech and the "Some Chicken! Some Neck!" Speech delivered before the Canadian Parliament. James Andrews explores the reasons why Churchill's rhetorical style contributed so greatly to Britain's resistance during the early dark days of the war. We see the grit and determination of Franklin Roosevelt in his memorable Declaration of War. We conclude a trilogy of wartime speeches with George Bush outlining the military defense of Saudi Arabia. We close with a different type of crisis:—energy—as addressed by Jimmy Carter and Robert Denton's assessment of his use of values to motivate the nation.

TWO WARTIME SPEECHES

Winston Churchill

(Transcribed from excerpts on the video, GREAT SPEECHES, VOLUME II)

ADDRESS TO THE DOMINION HIGH COMMISSIONERS AND ALLIED COUNTRIES' MINISTERS CONFERENCE
(St. James Palace, London, England, June 12, 1941)

What tragedies, what horrors, what crimes has Hitler and all that Hitler stands for brought upon Europe and the world! The concentration camps are overcrowded. Every dawn the firing parties are at their work. A vile race of quislings—to use the new word which will carry the scorn of mankind down the centuries—is hired to fawn upon the conqueror, to collaborate in his designs, and to enforce his rule upon their fellow countrymen, while grovelling low themselves. Such is the plight of once glorious Europe, and such are the atrocities against which we are in arms.

It is upon this foundation that Hitler, with his tattered lackey Mussolini at his tail and Admiral Darlof frisking at his side, pretends to build out of hatred, appetite, and racial assertion a new order for Europe. Never did so mocking a fantasy obsess the mind of mortal man. We cannot tell what the course of this fell war will be as it spreads remorseless through ever-wider regions. We know it will be hard; we expect it will be long; we cannot predict or measure its episodes or its tribulations. But one thing is certain, one thing is sure, one thing stands out stark and undeniable, massive and unassailable, for all the world to see. It will not be by German hands that the structure of Europe will be rebuilt or the union of the European family achieved. In every country, into which the German armies and the Nazi police have broken there has sprung up from the soil a hatred of the German name and a contempt for the Nazi creed which the passage of hundreds of years will not efface from human memory. We cannot yet see how deliverance will come, or when it will come, but nothing is more certain than that every trace of Hitler's footsteps, every stain of his infected and corroding fingers will be sponged and purged and, if need be, blasted from the surface of the earth.

He may spread his course far and wide, and carry his curse with him; he may break into Africa or into Asia. But it is with us here, in this island fortress, that he will have to reckon and settle in the end. We shall strive to resist him by land and sea. We shall be on his track wherever he goes. Our air power will continue to teach the German homeland that war is not all loot and triumph.

We shall aid and stir the people of every conquered country to resistance and revolt. We shall break up and derange every effort which Hitler makes to systematize and consolidate his subjugation. He will find no peace, no rest, no halting-place, no parley. And if, driven to desperate hazards, he attempts the invasion of the British Isles, as well he may, we shall not flinch from the supreme trial. With the help of God, of which we must all feel daily conscious, we shall continue steadfast in faith and duty till our task is done.

SOME CHICKEN! SOME NECK!

ADDRESS TO THE JOINT SESSION OF
THE CANADIAN PARLIAMENT
(Ottawa, Canada, December 30, 1941)

Sir, we did not make this war. We did not seek it. We did all we could to avoid it. We did too much to avoid it. We went so far in trying to avoid it as to be almost destroyed by it when it broke upon us, but that dangerous corner has been turned. And with every month and every year that passes we shall confront the evildoers with weapons as plentiful, as sharp and as destructive as those with which they have sought to establish their hateful domination.

We have been concerting the United Pacts and Resolves of more than thirty states and nations to fight on in unity together. And in fidelity, one with another, without any thought except the total and final excapation of the Hitler tyranny, of the Japanese frenzy, and the Mussolini flop.

There will be no halting or half measures. There will be no compromise or parley. These gangs of bandits have sought to darken the light of the world, have sought to stand between the common people of all the lands, and their march forward into their inheritance. They shall, themselves, be cast into the pit of death and shame and only when the earth has been cleansed and purged of their crimes and of their villainies will we turn from the task which they have forced upon us—a task which we were reluctant to undertake, but which we shall now most faithfully and punctiliously discharge.

When I warned them that Britain would fight on alone whatever they did, their generals told their Prime Minister and his divided cabinet, "In three weeks, England will have her neck wrung like a chicken." Some chicken! Some neck!

"ALL WILL COME RIGHT"

Winston Spencer Churchill's Wartime Speeches

Every stain of his infected and corroding fingers will be sponged.

CRITIC: James R. Andrews

WALKING WITH DESTINY: CHURCHILL THE POLITICIAN

In September of 1939, Germany invaded and quickly subdued Poland, triggering declarations of war by England and France whose governments had tried so hard to avoid war at almost any cost. At first there was a lull in the fighting, a "phoney war" people called it. By May of 1940, however, the war was anything but phoney, and the famous "blitzkrieg" or "lightening war," was being waged with ferocity and success by the Nazi legions. Disaster loomed for the Allies. Winston Churchill himself described the situation:

"Now at last the slowly gathered, long-pent-up-fury of the storm broke upon us. Four or five millions of men met each other in the first shock of the most merciless of all the wars of which record has been kept. Within a week the front in France...was to be irretrievably broken. Within three weeks the long-famed French Army was to collapse in rout and ruin, and the British Army to be hurled into the sea with all its equipment lost. Within six weeks we were to find ourselves alone, almost disarmed, with triumphant Germany and Italy at our throats, with the whole of Europe in Hitler's power.... It was amid these facts and looming prospects that I entered upon my duties as Prime Minister."[1]

A lesser man might have felt overwhelmed, or at least apprehensive, at undertaking the leadership of beleaguered Britain at this point in history. Churchill, however, was supremely confident of his own abilities and entered into his new duties "with a profound sense of relief" that now, at last, he was directing Britain's affairs. He reported that he "felt as if I were walking with Destiny, and all my past life had been but a preparation for this hour and for this trial."[2]

The past life of Winston Spencer Leonard Churchill had, indeed, been an extraordinary one. Born in 1874 at Blenheim Palace, the seat of his grandfather, the Duke of Marlborough, he was the son of a rising British politician, Lord Randolph Churchill and the beautiful American socialite, Jennie Jerome. He grew up at a time when the British Empire was at the zenith of its power and prestige, its outposts covering the globe. Young Winston was a poor scholar, earning the lowest grades in his class at Harrow and just squeaking into Sandhurst (Britain's West Point) on his second try at the entrance examinations, although he did show a genuine facility for language even as a boy and was known to dash off essays for his less facile Harrow classmates. Commissioned a cavalry officer in the Fourth Hussars in 1894, a year before his father's death, Winston Churchill launched his early career as a journalist and soldier.

As a war correspondent he covered the guerrilla warfare in Cuba and then went with his regiment to India. There he indulged his passion for polo and immersed himself in the writings of England's great literary historians, as well as reading widely and deeply in both classical and later literature. He saw extensive action in the Khyber Pass, sent dispatches back to the London papers, and wrote his first book.[3] In 1898 he was in Egypt and managed to participate in—and write about—the battle of Omdurman, the last great cavalry charge in history. The next year he ran for, and lost, a seat in the House of Commons; he returned to South Africa to cover the Boer war.

Through his writings, Churchill's own exploits had become known in England. Then, in 1899, he was captured by the Boers. "Before I had been an hour in captivity," he later wrote, "I resolved to escape."[4] And escape he did! Reports of his sensational escapade reached England to which he returned in 1900 in order to campaign for Parliament. Elected to the House of Commons as Member for Oldham, he began his long political career.

Over the next forty years, Churchill's political fortunes rose and fell. He started out as a member of the Conservative (Tory) Party and then switched to the Liberals in 1904. In 1908, at age 33, he joined the Cabinet as President of the Board of Trade. He subsequently became Home Secretary and then First Lord of the Admiralty. Stripped of this position after the failure of a campaign to knock Turkey out of World War I by seizing the Dardanelles, Churchill donned his uniform once more and returned to the front. After an enquiry had cleared Churchill of the major responsibility for the Dardanelles fiasco, he returned to the Cabinet as Secretary for War and Air and then, after the war as Colonial Secretary. Disenchanted with the Liberal Party, he rejoined the Conservatives and in 1924 became Chancellor of the Exchequer in the Tory Government. Throughout the twenties, Churchill's suspicion of Germany grew; but in 1931 he broke with his Party's leaders over the issue of what to do with India and was outside the circle of power until World War II began.

Through all of these twists and turnings, Churchill seemed always to be at the center of some political storm. As a young politician he dismayed his fellow aristocrats by advocating social reform and attacking the power of the House of Lords. He upset the established naval powers by advocating reforms, and was greeted with scorn when he proposed a new weapon which developed into the modern tank. He favored Home Rule for Ireland, supported the anti-Bolshevik counter-revolutionaries in Russia, and opposed plans that would lead eventually to an independent India. Flamboyant and impulsive, he gained notoriety, as Home Secretary, by personally leading a police attack on a group of anarchists. He learned to fly a plane. He sought out Lawrence of Arabia for advice on the Middle East. He was hit by a car while crossing a busy New York street. He gained and then lost a fortune on Wall Street. Some hated him, some found him a terrible nuisance, but no one ever accused him of being dull.

For this energetic, opinionated, adventurous figure, the 1930's were a trial. These "wilderness years" were marked for Churchill by exclusion from office and by the frustration of being ignored or dismissed. Widespread, international depression and the growth of fascist dictatorships undermined political stability and threatened the peace of the world. The economic chaos in Germany gave the Nazis their chance, and Hitler was installed as Chancellor early in 1933. In Italy, Mussolini, who first achieved office in 1922 had, by the 1930's, assumed dictatorial power and ruled through his Fascist Party. In the Far East, Japan's invasion of Manchuria demonstrated that the League of Nations was totally ineffective in combatting aggression.

In Britain, pacifism was popular; and while Germany introduced conscription and began systematically to rearm, by 1935, 100,000 Britons had taken the "Peace Pledge" renouncing war. Even if the Government had been eager to do so, which it was not, rearmament was not popular. Churchill found himself in a small minority who warned of the growing power of Nazi Germany and implored the Government to take action to improve the air force. The Prime Minister, Stanley Baldwin, voiced the sentiments of many when he remarked that, with all his gifts, Winston lacked judgment and wisdom. That was why, Baldwin observed, "while we delight to listen to him in this House we do not take his advice." [5] Churchill himself, recognized his impotence. As he later sadly observed, "I...went to Parliament from time to time to deliver warning speeches, which commanded attention, but did not, unhappily, wake to action the crowded, puzzled Houses which heard them." [6]

Baldwin's successor, Neville Chamberlain, hoped to "get on terms with the Germans" and appeared to be willing to go to great lengths to do so. [7] As Germany absorbed Austria into the Reich and menaced Czechoslovakia, Chamberlain met with Hitler in Munich and returned to England with an agreement that, he told cheering crowds, brought "peace in our time." While the Prime Minister was being lauded by the King and supported in Parliament, Churchill rose to call the agreement "a total and unmitigated defeat." [8] Lady Astor called out, "Nonsense," but events were soon to prove Churchill right. Hitler gobbled up Czechoslovakia and, by the time his armies finally invaded Poland, Britain had come to realize that Churchill's prophecies were to be fulfilled.

POWERS OF GLOWING SPEECH: CHURCHILL THE SPEAKER

As Churchill's life before his great ministry began might have been seen as a preparation for the tremendous task he undertook, so his development as a speaker can be viewed as a prelude to his monumental World War II speeches.

Churchill, many believed, was a natural writer; but as a speaker, he had flaws. He always preferred to give a set speech, well prepared and well rehearsed, than to improvise his remarks during the course of debate. "I never had the practice which comes to young men at the University," he lamented, "of speaking in small debating societies impromptu upon all sorts of subjects." [9] Nevertheless, his first speech to the House of Commons—the Maiden speech—was generally considered a success even though a Liberal newspaper, opposed to Churchill's imperialist position in the debate, described him as "a medium-sized, undistinguished young man, with an unfortunate lisp in his voice." [10] The lisp he never overcame; and, while he always had his critics and political enemies, his speaking was rarely to be characterized as undistinguished.

He took great pains in preparation of his speeches and, owing to his fear of being unable to react quickly, prepared as best he could even rebuttals he intended to deliver for speeches that he hadn't yet heard. This gift of "inspired and accurate prevision," as Violet Bonham Carter called it, generally stood him in good stead and lead to his "mastery of debate." [11]

What struck most observers was his ability to use language to convey the deeper meaning of events, language that was consistently striking and memorable. As the critics Carroll Arnold and Frederick Haberman observed, "He had no equal when the need was to find the public meaning of major events, to place that meaning in historical perspective, and to give such conceptions concise and ennobling or attaining expression."[12] Churchill, in short, rose to the occasion.

Over time, Churchill tried out language in various contexts, and finally used it in just the right way at the right time. In his speech to the House of Commons on May 13, 1941, for example, Churchill told the members of Parliament and, indeed, the whole country what he had told his new cabinet, "I have nothing to offer but blood, toil, tears, and sweat."[13] No one noticed, or cared, that he had used the same phrase a few years before in an article on the Spanish Civil War. The phrase struck just the right note at just the right time in this speech, and became one of the most memorable phrases in our language.[14]

Timing was, indeed, a vital factor in Churchill's use of language. Manfried Wiedhorn, in writing about Churchill's style, was of the opinion that "Churchill had always been his best in adversity." Professor Wiedhorn observed that "Eras of 'good feeling' or, if you will complacency, are not likely to produce either the passions or audience—in short, the occasion—for major works."[15]

In the early, dark days of World War II, Churchill certainly was given the occasion. As an historian, Churchill always was ready to draw a moral from events; and, if this made him less objective than his critics liked, he sought always to *use* history to shape the way present generations saw the world and to encourage them to react to problems in a way consistent with the lessons drawn from the past. He saw his mission, as one critic put it, "to preserve the ancient tradition of Britain and the English-speaking peoples."[16] At a time when that tradition was imperiled, Churchill's language came to its defense.

Churchill's was a language with punch to it. He hated the cumbersome circumlocutions used to describe simple things or ideas. He thought the language had a "magic and a music," and he hated it to be loaded down with pompous phrases. As Prime Minister he quickly changed the name of the "Local Defense Volunteers" to the "Home Guard;" and he ridiculed bureaucrats who spoke of homes as "accommodation units," by favoring the House of Commons with a little song: "Accommodation unit, sweet accommodation unit. There's no place like accommodation unit."[17] When speaking of the threat of invasion in 1940, Churchill spoke to the British people in the plain, blunt strength of Old English: "We shall fight on the beaches; we shall fight on the landing grounds, we shall fight in the fields and in the streets, we shall fight in the hills; we shall never surrender." In this passage, only the Norman-French word, "surrender" is of foreign derivation.[18]

To our contemporary ears, much of Churchill's language may seem old fashioned. To his audience, however, he was, in the words of Lord Birkett, "a survivor from the golden age of oratory."[19]

President Kennedy once observed that Churchill "mobilized the resources of the English language, proving that the word was mightier than the sword."[20] In the analysis of the two speeches which follows later in this essay, we will examine more precisely how Churchill's language, personality, and sense of history combined to make him, as the Archbishop of Canterbury wrote in his diary, "the man of the hour," whose "powers of glowing speech are a great public asset."[21]

BRITAIN AT BAY: THE RHETORICAL SITUATION

In the thirteen months between his assumption of the Premiership and the delivery of the first speech on the videotape, "Great Speeches, Volume II," Churchill presided over one of the most terrible and potentially disheartening periods in British history. On June 18, 1940, Churchill told the nation in a radio broadcast, that "the Battle of France is over. I expect that the Battle of Britain is about to begin.... Hitler knows that he will have to break us in this Island or lose the war."[22] The Nazi plan to break the island was first by massive bombing, Operation Eagle, followed by an invasion, Operation Sea Lion. Bombing began in the summer of 1940 and intensified in August.

Then, on September 7, the "Blitz" began with 320 bombers attacking London by day and another 250, guided by the fires burning in the city, renewing the assault at night. Over 1000 were dead at the end of this terrible raid. The intense raids continued for over a week, but the English were not broken in their island. Churchill, reminding his radio audience of Britain's defiance of the Spanish Armada and Napoleon's Grand Army, lashed out at the "cruel, wanton, indiscriminate bombings of London" as part of Hitler's plan to "cow the people." The plan, however, had turned on Hitler, and "what he has done is to kindle a fire in British hearts," a fire that would "burn with a steady and consuming flame until the last vestiges of Nazi Tyranny have been burnt out in Europe..." Churchill did not know, he told his listeners, when the "great ordeal" would be ended, but he did know that the British would endure it with "composure and fortitude," and triumph at the last.[23]

From July until the end of 1940 over 23,000 civilians were killed in the blitz. But the Royal Air Force gradually gained air supremacy, and by the end of the year it was apparent that Germany had scrapped any invasion plans. The blitz continued into 1941, but after May subsided as Hitler marshalled his forces for an attack on Russia.

Beginning in 1940, Churchill concentrated on increasing American involvement in the war. President Roosevelt was sympathetic, but the political climate in the United States forced him to move cautiously. After his re-election as President in 1940, Roosevelt conceived of the "lend-lease" scheme whereby American war material could be sent to Britain with the understanding that "when the show was over we would get repaid in kind sometime." Asserting that "the best defense of Great Britain is the best defense of the United States," Roosevelt argued that "munitions, ships," and "guns," would be put to better use by giving them to Britain "than if they were kept in storage here."[24] The President's Lend-Lease Act was passed in March, and Churchill cabled the President, "Our blessings from the whole British Empire go out to you and the American nation for this very present help in time of trouble."[25]

Throughout 1941, Churchill sought close ties with the United States, hopefully anticipating American entry into the war. Roosevelt was friendly, but still careful. Churchill invited the President to send a representative to the Dominion High Commissioners and Allied Countries' Ministers Conference, the setting of the first Churchill speech, but FDR declined.[26]

Although the horror of the blitz had abated, the war outlook was still very grim when Churchill spoke to the Dominion representatives in a speech that was also broadcast over the radio. Just two days before, the Prime Minister was forced to explain the British defeat in Crete to the House of Commons; and the campaign in Northern Africa was yet to be put into motion. Britain was still alone with very little in the way of tangible, dramatic success to bolster spirits.

The situation had modified somewhat by the end of year when Churchill travelled to the United States and Canada and delivered the second speech on the video to the Canadian Parliament (December 30, 1941). Germany had invaded Russia, and Britain was straining her own resources to help the Soviet Union. The Nazi U-boats were taking a heavy toll of shipping in the North Atlantic, although the participation of the American navy in protecting convoys and the frantic ship building program were beginning to turn the tide in favor of Britain. But the great event that made all the difference was the entry of the United States into the war on December 8, 1941, the day after the Japanese attack on Pearl Harbor. Churchill was immensely relieved and said, "to have the United States at our side was to me the greatest joy." On the night of December 8, Churchill "went to bed and slept the sleep of the saved and thankful."[27]

The Prime Minister immediately arranged with the President, with whom he had met and established the most cordial relations in August, to come to Washington for a conference. After eight days at sea, the battleship, *Duke of York*, arrived at Hampton Roads; and Churchill proceeded immediately to Washington. During his almost three weeks in the White House, Churchill met with Roosevelt, gave a speech to a joint session of Congress, and made a short trip to Canada where he conferred with the War Cabinet and delivered the Ottawa speech, the second Churchill speech considered here. Despite the entry of the United States, the prospects for the Allies were not glowing; and, indeed, 1942 was to bring depressing military reversals. From a rhetorical point of view, the situation was more hopeful—Britain, after all, no longer stood alone—but, with her American ally. However, she was now menaced in the Far East as well as in Europe, and after two bloody, draining years, German power on the continent did not appear to be diminished. Clearly, a long hard road still stretched ahead.

"ALL WILL COME RIGHT": CHURCHILL'S SPEECHES

In understanding the impact of Churchill's speeches, it is necessary first to understand the unspoken role of Churchill's own personality that is implied in these two speeches; and, indeed, in all of the Prime Minister's war speeches. Primarily, in the public mind, Churchill was the statesman who had rightly diagnosed Hitler's intentions and had called for firm action during those years in the wilderness. Churchill had, by the time he took office, established his reputation as a prophet who could see the turn events would take. His ability to predict, while not always correct, was seen by his audiences as exceptional and accurate. So Churchill's vision of the future had to be credited, given his past performance. Churchill's power to convince his audiences that "all will come out right," was greatly enhanced by their recollection that, in the past, when political leaders predicted the consequences of policies only Churchill was right.

Secondly, in the first long dismal months of the war, Churchill had never given the slightest indication that Britain would be overcome. He became the symbol of the indomitable; with courage that never faltered, sheer determination to control events, and the steadfast belief that they could be controlled. Harold Nicholson, after listening to Churchill, wrote to his wife in June of 1940, "I feel so much in the spirit of Winston's great speech that I could face a world of enemies," and one of Churchill's associates was of the opinion that "he seems to have enough courage for everybody."[28] His message to the Allied and Dominion Ministers that "we shall continue steadfast in our faith and duty till our task is done," then, was one that he had been sending without hesitation or qualification for over a year and one that all who heard him had come to associate with him personally.[29]

The most famous line in the Ottawa speech derives its force from the fact that Churchill had become almost synonymous with Britain itself. Describing the prognosis given the French Government by the defeatist French generals that England would have its neck wrung like a chicken, Churchill relishes the conclusion, "Some chicken! Some neck!" The image of Churchill himself, solid, planted firmly at the rostrum facing his audience—and facing the enemy—submitting to having his neck wrung submissively is so ludicrous as to bring gales of laughter from his listeners.

So Churchill's *ethos*, the image that he projected for his audiences, formed as it was by his past performance as profit and as unshakeable personification of Great Britain, was a crucial factor in enhancing his persuasiveness in both these speeches.

Churchill's rhetorical purpose in speaking during the time these speeches were given was clear. Two days after the June 12 speech, he observed in a telegram to President Roosevelt, "People must have hope to face the long haul that lies ahead."[30] To meet this purpose, to give people hope, Churchill developed a rhetorical strategy that was based on structuring and explaining what had happened and what was happening in such a way that his audiences' perception of the realities of events made it possible for them to see, as Churchill did, the ultimate—and triumphant—outcome. In achieving this, Churchill relied on fundamental conceptions of the struggle between good and evil, using an organizational pattern and appropriate language to picture this struggle and its final result.

Michael Osborn, a rhetorical critic and theorist, maintains that "none has been more aware of the potential power" of language used to construct basic images (Osborn calls them "archetypal metaphors") than was Winston Churchill. Osborn suggests that "in moments of great crisis, when society is in upheaval...the speaker must turn to the bedrock of symbolism, the archetype, which represents the unchanging essence of human identity."[31] Churchill's ability to construct these basic images through his language served him well in portraying good and evil.

In the speech to the High Commissioners, for example, Churchill early on establishes a series of contrasts that make use of basic human values. The privacy and peacefulness of the home is destroyed by the "all pervading secret political police;" religious beliefs are "affronted, persecuted or oppressed," by a "fantastic paganism" whose aim is to "perpetuate the worship and sustain the tyranny of one abominable creature [Hitler]." In the Ottawa speech, Churchill clearly employs the vision of light, the archetypical metaphor that has always stood for good, as against the darkness and evil of the enemy: the "gang of bandits have sought to darken the light of the world." The image of marching forward, universally symbolizing progress, and the image of cleanliness and purity contrasted to the filth and stain of corruption, are also powerful metaphors used by Churchill as he identifies the Allied cause with the forces of good. The Nazis, he says, have "sought to stand between the common people of all the lands and their march forward into their inheritance." These evil men will finally "be cast into the pit of death and shame," and Britain and her allies will continue the fight until "the earth has been cleansed and purged of their crimes and their villainy."[32]

The use of these basic images is in concert with Churchill's depiction of the enemy as totally vile. The invective, the verbal abuse of Hitler and the Nazis, is intense. Examples of this depiction can be seen in the passages already cited: Hitler the "abominable creature," the "gang of bandits," the criminals and villains. The High Commissioners speech contains the passage that expresses the determination of Britain to fight until "every stain of his [Hitler's] infected and corroding fingers" will be sponged, purged, or blasted form the earth.

Churchill's characterization of Hitler's allies is also in stark contrast with the forces ranged on the side of Britain and her Empire. In the speech given to the High

Commissioners, the Prime Minister describes those in conquered countries who have allowed themselves to become Nazi puppets as a "vile race of quislings," a word that derives from Vidkun Quisling, the name of the head of the State Council of Norway who collaborated with the Nazis during the German occupation. Italy's Mussolini is a "tattered lackey," and the French admiral Darlan is seen as a pet dog, "frisking" by Hitler's side. These traitors, Churchill makes clear, are not the real representatives of their countries. "Every dawn German volleys crack," and those who continue to resist the tyranny of Hitler are shot by firing squads, making "the great sacrifice for faith and country." In Ottawa, Churchill pays tribute to those "Frenchmen there were who would not bow the knee," and now, in exile, are allied with Britain under the leadership of General de Gaulle.

The war is being fought, then, against the "atrocities" and "ruthless savagery" of "slavish conquerors." It is being fought by those of "good heart," men and women who, trusting in God's help, will remain "true and faithful comrades." Churchill's language portrays a fight to the death against the forces of total evil, and surely this vision of the conflict could lead no one to entertain compromise or surrender.

Those who fight against Hitler are not only good, but strong, as well. Joseph Stalin is the "warrior leader" of Russia; the Dutch are "valiant, stout-hearted." The Royal Rifles of Canada and the Winnipeg Grenadiers defense of Hong Kong "crowned with military honor the reputation of their native land;" and the British themselves, "a tough and hardy lot," had "not journeyed all the way across the centuries, across the oceans, across the mountains, across the prairies, because we are made of sugar candy." The end result of such toughness of mind and spirit is that "if anybody likes to play rough we can play rough, too." This assertion produced cheers from the parliamentary audience.

Churchill also made a determined effort in these speeches to convince his audience that the war may be seen both realistically and hopefully. In both speeches, Churchill briefly reviews the past. There is no blinking at the fact that the Nazi war machine had been efficient and victorious. The "tragedies...horrors... crimes" that Britain and the rest of Europe had endured were real, as was the "plight of once glorious Europe." In the High Commissioners speech, Churchill is less specific about how victory is to be achieved than he is in his assertion that victory will come. While assuring his allies and supporters that triumph is ultimate, he is careful to point out that "we know it will be hard, we expect it will be long," and that it will only be achieved by "ceaseless and unwearying effort." In this speech Churchill reviews what little good news there is, "how far we have travelled since those breathless days of June a year ago." Britain had achieved air supremacy, and the Royal Navy commanded the seas. The blitz had destroyed neither British industry nor the British spirit; more help was coming from the United States, and the army was growing stronger. Thus, he could encourage his listeners to, "Lift up your hearts," and assure them that "All will come right;" while, at the same time, reminding them that it is only "Out of the depth of sorrow and sacrifice," that "will be born again the glory of mankind."

The Ottawa speech enlarges on this pattern of realism allied with hope: a recognition that there had been disastrous setbacks, that there were tremendous military hurdles to overcome, but that the momentum was with the Allies and victory must ultimately come. In this speech he was, at times, specific concerning such matters as the buildup of military strength. But, the most striking depiction of the future comes at the end of the speech when he discusses the three developing phases of the war. Here can be seen Churchill's sense of historical forces, his reliance on his own ethos, and the combining of realistic assessment with the triumphant prediction. The preparation phase entailed gathering strength while encountering determined opposition and promises "heavy fighting," with the implication that temporary reverses and set backs might have to be endured. The liberation phase, in which conquered territories would be recovered, called for continued exertion on the part not only of the Allied armies in the field, but also by those underground forces in the occupied countries. The assault phase entailed the conquest of the homelands of the enemy. This clear movement to victory, as certain as Churchill was that it would proceed, was not to be taken in any way for granted. "You will notice," he told his Canadian audience, "that I have not attempted to assign any time limits to the various phases. These time limits depend upon our exertions, upon our achievements, and on the hazardous and uncertain course of the war." The final note sounded in the speech is a statement of determination and confidence, but, Churchill tempered that call for victory with the reminder that the task ahead could not be underrated in its "tremendous difficulties and perils;" the "cost" and "suffering" would be great.

It is very difficult for anyone reading speeches over fifty years after they have been given to experience the nature and depth of the feelings of those who originally heard them. Knowing as we do that things did "come out right" and living in a world that has changed so much from the world of 1940, it is hard to imagine the uncertainty, the apprehension, the dread of those who went through World War II. But, one must try to understand that experience if one is to appreciate the monumental quality of Churchill's efforts. The events through which they were living were not as clear to them as they can be to us as we look back. Churchill's task was to make these events meaningful and to give, along with meaning, a reason for coping and the means to cope with the welter of happenings. His majestic and compelling language was meant to shape the views of those who heard it so that they could understand the tumultuous events through which they were passing and could direct their energies and actions in ways that would, in the immediate future, assure victory and would, ultimately, preserve the values of their culture.

Through the power of his own ethos, through his dramatic depiction of the war as a death struggle between good and evil, through his confident assertion of growing strength—both moral and physical, through his recognition of harsh realities coupled with determined faith in inevitable triumph, Churchill was able to direct his audiences' energies and actions. Winston Spencer Churchill, in these speeches and the others that he delivered in the early years of the war, brought his unique rhetorical powers forcefully to bear and made weapons of words.

James R. Andrews is chairman of the Speech Communication Department and professor at Indiana University, Bloomington.

NOTES

1. Winston S. Churchill, *Their Finest Hour* (Boston: Houghton Mifflin, 1949), pp. 3-4.
2. Winston S. Churchill, *The Gathering Storm* (Boston: Houghton Mifflin, 1948), p. 667.
3. Churchill was a prolific writer. In his lifetime he wrote over 160 books or pamphlets, over 60 forewords or contributions to other books, and more than 800 newspaper articles. See Frederick Woods, ed., *Young Winston's Wars* (New York: Viking Press, 1972), p. xiii.

4. Woods, *Young Winston's Wars*, p. 178.
5. Martin Gilbert, *Winston Churchill: The Wilderness Years* (Boston: Houghton Mifflin, 1983), p. 155.
6. Churchill, *The Gathering Storm*. p. 74.
7. Alfred F. Havinghurst, *Twentieth Century Britain* (Evanston, Illinois: Row, Peterson), p. 268.
8. Winston Churchill, "On the Munich Agreement," in *An Historical Anthology of Select British Speeches*, ed. Donald C. Bryant, Carroll C. Arnold, Frederick W. Haberman, Richard Murphy, Karl R. Wallace (New York: Ronald Press, 1967), p. 524.
9. Cited in William Manchester, *The Last Lion: Winston Spencer Churchill: Visions of Glory, 1874-1932* (Boston: Little, Brown, 1983), p. 342.
10. Manchester, p. 344.
11. Violet Bonham Carter, *Winston Churchill: An Intimate Portrait* (New York: Harcourt, Brace and World, 1965), p. 61.
12. Bryant, et. al., *Historical Anthology*, p. 521.
13. Winston S. Churchill, "I have nothing to offer but blood, toil, tears, and sweat, *A Treasury of the World's Great Speeches*, ed. Houston Peterson (New York: Grolier, 1965), p. 774.
14. See Manfried Wiedhorn, Churchill The Phrase Forger," *Quarterly Journal of Speech* 58 (April 1972): pp. 161-74.
15. Wiedhorn, "Churchill The Phrase Forger," p. 174.
16. Charles Lomas, "Winston Churchill: Orator-Historian," *Quarterly Journal of Speech* 44 (April 1958): p. 160.
17. Manchester, *Last Lion*, p. 30.
18. Robert McCrum, William Cran, Robert MacNeil, *The Story of English* (New York: Viking Press, 1986), p. 62.
19. cited in Bryant, et. al, *Historical Anthology*, p. 521.
20. cited in Piers Brandon, *Winston Churchill* (New York: Harper & Row, 1984), p. 144.
21. Martin Gilbert, *Finest Hour, 1939-41*, vol. VI of *Winston S Churchill* (Boston: Houghton Mifflin, 1983), p. 696.
22. "Finest Hour," June 18, 1941, *Sir Winston Churchill: Selections From His Writings and Speeches*, Guy Boas, ed. (London: Macmillan, 1966), p. 185.
23. "Prospect of Invasion," September 11, 1940, Boas, *Selections*, pp. 195-6.
24. Basil Rauch, ed., *Franklin D. Roosevelt: Selected Speeches, Messages, Press Conferences, and Letters*. (New York: Holt, Rinehart and Winston, 1957), pp. 270-1.
25. Doc. 43, "Churchill to Roosevelt," March 9, 1941, *Roosevelt and Churchill: Their Secret Wartime Correspondence*. eds. Francis Lowenheim, Harold Langley, Manfred Jonas (New York: E. P. Dutton, 1975), p. 131.
26. *Secret Wartime Correspondence*, p. 146.
27. Winston S. Churchill, *The Grand Alliance*, (Boston: Houghton Mifflin, 1950), pp. 607-8.
28. Gilbert, *Finest Hour*, p. 469, p. 653.
29. Quotations from the speech to the Dominion High Commissioners and from the speech to the Canadian Parliament are taken from the texts that appear in this volume.
30. Gilbert, *Finest Hour*, p. 1109.
31. Michael Osborn, "Archetypal Metaphor as Rhetoric: The Light-Dark Family," *Quarterly Journal of Speech* 53 (April 1967): pp. 119-20.
32. For a full discussion of metaphors in Churchill's war speeches see William E. Rickert, "Winston Churchill's Archetypal Metaphors: A Mythopoetic Translation of World War II," *Central States Speech Journal* 28 (Summer 1977): pp. 106-112.

DECLARATION OF WAR

Franklin D. Roosevelt

Joint Session of Congress, Washington, D.C., December 8, 1941
(Transcribed from the video, GREAT SPEECHES, VOLUME V)

Mr. Vice President, Mr. Speaker, Members of the Senate and the House of Representatives:

Yesterday, December 7, 1941—a date which will live in infamy—the United States of America was suddenly and deliberately attacked by naval and air forces of the Empire of Japan.

The United States was at peace with that nation and, at solicitation of Japan, still in conversation with its Government and its Emperor looking toward the maintenance of peace in the Pacific. Indeed, one hour after Japanese air squadrons had commenced bombing in the American island of Oahu, the Japanese Ambassador to the United States and his colleague delivered to our Secretary of State a formal reply to a recent American message. And while this reply stated that it seemed useless to continue the existing diplomatic negotiations, it contained no threat or hint of war or of armed attack.

It will be recorded that the distance of Hawaii from Japan makes it obvious that the attack was deliberately planned many days or even weeks ago. During the intervening time, the Japanese Government has deliberately sought to deceive the United States by false statements and expressions of hope for continued peace.

The attack yesterday on the Hawaiian Islands has caused severe damage to American naval and military forces. I regret to tell you that very many American lives have been lost. In addition, American ships have been reported torpedoed on the high seas between San Francisco and Honolulu.

Yesterday the Japanese Government also launched an attack against Malaya.

Last night Japanese forces attacked Hong Kong.

Last night Japanese forces attacked Guam.

Last night Japanese forces attacked the Philippine Islands.

Last night the Japanese attacked Wake Island.

And this morning the Japanese attacked Midway Island.

Japan has, therefore, undertaken a surprise offensive extending throughout the Pacific area. The facts of yesterday and today speak for themselves. The people of the United States have already formed their opinions and well understand the implications to the very life and safety of our nation.

As Commander in Chief of the army and navy I have directed that all measures be taken for our defense. But always will our whole nation remember the character of the onslaught against us. No matter how long it may take us to overcome this premeditated invasion, the American people in their righteous might will win through to absolute victory. I believe that I interpret the will of the Congress and of the people when I assert that we will not only defend ourselves to the uttermost but will make it very certain that this form of treachery shall never again endanger us.

Hostilities exist. There is no blinking at the fact that our people, our territory and our interests are in grave danger. With confidence in our armed forces—with the unbounding determination of our people—we will gain the inevitable triumph—so help us God.

I ask that the Congress declare that since the unprovoked and dastardly attack by Japan on Sunday, December 7, 1941 a state of war has existed between the United States and the Japanese Empire.

DEFENSE OF SAUDI ARABIA

George Bush

White House, Washington, D.C., August 8, 1990 (Transcribed from the video, GREAT SPEECHES VOLUME VI)

In the life of a nation, we're called upon to define who we are and what we believe. Sometimes these choices are not easy. But today as President, I ask for your support in a decision I've made to stand up for what's right and condemn what's wrong, all in the cause of peace.

At my direction, elements of the 82nd Airborne Division as well as key units of the United States Air Force are arriving today to take up defensive positions in Saudi Arabia. I took this action to assist the Saudi Arabian Government in the defense of its homeland. No one commits America's Armed Forces to a dangerous mission lightly, but after perhaps unparalleled international consultation and exhausting every alternative, it became necessary to take this action. Let me tell you why.

Less than a week ago, in the early morning hours of August 2nd, Iraqi Armed Forces, without provocation or warning, invaded a peaceful Kuwait. Facing negligible resistance from its much smaller neighbor, Iraq's tanks stormed in blitzkrieg fashion through Kuwait in a few short hours. With more than 100,000 troops, along with tanks, artillery, and surface-to-surface missiles, Iraq now occupies Kuwait. This aggression came just hours after Saddam Hussein (President of Iraq) specifically assured numerous countries in the area that there would be no invasion. There is no justification whatsoever for this outrageous and brutal act of aggression.

A puppet regime imposed from the outside is unacceptable. The acquisition of territory by force in unacceptable. No one, friend or foe, should doubt our desire for peace; and no one should underestimate our determination to confront aggression.

Four simple principles guide our policy. First, we seek the immediate, unconditional, and complete withdrawal of all Iraqi forces from Kuwait. Second, Kuwait's legitimate government must be restored to replace the puppet regime. And third, my administration, as has been the case with every President from President Roosevelt to President Reagan, is committed to the security and stability of the Persian Gulf. And fourth, I am determined to protect the lives of American citizens abroad.

Immediately after the Iraqi invasion, I ordered an embargo of all trade with Iraq and, together with many other nations, announced sanctions that both froze all Iraqi assets in this country and protected Kuwait's assets. The stakes are high. Iraq is already a rich and powerful country that possesses the world's second largest reserves of oil and over a million men under arms. It's the fourth largest military in the world. Our country now imports nearly half the oil it consumes and could face a major threat to its economic independence. Much of the world is even more dependent upon imported oil and is even more vulnerable to Iraqi threats.

We succeeded in the struggle for freedom in Europe because we and our allies remain stalwart. Keeping the peace in the Middle East will require no less. We're beginning a new era. This new era can be full of promise, an age of freedom, a time of peace for all peoples. But if history teaches us anything, it is that we must resist aggression or it will destroy our freedoms. Appeasement does not work. As was the case in the 1930's, we see in Saddam Hussein an aggressive dictator threatening his neighbors. Only 14 days ago, Saddam Hussein promised his friends he would not invade Kuwait. And 4 days ago, he promised the world he would withdraw. And twice we have seen what his promises mean: His promises mean nothing.

In the last few days, I've spoken with political leaders from the Middle East, Europe, Asia, and the Americas; and I've met with Prime Minister Thatcher (of the United Kingdom), Prime Minister Mulroney (of Canada), and NATO Secretary General Woerner. And all agree that Iraq cannot be allowed to benefit from its invasion of Kuwait.

We agree that this is not an American problem or a European problem or a Middle East problem: it is the world's problem. And that's why, soon after the Iraqi invasion, the United Nations Security Council, without dissent, condemned Iraq, calling for the immediate and unconditional withdrawal of its troops from Kuwait. The Arab world, through both the Arab League and the Gulf Cooperation Council, courageously announced its opposition to Iraqi aggression. Japan, the United Kingdom, and France, and other governments around the world have imposed severe sanctions. The Soviet Union and China ended all arms sales to Iraq.

And this past Monday, the United Nations Security Council approved for the first time in 23 years mandatory sanctions under chapter VII of the United Nations Charter. These sanctions, now enshrined in international law, have the potential to deny Iraq the fruits of aggression while sharply limiting its ability to either import or export anything of value, especially oil.

I pledge here today that the United States will do its part to see that these sanctions are effective and to induce Iraq to withdraw without delay from Kuwait.

But we must recognize that Iraq may not stop using force to advance its ambitions. Iraq has massed an enormous war machine on the Saudi border capable of initiating hostilities with little or no additional preparation. Given the Iraqi government's history of aggression against its own citizens as well as its neighbors, to assume Iraq will not attack again would be unwise and unrealistic.

And therefore, after consulting with King Fahd (of Saudi Arabia), I sent Secretary of Defense Dick Cheney to discuss cooperative measures we could take. Following those meetings, the Saudi Government requested our help, and I responded to that request by ordering U.S. air and ground forces to deploy to the Kingdom of Saudi Arabia.

Let me be clear: The sovereign independence of Saudi Arabia is of vital interest to the United States. This decision, which I shared with the congressional leadership, grows out of the longstanding friendship and security relationship between the United States and Saudi Arabia. U.S. forces will work together with those of Saudi Arabia and other nations to preserve the integrity of Saudi Arabia and to deter further Iraqi aggression. Through their presence, as well as through training and exercises, these multinational forces will enhance the overall capability of Saudi Armed Forces to defend the Kingdom.

I want to be clear about what we are doing and why. America does not seek conflict, nor do we seek to chart the destiny of other nations. But America will stand by her friends. The mission of our troops is wholly defensive. Hopefully, they will not be needed long. They will not initiate hostilities, buy they will defend themselves, the Kingdom of Saudi Arabia, and other friends in the Persian Gulf.

We are working around the clock to deter Iraqi aggression and to enforce U.N. sanctions. I'm continuing my conversations with world leaders. Secretary of Defense Cheney has just returned from valuable consultations with President Mubarak of Egypt and King Hassan of Morocco. Secretary of State Baker has consulted with his counterparts in many nations, including the Soviet Union, and today he heads for Europe to consult with President Özal of Turkey, a staunch friend of the United States. And he'll then consult with the NATO Foreign Ministers.

I will ask oil-producing nations to do what they can to increase production in order to minimize any impact that oil flow reductions will have on the world economy. And I will explore whether we and our allies should draw down our strategic petroleum reserves. Conservation measures can also help; Americans everywhere must do their part. And one more thing: I'm asking the oil companies to do their fair share. They should show restraint and not abuse today's uncertainties to raise prices.

Standing up for our principles will not come easy. It may take time and possibly cost a great deal. But we are asking no more of anyone than of the brave young men and women of our Armed Forces and their families. And I ask that in the churches around the country prayers be said for those who are committed to protect and defend America's interest.

Standing up for our principle is an American tradition. As it has so many times before, it may take time and tremendous effort, but most of all, it will take unity of purpose. As I've witnessed throughout my life in both war and peace, America has never wavered when her purpose is driven by principle. And in this August day, at home and abroad, I know she will do no less.

Thank you, and God bless the United States of America.

ENERGY CRISIS (MALAISE) SPEECH

Jimmy Carter

White House, Washington, D.C., July 15, 1979 (Transcribed from the video, GREAT SPEECHES, VOLUME VII)

Good evening. This is a special night for me. Exactly three years ago on July 15, 1976, I accepted the nomination of my party to run for President of the United States. I promised you a President who is not isolated from the people, who feels your pain and who shares your dreams and who draws his strength and his wisdom from you.

During the past three years, I've spoken to you on many occasions about national concerns: the energy crisis, reorganizing the Government, our nation's economy and issues of war and especially peace. But over those years the subjects of the speeches, the talks and the press conferences have become increasingly narrow, focused more and more on what the isolated world of Washington thinks is important.

Gradually you've heard more and more about what the Government thinks, or what the Government should be doing and less and less about our nation's hopes, our dreams and our vision of the future.

Ten days ago I had planned to speak to you again about a very important subject—energy. For the fifth time I would have described the urgency of the problem and laid out a series of legislative recommendations to the Congress, but as I was preparing to speak I began to ask myself the same question that I now know has been troubling many of you: Why have we not been able to get together as a nation to resolve our serious energy problem?

It's clear that the true problems of our nation are much deeper—deeper than gasoline lines or energy shortages. Deeper, even, than inflation or recession. And I realize more than ever that as President I need your help, so I decided to reach out and to listen to the voices of America. I invited to Camp David people from almost every segment of our society: business and labor; teachers and preachers; governors, mayors and private citizens.

And then I left Camp David to listen to other Americans. Men and women like you. It has been an extraordinary 10 days and I want to share with you what I've heard.

First of all, I got a lot of personal advice. Let me quote a few of the typical comments that I wrote down.

This from a Southern Governor: "Mr. President, you're not leading this nation, you're just managing the Government."

"You don't see the people enough anymore."

"Some of your Cabinet members don't seem loyal. There's not enough discipline among your disciples."

"Don't talk to us about politics or the mechanics of government, but about an understanding of our common good."

"Mr. President, we're in trouble. Talk to us about blood and sweat and tears. If you lead, Mr. President, we will follow."

Many people talked about themselves and about the condition of our nation. This from a young woman in Pennsylvania: "I feel so far from government. I feel like ordinary people are excluded from political power." And this from a young Chicano: "Some of us have suffered from recession all our lives. Some people have wasted energy but others haven't had anything to waste." And this from a religious leader: "No material shortage can touch the important things like God's love for us or our love for one another."

And I like this one particularly from a black woman who happens to be the Mayor of a small Mississippi town: "The big shots are not the only ones who are important. Remember, you can't sell anything on Wall Street unless someone digs it up somewhere else first."

This kind of summarized a lot of other statements: "Mr. President, we are confronted with a moral and a spiritual crisis."

Several of our discussions were on energy, and I have a notebook full of comments and advice. I'll read just a few.

"We can't go on consuming 40 percent more energy than we produce. When we import oil, we are also importing inflation plus unemployment. We've got to use what we have. The Middle East has only 5 percent of the world's energy, but the United States has 24 percent."

And this is one of the most vivid statements: "Our neck is stretched over the fence and OPEC has the knife."

"There will be other cartels and other shortages. American wisdom and courage right now can set a path to follow in the future."

This was a good one: "Be bold, Mr. President. We may make mistakes, but we are ready to experiment."

And this one from a labor leader got to the heart of it: "The real issue is freedom. We must deal with the energy problem on a war footing."

And the last that I'll read: "When we enter the moral equivalent of war, Mr. President, don't issue us beebee guns."

These 10 days confirmed my belief in the decency and the strength and the wisdom of the American people, but it also bore out some of my long-standing concerns about our nation's underlying problems. I know, of course, being President, that Government actions and legislation can be very important.

That's why I've worked hard to put my campaign promises into law, and I have to admit with just mixed success. But after listening to the American people I have been reminded again that all the legislature in the world can't fix what's wrong with America.

So I want to speak to you first tonight about a subject even more serious than energy or inflation. I want to talk to you right now about a fundamental threat to American democracy.

I do not mean our political and civil liberties. They will endure. And I do not refer to the outward strength of America—the nation that is at peace tonight everywhere in the world with unmatched economic power and military might. The threat is nearly invisible in ordinary ways. It is a crisis of confidence. It is a crisis that strikes at the very heart and soul and spirit of our national will.

We can see this crisis in the growing doubt about the meaning of our own lives and in the loss of a unity of purpose for our nation.

The erosion of our confidence in the future is threatening to destroy the social and the political fabric of America. The confidence that we have always had as a people is not simply some romantic dream or a proverb in a dusty book that we read just on the

Fourth of July. It is the idea which founded our nation and has guided our development as a people. Confidence in the future has supported everything else—public institutions and private enterprise, our own families and the very Constitution of the United States. Confidence has defined our course and has served as a link between generations.

We've always believed in something called progress. We've always had a faith that the days of our children would be better than our own.

Our people are losing that faith. Not only in Government itself, but in the ability as citizens to serve as the ultimate rulers and shapers of our democracy. As a people, we know our past and we are proud of it. Our progress has been part of the living history of America, even the world. We always believed that we were part of a great movement of humanity itself called democracy, involved in the search for freedom. And that belief has always strengthened us in our purpose. But just as we are losing our confidence in the future, we are also beginning to close the door on our past.

In a nation that was proud of hard work, strong families, close-knit communities and our faith in God, too many of us now tend to worship self-indulgence and consumption. Human identity is no longer defined by what one does but by what one owns.

But we've discovered that owning things and consuming things does not satisfy our longing for meaning.

We've learned that piling up material goods cannot fill the emptiness of lives which have no confidence or purpose. The symptoms of this crisis of the American spirit are all around us. For the first time in the history of our country a majority of our people believe that the next five years will be worse than the past five years. Two-thirds of our people do not even vote. The productivity of American workers is actually dropping and the willingness of Americans to save for the future has fallen below that of all other people in the Western world.

As you know there is a growing disrespect for Government and for churches and for schools, the news media and other institutions. This is not a message of happiness or reassurance but it is the truth. And it is a warning. These changes did not happen overnight. They've come upon us gradually over the last generation. Years that were filled with shocks and tragedy.

We were sure that ours was a nation of the ballot, not the bullet, until the murders of John Kennedy and Robert Kennedy and Martin Luther King, Jr. We were taught that our armies were always invincible and our causes were always just only to suffer the agony of Vietnam. We respected the Presidency as a place of honor until the shock of Watergate. We remember when the phrase "sound as a dollar" was an expression of absolute dependability until 10 years of inflation began to shrink our dollar and our savings. We believed that our nation's resources were limitless until 1973, when we had to face a growing dependence on foreign oil.

These wounds are still very deep. They have never been healed.

Looking for a way out of this crisis, our people have turned to the Federal Government and found it isolated from the mainstream of our nation's life. Washington, D.C., has become an island. The gap between our citizens and our Government has never been so wide. The people are looking for honest answers, not easy answers, clear leadership, not false claims and evasiveness and politics as usual. What you see too often in Washington and elsewhere around the country is a system of government that seems incapable of action.

You see a Congress twisted and pulled in every direction by hundreds of well-financed and powerful special interests. You see every extreme position defended to the last vote, almost to the last breath, by one unyielding group or another.

You often see a balance and a fair approach that demands sacrifice, a little sacrifice from everyone abandoned like an orphan without support and without friends.

Often you see paralysis and stagnation and drift. You don't like it.

And neither do I.

What can we do? First of all, we must face the truth and then we can change our course. We simply must have faith in each other. Faith in our ability to govern ourselves and faith in the future of this nation. Restoring that faith and that confidence to America is now the most important task we face.

It is a true challenge of this generation of Americans. One of the visitors to Camp David last week put it this way: We've got to stop crying and start sweating; stop talking and start walking; stop cursing and start praying. The strength we need will not come from the White House but from every house in America.

We know the strength of America. We are strong. We can regain our unity. We can regain our confidence. We are the heirs of generations who survived threats much more powerful and awesome than those that challenge us now.

Our fathers and mothers were strong men and women who shaped a new society during the Great Depression, who fought world wars and who carved out a new charter of peace for the world. We ourselves are the same Americans who just 10 years ago put a man on the moon. We are the generation that dedicated our society to the pursuit of human rights and equality.

And we are the generation that will win the war on the energy problem, and in that process rebuild the unity and confidence of America. We are at a turning point in our history. There are two paths to choose. One is the path I've warned about tonight—the path that leads to fragmentation and self-interest. Down that road lies a mistaken idea of freedom.

The right to grasp for ourselves some advantage over others. That path would be one of constant conflict between narrow interests ending in chaos and immobility. It is a certain route to failure.

All the traditions of our past, all the lessons of our heritage, all the promises of our future point to another path: the path of common purpose and the restoration of American values. That path leads to true freedom for our nation and ourselves. We can take the first steps down that path as we begin to solve our energy problem. Energy will be the immediate test of our ability to unite this nation.

And it can also be the standard around which we rally. On the battlefield of energy we can win for our nation a new confidence, and we can seize control again of our common destiny.

In little more than two decades we've gone from a position of energy independence to one in which almost half the oil we use comes from foreign countries at prices that are going through the roof. Our excessive dependence on OPEC has already taken a tremendous toll on our economy and our people. This is the direct cause of the long lines which have made millions of you spend aggravating hours waiting for gasoline., It's a cause of the increased inflation and unemployment that we now face.

This intolerable dependence on foreign oil threatens our economic independence and the very security of our nation.

The energy crisis is real. It is worldwide. It is a clear and present danger to our nation. These are facts and we simply must face them. What I have to say to you now about energy is simple and vitally important.

Point 1: I am tonight setting a clear goal for the energy policy of the United States. Beginning this moment, this nation will never use more foreign oil than we did in 1977. Never. From now on every new addition to our demand for energy will be met from our own production and our own conservation.

The generation-long growth in our dependence on foreign oil will be stopped dead in its tracks right now.

And then reversed as we move to the 1980's. For I am tonight setting the further goal of cutting our dependence on foreign oil by one-half by the end of the next decade—a saving of over four and a half million barrels of imported oil per day.

Point 2: To insure that we meet these targets, I will use my Presidential authority to set import quotas. I am announcing tonight that for 1979 and 1980 I will forbid the entry in this *[sic]* into this country of one drop of foreign oil more than these goals allow. These quotas will insure a reduction in imports even below the ambitious levels we set at the recent Tokyo summit.

Point 3: To give us energy security, I am asking for the most massive peacetime commitment of funds and resources in our nation's history to develop America's own alternative sources of fuel from coal, from oil shale, from plant products for gasohol, from unconventional gas, from the sun. I propose the creation of an Energy Security Corporation to lead this effort to replace 2 1/2 million barrels of imported oil per day by 1990. The corporation will issue up to $5 billion in energy bonds, and I especially want them to be in small denominations so that average Americans can invest directly in America's energy security.

Just as a similar synthetic rubber corporation helped us win World War II, so will we mobilize American determination and ability to win the energy war. Moreover, I will soon submit legislation to congress calling for the creation of this nation's first solar bank, which will help us achieve the crucial goal of 20 percent of our energy coming from solar power by the year 2000.

These efforts will cost money, a lot of money. And that is why Congress must enact the windfall profits tax without delay. It will be money well spent. Unlike the billions of dollars that we shift to foreign countries to pay for foreign oil, these funds will be paid by Americans to Americans. These funds will go to fight, not to increase, inflation and unemployment.

Point 4: I'm asking Congress to mandate—to require as a matter of law—that our nation's utility companies cut their massive use of oil by 50 percent within the next decade and switch to other fuels, especially coal, our most abundant energy source.

Point 5: To make absolutely certain that nothing stands in the way of achieving these goals, I will urge Congress to create an energy mobilization board which, like the War Production Board in World War II, will have the responsibility and authority to cut through the red tape, the delays and the endless roadblocks to completing key energy projects.

We will protect our environment. But when this nation critically needs a refinery or pipeline, we will build it.

Point 6: I am proposing a bold conservation program to involve every state, county and city, and every average American in our energy battle. This effort will permit you to build conservation into your homes and your lives at a cost you can afford. I ask Congress to give me authority for mandatory conservation and for standby gasoline rationing.

To further conserve energy, I'm proposing tonight an extra $10 billion over the next decade to strengthen our public transportation systems. And I'm asking you, for your good and for your nation's security, to take no unnecessary trips, to use car pools or public transportation whenever you can, to park your car one extra day per week, to obey the speed limit and to set your thermostats to save fuel. Every act of energy conservation like this is more than just common sense. I tell you it is an act of patriotism.

Our nation must be fair to the poorest among us so we will increase aid to needy Americans to cope with rising energy prices.

We often think of conservation only in terms of sacrifice. In fact it is the most painless and immediate way of rebuilding our nation's strength. Every gallon of oil each one of us saves is a new form of production that gives us more freedom, more confidence, that much more control over our own lives so that solution of our energy crisis can also help us to conquer the crises of the spirit in our country. It can rekindle our sense of unity, our confidence in the future, and give our nation and all of us individually a new sense of purpose.

You know we can do it. We have the natural resources. We have more oil in our shale alone than several Saudi Arabias. We have more coal than any nation on earth. We have the world's highest level of technology. We have the most skilled work force, with innovative genius.

And I firmly believe that we have the national will to win this war.

I do not promise you that this struggle for freedom will be easy. I do not promise a quick way out of our nation's problems when the truth is that the only way out is an all-out effort. What I do promise you is that I will lead our fight, and I will enforce fairness in our struggle and I will insure honesty. And above all, I will act. We can manage the short-term shortages more effectively—and we will. But there are no short-term solutions to our long-range problems.

There is simply no way to avoid sacrifice. Twelve hours from now I will speak again, in Kansas City, to expand and to explain further our energy program. Just as a search for solutions to our energy shortages has now led us to a new awareness of our nation's deeper problems, so our willingness to work for those solutions in energy can strengthen us to attack those deeper problems.

I will continue to travel this country to hear the people of America. You can help me to develop a national agenda for the 1980's. I will listen and I will act. We will act together.

These were the promises I made three years ago and I intend to keep them. Little by little we can and we must rebuild our confidence. We can spend until we empty our treasuries and we may summon all the wonders of science, but we can succeed only if we tap our greatest resources: America's people, America's values and America's confidence.

I have seen the strength of America in the inexhaustible resources of our people. In the days to come let us renew that strength in the struggle for an energy-secure nation.

In closing, let me say this: I will do my best, but I will not do it alone. Let your voice be heard. Whenever you have a chance, say something good about our country. With God's help and for the sake of our nation, it is time for us to join hands in America.

Let us commit ourselves together to a rebirth of the American spirit. Working together with our common faith, we cannot fail.

Thank you and good night.

BEARING BAD TIDINGS

A Value Analysis of Jimmy Carter's "Crisis of Confidence" Speech

The erosion of our confidence in the future is threatening to destroy the social and political fabric of America.

CRITIC: Robert E. Denton, Jr.

In a matter of months, Jimmy Carter went from "Jimmy Who?" to President of the United States. Running as an outsider, Carter won not because of traditional party politics or issues, but primarily because of his personal values. He claimed that America needed a government as good, as kind and as decent as its citizens. In the nation's post-Watergate era of deception, guilt and sense of fraud, the nation needed cleansing and purification.

During the Presidential campaign of 1976, Carter seemed like "one of us," a common man and a caring guardian of traditional American values. Once elected, however, Carter became very parental in tone and approach. He acted like the election was a mandate to redeem us, not just to govern us. Carter thought it was possible to be both preacher and politician, missionary and chief-legislator. Little did he realize that this approach to the presidency would generate public feelings of resentment and perceptions of incompetence.

For many political observers, Carter's "Crisis of Confidence" national address of July 15, 1979, was the pivotal point of his presidency. For Carter, it was a call for a new beginning and heroic leadership. For the nation it became a moment of national chiding and frustration. A value analysis of the address reveals Carter's beliefs about the role of government and the duties of presidential leadership. These beliefs, however, run counter to popular notions of democratic government and public expectations of leadership. As a result, Carter's values and beliefs about our country and his competency, specifically, became the central issues of the 1980 presidential campaign.

VALUE ANALYSIS AS CULTURAL CRITICISM

Roderick Hart (1990) argues that "rhetoric never escapes the influence of culture."[1] Elements of our culture are imbedded in our language.

Hart identifies three important dimensions of cultural criticism: values, myths and fantasy themes.[2] Values are our core beliefs about right and wrong and how we should live our lives in relation to others as individuals, as communities and as a nation. Myths are stories of "exceptional people doing exceptional things" which serve as moral guides of social and private behavior. Fantasy themes are short, abbreviated myths whose story lines reinforce idealized or cherished lessons of the past.

At the heart of value analysis is the attempt to discover the ways people give meanings to their messages.[3] For our purposes, values express judgments about how things are and should be. Identifying values is one way people make sense of the world. Through value analysis, we also discover how people define their culture. Thus, value statements are socially significant.

Within a particular text, the critic must identify positive and negative values stated as well as values that may be implied from the text. The cluster of values provide an orientation or worldview of the orator.

There are numerous value systems within a culture or society: religious, social, economic and political to name only a few. American political values range from the most philosophical (i.e., freedom, liberty, equality, natural laws, rationality, etc.) to more specific notions about one's relationship to government (i.e., democracy, constitution, two-party system, etc.).[4]

Presidential speeches are public statements of political values that express our hopes and dreams, define who we are and how we relate to one another. We begin learning at a very early age the values that are the basis of our form of government. In addition to our parents and teachers, public officials such as the president also serve an important role in developing and reinforcing our political values. "The President," according to presidential scholar Mary Stuckey, "has become the nation's chief storyteller, its interpreter-in-chief. He tells us stories about ourselves, and in so doing he tells us what sort of people we are, how we are constituted as a community. We take from him not only our policies but our national self-identity."[5] Thus, presidential discourse lends itself well to the study of American political values.

CARTER'S VIEW OF GOVERNMENT

Carter began his campaign biography, *Why Not the Best*, with a quote from Reinhold Niebuhr that perhaps best summarizes his view of government: "The sad duty of politics is to establish justice in a sinful world."[6] In the first chapter of this short book, Carter poses two questions that formed the basis of his presidential campaign. "Can our government be honest, decent, open, fair, and compassionate?" and "Can our government be competent?"[7] The first question suggests the preferred values of government. The latter question provides the clue to achieving the stated values—strong leadership.

Early in his campaign biography, Carter reflects upon the challenges and difficulties faced by members of the First Continental Congress in 1774. He notes that people of that time "were also discouraged, disillusioned, and confused. But these early leaders acted with purpose and conviction."[8] He argues that America can "restore in our country what has been lost—*if* we have understandable purposes and goals and a modicum of bold and inspired leadership. Our government can express the highest common ideals of human beings—*if* we demand of government true standards of excellence."[9]

In the wake of Watergate, the public was daily bombarded with reports of scandal and government wrongdoing. Public distrust and contempt for government and politicians reached an all time high. During the presidential campaign of 1976, Carter diagnosed a fundamental corruption at the heart of our governmental process. Congress no longer acted in the public interest, but showed undue concern for individual member's own reelection.[10] As a result, special interests dominated the political process. Interest groups had greater access to members of congress and received more attention from government than private citizens. In his memoirs, Carter writes that "it was obvious that our nation would have to resolve many such serious questions, which had long been ignored or deliberately avoided because of the incompatibility of the White House and Congress, fear of special-interest lobbies, or concern about the next election."[11]

For Carter, it was important for elected officials to represent the people and balance special interests with public interests.[12] Carter claims he "learned the hard way that there was no party loyalty or discipline when a complicated or controversial issue was at stake."[13] Electoral politics should be separate from policy-making. For Carter, it is more noble to do what is "right" than what is merely "political."

Thus, according to Charles Jones, Carter had "antipolitical attitudes" and benefited from an "anti-Washington mood" prevalent during the post-Watergate era, especially during the 1976 presidential campaign.[14] He believed the nation faced many difficult social and moral problems. Our government had failed to address our social ills. In effect, Carter argued that our very form of democratic government was part of the problem and could not adequately address national issues. Carter represented more "idealistic" beliefs and tendencies toward the role of government and the responsibilities of presidential leadership.

CARTER'S VIEW OF THE ROLE OF THE PRESIDENCY

If government is unable to solve the nation's problems, then it is the responsibility of the president to do so. Carter espoused the "great man" concept of the presidency which holds that the president must serve as the moral and spiritual leader of the people. In 1976, Carter reportedly told Bill Moyers that "there is only one person in this nation who can speak with a clear voice to the American people. There's only one person who can set a standard of ethics and morality...or call on the American people to make a sacrifice...or answer difficult questions or propose and carry out bold programs, ...and that's the president."[15] Although citizens have the right to inform elected officials of their opinions, "ultimately, public officials have to decide what action to take for the public good."[16]

As a result of his "heroic" view of the presidency, Carter believed that issues, policy and programs should originate in the executive office and be sent over to Congress for deliberation, not the other way around. "Carter thought Congress should support the president," according to Charles Jones, "because he spent time on an issue, demonstrated public support and personally avoided the strictly political."[17]

From the beginning of his presidency, Carter had a strong sense of urgency and leadership expressed through images of fear and war. Carter's first energy message called for action that would be, "the moral equivalent of war." Almost every presidential message spoke of crisis. Even his very positive theme of human rights was often contrasted with the evil Russian empire and states of the Middle East. Carter was always prepared to "get tough" if necessary to handle domestic or international issues.

Because of Carter's lack of trust in Congress and "politics as usual," he adopted a confrontational style of leadership that put pressure on Congress by labeling his proposals "most important" and "critical." Carter's perspective of leadership contributed to an environment of crisis and confrontation. The dynamics leading up to his national address on July 15, 1979, illustrate well Carter's intensive crisis management style.

SITUATIONAL DYNAMICS PRIOR TO THE SPEECH

In late June of 1979, while President Carter was in Tokyo for a summit conference with leaders from Japan and Western Europe, "all the news from home was bad."[18] Fuel prices climbed; long gas lines were formed at stations; and Carter's public approval ratings sank to an all time low. Instead of taking a short vacation in Hawaii upon his return from the summit, Carter went straight to Camp David to prepare a speech designed to push Congress to pass his energy program.

While working several days on the speech draft, Carter reviewed some public opinion poll data prepared by Pat Caddell (a political pollster and personal advisor) about American attitudes toward government and various other issues. Caddell's polls revealed that the central problem in America transcended the issue of energy. Most Americans thought that the government and the oil industries were incompetent and dishonest. People had lost trust in major American political and social institutions and even in themselves. Citizens were fearful of America's future and that of their children. Public alienation and rejection were growing to a dangerous level. Thus, Caddell advised Carter to broaden the scope of his message to focus on national and patriotic themes.[19]

After some reflection and consultation with family and staff members, Carter canceled his national address without explanation. Three days later, word leaked out that Carter had invited 134 guests to Camp David to meet in small groups over a ten day period to discuss national problems and his administration. People came from the broad occupational areas of politics, religion, business, select interest groups, academia and from a small circle of personal friends.

Carter determined to start anew, to readdress the focus and structure of his administration. He sensed he had lost contact with the American people, the ultimate source of his philosophical concerns of caring and compassion and had gotten bogged down in the details of daily government. At this critical point in American history, he believed he had to provide moral leadership for the nation by dramatizing the importance and seriousness of his own concern about the nation's future. He even took a couple of unannounced trips to private homes in Pennsylvania and West Virginia to talk to private citizens.

Carter's retreat at Camp David was high drama. It created an aura of national nervousness, crisis and high expectations. There was speculation about the president's emotional and physical health. Even the value of the dollar dropped. The political risks were high. Carter had to give an outstanding performance or the whole spectacle would confirm his inability to lead the nation.

The president returned from Camp David on Saturday night and practiced the speech several times on Sunday. By the evening of July 15, 1979, Carter was prepared to give a thirty-two minute speech that would make or break his presidency.

THE SPEECH

More than half of the address focused on the ills and problems of America. The conclusion Carter reached from his discussions at Camp David was that America was "confronted with a moral and a spiritual crisis."

Early in the address, Carter acknowledged his failure to provide adequate leadership for the nation. He had become "isolated from the people" and "increasingly narrow, focused more and more on what the isolated world of Washington thinks is important." He articulated his faults by quoting from people who had attended the Camp David meetings: "You're not leading this nation, you're just managing the Government...."

You don't see the people enough anymore.... Don't talk to us about politics or the mechanics of government, but about an understanding of our common good."

These early self-criticisms quickly transformed into an anti-Washington tirade about "a fundamental threat to American democracy" that "is threatening to destroy the social and the political fabric of America." He noted a "growing disrespect for Government" and characterized the federal government as "isolated from the mainstream of our nation's life." Washington had become an island. "The gap between our citizens and our Government has never been so wide.... You see a Congress twisted and pulled in every direction by hundreds of well-financed and powerful special interests.... You often see paralysis and stagnation and drift."

Carter also chided the public for failing to fulfill its civic obligations. "Our people are losing that faith. Not only in government itself, but in their ability as citizens to serve as the ultimate rulers and shapers of our democracy....too many of us now tend to worship self-indulgence and consumption. Human identity is no longer defined by what one does but by what one owns.... Two-thirds of our people do not even vote. The productivity of American workers is actually dropping and the willingness of Americans to save for the future has fallen below that of all other people in the Western world."

Carter attempts to define the current situation as one of crisis and urgency. He uses the specific term "crisis" eight times throughout the speech. In a very direct way Carter informs the audience, "I want to talk to you right now about a fundamental threat to American democracy.... The threat is nearly invisible in ordinary ways. It is a crisis of confidence. It is a crisis that strikes at the very heart and soul and spirit of our national will." We must act now to avoid "failure," "chaos," and "immobility," and to protect our "economic independence and the very security of our nation." Carter claims the crisis is "a clear and present danger to our nation."

Throughout the address, Carter offers to provide the moral leadership necessary to restore faith and confidence in America. "The people are looking for honest answers, not easy answers, clear leadership, not false claims and evasiveness and politics as usual." He calls for national faith and a restoration of values. "We simply must have faith in each other.... All the traditions of our past, all the lessons of our heritage, all the promises of our future point to another path: the path of common purpose and the restoration of American values." By quoting a visitor to Camp David, Carter challenges Americans to "stop crying and start sweating; stop talking and start walking; stop cursing and start praying." Carter makes a bold commitment to action. "What I do promise you is that I will lead our fight and I will enforce fairness in our struggle and I will insure honesty. And above all, I will act." In the final third of the speech, Carter announced a six-point program to deal with the energy crisis. In outlining the proposals, Carter was direct and specific demonstrating presidential forcefulness and initiative. (See the six points outlined by Carter on pages 135 and 136 in the previous transcript.)

At the time, Carter believed the speech was a success. In his memoirs Carter relates, "it was one of my best speeches, and the response to it was overwhelmingly positive. Intrigued by the mystery of what I would say, about one hundred million people had listened—perhaps the largest American audience I ever had."[20] President Carter wanted to portray himself as leader of the people, above the petty politics of daily Washington life. What the people heard, however, was a statement of failure. The government had failed. It would not or could not solve the nation's problems. The people failed. We no longer had the faith, the courage or the national interest to make sacrifices to solve future problems. In short, both government and the citizens were the problem—not Carter.

Analysis of the speech reveals Carter's anti-government views, the general moral morass of American society and the need for strong leadership. These positions counter the more traditional values of American democracy. Carter challenged the notions that the American system of government is the best on earth, that Americans are moral and compassionate and that the people are able to lead themselves.

CONCLUSION

According to Roderick Hart, Carter's July 15, 1979, address was really about his views of American values—views that ran counter to what Americans believed or wanted to hear.[21] In effect, Carter questioned our economic bases of success, our sense of historical destiny and our own self-competence. Hart observes, "the speech came to symbolize not what was wrong with America but what was wrong with Jimmy Carter: too philosophical for a practical people, too introspective for an outward-looking nation, too melancholy for a country of idealists."[22]

David Beisel prophetically wrote in 1977 that "America wanted presidential candidates who were honest, caring family men, able to create the illusion of caring and nurturance without stimulating the anxiety which would be provoked by vigorously attacking the many serious problems confronting America and by initiating far-reaching fundamental reforms in American society."[23] Candidate Carter was right for the times and mood of the country. As president, Carter became too parental and too challenging, confronting one perceived crisis after another both at home and abroad.

It is important to remember that America had just gotten rid of Nixon, the "imperial" president. We replaced the "royal" president with the "stern" father. We wanted nurturance, Carter suggested reform. We wanted hope, Carter provided despair. We wanted a plan, Carter delivered a sermon. We wanted reassurance, Carter scolded us. We wanted escape, Carter provided reality. According to presidential scholar Charles Jones, "we are prepared to listen to a politician who wants to do the right thing, but we may well abandon him or her just when our support is needed most."[24] By the presidential campaign of 1980, Americans wanted to follow the beat of a different drummer, Ronald Reagan. The election was our democratic way of "killing the messenger."

Robert E. Denton, Jr. is professor and chairperson of the Department of Communication Studies at Virginia Polytechnic Institute and State University.

NOTES

1. Roderick P. Hart, *Modern Rhetorical Criticism* (Glenview, IL: Scott, Foresman/Little Brown, 1990), p. 305.
2. *Ibid*, pp. 303-339.
3. Malcolm O. Sillars, *Messages, Meanings, and Culture: Approaches to Communication Criticism* (New York: HarperCollins, 1991), p. 128.
4. For examples of such American values, see Hart, pp. 310-311,

5. Mary E. Stuckey, *The President as Interpreter-In-Chief* (New Jersey: Chatham House Publishers, 1991), p. 1.

6. Jimmy Carter, *Why Not the Best?* (Nashville, TN: Broadman Press, 1975), p. 1.

7. *Ibid,* p. 2.

8. *Ibid,* p. 11.

9. *Ibid,* p. 11.

10. See Charles O. Jones, *The Trusteeship Presidency* (Baton Rouge, LA: Louisiana State University Press, 1988), pp. 1-9 and Jimmy Carter, *Keeping Faith* (New York: Bantam Books, 1982), pp. 66-124.

11. Carter, *Keeping Faith*, p. 66.

12. Jones, pp. 6-9.

13. Carter, *Keeping Faith*, p. 80.

14. Jones, p. 210.

15. Betty Glad, *Jimmy Carter* (New York: W.W. Norton & Co., 1980), p. 347.

16. Carter, *Keeping Faith*, p. 80.

17. Jones, p. 84.

18. Carter, *Keeping Faith*, p. 114.

19. For various explanations and descriptions, see Carter, *Keeping Faith,* pp. 114-121 and Glad, pp. 444-446.

20. Carter, *Keeping Faith*, p. 121.

21. Hart, p. 313.

22. *Ibid,* p. 313.

23. David Beisel, "Toward Psychohistory of Jimmy Carter," in *Jimmy Carter and American Fantasy,* Lloyd deMause and Henry Sbel, Editors (New York: Institute for Psychohistory, 1977), p. 81.

24. Jones, pp. 216-217.

CHAPTER 5:
Accusation and Defense

Their ideas challenged, their principles questioned, or their country's actions and motives assaulted, the political leaders face the ultimate test of leadership. The success of their responses frequently dictates the future of their careers. Accusation and defense provides the real color of political discourse.

We begin with Douglas MacArthur's Farewell Address to Congress. His defiance of the President's policies in Korea prompted Truman's decision to relieve him of duty. Richard Nixon defended against charges of financial indiscretion and saved his political future with his "Checkers" speech. The essay by Martha Cooper focuses on his defense and details the preparation for this early, politically effective use of the television medium. Adlai Stevenson gave a well-crafted presentation as the world stood on the brink of war and critic James McBath examines his efforts in the U.N. Cuban Missile Crisis Debate. A series of three Watergate era speeches begins with Richard Nixon's televised explanation of the events surrounding this controversial scandal. Next we include the speech which brought national prominence to Barbara Jordan, her statement on the Nixon Articles of Impeachment. Patricia Witherspoon's essay discusses the construction of this classic statement which appropriately draws its support from the writings of the framers of the Constitution. In the Presidential Resignation Speech of Richard Nixon we see his final defense of his career and Richard Katula evaluates the effectiveness of his apology. We conclude with Jeane Kirkpatrick's stinging attack on the Soviet Union during the United Nation's deliberation of the KAL 007 Airline Disaster.

FAREWELL ADDRESS

Douglas MacArthur

Joint Session of Congress, Washington, D.C., April 19, 1951 (Transcribed from the video, GREAT SPEECHES, VOLUME I)

Mr. President, Mr. Speaker, and distinguished Members of the Congress, I stand on this rostrum with a sense of deep humility and great pride; humility in the wake of those great American architects of our history who have stood here before me, pride in the reflection that this home of legislative debate represents human liberty in the purest form yet devised. Here are centered the hopes, and aspirations, and faith of the entire human race.

I do not stand here as advocate for any partisan cause, for the issues are fundamental and reach quite beyond the realm of partisan consideration. They must be resolved on the highest plane of national interest if our course is to prove sound and our future protected. I trust, therefore, that you will do me the justice of receiving that which I have to say as solely expressing the considered viewpoint of a fellow American. I address you with neither rancor nor bitterness in the fading twilight of life with one but, with but one purpose in mind—to serve my country.

The issues are global and so interlocked that to consider the problems of one sector, oblivious to those of another, is but to court disaster for the whole. While Asia is commonly referred to as the gateway to Europe, it is no less true that Europe is the gateway to Asia, and the broad influence of the one cannot fail to have its impact upon the other.

There are those who claim our strength is inadequate to protect on both fronts—that we cannot divide our effort. I can think of no greater expression of defeatism. If a potential enemy can divide his strength on two fronts, it is for us to counter his effort. The communist threat is a global one. Its successful advance in one sector threatens the destruction of every other sector. You cannot appease or otherwise surrender to communism in Asia without simultaneously undermining our efforts to halt its advance in Europe.

Beyond pointing out these general truisms, I shall confine my discussion to the general areas of Asia. Before one may objectively assess the situation now existing there, he must comprehend something of Asia's past and the revolutionary changes which are [sic]...which have marked her course up to present. Long exploited by the so-called colonial powers, with little opportunity to achieve any degree of social justice, individual dignity, or a higher standard of life such as guided our own noble administration of the Philippines, the peoples of Asia found their opportunity in the war just past to throw off the shackles of colonialism, and now seen the [sic]...see the dawn of new opportunity, a heretofore unfelt dignity and the self-respect of political freedom.

Mustering half of the earth's population and 60 percent of its natural resources, these peoples are rapidly consolidating a new force, both moral and material, with which to raise the living standard and erect adaptations of the design of modern progress to their

own distinct cultural environments. Whether one adheres to the concept of coloniza-
tion or not, this is the direction of Asian progress and it may not be stopped. It is a
corollary to the shift of the world economic frontiers, as the whole epicenter of world
affairs rotates back toward the era [sic]... area whence it started. In this situation it
becomes vital that our own country orient its policies in consonance with this basic
evolutionary condition rather than pursue a course blind to the reality that the colonial
era is now past and the Asian peoples covet the right to shape their own free destiny.
What they seek now is friendly guidance, understanding, and support, not imperious
direction; the dignity of equality, and not the shame of subjugation. Their prewar
standard of life, pitifully low, is infinitely lower now in the devastation left in war's
wake. World ideologies play little part in Asian thinking and are little understood.
What the peoples strive for is the opportunity for a little more food in their stomachs,
a little better clothing on their backs, a little firmer roof over their heads, and the
realization of the normal nationalist urge for political freedom. These political-social
conditions have but an indirect bearing upon our own national security, but do form
a backdrop to contemporary planning which must be thoughtfully considered if we are
to avoid the pitfalls of unrealism.

Of more direct and immediate bearing upon our national security are the changes
wrought in the strategic potential of the Pacific Ocean in the course of the past war.
Prior thereto, the western strategic frontier of the United States lay on the littoral line
of the Americas with an exposed island salient extending out through Hawaii, Midway,
and Guam to the Philippines. That salient proved not an outpost of strength but an
avenue of weakness along which the enemy could and did attack. The Pacific was a
potential area of advance for any predatory force intent upon striking at the bordering
land areas.

All this was changed by our Pacific victory. Our strategic frontier then shifted to
embrace the entire Pacific Ocean which became a vast moat to protect us as long as we
held it. Indeed, it acts as a protective shield for all of the Americas and all free lands of
the Pacific Ocean area. We control it to the shores of Asia by a chain of islands extending
in an arc from the Aleutians to the Mariannas held by us and our free allies.

From this island chain we can dominate with sea and air power every Asiatic port
from Vladivostok to Singapore with sea and air power, every port, as I said, from
Vladivostok to Singapore and prevent any hostile movement into the Pacific. Any
predatory attack from Asia must be an amphibious effort. No amphibious force can be
successful without control of the sea lanes and the air over those lanes in its avenue of
advance. With naval and air supremacy and modest ground elements to defend bases
any major attack from continental Asia toward us or our friends [sic] Pacific would be
doomed to failure. Under such conditions the Pacific no longer represents menacing
avenues of approach for a prospective invader—it assumes instead the friendly aspect
of a peaceful lake. Our line of defense is a natural one and can be maintained with a
minimum of military effort and expense. It envisions no attack against anyone nor does
it provide the bastions essential for offensive operations, but properly maintained
would be an invincible defense against aggression.

The holding of this littoral defense line in the western Pacific is entirely dependent
upon holding all segments thereof, for any major breach of that line by an unfriendly
power would render vulnerable to determined attack every other major segment. This
is a military estimate as to which I have yet to find a military leader who will take
exception.

For that reason I have strongly recommended in the past as a matter of military urgency that under no circumstances must Formosa fall under communist control. Such an eventuality would at once threaten the freedom of the Philippines and the loss of Japan, and might well force our western frontier back to the coasts of California, Oregon, and Washington.

To understand the changes which now appear upon the Chinese mainland, one must understand the changes in Chinese character and culture over the past 50 years. China up to 50 years ago was completely nonhomogeneous, being compartmented into groups divided against each other. The war-making tendency was almost nonexistent, as they still followed the tenets of the Confucian ideal of pacifist culture. At the turn of the century, under the regime of Chan So Lin, efforts toward greater homogeneity produced the start of a nationalist urge. This was further and more successfully developed under the leadership of Chiang Kai-shek but has been brought to its greatest fruition under the present regime, to the point that it has now taken on the character of a united nationalism of increasingly dominant aggressive tendencies. Through these past 50 years, the Chinese people have thus become militarized in their concepts and in their ideals. They now constitute excellent soldiers with competent staffs and commanders. This has produced a new and dominant power in Asia which for its own purposes is allied with Soviet Russia, but which in its own concepts and methods has become aggressively imperialistic with a lust for expansion and increased power normal to this type of imperialism. There is little of the ideological concept either one way or another in the Chinese make-up. The standard of living is so low and the capital accumulation has been so thoroughly dissipated by war that the masses are desperate and avid to follow any leadership which seems to promise the alleviation of local stringencies. I have from the beginning believed that the Chinese Communists' support of the North Koreans was the dominant one. Their interests are at present parallel to those of the Soviet, but I believe that the aggressiveness recently displayed not only in Korea, but also in Indochina and Tibet and pointing potentially toward the south, reflects predominantly the same lust for the expansion of power which has animated every would-be conqueror since the beginning of time.

The Japanese people since the war have undergone the greatest reformation recorded in modern history. With a commendable will, eagerness to learn, and marked capacity to understand, they have from the ashes left in war's wake, erected in Japan an edifice dedicated to the primacy of individual liberty and personal dignity, and in the ensuing process there has been created a truly representative government committed to the advance of political morality, freedom of economic enterprise and social justice. Politically, economically and socially Japan is now abreast of many free nations of the earth and will not again fail the universal trust. That it may be counted upon to wield a profoundly beneficial influence over the course of events in Asia is attested by the magnificent manner in which the Japanese people have met the recent challenge of war, unrest, and confusion surrounding them from the outside, and checked communism within their own frontiers without the slightest slackening in their forward progress. I sent all four of our occupation divisions to the Korean battle front without the slightest qualms as to the effect *[sic]* the resulting power vacuum upon Japan. The results fully justified my faith. I know of no nation more serene, orderly, and industrious—nor in which higher hopes can be entertained for future constructive service in the advance of the human race.

Of our former ward...of our former ward of our former ward the Philippines, we can look forward in confidence that the existing unrest will be corrected and a strong and healthy nation will grow in the longer aftermath of war's terrible destructiveness. We must be patient and understanding and never fail them, as in our hour of need they did not fail us. A Christian nation, the Philippines stand as a mighty bulwark of Christianity in the Far East, and its capacity for high moral leadership in Asia is unlimited.

On Formosa, the Government of the Republic of China, has had the opportunity to refute by action much of the malicious gossip which so undermined the strength of its leadership on the Chinese mainland. The Formosan people are receiving a just and enlightened administration with majority representation on the organs of government; and politically, economically and socially they appear to be advancing along sound and constructive lines.

With this brief insight into the surrounding areas I now turn to the Korean conflict. While I was not consulted prior to the President's decision to intervene in support of the Republic of Korea, that decision, from a military standpoint, proved a sound one as we, as I say, proved a sound one as we hurled back the invaders and decimated his forces. Our victory was complete and our objectives within reach when Red China intervened with numerically superior ground forces. This created a new war and an entirely new situation, a situation not contemplated when our forces were committed against the North Korean invaders; a situation which called for new decisions in the diplomatic sphere to permit the realistic adjustment of military strategy. Such decisions have not been forthcoming.

While no man in his right mind would advocate sending our ground forces into continental China and such was never given a thought, the new situation did urgently demand a drastic revision of strategic planning if our political aim was to defeat this new enemy as we had defeated the old.

Apart from the military need as I saw it to neutralize the sanctuary protection given the enemy north of the Yalu, I felt that military necessity in the conduct of the war made necessary, first, the intensification of our economic blockade against China; two, the imposition of a naval blockade against the China coast; three, removal of restrictions on air reconnaissance of China's coastal areas and of Manchuria; four, removal of restrictions on the forces of the Republic of China on Formosa with logistical support to contribute to their effective operations against the common enemy.

For entertaining these views, all professionally designed to support our forces committed to Korea and bring hostilities to an end with the least possible delay and at a saving of countless American and Allied lives, I have been severely criticized in lay circles, principally abroad, despite my understanding that from a military standpoint the above views have been fully shared in past by practically every military leader concerned with the Korean campaign, including our own Joint Chiefs of Staff.

I called for reinforcements, but was informed that reinforcements were not available. I made clear that if not permitted to destroy the enemy build-up bases north of the Yalu; if not permitted to utilize the friendly Chinese force of some 600,000 men on Formosa; if not permitted to blockade the China coast to prevent the Chinese Reds from getting succor from without; and if there were to be no hope of major reinforcements, the position of the command from the military standpoint forbade victory. We could hold in Korea by constant maneuver and at an approximate area where our supply line advantages were in balance with the supply line disadvantages of the enemy, but we could hope at best for only an indecisive campaign, with its terrible and constant attrition upon our forces if the enemy utilized his full military potential. I have constantly called for the new political decisions essential to a solution. Efforts have been made to distort my position. It has been said, in effect, that I was a warmonger. Nothing could be further from the truth. I know war as few other men now living know it, and nothing to me...and nothing to me is more revolting. I have long advocated its complete abolition as its very destructiveness on both friend and foe has rendered it useless as a means of settling international disputes. Indeed, on the 2nd day of September 1945, just following the surrender of the Japanese Nation on the battleship Missouri, I formally cautioned as follows:

> Men since the beginning of time have sought peace. Various methods through the ages have been attempted to devise an international process to prevent or settle disputes between nations. From the very start, workable methods were found insofar as individual citizens were concerned, but the mechanics of an instrumentality of larger international scope have never been successful. Military alliances, balances of power, leagues of nations, all in turn failed, leaving the only path to be by way of the crucible of war. The utter destructiveness of war now blots out this alternative. We have had our last chance. If we will not devise some greater and more equitable system, Armageddon will be at our door. The problem basically is theological and involves a spiritual recrudescence and improvement of human character that will synchronize with our almost matchless advances in science, art, literature, and all material and cultural developments of the past 2,000 years. It must be of the spirit if we are to save the flesh.

But once war is forced upon us, there is no other alternative than to apply every available means to bring it to a swift end. War's very object is victory—not prolonged indecision. In war there is no substitute for victory. There are some who for varying reasons would appease Red China. They are blind to history's clear lessons. For history teaches with unmistakable emphasis that appeasement but begets new and bloodier war. It points to no single instance where this end has justified that means—where appeasement has led to more than a sham peace. Like blackmail, it lays the basis for new and successively greater demands, until, as in blackmail, violence becomes the only other alternative. Why my soldiers asked of me, surrender military advantages to an enemy in the field? I could not answer. Some may say to avoid spread of the conflict into an all-out war with China; others, to avoid Soviet intervention. Neither explanation seems valid. For China is already engaging with the maximum power it can commit and the Soviet will not necessarily mesh its actions with our moves. Like a cobra, any new enemy will more likely strike whenever it feels that the relativity in military or other potential is in its favor on a worldwide basis.

The tragedy of Korea is further heightened by the fact that as military action is confined to its territorial limits, it condemns that nation, which it is our purpose to save, to suffer the devastating impact of full naval and air bombardment, while the enemy's sanctuaries are fully protected from such attack and devastation. Of the nations of the world, Korea alone, up to now, is the sole one which has risked its all against communism. The magnificence of the courage and fortitude of the Korean people defies description. They...they have chosen to risk death rather than slavery. Their last words to me were "Don't scuttle the Pacific."

I have just left your fighting sons in Korea. They have met all tests there and I can report to you without reservation they are splendid in every way. It was my constant effort to preserve them and end this savage conflict honorably and with the least loss of time and a minimum sacrifice of life. Its growing bloodshed has caused me the deepest anguish and anxiety. Those gallant men will remain often in my thoughts and in my prayers always.

I am closing my 52 years of military service. When I joined the Army even before the turn of the century, it was the fulfillment of all my boyish hopes and dreams. The world has turned over many times since I took the oath on the plain at West Point, and the hopes and dreams have long since vanished. But I still remember the refrain of one of the most popular barrack ballads of that day which proclaimed most proudly that— "Old soldiers never die; they just fade away." And like the old soldier of that ballad, I now close my military career and just fade away—an old soldier who tried to do his duty as God gave him the light to see that duty.

Good-by.

THE CHECKERS SPEECH

Richard M. Nixon

Los Angeles, California, September 23, 1952 (Transcribed from the video, GREAT SPEECHES, VOLUME II)

My fellow Americans: I come before you tonight as a candidate for the Vice Presidency and as a man whose honesty and integrity has been questioned. The usual political thing to do when charges are made against you is to either ignore them or to deny them without giving details. I believe we've had enough of that in the United States, particularly with the present Administration in Washington D.C. To me the office of the Vice Presidency of the United States is a great office, and I feel that the people have got to have confidence in the integrity of the men who run for that office and who might obtain it. I have a theory, too, that the best and only answer to a smear or to an honest misunderstanding of the facts is to tell the truth, and that's why I'm here tonight. I want to tell you my side of the case.

I'm sure that you have read the charge and you've heard it that I, Senator Nixon, took $18,000 from a group of my supporters.

Now, was that wrong? The question is was it morally wrong? I say that it was morally wrong if any of that $18,000 went to Senator Nixon for my personal use. I say that it was morally wrong if it was secretly given and secretly handled, and I say that it was morally wrong if any of the contributors got special favors for the contributions that they made.

It was not a secret fund. As a matter of fact, when I was on "Meet the Press," some of you may have seen it last Sunday—Peter Edson came up to me after the program and he said, "Dick, what about this fund we hear about?" And I said, "Well, there's no secret about it. Go out and see Dana Smith, who was the administrator of the fund." And I gave him his address, and I said you will find that the purpose of the fund simply was to defray political expenses that I did not feel should be charged to the Government.

And third, let me point out, and I want to make this particularly clear, that no contributor to this fund, no contributor to any of my campaigns, has ever received any consideration that he would not have received as an ordinary constituent. I just don't believe in that and I can say that never, while I have been in the Senate of the United States, as far as the people that contributed to this fund are concerned, have I made a telephone call for them to an agency, or have I gone down to an agency in their behalf. And the records will show that, the records which are in the hands of the Administration.

Well, then some of you will say and rightly, "Well, what did you use the fund for, Senator? Why did you have to have it?" Let me tell you in just a word how a Senate office operates. First of all, a Senator gets $15,000 a year in salary. He gets enough money to pay for one trip a year, a round trip that is, for himself and his family between his home and Washington D.C. And then he gets an allowance to handle the people that work in his office, to handle his mail. And the allowance for my State of California is enough to hire 13 people. And let me say, incidentally, that that allowance is not paid to the

Senator—it's paid directly to the individuals that the Senator puts on his payroll. But all of these people and all of these allowances are for strictly official business. Business, for example, when a constituent writes in and wants you to go down to the Veteran's Administration and get some information about his G.I. policy—items of that type, for example.

But there are other expenses which are not covered by the Government, and I think I can best discuss those expenses by asking you some questions. Do you think that when I or any other Senator makes a political speech, has it printed, should charge the printing of that speech and the mailing of that speech to the taxpayers? Do you think, for example, when I or any other Senator makes a trip to his home state to make a purely political speech that the cost of that trip should be charged to the taxpayers? Do you think when a Senator makes political broadcasts or political television broadcasts, radio or television, that the expense of those broadcasts should be charged to the taxpayers? Well, I know what your answer is. The same answer that audiences give me whenever I discuss this particular problem. The answer is, "no." The taxpayers shouldn't be required to finance items which are not official business but which are primarily political business.

But then the question arises, you say, "Well, how do you pay for these and how can you do it legally?" And there are several ways that it can be done, incidentally, and that it is done legally in the United States Senate and the Congress. The first way is to be a rich man. I don't happen to be a rich man so I couldn't use that way. Another way that is used is to put your wife on the payroll. Let me say, incidentally, that my opponent, my opposite number for the Vice Presidency on the Democratic ticket does have his wife on the payroll, and has had it, her on his payroll for the ten years...for the past ten years.

Now just let me say this. That's his business and I'm not critical of him for doing that. You will have to pass judgment on that particular point. But I have never done that for this reason. I have found that there are so many deserving stenographers and secretaries in Washington that needed the work that I just didn't feel it was right to put my wife on the payroll. My wife's sitting over here. She's a wonderful stenographer. She used to teach stenography and she used to teach shorthand in high school. And I'm proud to say tonight that in the six years I've been in the House and the Senate of the United States, Pat Nixon has never been on the government payroll.

Well, there are other ways that these finances can be taken care of. Some who are lawyers, and I happen to be a lawyer, continue to practice law. But I haven't been able to do that. I'm so far away from California that I've been so busy with my Senatorial work that I have not engaged in any legal practice. And also as far as law practice is concerned, it seemed to me that the relationship between an attorney and the client was so personal that you couldn't possibly represent a man as an attorney and then have an unbiased view when he presented his case to you in the event that he had one {before the Government}. And so I felt that the best way to handle these necessary political expenses of getting my message to the American people and the speeches I made—the speeches that I had printed, for the most part, concerned this one message of exposing this Administration, the Communism in it, the corruption in it—the only way that I could do that was to accept the aid which people in my home state of California who contributed to my campaign and who continued to make these contributions after I was elected were glad to make. And let me say I am proud of the fact that not one of them has ever asked me for a special favor. I am proud of the fact that not one of them has ever asked me to vote on a bill other than of *[sic]* my own conscience would dictate. And I am proud of the fact that the taxpayers by subterfuge or otherwise have never paid one dime for expenses which I thought were political and shouldn't be charged to the taxpayers.

Let me say, incidentally, that some of you may say, "Well, that's all right, Senator; that's your explanation, but have you got any proof?" And I'd like to tell you this evening that just an hour ago we received an independent audit of this entire fund. I suggested to Gov. Sherman Adams, who is the chief of staff of the Dwight Eisenhower campaign that an independent audit and legal report be obtained. And I have that audit here in my hand. It's an audit made by the Price, Waterhouse and Co. Firm, and the legal opinion by Gibson, Dunn & Crutcher, lawyers in Los Angeles, the biggest law firm and incidentally one of the best ones in Los Angeles.

I'm proud to be able to report to you tonight that this audit and this legal opinion is being forwarded to General Eisenhower. And I'd like to read to you the opinion that was prepared by Gibson, Dunn & Crutcher and based on all the pertinent laws and statutes, together with the audit report prepared by the certified public accountants.

> It is our conclusion that Senator Nixon did not obtain any financial gain from the collection and disbursement of the fund by Dana Smith; that Senator Nixon did not violate any Federal or state law by reason of the operation of the fund, and that neither the portion of the fund paid by Dana Smith directly to third persons nor the portion paid to Senator Nixon to reimburse him for designated office expenses constituted income to the Senator which was either reportable or taxable as income under applicable tax laws. Signed Gibson, Dunn & Crutcher by Alma H. Conway.

Now that, my friends, is not Nixon speaking, but that's an independent audit which was requested because I want the American people to know all the facts and I'm not afraid of having independent people go in and check the facts, and that is exactly what they did.

"{How can we} believe what you say? After all, is there a possibility that maybe you got some sums in cash? Is there a possibility that you may have feathered your own nest?"

And so now what I am going to do—and incidentally this is unprecedented in the history of American politics—I am going at this time to give to this television and radio audit *[sic]*...audience a complete financial history; everything I've earned; everything I've spent; everything I owe. {And I} want you to know the facts. I'll have to start early. I was born in 1913. Our family was one of modest circumstances and most of my early life was spent in a store out in East Whittier. It was a grocery store—one of those family enterprises. The only reason we were able to make it go was because my mother and dad had five boys and we all worked in the store.

I worked my way through college and to a great extent through law school. And then, in 1940, probably the best thing that ever happened to me happened, I married Pat— sitting over here. We had a rather difficult time after we were married, like so many of the young couples who may be listening to us. I practiced law; she continued to teach school. Then, in 1942, I went into the service. Let me say that my service record was not a particularly unusual one. I went to the South Pacific. I guess I'm entitled to a couple of battle stars. I got a couple of letters of commendation but I was just there when the bombs were falling and then I returned...I returned to the United States and in 1946 I ran for the Congress.

When we came out of the war, Pat and I—Pat during the war had worked as a stenographer and in a bank and as an economist for a Government agency—and when we came out the total of our savings from both my law practice, her teaching and all the time that I was in the war—the total for that entire period was just a little less then ten thousand dollars. Every cent of that, incidentally, was in Government bonds.

Well, that's where we start when I go into politics. Now what have I earned since I went into politics? Well, here it is—I jotted it down, let me read the notes. First of all I've had my salary as a Congressman and as a Senator. Second, I have received a total in this past six years of $1600.00 from estates which were in my law firm at the time that I severed my connection with it. And, incidentally, as I said before, I have not engaged in any legal practice and have not accepted any fees from business that came into the firm after I went into politics. I have made an average of approximately $1500.00 a year from non-political speaking engagements and lectures. Then, fortunately, we've inherited a little money. Pat sold her interest in her father's estate for $3,000.00 and I inherited $1500.00 from my grandfather. We lived rather modestly. For four years we lived in an apartment in Park Fairfax, in Alexandria, Virginia. The rent was eighty dollars a month, and we saved for the time that we could buy a house. Now, this will surprise you, because it is so little, I suppose, as standards generally go, of people in public life. First of all, we've got a house in Washington which cost $41,000.00 and on which we owe $20,000.00. We have a house in Whittier, California, which cost $13,000.00 and on which we owe $3,000.00. My folks are living there at the present time.

I have just $4,000.00 in life insurance plus my G.I. policy which I've never been able to convert and which will run out in two years. I have no life insurance whatever on Pat. I have no life insurance on our two youngsters, Patricia and Julie. I own a 1950 Oldsmobile car. We have our furniture. We have no stocks and bonds of any type. We have no interest of any kind, direct or indirect, in any business.

Now, that's what we have. What do we owe? Well, in addition to the mortgage, the $20,000.00 mortgage on the house in Washington, the $10,000.00 one on the house in Whittier, I owe $4500.00 to the Riggs Bank in Washington D.C., with interest four and a half per cent. I owe $3500.00 to my parents and the interest on that loan which I pay regularly, because it's the part of the savings they made through the years they were working so hard, I pay regularly four per cent interest. And then I have a $500 loan which I have on my life insurance.

That's what we have. It isn't very much but Pat and I have the satisfaction that every dime that we've got is honestly ours. I should say this—that Pat doesn't have a mink coat. But she does have a respectable Republican cloth coat, and I always tell her that she'd look good in anything.

One other thing I probably should tell you because if I don't they'll probably be saying this about me too, we did get something—a gift—after the election. A man down in Texas heard Pat on the radio mention the fact that our two youngsters would like to have a dog. And, believe it or not, the day before we left on the campaign trip we got a message from Union Station in Baltimore saying they had a package for us. We went down to get it. You know what it was? It was a little cocker spaniel dog in a crate that he'd sent all the way from Texas. Black and white spotted. And our little girl—Trisha, the six-year-old—named it Checkers. And you know, the kids, like all kids, love the dog and I just want to say this right now, that regardless of what they say about it, we're gonna keep it.

It isn't easy to come before a nationwide audience and bare your life as I've done. But I want to say some things before I conclude. First of all, you have read in the papers about other funds now. Mr. Stevenson, apparently, had a couple. One of them in which a group of business people paid and helped to supplement the salaries of state employees. Here is where the money went directly into their pockets.

And I think that what Mr. Stevenson should do should be to come before the American people as I have, give the names of the people that contributed to that fund; give the names of the people who put this money into their pockets at the same time that they were receiving money from their state government, and see what favors, if any, they gave out for that.

I don't condemn Mr. Stevenson for what he did. But until the facts are in there is a doubt that will be raised. And as far as Mr. Sparkman is concerned, I would suggest the same thing. He's had his wife on the payroll. I don't condemn him for that. But I think that he should come before the American people and indicate what outside sources of income he has had. I would suggest that under the circumstances both Mr. Sparkman and Mr. Stevenson should come before the American people as I have and make a complete financial statement as to their financial history. And if they don't it will be an admission that they have something to hide, and I think you will agree with me.

Because, folks, remember, a man that's to be President of the United States, a man that's to be Vice President of the United States must have the confidence of all the people. And that's why I'm doing what I'm doing, and that's why I suggest that Mr. Stevenson and Mr. Sparkman, since they are under attack, should do what they're doing.

Now, let me say this: I know that this is not the last of the smears. In spite of my explanation tonight other smears will be made; others have been made in the past. And the purpose of the smears, I know, is this—to silence me, to make me let up. Well, they just don't know who they're dealing with. I'm going to tell you this: I remember in the dark days of the Hiss Case some of the same columnists, some of the same radio commentators who are attacking me now and misrepresenting my position were violently opposing me at the time I was after Alger Hiss. But I continued the fight because I knew I was right. And I can say to this great television and radio audience that I have no apologies to the American people for my part in putting Alger Hiss where he is today. And as far as this is concerned, I intend to continue the fight.

Why do I feel so deeply? Why do I feel that in spite of the smears, the misunderstanding, the necessity for a man to come up here and bare his sole as I have? Why is it necessary for me to continue this fight? And I want to tell you why, because you see, I love my country. And I think my country is in danger and I think the only man that can save America at this time is the man that's running for President on my ticket—Dwight Eisenhower.

You say, "Why do I think it's in danger?" And I say look at the record. Seven years of the Truman-Acheson Administration and what's happened? Six hundred million people lost to the Communists, and a war in Korea in which we have lost 117,000 American casualties. And I say to all of you that a policy that results in a loss of 600,000,000 people to the Communists and a war which costs us 117,000 American casualties isn't good enough for America. And I say that those in the State Department that made the mistakes which caused that war and which resulted in those losses should be kicked out of the State Department just as fast as we get 'em out of there.

And let me say that I know Mr. Stevenson won't do that, because he defends the Truman policy and I know that Dwight Eisenhower will do that, and that he will give America the leadership that it needs.

Take the problem of corruption. You've read about the mess in Washington. Mr. Stevenson can't clean it up because he was picked by the man, Truman, under whose Administration the mess was made. You wouldn't trust a man who made the mess to clean it up—that's Truman. And by the same token you can't trust the man who was picked by the man that made the mess to clean it up—and that's Stevenson. And so I say, Eisenhower, who owes nothing to Truman, nothing to the big city bosses, he is the man that can clean up the mess in Washington.

Take Communism. I say that as far as that subject is concerned, the danger is great to America. In the Hiss case they got the secrets which enabled them to break the American secret State Department code. They got secrets in the atomic bomb case which enabled 'em to get the secret of the atomic bomb, five years before they would have gotten it by their own devices. And I say that any man who called the Alger Hiss case a "red herring" isn't fit to be President of the United States. I say that a man who like Mr. Stevenson has pooh-poohed and ridiculed the Communist threat in the United States—he said that they are phantoms among ourselves; he's accused us that have attempted to expose the Communists of looking for Communists in the Bureau of Fisheries and Wildlife—I say that a man who says that isn't qualified to be President of the United States. And I say that the only man who can lead us in this fight to rid the Government of both those who are Communist and those who have corrupted this Government is Eisenhower, because Eisenhower, you can be sure, recognizes the problem and he knows how do deal with it.

Now let me say that, finally, this evening I want to read to you just briefly excerpts from a letter which I received, a letter which, after all this is over, no one can take away from us. It reads as follows:

Dear Senator Nixon,

Since I'm only 19 years of age I can't vote in this Presidential election but believe me if I could you and General Eisenhower would certainly get my vote. My husband is in the Fleet Marines in Korea. He's a corpsman on the front lines and we have a two-month-old son he's never seen. And I feel confident that with great Americans like you and General Eisenhower in the White House, lonely Americans like myself will be united with their loved ones now in Korea.

I only pray to God that you won't be too late. Enclosed is a small check to help you in your campaign. Living on $85 a month it is all I can afford at present. But let me know what else I can do.

Folks, it's a check for ten dollars, and it's one that I will never cash. And just let me say this, we hear a lot about prosperity these days but I say, why can't we have prosperity built on peace rather than prosperity built on well, war? Why can't we have prosperity and an honest government in Washington D.C., at the same time? Believe me we can, and Eisenhower is the man that can lead this crusade.

I know that you wonder whether or not I am going to stay on the Republican ticket or resign. Let me say this: I don't believe that I ought to quit because I'm not a quitter.

And, incidentally, Pat's not a quitter. After all, her name was Patricia Ryan and she was born on St. Patrick's Day, and you know the Irish never quit.

But the decision, my friends, is not mine. I would do nothing that would harm the possibilities of Dwight Eisenhower to become President of the United States. And for that reason I am submitting to the Republican National Committee tonight through this television broadcast the decision which it is theirs to make. Let them decide whether my position on the ticket will help or hurt them. And I am going to ask you to help them decide. Wire and write the Republican National Committee whether you think I should stay on or whether I should get off.

Just let me say this last word. Regardless of what happens I'm going to continue this fight. I'm going to campaign up and down in America until we drive the crooks and the Communists and those that defend them out of Washington. And remember folks, Eisenhower is a great man, believe me. He's a great man. And a vote for Eisenhower is a vote for what's good for America.

ETHOS, A CLOTH COAT AND A COCKER SPANIEL

Richard Nixon's Checkers Speech

The kids love the dog and I just want to say this right now . . . we're gonna keep it.

CRITIC: Martha Cooper

On September 23, 1952, Richard Nixon spoke to the largest television viewing audience amassed by any politician prior to that time. He spoke in defense of himself. The success of his speech not only allowed him to remain a viable candidate for the Vice Presidency, but catapulted him into the national spotlight as a credible politician for the next twenty years. The Checkers Speech is a study in the skillful construction of *ethos*, the personal character of the speaker. We can examine both the context for Nixon's speech and the speech itself for a more complete understanding of how this rhetorical event shaped the *ethos* of Richard Nixon.

Before examining either his speech or the context, however, it is helpful to recall the nature of *ethos* as a means of persuasion. Aristotle explained that:

> Persuasion is achieved by the speaker's personal character when the speech is so spoken as to make us think him credible.... This kind of persuasion, like the others, should be achieved by what the speaker says, not by what people think of this character before he begins to speak. It is not true, as some writers assume in their treatises on rhetoric, that the personal goodness revealed by the speaker contributes nothing to his power of persuasion; on the contrary, his character may almost be called the most effective means of persuasion he possesses.[1]

Thus, we can recall from Aristotle the importance of *ethos* as a means of persuasion. Furthermore, because *ethos* is constructed during the spoken act, it is a product of artistic proof, rather than an inartistic proof. As Aristotle explained, inartistic proofs such as witnesses, written contracts and so forth are merely used by speakers, while artistic proofs must be invented by speakers.[2] In other words, artistic proofs involve the construction of arguments by carefully weaving together claims and supporting materials and framing those elements in appropriate language that is arranged and presented strategically. Thus our examination of Nixon's speech must include an investigation of several aspects of his presentation in order to uncover the construction of *ethos*.

In addition to providing direction regarding where to look for the construction of *ethos*, Aristotle's comments on the subject also suggest what to look for. He noted that "there are three things which inspire confidence in the orator's own character...: good sense, good moral character and goodwill."[3] Hence, we will look for aspects of the speech that illustrate Nixon's sensibleness, his moral values and his regard for the audience. But how can we determine if those qualities are good? In other words, what is the appropriate standard for "goodness?" Here too, Aristotle provided direction. He argued that the audience provides the standard. Whatever the audience believes to be virtuous is what the speaker must maintain as virtuous if he or she is to be successful in establishing *ethos*.[4] To understand the nature of Nixon's audience, it is important to begin with an examination of the context for the speech.

SITUATION: THE LOSS OF CREDIBILITY

The context for the Checkers Speech provides insight into both the nature of Nixon's audience and the exigence that provoked his defense. We can begin by exploring the general context for the speech and then consider the more immediate events surrounding Nixon's defense of himself.

On the domestic scene, the year of 1952 was one of prosperity. The Gross National Product was rising, employment was high and inflation was low. Industries producing relatively new consumer goods like freezers, televisions and a variety of home appliances, were booming. John Kenneth Galbraith's book, *American Capitalism*, was a best seller, reinforcing the idea that the capitalist system that had furnished the goods necessary for victory in World War II was still working and providing a system by which common people could participate in the American dream.

Amidst their feeling of personal prosperity, many Americans sensed an uneasy transition in the political arena. Truman was a lame duck, and all indications were that after controlling the White House for twenty years, the Democrats were likely to lose to the Republican candidate for President in 1952. The Republican's nominee was the popular veteran of World War II, General Dwight D. Eisenhower; his running mate was a young Senator from California, Richard Nixon. Even though Nixon was not a household name and Vice Presidential candidates rarely attract the attention paid to Presidential candidates, polls at the time showed that more voters recognized Nixon's name than recognized the name of the Democratic nominee for President, Adlai Stevenson.

The issues during the 1952 campaign were three-fold: (1) the Korean War, (2) Communism and (3) Corruption.[5] Many Americans were tiring of the unofficially declared war in Korea but at the same time were concerned about the Communist menace that seemed to be threatening to overrun all parts of the world, including Korea. Stalin, still alive and reigning as the head of the Soviet government, was perceived by many as a ruthless and oppressive leader whose objective was to encircle the world with an iron curtain. Revelations concerning how the Soviets had acquired the expertise to detonate their own nuclear weapons, thus destroying the American monopoly on the tools of ultimate destruction, fueled the fires of the Cold War and the fears of some that Communists had infiltrated the breadth of American society. For several years, Senator Joseph McCarthy had led investigations of alleged lists of Communists in the circles of Hollywood, the academy and government alike. Similarly, the Republican party had targeted corruption as an issue, and pointed to members of the Truman administration who accepted kickbacks in return for influence. Examples included officials who regularly accepted 5% of the take in return for government contracts and a White House secretary who had accepted a gift of a $9,000.00 mink coat.

Nixon, the Republican's Vice Presidential candidate, had pursued all three of the major issues, but was particularly effective in his charges regarding Communism and corruption. His selection for the ticket was somewhat surprising considering his youth,

39 years, and his relative inexperience in politics, 6 years.[6] However, his constituency, the people of California, represented a key state for a national election and a geographic area of the country that was growing in political importance. In addition, his role in exposing Alger Hiss as a Communist who had given secrets to the Soviets had given him national exposure as an able opponent of Communism and a defender of traditional America.

The Hiss case had been particularly important because as a well-bred Eastern intellectual with many friends among the party in power, Hiss had received the continuing support of many Democrats, including the then Secretary of State Dean Acheson and even President Truman. Nixon's persistence in the Hiss case had led to revelations regarding events like the hiding of microfilm in hollowed-out pumpkins that read more like an inexpensive spy novel than the behavior of a Harvard educated lawyer. Even though the statute of limitations had run out by the time the Hiss story was revealed, Nixon's persistence, though unpopular to many during the height of the Hiss investigation, had led to a perjury conviction. Thus, Nixon's role in the campaign against Communism and corruption helped place him on the ticket that claimed it would "clean up the mess in Washington." Although General Eisenhower was perhaps not as enthusiastic about the charges of corruption and Communism among the Democratic party, the more conservative wing of the Republican party, headed by Robert Taft, had found in Nixon a man who they believed could level the charges effectively.

In September of 1952, Eisenhower and Nixon were winning the campaign battle. Their pursuit of the issues of Korea, Communism, and corruption was catching on, and victory in November appeared likely. It was within this context, that the immediate events necessitating the Checkers Speech occurred. One of the most comprehensive, even if potentially biased, accounts of the events leading to Nixon's speech, is found in his autobiography.[7] According to Nixon, he was first asked about a political fund on September 14, following an appearance on "Meet the Press." At that time he explained that Dana Smith, a Los Angeles attorney, had collected and controlled the disbursement of funds donated by California businessmen to assist Nixon in meeting expenses associated with his representation of the people of California. After providing that explanation, Nixon planned a whistle-stop campaign trip that was to begin in California and continue northward along the Pacific coast.

On Wednesday, September 17, Nixon held a rally in Pomona, California. The next morning he boarded the campaign train that was scheduled to stop at towns and small cities throughout the central valley of California where Nixon would deliver brief campaign addresses. That same morning the New York *Post* carried a front page headline that read "Secret Nixon Fund" and a second page headline that read "Secret Rich Men's Trust Fund Keeps Nixon in Style Far Beyond His Salary." The accompanying story suggested that the fund was probably illegal and insinuated that Nixon might be guilty of the same type of corruption of which he had been accusing his opponents. As word of the story reached the West coast, more and more hecklers began turning out when Nixon's train stopped for his appearances. Throughout the first day of the whistle-stop tour, Nixon refused to give the charge credence by responding to the hecklers or discussing the fund.

That evening, Nixon consulted his advisors and worried about not yet hearing from Eisenhower concerning the matter, but resolved to continue campaigning without succumbing to the hecklers. The next morning, Friday the 19th, that resolve was broken at a stop in Marysville, California. In response to a jibe from the audience to "tell us about the $16,000.00," Nixon provided an impromptu explanation that was met with cheers and applause. That evening, Nixon received word that the New York *Herald Tribune* intended to print an editorial the next morning that would argue that Nixon should resign from the ticket because of the secret fund. Nixon's confidence was shaken as the *Herald Tribune* was the most influential Republican newspaper in the East, unlike the *Post* that had originally run the fund story. Whereas earlier he had considered the story about the fund to be an annoyance, now he realized that the story could lose him his position on the ticket, or worse yet, cost Eisenhower the election.

Nixon's loss of confidence was shared by many influential Republicans and other opinion leaders across the country. The next day, Saturday, September 20, the rumors regarding impending disaster that reached Nixon's train came fast and furiously. Eisenhower's advisors, accompanying him on a similar whistle-stop tour in the Midwest, were reported as almost unanimous in their agreement that Nixon should withdraw from the campaign. Telegrams concerning the fund that were reaching the Eisenhower train were running about fifty-fifty in favor of Nixon's resignation. Ninety percent of the press traveling with Eisenhower opposed retaining Nixon; the figure was representative of the response to the fund by the press throughout the country.[8] The reasoning for the strong negative reaction was made clear by Costello ten years later: "If the Democrats could make the imputation of scandal stand, it might be that the fire had gone out of Ike's whole campaign."[9]

Despite the apparent desperation of the situation and the absence of any formal response from Eisenhower, on Saturday Nixon began to defend himself in earnest. Bolstered by a message of support from Taft and counsel from his advisors on the train, Nixon released a fact-sheet concerning the fund that afternoon and continued his impromptu defense at stops throughout the day. In Eugene, Oregon, for example, he explained that his wife had never received a mink coat but wore a respectable cloth coat. As the campaign day drew to a close, Nixon and his advisors conferred. They agreed that his only option was to explain the fund to the people and defend himself as he had been doing at the stops earlier that day, but they were equally convinced that he needed a national platform for his explanation.

On Sunday, September 21, Nixon received a telegram from Harold Stassen, a prominent Republican, urging him to resign from the ticket and including the draft of a resignation speech. Shortly thereafter, Dewey called to suggest that he take the initiative to appear on national television to explain the fund and if the results of the broadcast were overwhelmingly favorable (9:1) remain on the ticket, but otherwise resign. That same day Eisenhower made a formal statement to the press, saying that he thought Nixon was "an honest man," but carefully avoiding any suggestion regarding either Nixon's retention or removal from the ticket. Nixon and his advisors, meanwhile, held strategy sessions to determine an appropriate course of action and how to secure broadcast time. That evening Eisenhower finally called Nixon to say that the Republican National Committee had bought one-half hour of television time for a broadcast Tuesday evening and advised Nixon to "tell them about everything you have ever received from the time you entered public life."[10] Nixon urgently requested Eisenhower's support, or at least some decision regarding whether or not he should remain on the ticket, but Eisenhower declined to make such a decision until after the broadcast was over. In the wee hours of Monday morning, Nixon held a press conference to announce the Tuesday broadcast and later caught a red-eye flight for Los Angeles, where the broadcast would take place.

During the flight and all day Monday, Nixon made notes for the upcoming speech. In his autobiography, Nixon described his purpose as follows: "I must not only remove any liability I might be to the ticket, I must become a positive asset."[11] More specifically, he recalled that the speech had to meet three requirements: (1) answer the immediate attack by explaining and defending the fund, (2) ward off further allegations by showing that he did not accrue personal profit and (3) launch a political counterattack. In addition, he resolved that there should be no press release of the text prior to the address in order to insure the maximum number of viewers Tuesday evening.

Nixon's initial notes for the speech were written on post cards during his flight to Los Angeles. He jotted down notes regarding Pat's cloth coat and other explanations he had used during the previous days of campaigning. In line with Eisenhower's admonishment to "tell them everything," he recalled the gift of a cocker spaniel from a Texas business man and noted the existence of "Checkers," the title by which the speech would be remembered later. Similarly, he noted Dewey's advice to involve the viewing audience and to ask them to send telegrams or letters with their judgment of the situation. While speculating about the monetary costs of performing official duties, he remembered a quotation from Abraham Lincoln concerning the common man and noted it.

As Nixon collected his thoughts and prepared various lines of argument, other sources began to furnish additional supporting materials. On Monday the Chicago *Tribune* disclosed the existence of a similar fund for Adlai Stevenson. Meanwhile Dana Smith was obtaining an audit of the Nixon fund from the accounting firm of Price Waterhouse and a legal assessment from a prestigious law firm in Los Angeles. Other aides were collecting the data regarding Nixon's financial history.

Nixon arrived in Los Angeles Monday afternoon, finding himself with only twenty-four hours to organize and practice his speech. Using skills he attributed to his experience as an intercollegiate debater, he continued to gather facts and prepared a lengthy outline on Tuesday, September 23.[12] Although Nixon was accustomed to preparing both a second and third draft of an outline and practicing sufficiently so as to deliver addresses without notes, time did not permit his usual routine. He did construct a second draft, from which he practiced the speech during a walk with a friend near his hotel. However, the third draft was never completed, and Nixon realized that the speech would have to be delivered from the five pages of notes that constituted the second draft of the outline.

At 4:30 p.m., Tuesday afternoon, Nixon had still not decided how to end the speech. He knew he wanted to ask the viewers to write or wire someone with their responses, but he was unsure of who should receive the responses. As he pondered the problem, the phone rang. It was Thomas Dewey, the person who had suggested the idea of audience response. However, Dewey was calling with a new suggestion for the conclusion of Nixon's speech. Dewey explained that Eisenhower's advisors thought that Nixon should resign at the end of the speech, and he explained that this suggestion represented Eisenhower's opinion as well. Met with Nixon's stunned silence, Dewey inquired: "What will you do?" Nixon's answer was startling: "I haven't the slightest idea—Tune in."[13]

With little more than half an hour before Nixon was to leave for the El Capitan Theater, where the broadcast was to be held, Nixon continued to agonize about the conclusion of the speech. His statement to Dewey characterized the final hour before the address. At the theater, the stage had been set by an advisor. The press and their stenographers were housed in a separate room furnished with closed-circuit television. Following a quick make-up job to cover any remnants of Nixon's five-o'clock shadow, a cameraman asked him what movements he planned to make. Nixon's answer was simple: "I haven't the slightest idea; just follow me."[4] On schedule, at 6:30 p.m. on the West coast, 9:30 p.m. in the East, Nixon began his speech to the cameras and a theater empty of the press, Eisenhower and his advisors, and the undecided public.

As the account of the events leading to Nixon's speech suggests, there were several audiences for Nixon's speech. The primary audience was the viewing and listening public, whom Nixon intended to ask for support. However, of just as much importance was the audience composed of Eisenhower, his advisors, and influential members of the Republican Party. For the final decision regarding Nixon's retention as a candidate lay with the Presidential candidate. Finally, the press who, given the events of the last five days, clearly held the power to influence the opinions of the other two audiences had to be persuaded.

The exigence for Nixon's speech was, as he had described, to persuade the audience that he was an asset rather than a liability. More specifically, his *ethos* had been called into question, and his challenge was to persuade his audiences that his personal character was intact, that he was a trustworthy man of good sense, good character, and good will. If he was successful, Nixon would remain a viable candidate; if not, his political career might end then and there.

The standards for acceptance of his plea was shaped by the times. He faced an audience who embraced traditional American values, like honesty, courage, individualism, morality, and so forth, but who had found those values shaken by recent revelations concerning both Communism and corruption in government. He faced an audience who was experiencing unequalled prosperity at the same time they were confronted with uncertainty regarding the continuing prominence of the democratic and capitalistic system. In short, he faced an audience that had everything, that abounded with all of the things that make us comfortable, but who was "yearning for something that was not there, but had once been there, for an older, simpler America without juvenile delinquents and genteel young men turning into Alger Hisses and five percenters and bewildering doctrines of limited warfare."[15]

SPEECH: THE CONSTRUCTION OF ETHOS

In an extended analysis of Nixon's speaking style that surveyed seventy-nine speeches delivered by Nixon at various points in his political career, Hart observed that "the public Nixon was one of the coolest rhetorical customers this nation has known... Nixon was a textbook persuader—certain when hosting friendly elements, equivocal otherwise."[16] The Checkers Speech is no exception to this conclusion. In the Checkers Speech, Nixon presented an image of himself as a man of good sense, good character and good will. We will explore how his speech established each of these components of *ethos*.

His appearance as a man of *good sense* was established by various aspects of the structure, content, and delivery of the speech. In his opening statement, Nixon suggested that he would take a rational approach to the topic by not following the "usual" course of ignoring the charge or denying it "without reference to details," but by contrasting the "truth" with the prevailing "misunderstanding of the facts." Hence he aroused the audience's expectation for a detailed and fact-filled presentation, from which they might make a considered judgment. The impression created was one of a sensible man who was willing to discuss the facts.

Nixon developed three main ideas in the body of the speech: (1) the fund was morally defensible; (2) his financial history showed him to be an honest man; (3) the Republican nominees could handle the issues in Washington more successfully than the Democratic nominees. Each of these ideas was structured in a way that reinforced his sensible approach to the topic. He provided three criteria for determining whether or not the fund was morally wrong, thereby inviting a reasonable and legalistic judgment of that issue. Similarly, his development of the second main idea resembled the pattern of assets and liabilities common to the objectively prepared balance sheet. Likewise his development of the final main idea followed a pattern in which the three issues targeted by the Republican Party—Korea, Corruption, and Communism—furnished the criteria by which to measure Eisenhower against Stevenson.

Just as his structuring of ideas fostered the impression of a rational approach, so Nixon's use of supporting material implied a factual approach to the topic. His explanation of the fund was supported with both testimony from a respectable accounting firm and legal opinion from a prestigious firm. Nixon revealed in his autobiography that he included testimony from these sources in part because he felt the mention of these firms would carry weight with Eisenhower's associates from business and finance."[16] Similarly, his litany of figures regarding salary, mortgages, and outstanding loans, along with details concerning Pat's coat and his children's dog contributed to the impression that he was presenting the facts to his audience. His disclosures regarding Sparkman's hiring of his wife and Stevenson's fund added to the fact-disclosing nature of the address

Moreover, Nixon's delivery frequently underscored the factual nature of his speech. In contrast to his usual unobtrusive use of his notes, whenever Nixon referred to "facts" he read directly from the script. A careful viewing reveals that he picked up the script and made it visible to the camera at several strategic points. He visibly read the opinion of Price Waterhouse, noting that "I have that audit here in my hand." Similarly, he punctuated his financial disclosures with the statement: "I jotted it down. Let me read the notes." Again the script was used as if it was tangible proof. Even in the conclusion, instead of summarizing the letter of support, he groped on the desk, producing a visible personal letter with a check attached. These nonverbal cues solidified the impression that "real proof" was being presented and contributed to the impression that Nixon was a man of good sense who was dealing with the issue in a rational manner that took the facts into account.

The force of Nixon's arguments, however, probably emerged more from their contribution to his appearance as a man of *good character* than as a man of good sense. After all, it was Nixon's character that had been challenged, not his knowledge or expertise. The content, delivery, and wording of his speech contributed directly to the impression of Nixon as a man of good character. The assessment of good moral character made by an audience often depends on the audience's comparison of their own values to the values embodied by the speaker. The audience's values probably paralleled the standard American values identified by Steele and Redding.[18] Given the combination of domestic prosperity and international crisis, the audience likely found comfort in values regarding the individual, Puritan and pioneer morality, effort and optimism, science and rationality, efficiency and practicality, achievement and success, quantification, material comfort, generosity and considerateness, rejection of authority, equality of opportunity, external conformity, sociality, humor, and patriotism.

A detailed analysis of Nixon's reliance on these traditional American values in the Checkers Speech is furnished by Henry McGuckin, Jr.[19] He points to a number of aspects of the content that illustrate these core values. For example, by making the propriety of the fund a moral question, Nixon uses the values of Puritan and pioneer morality. In the midst of Nixon's explanation of how a Senator's office works, he referred to going down to the Veteran's Administration to get some information about a GI policy, thus invoking the value of the individual. Not putting his wife on the payroll when there were so many other deserving stenographers who needed to work implied the value of considerateness and generosity. His story of his parent's small grocery that made a go of it because the boys worked reminded the audience of the values of effort, optimism, achievement and success. In all, McGuckin identifies 39 instances in which Nixon identified with particular values, the most frequent being, Puritan morality and equality. The effect, as noted by a rhetorical critic at the time, was the representation of Nixon "as a common man, harassed by the same troubles as other common men, possessed of the virtues most admired by common men."[20]

An examination of the wording and delivery of the speech exposes how these two aspects of Nixon's presentation contributed to his identification with the values likely to create a positive impression of his character. Several detailed studies of Nixon's language usage have verified that he used common language that was easily understood in the Checkers Speech. For example, Gibson and Felkins calculated the type/token ratio for the speech and, finding the ratio to be lower than that usually found in public speaking classes, concluded that "Nixon was using a very simple, basic, and potentially emotional form of language."[21] His common and repeated use of words like "you," "wrong," "people," "think" and "I" gave the speech a sociable, personal tone that emphasized the value of sociability and reinforced his identification with the values of common people.

In addition to the informality of Nixon's wording, the language used also reinforced some of the core values specifically. Gibson and Felkins found that the speech scored high in its use of words associated with legality, sensitivity, virtue, and association.[22] The legality of his language probably conveyed a sense of rational objectivity. The virtues emphasized in his language included honesty, sociality, and patriotism. His sensitivity and association portrayed him as a decent and likable man. Similarly, Hart's analysis of Nixon's use of language in the Checkers Speech revealed a high degree of forthrightness and equivocality.[23] The value of forthrightness is obvious. His equivocality suggested that he was being objective, rather than making absolute and rash statements. For example, he frequently explained that he would not make harsh judgments regarding the actions of Stevenson or Sparkman, but the audience was free to do so.

The informal language of the speech was probably the result of Nixon's extemporaneous method of delivery that depended on his practiced use of an outline. Several aspects of his delivery reinforced his image as a participant in the American dream. His conversational tone accompanied by frequent eye contact and a limited dependency on his notes gave the impression of spontaneity and honesty. The fact that he sat behind the desk for most of the speech, rising only when he seemed to be carried away by the passion he held for his country, gave his presentation a casual, conversational flavor.

His gestures suggesting honesty, openness, and family loyalty combined to foster this identification with Puritan and pioneer morality. During his explanations of the fund and his financial history, his frequent use of open hand gestures conveyed a sense of disclosure, as opposed to his pointing and clinched fist gestures when he discussed the issues of Korea, Communism, and corruption. His wide-eyed look as he explained that no matter what happened he wouldn't take Checkers away from his children mirrored the sincere promise of a loving father, and his magnanimous smile whenever he referred to his wife cast him as an admiring husband. McGuckin pointed out that the occasional breaks in his voice and his pitch revealed emotional strain, an impression that helped identify him as sincere [24]

Similarly, several aspects of the set and movements of the camera emphasized core values. McGuckin noted:

> [The speech] was aided by the television setting of a home library or study with a desk— symbols of success. His dress in an ordinary business suit demonstrated equality and external conformity. The presence of his wife, also simply attired, attested to his sociality— family togetherness in this case.[25]

Certainly, the shots of his wife, in rapt and admiring attention, conveyed a similar sense of success and loyalty. The camera shots that zoomed in and moved out provided the viewer with a sense that he or she was in the room with Nixon, adding to the casual and common aura of the speech.

In sum, then, Nixon appeared to be a man of good moral character because his arguments, his wording, and his style of presentation epitomized core American values, the same values that his audience would use to measure the goodness of his character.

In addition to conveying a sense of himself as of good sense and good character, Nixon was also successful in presenting himself as a man of *good will* in the Checkers speech. The content, delivery and structure of the speech worked together to foster the type of audience interaction that would assure viewers that Nixon had their best interests in mind.

In the conclusion of the speech, Nixon makes his strongest appeal for audience interaction. Following his explanation that although he did not intend to quit the decision was not his alone, Nixon asked the viewers to write or wire their advice to the Republican National Committee. He placed the power to influence the decision about his political future squarely in the hands of his primary audience. In doing so, he implied not only respect for their decision but confidence in their ability to weigh the facts as presented.

The identification with the audience that Nixon had accomplished through his use of informal wording and a conversational style of delivery throughout the speech affirmed his respect for the audience. By not using language or nonverbal cues that either distanced himself from them or condescended to them, he appeared to share and promote their interests. Similarly, the structural device he used as a transition throughout the speech encouraged audience participation and signalled his empowering the audience with the means to reach a rational decision. His most common transition was the rhetorical question. For example, as he made his explanation of the fund, he asked repeatedly: "Do you think that when I or any other Senator makes a political speech, has it printed, should charge the printing of that speech to the taxpayers?" "Do you think, for example, when I or any other Senator makes a trip to his home State to make a purely political speech that the cost of that trip should be charged to the taxpayers?" "Do you think when a Senator makes political broadcasts or political television broadcasts, radio or television, that the expense of those broadcasts should be charged to the taxpayers?" Nixon's structural technique gave his listeners a sense of participation by giving them the questions and deftly influenced their judgment by immediately providing the answers to those questions.

In addition, Nixon invited the audience to participate in making judgments about the political candidates for the Democratic party. Following his disclosure that Sparkman had had his wife on the payroll for years, he said, "you will have to pass judgment on that particular point." Similarly, following his disclosure regarding Stevenson's fund, he suggested that Stevenson "should come before the American people" and make a "complete financial statement." Thus, he again appeared to support the audience's best interests by encouraging them to make judgments.

CONCLUSION

Because Nixon called for a formal response in his conclusion, the Checkers Speech provides a unique opportunity for assessing its effectiveness according to the responses from his various audiences. All three of Nixon's audiences responded favorably to the speech.

Because Nixon had run out of time on the broadcast and failed to give the address of the Republican National Party's headquarters, wires and letters were addressed to a variety of places, including Eisenhower's train, Nixon's train, Dana Smith's office, and local Republican offices. According to one account:

> Western Union officials said they had never handled as many wires as they did that night. It was a month before the Republican National Committee, using a hundred volunteers, could get the mail opened and sorted...enough contributions poured in—mostly in amounts of one dollar or less—to pay sixty thousand dollars of the seventy-five thousand dollar cost of the telecast.[26]

An analysis of the written responses, now archived at Whittier College, Nixon's alma mater, revealed that responses came from "throughout the forty-eight states and the then territories of Alaska and Hawaii and the Commonwealth of Puerto Rico."[27] According to O'Brien and Jones, the respondents were "representative of the population as a whole," in terms of demographic characteristics. Eighty percent of the responses were sent before Eisenhower made his official announcement that Nixon would stay on the ticket. The ratio of telegraphed responses was 200 to one in favor of Nixon's retention; the ratio of responses by letter and post card was 74 to one in favor of Nixon's retention. Over half of all the responses focused on Nixon's character, praising him for his honesty, courage, sincerity, patriotism, and devotion to his family.

The reaction of Nixon's primary audience, the general viewing public, demonstrates the effectiveness of his speech. The audience's praise indicates that his attempt to identify with traditional American values in a presentation that was not only oriented to the common man and woman but also empowered the common man and woman to participate in a political decision was effective. As O'Brien and Jones put it:

> [He] had succeeded in projecting an image of himself to which [the audience] could respond. As evidenced by listener responses, Nixon was perceived as embodying the ideals of honesty, sincerity, trustworthiness, love of family and of the common man. They saw him as a man who shared their own feelings, thought as they thought, and valued what they valued…. [I]n their responses they seemed to say, "We trust him; we believe in him because he is one of us."[28]

The response of the general listening public undoubtedly acted as an inartistic proof of Nixon's *ethos* for his other primary audience, Eisenhower and his advisors. However, journalistic accounts of Eisenhower's immediate reaction to the speech are worth noting. Goldman recalled that Eisenhower and his wife, Mamie, watched the broadcast in a Cleveland auditorium where the General was scheduled to speak that night. "At the conclusion Mrs. Eisenhower was weeping and the General was obviously trying to control his emotions."[29] Later accounts from sources less supportive of Nixon have suggested that Eisenhower was only lukewarm in his response.[30] After all, Eisenhower had expected Nixon to resign at the end of the speech. By asking the public to write the Republican National Party, Nixon had, in a sense, usurped Eisenhower's power to decide the fate of the ticket. Regardless of the direction or intensity of Eisenhower's personal reaction, however, the speech and the favorable public response made his decision regarding Nixon's retention clear. That night Eisenhower revised the text of the speech he was to give to include a reference to Nixon's courage in a tough situation. Two days later, at a rally in Wheeling, West Virginia, Eisenhower announced that Nixon would remain the Republican nominee for the Vice Presidency.

The press, Nixon's final audience, exhibited a mixed reaction to the speech. Pro-Stevenson papers tended to echo the reservations voiced by the very few negative responses from the public. Some explained that although Nixon had proved himself to be honest and sincere he showed a lack of political expertise by ever having involved himself with such a fund. Others charged that his speech was too evasive, noting that he had failed to answer the real charge.

Two noted rhetorical critics explained a similar reservation in their critiques of the speech. Barnet Baskerville argued that Nixon created merely an "illusion of proof" by providing supporting data that was not relevant to the claims he was making.[31] For example, the opinion of the legal firm of Gibson, Dunn & Crutcher simply proved there was no illegality in the operation of the fund, not that the fund's existence was morally acceptable. Similarly, Frederick Haberman charged that Nixon's reasoning was unsound.[32] For example, Nixon's explanation that the fund was used for political expenses that shouldn't be borne by the taxpayers illustrated a false dilemma because obviously other Senators managed to pay for their political expenses without resorting to such a fund. Such negative reactions imply that these audience members were applying more stringent standards for evaluating Nixon's image as a man of good sense. For them, using a structural pattern and sources of evidence that suggested reasonableness was insufficient. The arguments needed to meet the tests of logical reasonableness as well. Because of the logical inadequacies of some of Nixon's arguments, the speech was less effective for this minority.

For the most part, however, the press covered the reaction to the speech more frequently than they conducted an analysis of the speech itself. Faced with an overwhelmingly positive reaction to the speech, commentaries in the press focused on the association of Nixon's positive image with the image of the Republican Party generally. The words of Scripps-Howard columnist, Robert Ruark, are illustrative:

> Tuesday night the nation saw a little man, squirming his way out of a dilemma, and laying bare his most-private hopes, fears and liabilities. This time the common man was a Republican, for a change...Dick Nixon...has suddenly placed the burden of old-style Republican aloofness on the Democrats.[33]

Thus, from the perspective of the press, Nixon had not only established his own ethos, but had reconstructed the *ethos* of the Republican Party as well.

Nixon's Checkers Speech provided a rhetorical answer to the loss of credibility he suffered from the charge of impropriety launched by the New York *Post*. His successful construction of *ethos* gave him the support of both Eisenhower and the American people at the same time that it deflected the more critical attention of the press. Less than two months later the Republican nominees, Eisenhower and Nixon, won the general election.

Martha D. Cooper, Ph.D., is an assistant professor of Speech at Northern Illinois University.

NOTES

1. Aristotle, *Rhetoric*, translated by W. Rhys Roberts (New York: Random House, 1954), 1356a.
2. Aristotle, 1355b.
3. Aristotle, 1378a.
4. Aristotle, 1367b.
5. Erie F. Goldman, *The Crucial Decade and After: America, 1945-1960* (New York: Vintage, 1960), p. 225.
6. Robert W. O'Brien and Elizabeth Jones, *The Night Nixon Spoke* (Los Alamitos, CA: Hwong, 1976), pp. 6-7.
7. Richard M. Nixon, *Six Crises* (New York: Doubleday, 1962). The primary source on which this review of the immediate events is based is Nixon's book.
8. O'Brien and Jones, p. 11.
9. William Costello, *The Facts About Nixon: An Unauthorized Biography* (New York: Viking, 1960), p. 104.
10. Richard Nixon, *Six Crises* (New York: Doubleday, 1962), p. 103.
11. Nixon, p. 102.
12. Ben Padrow and Bruce Richards, "Richard Nixon...His Speech Preparation," *Communication Quarterly* 7 (1959), 11.
13. Nixon, p. 110.
14. Nixon, p. 112.
15. Goldman, p. 218. His characterization is based on a widely circulated and popular editorial written by Louis B. Seltzer, of *The Cleveland Press*.

16. Roderick P. Hart, "Absolutism and Situation: Prolegomena to a Rhetorical Biography of Richard M. Nixon," *Communication Monographs* 43 (1976), 223.

17. Nixon, p. 108.

18. Edward D. Steele and W. Charles Redding, "The American Value System: Premises for Persuasion," *Western Speech Journal* 26 (1962), 83-91.

19. Henry McGuckin, Jr., "A Value Analysis of Richard Nixon's 1952 Campaign Fund Speech," *Southern Speech Journal* 33 (1968), 259-69. The examples used in this paragraph are drawn primarily from McGuckin's critique. A table summarizing his findings can be found on pp. 267-8 of the essay.

20. Frederick W. Haberman, "The Election of 1952: A Symposium," *Quarterly Journal of Speech* 38 (1952), 407.

21. James W. Gibson and Patricia K. Felkins, "A Nixon Lexicon," *Western Speech Communication Journal* 38 (1974), 190-8.

22. Gibson and Felkins, 196.

23. Hart, 223.

24. McGuckin, 268.

25. McGuckin, 262.

26. Goldman, p. 231.

27. O'Brien and Jones. This paragraph is based on the analysis of listener response conducted by O'Brien and Jones. See, specifically, pp. 14, 39, 41, and 54.

28. O'Brien and Jones, p. 13.

29. Goldman, p. 230.

30. Bruce Mazlish, *In Search of Nixon* (New York: Basic Books, 1972), p. 100.

31. Barnet Baskerville, "The Illusion of Proof," *Western Speech* 25 (1961), 236-42.

32. Frederick W. Haberman, "The Election of 1952: A Symposium," *Quarterly Journal of Speech* 38 (1952), 406-7.

33. Qtd. by Goldman, p. 233.

CUBAN MISSILE CRISIS DEBATE

Adlai Stevenson

United Nations Security Council, New York City, October 25, 1962
(Transcribed from the video, GREAT SPEECHES, VOLUME II)

Mr. President, members of the Council, today we must address our attention to the realities of the situation posed by the build-up of nuclear striking power in Cuba. In this connection I want to say at the outset that the course adopted by the Soviet Union yesterday to avoid direct confrontations in the zone of quarantine are welcome to my Government. We also welcome the assurance by Chairman Khrushchev in his letter to Earl Russell that the Soviet Union will take no reckless decisions with regard to this crisis. And we welcome most of all the report that Mr. Khrushchev has agreed to the proposals advanced by the Secretary-General. Perhaps that report will be confirmed here today.

My Government is most anxious to effect a peaceful resolution of this affair. We continue to hope that the Soviet Union will work with us to diminish the—not only the new danger which has suddenly shadowed the peace but all of the conflicts that divide the world.

I shall not detain you with any detailed discussion of the Soviet and the Cuban responses to our complaint. The speeches of the communist delegates were entirely predictable. I shall make brief comment on some points suggested by these speeches and some other points which may have arisen in the minds of Members of the United Nations.

Both Chairman Khrushchev, in his letter to Earl Russell, and Ambassador Zorin, in his remarks to this Council, argued that this threat to the peace had been caused not by the Soviet Union and Cuba but by the United States.

We are here today, and have been this week, for one single reason: because the Soviet Union secretly introduced this menacing offensive military build-up into the island of Cuba while assuring the world that nothing was further from their thoughts.

The argument, in its essence, of the Soviet Union it *[sic]* is that it was not the Soviet Union which created this threat to peace by secretly installing these weapons in Cuba, but that it was the United States which created this crisis by discovering and reporting these installations. This is the first time, I confess, that I have ever heard it said that the crime is not the burglar but the discovery of the burglar, and that the threat is not the clandestine missiles in Cuba but their discovery and the limited measures taken to quarantine further infection. The peril arises not because the nations of the Western Hemisphere have joined together to take necessary action in their self-defense but because the Soviet Union has extended its nuclear threat into the Western Hemisphere.

I noted that there is still at least some delegates in the Council, possibly I suspect very few, who say that they don't know whether the Soviet Union has in fact built in Cuba installations capable of firing nuclear missiles over ranges from 1,000 to 2,000 miles. As I say, Chairman Khrushchev did not deny these facts in his letter to Earl Russell, nor

171

did Ambassador Zorin on Tuesday evening, and, if further doubt remains on this score, we shall gladly exhibit photographic evidence to the doubtful.

One other point I'd like to make, Mr. President and gentlemen, is to invite attention to the casual remark of the Soviet representative claiming that we have thirty-five bases in foreign countries. The facts are that there are missiles comparable to these being placed in Cuba with the forces of only three of our allies. They were only established there by a decision of the Heads of Government meeting in December 1957, which was compelled to authorize such arrangements by virtue of a prior Soviet decision to introduce its own missiles capable of destroying the countries of Western Europe.

In the next place, there are some troublesome questions in the minds of Members that are entitled to serious answers. There are those who say that, conceding the fact that the Soviet Union has installed these offensive missiles in Cuba, conceding the fact that this constitutes a grave threat to the peace of the world, why was it necessary for the nations of the Western Hemisphere to act with such speed? Why could not the quarantine against the shipment of offensive weapons have been delayed until the Security Council and the General Assembly had a full opportunity to consider this, the situation and make recommendations? Let me remind the Members that the United States was not looking for some pretext to raise the issue of the transformation of Cuba into a military base. On the contrary, the United States made no objection whatever to the shipment of defensive arms by the Soviet Union to Cuba, even though such shipments offended the traditions of this hemisphere. Even after the first hard intelligence reached Washington concerning the change in the character of Soviet military assistance to Cuba, the President of the United States responded by directing an intensification of surveillance. And only after the facts and the magnitude of the build-up had been established beyond all doubt did we begin to take this limited action of barring only those nuclear uh...uh only these nuclear weapons, equipment and aircraft.

To understand the reasons for this prompt action, it is necessary to understand the nature and the purposes of this operation. It has been marked, above all, by two characteristics: speed and stealth. As the photographic evidence makes clear, the installation of these missiles, the erection of these missile sites, has taken place with extraordinary speed. One entire complex was put up in 24 hours. This speed need not only...not only demonstrates the methodical organization and the careful planning involved, but it also demonstrates a premeditated attempt to confront this hemisphere with a *fait accompli*. By quickly completing the whole process of nuclearization of Cuba, the Soviet Union would be in a position to demand, that the *status quo* be maintained and left undisturbed—and, if we were to have delayed our counteraction, the nuclearization of Cuba would have been quickly completed.

This is not a risk which this hemisphere is prepared to take. When we first detected the secret offensive installations, could we reasonably be expected to have notified the Soviet Union in advance, through the process of calling the Security Council, that we had discovered its perfidy, and then to have done nothing but wait while we debated, and then have waited further while the Soviet representative in the Security Council vetoed a resolution, as he has already announced he will do? In different circumstances, we would have, but today we are dealing with dread realities and not with wishes.

One of the sites, as I have said, was constructed in 24 hours. One of these missiles, can be armed with its nuclear warhead in the middle of the night, pointed at New York, and landed above this room five minutes after it was fired. No debate in this room could affect in the slightest the urgency of these terrible facts or the immediacy of the threat to the peace. There was only one way to deal with that urgency and, and with that immediacy, and that was to act, and to act at once, but with the utmost restraint consistent with the urgency of the threat to the peace; and we came to the Security Council, I would remind you, immediately…immediately, and concurrently with the O.A.S. We didn't even wait for the O.A.S. to meet and to act. We came here at the same time.

We immediately put into process the political machinery that we pray will achieve a solution of this grave crisis, and we did not act until the American Republics had acted to make the quarantine effective. We did not shirk our duties to ourselves, to the hemisphere, to the United Nations or to the world.

We are now in the Security Council on the initiative of the United States, precisely because having taken the hemispheric action which has been taken, we wish political machinery, the machinery of the United Nations, to take over to reduce these tensions and to interpose itself to eliminate this aggressive threat to the peace and to insure the removal from this hemisphere of offensive nuclear weapons and the corresponding lifting of the quarantine.

There are those who say that the quarantine is an inappropriate and extreme remedy; that the punishment does not fit the crime. But I ask those who take this position to put themselves in the position of the Organization of American States; to consider what you would have done in the face of the nuclearization of Cuba. Were we to do nothing until the knife was sharpened? Were we to stand idly by until it was at our throats? What were the alternatives available? On the one hand, the O.A.S. might have sponsored an invasion or destroyed the bases by an air strike, or imposed a total blockade on all imports into Cuba, including medicine and food. On the other hand, the O.A.S. and the United States might have done nothing. Such a course would have confirmed the greatest threat to the peace of the Americas known to history and would have encouraged the Soviet Union in similar adventures in other parts of the world. And it would have discredited our will, our determination to live in freedom and to reduce, not increase, the perils of this nuclear age.

The course we have chosen seems to me perfectly graduated to meet the character of the threat. To have done less would have been to fall [sic] ah to fail in our obligation to peace.

To those who say that a limited quarantine was too much in spite of the provocation and the danger, let me tell you a story, attributed, like so many stories of our American stories to Abraham Lincoln, about the passerby out in my part of the country who was charged by a farmer's ferocious boar. He picked up a pitchfork and met the boar head on; it died and the irate farmer denounced him and asked him why he didn't use the blunt end of the pitchfork and the man replied, "Why didn't the boar attack me with his blunt end."

Some here have attempted to question the legal basis of the defensive measures taken by the American Republics to protect the Western Hemisphere against Soviet long-range nuclear missiles, and I would gladly expand on our position on this but in view of the proposal now before us, presented last night by the Secretary-General, perhaps that is a matter and a discussion, in view of its complexity and length, could be more fruitfully delayed to a later time.

Finally, let me say that no twisting of logic, no distortion of words can disguise the plain, the obvious, the compelling commonsense conclusion that the installation of

nuclear weapons by stealth, weapons of mass destruction in Cuba, poses a dangerous
threat to the peace, a threat which contravenes Article 2, paragraph 4 and a threat which
the American Republics are entitled to meet, as they have done, with appropriate
regional defensive methods.

Nothing has been said by the representatives of the communist States here which
alters the basic situation. There is one fundamental question to which I solicit
your...your attention. The question is this: what actions serve to strengthen the world's
hope of peace? Can anyone claim that the introduction of long-range nuclear missiles
into Cuba strengthens the peace? Can anyone claim that the speed and stealth of this
operation strengthens the peace? Can anyone suppose that this whole undertaking is
anything more than an audacious effort to increase the nuclear striking power of the
Soviet Union against the United States and thereby magnify its frequently reiterated
threats against Berlin? When we are about to debate how to stop the dissemination of
nuclear weapons, does their introduction in a new hemisphere by an by [sic] outside
State advance sanity and peace? Does anyone suppose that if this Soviet adventure
should go unchecked, the Soviet Union would refrain from similar adventures in other
parts of the world?

The one action in the last few days which has strengthened the peace is the
determination to stop this further spread of weapons in this hemisphere. In view of the
situation that now confronts us, and the proposals made here yesterday by the Acting
Secretary-General, I am not going to further extend my remarks this afternoon. I wish
only to conclude by reading to the members of the Council a letter from the President
of the United States which was delivered to the Acting Secretary General just a few
minutes ago in reply to his appeal of last night. He said to Mr. U Thant:

> I deeply appreciate the spirit which prompted your message of yesterday. As we made clear
> in the Security Council, the existing threat was created by the secret introduction of
> offensive weapons into Cuba, and the answer lies in the removal of such weapons. In your
> message, in your statement to the Security Council last night, you have made certain
> suggestions and have invited preliminary talks to determine whether satisfactory arrange-
> ments can be assured. Ambassador Stevenson is ready to discuss promptly these arrangements
> with you. I can assure you of our desire to reach a satisfactory and a peaceful solution of this
> matter.

Signed "John F. Kennedy." I have nothing further to say at this time, Mr. President.
(Ambassador Zorin presents the Soviet response.)

(Stevenson continues): Mr. Zorin and gentlemen, I want to say to you, Mr. Zorin,
that I don't have your talent for obfuscation, for distortion, for confusing language and
for double-talk—and I must confess to you that I am glad I don't. But if I understood
what you said, you said that my position had changed: that today I was defensive
because we didn't have the evidence to prove our assertions that your Government had
installed long-range missiles in Cuba. Well, let me say something to you, Mr.
Ambassador: We do have the evidence. We have it, and it's clear and incontrovertible.
And let me say something else: Those weapons must be taken out of Cuba.

And next, let me say to you with a [sic] that if I understood you—with a trespass on
credulity that excels your best—you said, that our position had changed since I spoke
here the other day because of the pressures of world opinion and a majority of the
United Nations. Well, let me say to you sir: You are wrong again. We have had no

pressure from anyone whatsoever. We came in here today to indicate our willingness to discuss Mr. U Thant's proposals—and that is the only change that has taken place. But let me also say to you, sir, that there has been a change. You, the Soviet Union, has sent these weapons to Cuba. You, the Soviet Union, has upset the balance of power in the world. You, the Soviet Union, has created this new danger—not the United States. And you asked, with a fine show of indignation, why the President didn't tell Mr. Gromyko on last Thursday about our evidence, at the very time that the [sic] that Mr. Gromyko was blandly denying to the President that the United [sic] that the USSR was placing such weapons on sites in the New World. Well, I'll tell you why: because we were assembling the evidence—and perhaps it would be instructive to the world to see how a Soviet official, how far he would go in perfidy. Perhaps we wanted to know if this country faced another example of nuclear deceit like that one a year ago when in stealth the Soviet Union broke the nuclear test moratorium. And, while you are asking, while we are asking questions, let me ask you, why your Government, your Foreign Minister, deliberately, cynically deceived us about the nuclear build-up in Cuba. And finally, the other day, Mr. Zorin, I remind you that you didn't deny the existence of these weapons. Instead, we heard that they had suddenly become defensive weapons. But today— again, if I heard you correctly—you now say they don't exist, or that we haven't proved they exist—with another fine flood of rhetorical scorn. All right, sir, let me ask you one simple question: Do you, Ambassador Zorin, deny that the USSR has placed and is placing medium and intermediate-range missiles and sites in Cuba? Yes or no? Don't wait for the translation. Yes or no?

(Zorin): Mr. Stevenson, would you continue your statement please? You will receive the answer in the due course, do not worry.

(Stevenson): I'm prepared to wait for my answer until Hell freezes over, if that's your decision. I am also prepared to present the evidence in this room.

THE WAR OR PEACE ALTERNATIVE

Adlai Stevenson's Cuban Missile Crisis Presentation

I am prepared to wait for my answer until Hell freezes over.

CRITIC: James H. McBath

On May 25, 1957, Oxford University conferred on Adlai Stevenson the honorary degree of Doctor of Civil Law. In his citation, the *Public Orator* said:

> I present to you Adlai Stevenson, amid the strains and stresses of national and international politics the champion of humanism in word and deed, and himself the source.

THE SPEAKER

Adlai Stevenson lived through a time of unusual turbulence in American history, and he was a participant in both its domestic and international dimensions. In an editorial, titled "First Gentleman of the World," *Life* said that Stevenson's death in July of 1965 left two vacuums to be filled. One was his role as head of the country's United Nations delegation, which Stevenson had once termed "the most complex embassy in the history of our diplomacy." The other vacuum was in American politics. "His campaigns for the Presidency," observed the editor, "changed the popular image of what a politician can be; his example improved the breed, perhaps permanently." [1]

Born to affluence and influence, Adlai Stevenson's roots went into the history of the Middle West of the 1830's. His maternal great-grandfather, Jesse Fell, who proposed Abraham Lincoln for the Presidency, also helped arrange the Lincoln-Douglas debates. His grandfather, the first Adlai Stevenson, served as Vice President in Grover Cleveland's second administration.

Following an undergraduate education at Princeton, Stevenson took his law degree at Northwestern University in 1929 and joined a leading law firm in Chicago. After two years practicing law, Stevenson turned to a career in public service. With the advantage of a private income, he was able to leave his law practice for long periods of time during the New Deal; he was one of Franklin D. Roosevelt's bright young lawyers in government service. When the United States entered the war, Stevenson went to Washington, D.C., as an aide to Navy Secretary Frank Knox. In February of 1945, he moved to the State Department, where, as an assist to Secretary Edward Stettinius, he helped in the creation of the United Nations. "After years of preoccupation with war," he said, "the satisfaction of having a part in the organized search for the conditions and mechanics of peace completed my circle." [2]

Of course, his circle was far from completed. When the forty-seven-year-old Stevenson returned to Illinois in 1947, there was nothing in his record to forecast that in five years he would become a central figure in American politics. In 1948 he was chosen by Illinois Democratic leaders to run for Governor against the Republican incumbent whose administration had been marred by scandal. Stevenson won by a record 572,000 votes and set about riding close herd over a heavily Republican legislature; in 1952 alone he vetoed no fewer than 134 bills.

His circle widened further in 1952. President Harry Truman had decided not to run again; and the winner of most Democratic presidential primaries was Tennessee's Senator Estes Kefauver, a lone-wolf liberal who was unacceptable to most national leaders. Casting about desperately for a candidate, the Democrats found Stevenson. From Truman's point of view, Stevenson was very nearly irresistible—a Middle Westerner who had led his ticket in a swing state, who had both statehouse and foreign-policy experience, and who was generally well liked.

Stevenson accepted the nomination with genuine reluctance. Of course no Democrat could have beaten Dwight Eisenhower in 1952. The most popular American war hero of the century rode into office on a wave of his own popularity and disenchantment with Democrats. Stevenson took the beating he had expected, and he was a graceful loser. In his concession speech to a roomful of supporters in Springfield, Illinois, he said: "Someone asked me as I came in, how I felt, and I was reminded of a story that a fellow townsman of ours used to tell—Abraham Lincoln. They asked him how he felt once after an unsuccessful election. He said he felt like a little boy who has stubbed his toe in the dark. He then said that he was too old to cry, but it hurt too much to laugh."

In 1956 Stevenson campaigned actively for the Democratic nomination, won it again, and launched an aggressive campaign. Facing a confident Dwight Eisenhower who was seeking a second term, he suffered a greater defeat than in 1952. After 1956 Stevenson practiced law, made speeches to wipe out campaign debts, and dutifully rebuffed his colleagues when they sought his permission to work for a third nomination. But at the 1960 convention he waited hopefully for a summons that never came. John F. Kennedy won the nomination and the Presidency. For Adlai Stevenson there remained the prospect of appointment to a position he coveted in Kennedy's cabinet. His friend, Norman Cousins, recalled a luncheon meeting with a group of newspaper editors:

> Suppose, one of them asked him, you were able, just by waving a magic wand, to do the one job in the world you wanted most to do, other than what you are now doing. What would it be?" "Other than the Presidency, of course," he said with a smile, "I suppose I would have to say it would be the job of U.S. Secretary of State. Assuming you could really be involved in making policy and not just be an administrator, that job, with its infinite complexities and challenges, is the one I would have to choose." [3]

Instead of being offered the job he really wanted, Stevenson was invited to head the United States delegation to the United Nations. If the role was less than Stevenson wanted, his friends argued that he was in a stronger position to influence American policy from a summit inside the UN than from any station outside the UN or outside the government. Stevenson accepted and served as his country's ambassador to the United Nations until the time of his death in 1965.

By the very nature of his position at the United Nations, Stevenson was a spokesman for national policy rather than a maker of policy. Nevertheless, through his stature and ability, he endowed the position with commanding authenticity. He was, in his own right, a respected world figure. Eric Severeid, of CBS Television News, observed:

Stevenson had to be the agent of American foreign policy at the UN, but, of course, he saw himself as something more than that. Too many crowds, in too many foreign countries, had adored and cheered him as a kind of universal symbol of peace, high thought and the goodness in man.[4]

As Stevenson was being buried in Illinois, a memorial service was held in the green-and-gold hall of the UN General Assembly in New York. More than two thousand colleagues and admirers gathered to hear tributes. Four speakers addressed the audience, including Secretary of State Dean Rusk. Stevenson, said Rusk, was a "universal man" whose "universality did not rest upon his being a prince among plain men, but upon his being a plain man even among princes." And then Rusk concluded, "Three presidents of the United States sent Adlai Stevenson to the United Nations. They sent you our best."[5]

BACKGROUND TO THE CRISIS

Through the late summer and early fall of 1962, reports from Cuban refugees and other sources indicated unusual Soviet military activity in Cuba, including the construction of missile installations. Intelligence reports said that about five thousand Soviet technicians were already in the country, with more men and sophisticated electronic equipment on the way by ship. At this point, President Kennedy issued a stern warning on the fourth of September that although there was "no evidence" of "significant offensive capability" in Cuban hands, "were it to be otherwise, the gravest issues would arise." The Soviet Union replied with a *Tass* statement on the 11th of September that the USSR had no need to deploy its nuclear weapons outside Soviet territory; it warned the United States to halt its "aggressive" threats against Cuba.

On October 14th, an American U-2 aircraft returned from Cuba with photographic evidence of a launching pad, associated buildings, and missiles on the ground. Subsequent reconnaissance overflights confirmed the construction of nine new missile sites with launching positions for twenty-four Soviet medium-range (1100-mile) and twelve intermediate-range (2200-mile) ballistic missiles. In addition, there were forty-two Ilyushin-28 Beagle tactical bombers (600-mile range), still unassembled. A small advisory group assembled by Kennedy (ExCom) assessed the challenge as an attempt to shift the global military and political balance of power. They saw the missile installation as a Cold War move to test American resolve and to discredit American strength and reliability as an ally. If it succeeded, reasoned Kennedy and ExCom, the Russians could then move boldly on West Berlin or in Latin America.[6]

Kennedy's first reaction was that the United States would have to act swiftly, probably with an air strike "to wipe them out" before the missile launching pads became fully operational. Stevenson said he thought there should be no air strike until the United States had exhausted every peaceful means of removing the threat.

Stevenson had to return to the UN while the ExCom continued its agonized debate. When he got back to Washington, he found to his vast relief that the air strike proposal had lost favor, mainly because Robert Kennedy had sharply opposed it. "A sudden air strike at dawn Sunday without warning," said the Attorney General, "would be a Pearl Harbor in reverse, and it would blacken the name of the United States in the pages of history" as a great power who attacked a small neighbor. In addition, a sneak air attack on Cuba might have made the Russians feel they had no alternative but to retaliate, perhaps even with nuclear weapons. So the group turned to the idea of a naval blockade, with which Stevenson agreed completely, because it gave Soviet Chairman Khrushchev time to take considered action. Equally important, it made backing down less difficult for him. It was decided to call the blockade a "quarantine," which sounded more like a medical necessity than a warlike act.

On Monday night, October 22, 1962, at 7:00 p.m., President Kennedy, speaking on television and radio, told the nation that the Soviet Union, despite its statements to the contrary, was building launching sites in Cuba for medium- and intermediate-range ballistic missiles capable of striking most major cities in the Western Hemisphere. He declared that "this urgent transformation of Cuba into an important strategic base...constitutes an explicit threat to the peace and security of all the Americas" and "cannot be accepted by this country." In "defense of our own security and that of the entire Western Hemisphere," President Kennedy announced the following steps:[7]

1. A naval and air quarantine on shipment of all "offensive" military equipment to Cuba and a turning back of all ships carrying such cargo to Cuba;
2. Increased aerial surveillance of Cuba;
3. Adoption of a policy that any nuclear missile launched from Cuba against any nation in the Western Hemisphere "would be deemed an attack by the Soviet Union on the United States, requiring a full retaliatory response upon the Soviet Union;"
4. Reinforcement of the American naval base at Guantanamo;
5. A call for an immediate meeting of the Organization of American States;
6. A call for an emergency of the UN Security Council;
7. A plea to Chairman Khrushchev to halt and eliminate the clandestine reckless and provocative threat to world peace."

At 7:30 p.m., Stevenson made a formal request for an emergency meeting of the Security Council. Attached to the request was a draft resolution calling for the immediate dismantling of Soviet missiles and the immediate removal, under UN observation of the missiles and Soviet bombers, for an end to the "quarantine" once the "offensive" weapons had been removed, and for negotiations between the United States and Russia "on measures to remove the existing threat." Thus, after Kennedy's Monday night speech, the scene shifted to the United Nations.

The United States, as the member that had requested the Security Council meeting, spoke first on October 23rd. With his reasoned eloquence, Stevenson put forward the American position.[8]

He announced to the Council that the Organization of American States had just unanimously adopted a resolution empowering OAS member states "to take all measures individually and collectively, including the use of armed force which they may deem necessary." Soon afterward, Stevenson concluded:

Since the end of the Second World War, there has been no threat to the vision of peace so profound, no challenge to the work of the Charter so fateful. The hopes of mankind are concentrated in this room.... Let [this day] be remembered, not as the day when the world came to the edge of nuclear war, but as the day when men resolved to let nothing thereafter stop them in their quest for peace.

Stevenson returned to the debate, providing the historical and political context for his subsequent persuasion. Stevenson revealed that the striking range of the nuclear warheads being installed in Cuba could reach targets as far north as the Hudson Bay in Canada, and far south as Peru. After establishing the existence of a serious threat to the Western Hemisphere, he developed two themes: (1) Communist policy was inimical to the United Nations and (2) The American response to the present threat was justified. To support the first premise, Stevenson traced the history of Soviet and American policy from the end of World War II until the present crisis period. He stated that "the ink was hardly dry on the Charter before Moscow began its war against the world of the United Nations." Moreover, the Soviets broke their promise to remove all troops from Romania, Bulgaria, Hungary, Poland, Eastern Germany, and Czechoslovakia, denying these people the rights of self-determination. Rejecting an open world, Russia has attempted to "impose its design of a Communist future;" and now Russian expansionism is in our neighborhood. The critical issue is that "Cuba has given the Soviet Union a bridgehead and staging area in this hemisphere."

Stevenson next turned to the appropriateness of the U.S. blockade and demand for removal of the missiles. He argued that if the United States and the UN did not stand firm in demanding that the Soviet Union remove its missiles from Cuba, we would be allowing the Soviets to achieve their objectives through intimidation and would be encouraging them to pursue expansion in the Western Hemisphere. The alternatives for the Soviet Union were clear: "Either remove all missiles from Cuba or enter into direct military conflict with the Organization of American States." This was the first positive statement of American intentions. President Kennedy, in his televised speech that previous night, had not mentioned the prospect of war if the missiles were not removed.

THE SPEECH

The speaking situation at the UN was well suited to Stevenson's presentational strengths. His long experience in addressing conferences while seated made this a familiar mode. The semi-circular seating arrangement enabled him to have full view of members of the immediate audience. The official nature of the occasion called for close attention to notes and manuscript. This worked to Stevenson's advantage as he was most comfortable with detailed written materials. His deputy at the UN recalled, "How he worried and worked over those speeches. Usually he would outline some ideas to someone on the staff, who would come up with a draft; then he would start redrafting (often completely), revising, polishing until the last hectic deadline."[9] Moreover, he was skilled at speaking from a manuscript or weaving copious notes into a finished composition. Finally, the use of a microphone as well as the nearness of other Security Council members permitted the low-keyed, conversational delivery that Stevenson preferred. In short, the speaking situation was tailor-made to his preferences and abilities.

Stevenson begins his speech of October 25th on a conciliatory note, welcoming Khrushchev's assurance that the Soviets will "take no reckless decisions" with regard to the crisis.[10] "My government," he adds, "is most anxious to effect a peaceful resolution of this affair." His listeners are told that he intends to make brief comment on some points suggested by speeches of the Communist delegates and other points that may have arisen in the minds of delegates. He brushes aside the Soviet allegation that the United States had created the crisis by discovering and reporting the missile installations: "This is the first time, I confess, that I have ever heard it said that the crime is not the burglar but the discovery of the burglar." Then, almost as if to invite rejoinder, he mentions that neither Khrushchev nor Zorin has denied the presence of Soviet missiles in Cuba. "And if further doubt remains on this score, we shall gladly exhibit photographic evidence to the doubtful."

In the body of his speech, Stevenson presses home four main points:

1. Installation of the missile sites has been marked by speed and stealth. The very speed of construction reveals careful planning and organization. "It also demonstrates a premeditated attempt to confront this hemisphere with a *fait accompli*."
2. The nuclear threat is genuine; today "we are dealing with dread realities." One of these missiles "can be armed with its nuclear warhead in the middle of the night, pointed at New York, and landed above this room five minutes after it was fired."
3. The American response has been measured and appropriate. We and the Organization of American States might have invaded Cuba, or we might have done nothing. Instead, "the course we have chosen seems to me perfectly graduated to meet the character of the threat."
4. Resolution of the crisis is a Soviet responsibility. As President Kennedy stated in his letter to the UN Acting Secretary-General, "The existing threat was created by the introduction of offensive weapons into Cuba, and the answer lies in the removal of such weapons."

Ambassador Zorin moves to the attack. The United States has no evidence to prove its contentions. The "aggressive intentions of the United States" are opposed by the "overwhelming majority" of delegations to the UN. Thus Stevenson, says Zorin, has been "forced to change his tone," to become defensive. Why has the United States not produced its evidence of missiles in Cuba? "Because there is no such evidence." The only evidence the United States possesses is "fake."

Stevenson's famous response begins with the words: "I want to say to you, Mr. Zorin, that I do not have your talent for obfuscation, for distortion, for confusing language, and for double-talk. And I must confess to you that I am glad I do not!" Then, stating the heart of his argument, Stevenson says, "We have it [the evidence], and it is clear and incontrovertible. And let me say something else those weapons must be taken out of Cuba."

The dramatic, televised confrontation, seen by millions, concludes with this exchange:

STEVENSON: "Finally, Mr. Zorin, I remind you that the other day you did not deny the existence of these weapons. But today, again, if I heard you correctly, you now say that they do not exist, or that we haven't proved they exist—and you say this with another fine flood of rhetorical scorn. All right, sir, let me ask you one simple question. Do you, Ambassador Zorin, deny that the USSR has placed and is placing medium- and intermediate-range missiles and sites in Cuba? Yes or no? Don't wait for the translation. Yes or no?"

ZORIN: "'I am not in an American courtroom, sir; and, therefore, I do not wish to answer a question that is put to me in the fashion in which a prosecutor puts questions. In due course, sir, you will have your answer."

STEVENSON: "You are in the courtroom of world opinion right now, and you can answer yes

or no. You have denied that they exist, and I want to know whether I have
understood you correctly.

ZORIN: "Will you please continue your statement, sir? You will have your answer in due
course."

STEVENSON: "I am prepared to wait for my answer until Hell freezes over, if that's your
decision. And I am also prepared to present the evidence in this room."

And with that, Stevenson revealed the photographs of the Russian missiles and sites,
with devastating effect. Several days later, after a successful naval blockade and further
negotiation between Washington and Moscow, Khrushchev ordered removal of the
missiles from Cuba.

EVALUATION

Stevenson's key rhetorical strategy is to identify the American response with the best
interests of other nations and of world peace itself. If he can accomplish this aim, the
moral position and actions of the United States will have international sanction. The
Soviet Union then will be universally regarded as indifferent to the interests of other
nations and a threat to world peace. Stevenson advances his plan in three ways: by
suggesting offensive nuclear arms in Cuba are more than a threat to the United States,
but are a danger to the entire Western Hemisphere; by implying that this Soviet action
is not an isolated case but rather a precursor to future aggressive action against other
nations; and by proposing that actions toward resolution of the missile crisis be viewed
as constructive steps to world peace.

While avoiding any limitations of the debate to a contest between the Soviet Union
and the United States, Stevenson fixes responsibility for the crisis: "The peril arises not
because the nations of the Western Hemisphere have joined together to take necessary
action in their self defense, but because the Soviet Union has extended nuclear threat
into the Western Hemisphere." To meet the common threat, he concludes, "the
American republics are entitled to meet, as they have done, with appropriate regional
defensive measures."

Stevenson then extends his argument from a Soviet threat to the Western Hemisphere to a future threat against other nations and ultimately to the peace of the world.
In his defense of the American response to the missiles, Stevenson implies that were the
Soviets to be left unchecked in Cuba, they would be encouraged to take similar actions
elsewhere. "Does anyone suppose," he asks, "that, if this Soviet adventure should go
unchecked, the Soviet Union would refrain from similar adventures in other parts of
the world?"

Stevenson's speech is marbled with references to world peace. He repeatedly links the
missile confrontation to the larger issues of international responsibility and peace:

There is one fundamental question to which I solicit your attention. The question is this:
What action serves to strengthen the world's hope for peace? Can anyone claim that the
introduction of long-range nuclear missiles into Cuba strengthens the hope for peace?

Can anyone claim that the speed and stealth of this operation strengthens the peace?

Can anyone suppose that this whole undertaking is anything more than an audacious
effort to increase the nuclear striking power of the Soviet Union against the United States
and thereby magnify its frequently reiterated threats against Berlin?

When we are about to debate how to stop the dissemination of nuclear weapons does their introduction into a new hemisphere by an outside state advance sanity and peace?

Not only does Stevenson portray the Soviet Union as a reckless aggressive power uninterested in peace, but he offers, in contrast, his country's sense of global responsibility:

We did not shirk our duties to ourselves, to the hemisphere, to the United Nations, or to the world.
To have done less would have been to fail in our obligation to peace.
Our job, Mr. Zorin, is to save the peace. And if you are ready to try, we are.

Stevenson's speech of October 25th is, in reality, two speeches. The former is a carefully crafted statement of American policy. Then comes Zorin's remarks, heavy with contempt for Stevenson's alleged lack of evidence and seeming reversal of position. Stevenson's rejoinder, his second appearance differs from the former in several essential respects.

First, the initial presentation is phrased in the language and cadences of diplomacy. We hear long, flowing sentences, little repetition, and no questions. The more impersonal "we" is used instead of "I" (in fact, twice as many "I's" appear in the second of the appearances). Fifty- and sixty-word sentences characterize carefully prepared manuscripts as do polished phrases: "We continue to hope that the Soviet Union will work with us to diminish not only the new danger which has suddenly shadowed the peace but all of the conflicts that divide the world." In contrast, the second presentation, which is clearly extemporaneous, is marked by short sentences, questions, and repetition of phrases. For example:

I have not finished my statement. I asked you a question. I have had to reply to the question.
You—the Soviet Union has sent these weapons to Cuba.
You—the Soviet Union has upset the balance of power in the world. You—the Soviet Union has created this new danger—not the United States.
These weapons, gentlemen—these launching pads—these planes—of which we have illustrated only a fragment....

Second, consider Stevenson's use of language. The message that our conclusions are based on observation, while the Soviet statements are unsupported assertions is conveyed by Stevenson's linguistic decisions. By a wide margin, perhaps by a ratio of ten to one, Stevenson's language in contrast to Zorin's suggests that our claims rely on "facts," "realities," "evidence." Thus, Stevenson argues that "the facts are that there are missiles" and "no twisting of logic, no distortion of words can disguise the plain, the obvious, the compelling commonsense conclusion that the installation of nuclear weapons by stealth, weapons of mass destruction, in Cuba poses a dangerous threat...."

Reinforcing the image of a logic-grounded, fact-oriented American policy, Stevenson relies heavily on specific, factual data. We hear about "launcher-erector mechanisms," "1,000-mile missiles," "concrete retaining walls," "weapons systems," "Beagle bombers," "launching pads," "nuclear warheads." Listeners can visualize Cuba as a fortress, bristling with armaments .

But linguistic choices can do more than convey an image. By the metrics of sentence structure, the most important points can be stressed. This is especially effective in the use of parallel structure. Through repetition of the same form, a single point can receive greater attention. Stevenson repeatedly uses parallel structure to signify the intensity of a claim. In discussing threats to peace, he asks:

> Can anyone claim that the introduction of long-range nuclear missiles in Cuba strengthens the peace? Can anyone claim that the speed and stealth of this operation strengthens the peace? Can anyone suppose that this whole undertaking is anything more than an audacious effort to increase the nuclear powers of the Soviet Union against the United States?

A third factor affecting Stevenson's persuasion is the quality of the man himself. Already a world figure when he became our ambassador to the United Nations, Stevenson was accorded a standing ovation by the delegates when he entered the hall in 1960. His role at the UN confirmed his entitlement to confidence and respect. His speeches were authoritative statements, marked by comprehensive research and incisive analysis, and undergirded by profound patriotism. Barbara Ward, the distinguished British economist, found Stevenson's love of country a source of personal strength: "This deep, unshakeable dedication to America's authentic greatness informed even his smallest acts of policy and diplomacy—the courtesy of his language, the warmth of his interest, the modesty of his bearing."[11]

A self-confessed intellectual—a rarity among politicians—Stevenson was warm and convivial.[12] His friends often spoke of his sense of humor, his appreciation of the absurd. He had an irrepressible urge to find a light side in serious subjects. His memorable charge to intellectuals—"eggheads of the world unite, you have nothing to lose but your yolks"—endeared him to the intelligentsia, if not to the average voter. One of his favorite anecdotes on informal occasions was about the middle-aged club woman who came up to him after a speech and said with a flutter in her voice: "Oh, Mr. Stevenson, your speech was superfluous." "Thank you, madam. I've been thinking about having it published posthumously." "Oh, won't that be nice," she replied, "the sooner the better."

Some of this humor was self-deprecating and dealt with his frustrated candidacies. He often mused: "A funny thing happened to me on the way to the White House." To a friend who had been elected president of a church association he wrote: "Congratulations on your election as president. I know from hearsay how satisfying that can be." Though regarded as an intellectual and basically serious-minded, Stevenson's ingrained sense of humor may have insulated him from the arrogance and stuffiness common to others in high office.

Contributing to his ethical persuasion was his faith in the United Nations. Indeed, a key premise of Stevenson's speeches at the UN was his personal commitment to "make the United Nations successful, to make this great experiment in international collaboration fulfill the dreams to its founders that one day reason would rule and mankind would be liberated from the everlasting scourge of war."[13] Informed listeners knew the strength of his allegiance to the ideal of international organization. To many Stevenson was not merely speaking at the UN; he was the UN speaking.

The powerful ethical stance may have permitted Stevenson to speak more forthrightly, more directly and sharply, than would have been possible by another American representative. But Stevenson, both long-time friend and symbol of the UN, was accorded by his listeners a latitude that permitted an undiluted statement of the argument. And the very comprehensiveness of his argument, and the way it was phrased and presented, created a lasting impression.

A FINAL WORD

It would be unrealistic to view Stevenson's performance at the UN as a decisive event. It was a significant, even critical, occurrence among a multitude of occurrences. "We shall never know," said Edward R. Murrow of another crossroad in events. "History does not disclose its alternatives." But we do know that, essential to the resolution of the missile crisis, was a clear understanding by both sides of the consequences of their subsequent actions. And it was important that other nations observe firsthand that communication in process. Adlai Stevenson on October 25, 1962, with the world as witness, made the issue of war or peace an unmistakable alternative for the Soviet Union.

Before his death in 1992 James H. McBath, Ph.D., was a professor of Communication Arts at the University of Southern California.

NOTES

1. *Life*, July 23, 1965, p. 4.
2. *Time*, July 23, 1965, pp. 20-21.
3. "Memories of A. E. S.," *Saturday Review*, July 31, 1965, p. 32.
4. "The Final Troubled Hours of Adlai Stevenson," *Look*, November 30, 1965, p. 84.
5. Quoted in Francis T. P. Plimpton, "They Sent You Our Best," in *As We Knew Adlai*, ed. Edward P. Doyle (New York: Harper & Row, Publishers, 1966), p. 256.
6. Robert F. Kennedy, a member of ExCom, provided an account of their deliberations in *Thirteen Days: A Memoir of the Cuban Missile Crisis* (New York: W. W. Norton, 1969).
7. The text of Kennedy's speech is from *The Cuban Crisis of 1962: Selected Documents and Chronology*, ed. David L. Larson (Boston: Houghton Mifflin Co., 1963), pp. 41-46.
8. "The Cuban Crisis," *Vital Speeches*, November 15, 1962, pp. 70-76.
9. Plimpton, p. 260.
10. For a text of the Stevenson-Zorin debate see "Has the U.S.S.R. Missiles in Cuba?" *Vital Speeches*, November 15, 1962, pp. 77-83.
11. "Affection and Always Respect," in *As We Knew Adlai*, p. 226.
12. A book rich in anecdotal material is Elizabeth Stevenson Ives and Hildegarde Dolson, *My Brother Adlai* (New York: William Morrow & Co., 1956).
13. Quoted in *An Ethic for Survival: Adlai Stevenson Speaks on International Affairs*, ed. Michael H. Prosser (New York: William Morrow & Co., 1969), p. 30.

WATERGATE

Richard M. Nixon

White House, Washington, D.C., April 30, 1973 (Transcribed from the video, GREAT SPEECHES, VOLUME VI)

I want to talk to you tonight from my heart on a subject of deep concern to every American.

In recent months, members of my Administration and officials of the Committee for the Re-election of the President, including some of my closest friends and most trusted aides, have been charged with involvement in what has come to be known as the Watergate affair. These include charges of illegal activity during and preceding the 1972 Presidential election and charges that responsible officials participated in efforts to cover up that illegal activity. The inevitable result of these charges has been to raise serious questions about the integrity of the White House itself. Tonight I wish to address those questions.

Last June 17, while I was in Florida trying to get a few days rest after my visit to Moscow, I first learned from news reports of the Watergate break-in. I was appalled at this senseless, illegal action, and I was shocked to learn that employees of the Re-election Committee were apparently among those guilty. I immediately ordered an investigation by appropriate Government authorities. On September 15, as you will recall, indictments were brought against seven defendants in the case.

As the investigations went forward, I repeatedly acked [sic]...asked those conducting the investigation whether there was any reason to believe that members of my Administration were in any way involved. I received repeated assurances that there were not. Because of these continuing reassurances, because I believed the reports I was getting, because I had faith in the persons from whom I was getting them, I discounted the stories in the press that appeared to implicate members of my Administration or other officials of the campaign committee.

Until March of this year, I remained convinced that the denials were true and that the charges of involvement by members of the White House Staff were false. The comments I made during this period; the comments made by my Press Secretary in my behalf, were based on the information provided to us at the time we made those comments. However, new information then came to me which persuaded me that there was a real possibility that some of these charges were true, and suggesting further that there had been an effort to conceal the facts both from the public, from you, and from me.

As a result, on March 21, I personally assumed the responsibility for coordinating intensive new inquiries into the matter, and I personally ordered those conducting the investigations to get all the facts and to report them directly to me, right here in this office. I again ordered that all persons in the Government or at the Re-election Committee should cooperate fully with the FBI, the prosecutors, and the grand jury. I also ordered that anyone who refused to cooperate in telling the truth would be asked to resign from government service. And, with ground rules adopted that would preserve the basic constitutional separation of powers between the Congress and the Presidency, I directed that members of the White House Staff should appear and testify voluntarily under oath before the Senate committee which was investigating Watergate. I was determined that we should get to the bottom of the matter, and that the truth should be fully brought out no matter who was involved.

At the same time, I was determined not to take precipitate action, and to avoid, if at all possible, any action that would appear to reflect on innocent people. I wanted to be fair. But I knew that in the final analysis, the integrity of this office—public faith in the integrity of this office—would have to take priority over all personal considerations.

Today, in one of the most difficult decisions of my Presidency, I accepted the resignations of two of my closest associates in the White House—Bob Haldeman, John Ehrlichman—two of the finest public servants it has been my privilege to know. I want to stress that in accepting these resignations, I mean to leave no implication whatever of personal wrongdoing on their part, and I leave no implication tonight of implication on the part of others who have been charged in this matter. But in matters as sensitive as guarding the integrity of our democratic process, it is essential not only that rigorous legal and ethical standards be observed, but also that the public, you, have total confidence that they are both being observed and enforced by those in authority and particularly by the President of the United States. They agreed with me that this move was necessary in order to restore that confidence.

Because Attorney General Kleindienst, though a distinguished public servant, my personal friend for 20 years, with no personal involvement whatever in this matter, has been a close personal and professional associate of some of those who are involved in this case, he and I both felt that it was also necessary to name a new Attorney General. The Counsel to the President, John Dean, has also resigned.

As the new Attorney General, I have today named Elliot Richardson, a man of unimpeachable integrity and rigorously high principle. I have directed him to do everything necessary to ensure that the Department of Justice has the confidence and the trust of every law abiding person in this country. I have given him absolute authority to make all decisions bearing upon the prosecution of the Watergate case and related matters. I have instructed him that if he should consider it appropriate, he has the authority to name a special supervising prosecutor for matters arising out of the case.

Whatever may appear to have been the case before, whatever improper activities may yet be discovered in connection with this whole sordid affair, I want the American people, I want you to know beyond the shadow of a doubt that during my term as President, justice will be pursued fairly, fully, and impartially, no matter who is involved. This office is a sacred trust and I am determined to be worthy of that trust.

Looking back at the history of this case, two questions arise: How could it have happened? Who is to blame?

Political commentators have correctly observed that during my 27 years in politics I have always previously insisted on running my own campaigns for office. But 1972 presented a very different situation. In both domestic and foreign policy, 1972 was a year of crucially important decisions, of intense negotiations, of vital new directions, particularly in working toward the goal which has been my overriding concern throughout my political career—the goal of bringing peace to America, peace to the world. And that is why I decided, as the 1972 campaign approached, that the Presidency should come first and politics second. To the maximum extent possible, therefore, I sought to delegate campaign operations, to remove the day-to-day campaign decisions from the President's office and from the White House. I also, as you recall, severely limited the number of my own campaign appearances.

Who, then, is to blame for what happened in this case? For specific criminal actions by specific individuals, those who committed those actions must, of course, bear the liability and pay the penalty. For the fact that alleged improper actions took place within the White House or within my campaign organization, the easiest course would be for me to blame those to whom I delegated the responsibility to run the campaign. But that would be a cowardly think to do. I will not place the blame on subordinates— on people whose zeal exceeded their judgment, and who may have done wrong in a cause they deeply believed to be right. In any organization, the man at the top must bear the responsibility. That responsibility, therefore, belongs here, in this office. I accept it. And I pledge to you tonight, from this office, that I will do everything in my power to ensure that the guilty are brought to justice, and that such abuses are purged from our political processes in the years to come, long after I have left this office.

Some people, quite properly appalled at the abuses that occurred, will say that Watergate demonstrates the bankruptcy of the American political system. I believe precisely the opposite is true. Watergate represented a series of illegal acts and bad judgments by a number of individuals. It was the system that has brought the facts to light and that will bring those guilty to justice—a system that in this case has included a determined grand jury, honest prosecutors, a courageous judge, John Sirica, and a vigorous free press.

It is essential now that we place our faith in that system and especially in the judicial system. It is essential that we let the judicial process go forward, respecting those safeguards that are established to protect the innocent as well as to convict the guilty. It is essential that in reacting to the excesses of others, we not fall into excesses ourselves. It is also essential that we not be so distracted by events such as this that we neglect the vital work before us, before this nation, before America, at a time of critical importance to America and the world.

Since March, when I first learned that the Watergate affair might, in fact, be far more serious than I had been led to believe, it has claimed far too much of my time and my attention. Whatever may now transpire in the case, whatever the actions of the grand jury, whatever the outcome of any eventual trials, I must now turn my full intention [sic] and I shall do so once again to the larger duties of this office. I owe it to this great office that I hold, and I owe it to you—to my country.

I know that as Attorney General, Elliot Richardson will be both fair and he will be fearless in pursing this case wherever it leads. I am confident that with him in charge, justice will be done.

There is vital work to be done toward our goal of a lasting structure of peace in the world—work that cannot what [sic] wait, work that I must do. Tomorrow, for example, Chancellor Brandt of West Germany will visit the White House for talks that are a vital element of "The Year of Europe," as 1973 has been called. We are already preparing for the next Soviet-American summit meeting later this year. This is also a year in which we are seeking to negotiate a mutual and balanced reduction of armed forces in Europe, which will reduce our defense budget and allow us to have funds for other purposes at home so desperately needed. It is the year when the United States and Soviet negotiators will seek to work out the second and even more important round of our talks on limiting nuclear arms, and of reducing the danger of a nuclear war that would destroy civilization as we know it. It is a year in which we confront the difficult tasks of maintaining peace in Southeast Asia and in the potentially explosive Middle East.

There is also vital work to be done right here in America: to ensure prosperity, and that means a good job for everyone who wants to work; to control inflation, that I know worries every housewife, everyone who tries to balance a family budget in America; to set in motion new and better ways of ensuring progress toward a better life for all Americans.

When I think of this office—of what it means—I think of all the things that I want to accomplish for this Nation, of all the things I want to accomplish for you.

On Christmas Eve, during my terrible personal ordeal of the renewed bombing of North Vietnam, which after 12 years of war, finally helped to bring America peace with honor, I sat down just before midnight. I wrote out some of my goals for my second term as President. Let me read them to you.

> To make it possible for our children, and for our children's children, to live in a world of peace. To make this country be more than ever a land of opportunity—of equal opportunity, full opportunity for every American. To provide jobs for all who can work, and generous help for those who cannot work. To establish a climate of decency, and civility, in which each person respects the feelings and the dignity and the God-given rights of his neighbor. To make this a land in which each person can dare to dream, can live his dreams—not in fear, but in hope—proud of his community, proud of his country, proud of what America has meant to himself and to the world.

These are great goals. I believe we can, we must work for them. We can achieve them. But we cannot achieve these goals unless we dedicate ourselves to another goal. We must maintain the integrity of the White House, and that integrity must be real, not transparent. There can be no whitewash at the White House.

We must reform our political process—ridding it not only of the violations of the law, but also of the ugly mob violence, and other inexcusable campaign tactics that have been too often practiced and too readily accepted in the past, including those that may have been a response by one side to the excesses or expected excesses of the other side. Two wrongs do not make a right.

I've been in public life for more than a quarter of a century. Like any other calling, politics has good people, and bad people. And let me tell you, the great majority in politics—in the Congress, in the Federal Government, in the State Government—are good people. I know that it can be very easy, under the intensive pressures of a campaign, for even well-intentioned people to fall into shady tactics—to rationalize this on the grounds that what is at stake is of such importance to the Nation that the end justifies the means. And both of our great parties have been guilty of such tactics in the past.

In recent years, however, the campaign excesses that have occurred on all sides have provided a sobering demonstration of how far this false doctrine can take us. The lesson is clear: America, in its political campaigns, must not again fall into the trap of letting the end, however great that end is, justify the means. I urge the leaders of both political parters [sic] parties, I urge citizens, all of you, everywhere, to join in working toward a new set of standards, new rules and procedures to ensure that future elections will be as nearly free of such abuses as they possibly can be made. This is my goal, I ask you to join in making it America's goal.

When I was inaugurated for a second term this past January 20, I made...gave each member of my Cabinet and each member of my senior White House Staff a special 4-year calendar, with each day marked to show the number of days remaining to the Administration. In the iscrip [sic] inscription on each calendar, I wrote these words: "The Presidential term which begins today consists of 1,461 days—no more, no less. Each can be a day of strengthening and renewal for America; each can add depth and dimension to the American experience. If we strive together, if we make the most of the challenge and the opportunity that these days offer us, they can stand out as great days for America, and great moments in the history of the world."

I looked at my own calendar this morning up at Camp David as I was working on this speech. It showed exactly 1,361 days remaining in my term. I want these to be the best days in America's history, because I love America. I deeply believe that America is the hope of the world. And I know that in the quality and wisdom of the leadership America gives lies the only hope for millions of people all over the world, that they can live their lives in peace and freedom. We must be worthy of that hope, in every sense of the word. Tonight, I ask for your prayers to help me in everything that I do throughout the days of my Presidency to be worthy of their hopes and of yours.

God bless America and God bless each and every one of you.

STATEMENT OF THE ARTICLES
ON IMPEACHMENT

Barbara Jordan

Committee on the Judiciary, House of Representatives, Washington, D.C., July 25, 1974 (Transcribed from the video, GREAT SPEECHES, VOLUME II)

Mr. Chairman, I join my colleague, Mr. Rangle, in thanking you for giving the junior members of this committee the glorious opportunity of sharing the pain of this inquiry. Mr. Chairman, you are a strong man and it has not been easy but we have tried as best we can to give you as much assistance as possible. Earlier today we heard the beginning of the preamble to the Constitution of the United States. "We the people"—it's a very eloquent beginning. But when that document was completed on the seventeenth of September in 1787, I was not included in that "We the people." I felt somehow for many years that George Washington and Alexander Hamilton just left me out by mistake. But through the process of amendment, interpretation, and court decision, I have finally been included in "We the people."

Today I am an inquisitor and hyperbole would not be fictional and would not overstate the solemnness that I feel right now. My faith in the Constitution is whole. It is complete. It is total and I am not going to sit here and be an idle spectator to the diminution, the subversion, the destruction of the Constitution.

"Who can so properly be the inquisitors for the nation as the representatives of the nation themselves?" "The subjects of its jurisdiction are those offenses which proceed from the misconduct of public men," and that's what we are talking about. In other words, from the abuse or violation of some public trust.

It is wrong, I suggest, it is a misreading of the Constitution for any member here to assert that for a member to vote for an Article of Impeachment means that that member must be convinced that the President should be removed from office. The Constitution doesn't say that. The powers relating to impeachment are an essential check in the hands of the body, the legislature, against and upon the encroachments of the Executive. The division between the two branches of the legislature, the House and the Senate, assigning to the one the right to accuse and to the other the right to judge, the framers of this Constitution were very astute. They did not make the accusers and the judges...and the judges the same person.

We know the nature of impeachment. We've been talking about it for a while now. "It is chiefly designed for the President and his high ministers' to somehow be called into account. It is designed to "bridle" the Executive if he engages in excesses. It is designed as a method of national "inquest into the conduct of public men." The framers confided in the Congress the power, if need be, to remove the President in order to strike a delicate balance between a President swollen with power and grown tyrannical, and preservation of the independence of the Executive. The nature of impeachment, a narrowly channeled exception to the separation of powers maxim; the Federal Convention of 1787 said that. It limited impeachment to "high crimes and misdemeanors" and discounted and opposed the term "maladministration." It is to be used only for great misdemeanors, so it was said in the North Carolina ratification convention—and in the Virginia ratification convention: "We do not trust our liberty to a particular branch. We need one branch to check the other."

"No one need be afraid" the North Carolina ratification convention; "No one need be afraid that officers who commit oppression will pass with immunity."

"Prosecutions of impeachments will seldom fail to agitate the passions of the whole community," said Hamilton in the *Federalist Papers, No. 65,* "We divided the parties more or less friendly or inimical to the accused." (I do not mean political parties in that sense.)

The drawing of political lines goes to the motivation behind impeachment; but impeachment must proceed within the confines of the constitutional term "high crimes and misdemeanors."

Of the impeachment process, it was Woodrow Wilson who said that "nothing short of the grossest offenses against the plain law of the land will suffice to give them speed and effectiveness. Indignation so great as to overgrow party interest may secure a conviction; but nothing else can."

Common sense would be revolted if we engaged upon this process for petty reasons. Congress has a lot to do: appropriations, tax reform, health insurance, campaign finance reform, housing, environmental protection, energy sufficiency, mass transportation. Pettiness cannot be allowed to stand in the face of such overwhelming problems. So today we're not being petty. We are trying to be big because the task we have before us is a big one.

This morning, in a discussion of the evidence, we are told that the evidence which purports to support the allegations of misuse of the CIA by the President is thin. We are told that that evidence is insufficient. What that recital of the evidence this morning did not include is what the President did know on June the 23rd, 1972. The President did know that it was Republican money, that it was money from the Committee for the Reelection of the President, which was found in the possession of one of the burglars arrested on June the 17th.

What the President did know on the twenty-third of June was the prior activities of E. Howard Hunt, which included his participation in the break-in of Daniel Ellsberg's psychiatrist, which included Howard Hunt's participation in the Dita Beard ITT affair, which included Howard Hunt's fabrication of cables designed to discredit the Kennedy administration.

We were further cautioned today that perhaps these proceedings ought to be delayed because certainly there would be new evidence forthcoming from the President of the United States. There has not even been an obfuscated indication that this committee would receive any additional materials from the President. The committee subpoena is outstanding, and if the President wants to supply that material, the committee sits here.

The fact is that on yesterday, the American people waited with great anxiety for eight hours, not knowing whether their President would obey an order of the Supreme Court of the United States.

At this point I would like to juxtapose a few of the impeachment criteria with some of the actions the President has engaged in.

Impeachment criteria—James Madison from the Virginia Ratification Convention: "If the President be connected in any suspicious manner with any person and there be grounds to believe that he will shelter him, he may be impeached."

We have heard time and time again that the evidence reflects the payment to defendants, money. The President had knowledge that these funds were being paid and these were funds collected for the 1972 presidential campaign.

We know that the President met with Mr. Henry Peterson twenty-seven times to discuss matters related to Watergate, and immediately thereafter met with the very persons who were implicated in the information Mr. Peterson was receiving. The words are: "If the President is connected in any suspicious manner with any person and there be grounds to believe that he will shelter that person, he may be impeached."

Justice Story: "Impeachment is attended, is intended for occasional and extraordinary cases where a superior power acting for the whole people is put into operation to protect their rights and rescue their liberties from violations."

We know about the "Houston Plan." We know about the break-in at the psychiatrist's office. We know that there were [sic] absolute complete direction on September 3 when the President indicated that a surreptitious entry had been made in Dr. Fielding's office after having met with Mr. Ehrlichman and Mr. Young. Protect their rights. Rescue their liberties from violation.

The Carolina Ratification Convention impeachment criteria: Those are impeachable "who behave amiss or betray their public trust."

Beginning shortly after the Watergate break-in and continuing to the present time, the President has engaged in a series of public statements and actions designed to thwart the lawful investigation by government prosecutors. Moreover, the President has made public announcements and assertions bearing on the Watergate case which the evidence will show he knew to be false—these assertions, false assertions: impeachable—those who misbehave, those who behave amiss or betray the public trust.

James Madison, again at the Constitutional Convention: "A President is impeachable if he attempts to subvert the Constitution."

The Constitution charges the President with the task of taking care that the laws be faithfully executed, and yet the President has counseled his aides to commit perjury, willfully disregard the secrecy of grand jury proceedings, conceal surreptitious entry, attempt to compromise a federal judge while publicly displaying his cooperation with the processes of criminal justice. A President is impeachable if he attempts to subvert the Constitution.

If the impeachment provision in the Constitution of the United States will not reach the offenses charged here, then perhaps that eighteenth century Constitution should be abandoned to a twentieth century paper shredder. Has the President committed offenses and planned and directed and acquiesced in a course of conduct which the Constitution will not tolerate? That's the question. We know that. We know the question. We should now forthwith proceed to answer the question. It is reason and not passion which must guide our deliberations, guide our debate, and guide our decision.

"WE THE PEOPLE"

Barbara Jordan's Statement before the House Judiciary Committee on the Impeachment of Richard M. Nixon

My faith in the Constitution is whole. It is complete. It is total.

CRITIC: Patricia D. Witherspoon

On August 9, 1974, Richard M. Nixon resigned as the 37th president of the United States. Threatened with impeachment because of his involvement in what became known as the "Watergate scandal," he left office after five and one-half years as the nation's Chief Executive. Each president since Nixon has had to deal with public and press scrutiny of the White House in response to the misuse and abuse of power attributed to the Nixon administration. Consequently, issues related to the use of presidential power continue to be of significant interest to those who study the American presidency and those whose lives are affected by presidential decisions.

Barbara Jordan, a Congresswoman from Texas, played an important role in the House of Representatives' attempt to determine whether President Nixon's actions between 1972 and 1974 were impeachable offenses. No analysis of her statement to the House Judiciary Committee during its impeachment hearings would be complete without first looking at the events which led to the President's confrontation with Congress in the Summer of 1974.

WATERGATE

On June 17, 1972, employees of the Committee for the Reelection of President Richard Nixon broke into the headquarters of the Democratic National Committee located in the Watergate office complex in Washington, D.C. The purpose of the break-in was to wiretap telephones to obtain information that might help Nixon's campaign efforts. The five would-be thieves were thwarted in their efforts by a security guard and were arrested in the building. One of those arrested was the head of security for the President's reelection committee.

Almost immediately a massive cover-up was organized by individuals holding high positions in the Nixon administration to distance the President and his campaign from the break-in. These individuals included the nation's Attorney General, John Mitchell, as well as White House Chief of Staff Robert Haldeman and other aides employed in the Office of the President. For over two years an "underground" network of these individuals, as well as the FBI and the CIA, attempted to conceal the White House's involvement in this and other illegal and unethical activities that had been planned to help propel the President into a second term of office. (Indeed, Nixon did win reelection in November, 1972, before these actions became public knowledge.)

Through a series of attempts by journalists, Congressional investigative committees, federal judges, and the Supreme Court, the conspiracy of secrecy eventually was uncovered. During months of interviewing and investigating, journalists for the Washington *Post* discovered attempts by White House aides to pay the Watergate defendants (those who came to trial for the break-in) for their silence and prevent their implicating anyone in the White House in the matter. Press reports prompted the U.S. Senate to create an investigative committee concerning the break-in and other alleged covert activities relating to political espionage. It was during televised hearings held by this committee that the nation was told by one White House staff member about an elaborate taping system in the White House. An aide to Nixon's Chief of Staff informed the Senate Watergate Committee that the system was used in the Oval Office and the Cabinet Room and that White House telephones used habitually by the President were tapped. This system was a surprise to many governmental officials who were unaware that their conversations and telephone calls had been taped.

Leon Jaworski, an eminent attorney from Texas, was named a Special Prosecutor by President Nixon to investigate and bring indictments against individuals responsible for illegal acts relating to the cover-up and other covert political activities. Ironically, Jaworski ultimately had to file suit against the President for withholding information—specifically, recordings of Nixon's private conversations that might contain evidence of crimes committed by associates of Nixon under indictment at the time.

On July 24, 1974, the Supreme Court issued an opinion through Chief Justice Warren Burger that, although a president did possess executive privileges of secrecy, that privilege "must yield to the demonstrated specific need for the evidence in a pending criminal trial."[1] Although some tapes had been delivered to the Special Prosecutor, others had not. Consequently, a number of White House tapes were turned over to the Special Prosecutor as a result of the Supreme Court's decision. One of the tapes released by the Court's ruling revealed that on June 23, 1972, six days after the illegal entry into the Watergate building, the President of the United States directed the CIA to halt an FBI investigation of the matter. This action clearly was an obstruction of justice, and the taped conversation has been referred to since that time as the "smoking gun," the evidence that Richard Nixon was involved in the cover-up of the break-in almost from its inception. This particular evidence was not yet available when the House Judiciary Committee began its deliberations on the issue of impeachment.

IMPEACHMENT PROCEEDINGS

The Constitution requires the House of Representatives, through one of its committees, to inquire into the conduct of the President if charges of misconduct are brought against him. If it is judged that significant evidence does exist, the House develops articles of impeachment for presentation to the Senate. The Senate then conducts a trial to determine if a president should be impeached, based on the evidence it has received.

During the spring and summer of 1974, the House Judiciary Committee, chaired by Peter Rodino of New Jersey, received and reviewed evidence about Richard Nixon's alleged misdeeds, including information that had become available during hearings conducted by the Senate Watergate Committee. Members perused large black notebooks of reading material in closed-door sessions. This material, compiled by attorneys hired by the Committee, consisted of evidence and the attorneys' evaluation of whether that evidence constituted a violation of the law.

On Wednesday evening, July 24, 1974, the House Judiciary Committee, comprised of 38 members, opened its deliberations to the public. Before a national television audience the Chairman of the Committee began the proceedings by solemnly stating:

> We have reached the moment when we are ready to debate resolutions whether or not the Committee should recommend that the House of Representatives adopt articles for the impeachment of Richard M. Nixon. Make no mistake about it. This is a turning point, whatever we decide. Our judgment is not concerned with an individual but with a system of Constitutional government....[2]

On the evening of the following day, July 25, Barbara Jordan, a junior Congresswoman from Texas, took her turn to address the Committee. It is important to look at the path that led her to this important juncture in her career before analyzing the statement she presented to her colleagues and the nation.

THE SPEAKER

Barbara Charline Jordan was born February 21, 1936, in Houston, Texas. Her father worked as a warehouse employee during her childhood and became a Baptist minister in 1949. Her mother was a respected orator in church circles prior to her marriage. A strong religious background was one factor in her upbringing that profoundly affected Jordan's life. As she has said, there "are certain values which are instilled in you about the way you treat your fellow man and fellow human beings that come out of that religious orientation."[3]

Her mother also engendered in her a sense of caring and compassion for other people as well as a sense of community. Additionally, she fondly recalls a grandfather who supported her goals and ambitions. In her words, "strong family support, good religious background, sense of self...were all values, principles articulated to me, driven into me, demonstrated to me which served me well."[4]

Jordan also had a father who valued education, particularly as a way for blacks to break the oppressive yoke of discrimination. She remembers him emphasizing that "...one thing no one can ever take from you is a good strong mind. So you ought to get as much education as you can."[5] He promised to finance as much education as she was willing to pursue.

In high school Jordan developed an interest in oratory and won numerous oratorical awards in local and statewide competitions. She became an outstanding debater at Texas Southern University where she received a baccalaureate degree in political science and history in 1956. During her senior year she began to think about career plans. For some time Jordan had wanted to be an attorney, and she announced to her debate coach that she wanted to apply to the Harvard University Law School. He dissuaded her from applying, however, candidly stating that the institution probably would not accept the graduate of a school that was relatively unknown to its administrators. He suggested she attend Boston University, make her mark there, and then attend Harvard's graduate school. In 1959 Barbara Jordan received her law degree from Boston University but she never pursued graduate work at Harvard.

Between 1960 and 1966, Jordan practiced law in Houston. Interested in the election of John Kennedy and fellow Texan Lyndon Johnson, she worked as a volunteer for the Democratic ticket in 1960. By the end of the campaign she had been bitten by the political "bug." Consequently, she ran for the Texas House of Representatives in 1962 and 1964, but she lost both elections. Believing she was the better candidate in each campaign, she was surprised at her first defeat and depressed by the second one. On the evening of her second defeat she contemplated moving out of Texas, realizing that perhaps the state was not ready for a black woman intent on a political career. However, in 1965 Harris County (Houston) reapportioned its legislative districts in response to Supreme Court rulings. Jordan resided in one of the newly created senatorial districts. While checking the precincts within it, she discovered that she had carried each of them in her previous races, so she ran for state Senator in her new district. In 1966 Ms. Jordan was elected to the Texas Senate and became the first black woman in history to sit in the Texas Legislature. In 1972 she was selected by her colleagues as President Pro Tempore and served as Governor for a Day. She became the first black woman in U.S. history to serve in such a capacity.

During her years in the Texas Senate, Jordan became known and respected for her knowledge of issues, her analytical skills, and her ability to communicate with a variety of constituencies in the legislative process. By 1972 she felt sufficiently confident in her public support and personal competence to run for the U.S. Congress.

In January, 1973, Barbara Jordan was sworn in as Congresswoman from the 18th District of Texas, and Richard Nixon was inaugurated for a second term as President of the United States. Her career in Washington was just beginning. Mr. Nixon and his administration, however, were becoming embroiled in charges of political scandals and cover-ups of unethical and illegal activities. During the next year and a half a series of events led to a presidential confrontation with Congress in the summer of 1974. For a few days in July of that year, the futures of Barbara Jordan and Richard Nixon were affected permanently by the public deliberations of the House of Representatives' Judiciary Committee. One would leave office in disgrace; the other would garner new respect from her colleagues, her party, and much of the nation.

THE STATEMENT

The House Judiciary Committee decided before the opening of its televised discussions to allow each member fifteen minutes for a prefatory statement. Jordan recalls in her autobiography that she opposed this practice, viewing it as unnecessary. She remembers suggesting to the Committee: "Let's deal with the issue and make a decision on the basis of the facts we have accumulated to this point. We don't need speechmaking."[6] However, there was little support for this sentiment and the statements began on the evening of July 24, 1974.

Continuing to believe that individual statements were "a waste of the country's time," she waited to prepare her remarks until three hours before the Committee convened on Thursday evening, July 25.[7] That evening it would be her turn to speak. The members were speaking in order of seniority and had been presenting their individual comments all that day and the previous evening.

At 6 p.m. she began writing, using "little disjointed notes" she had taken while reading a variety of sources about the nature and process of impeachment.[8] In her words:

I jotted down from this note and from that note and from this other note, and sent each page out to Marian (her secretary) when it was finished. I had already had my legislative assistant Bob Alcock parallel statements on impeachment—historical documents, Constitutions of the Confederacy, whenever impeachment had been talked about—against some, of the offenses by Richard Nixon that we had talked about. So I also had that chart, that comparison about what had been said and what it was that Richard Nixon had done.[9]

The result of her efforts was four annotated pages of notes and four pages of a chart which juxtaposed historical impeachment criteria and the President's actions under scrutiny.

Before analyzing the message Jordan developed and presented, it is important to note that her statement is different from other speeches examined in this text. It was presented as one set of remarks within a series of statements by 37 other individuals. Each member of the House Judiciary Committee spoke from his or her seat during the deliberations. Due to the solemnity of the proceedings there was no applause after each statement was presented. The following analysis considers the unique characteristics of the occasion and the audience that affected the message presented by Ms. Jordan to colleagues, reporters, other observers, and the television audience.

When analyzing the elements of any speech, a critic must look at the choices the speaker made to create a message appropriate to the audience, the occasion, and the purpose of the communication. This analysis discusses the thesis of Barbara Jordan's statement; the materials and appeals used to support the thesis and persuade the audience; the clear and vivid language used to communicate her opinions; and the elements of delivery which she effectively utilized.

Congresswoman Jordan's statement to the House Judiciary Committee is an excellent example of the use of logical proof in persuasive discourse. Shortly before Jordan began to prepare her statement, her assistant asked if she had decided what to say. "I'm going to come out for impeachment," she responded. "I have decided I am going to do that, and I am going to say why."[10] The main thesis of her statement, therefore, was that the House Judiciary Committee should approve articles of impeachment against Richard Nixon. This analysis begins by presenting an overview of its contents which formed the justification for her thesis.

Barbara Jordan was one of two blacks on the House Judiciary Committee in 1974. As she listened to the prefatory statements of her colleagues on July 24 and 25, she realized that many of them quoted the Constitution's Preamble: "We the People of the United States...." Jordan was struck with the significance of that beginning. When the Constitution was completed in September, 1787, blacks were not considered citizens; and, therefore, were not included in that phrase. To capture the audience's attention, establish her credibility, and lead into the body of the speech, Jordan's introduction reminded the audience that the Constitution, which had originally excluded her from its precepts, was about to be cited by her as evidence in support of the impeachment of a president. As she emphasized: "Today I am an inquisitor." Moreover, despite, or perhaps because of, a 200-year struggle to include equal rights for blacks in its protective paragraphs, Jordan declared: "My faith in the Constitution is whole. It is complete. It is total. I am not going to sit here and be an idle spectator to the diminution, the subversion, the destruction of the Constitution." At this point in the statement she chose to present an overview of the impeachment process, not necessarily to enlighten her colleagues who had been studying the process for months, but to inform citizens viewing the historical proceedings—citizens who most likely were not well-versed in Constitutional law.

Having spent weeks and months reviewing the Constitutional process of impeachment and the evidence against Richard Nixon, Jordan succinctly summarized the definition and the purpose of impeachment and the reasons behind it. There was no venting of political partisanship, but careful reference to the words of those who established and explained the process in the Constitution and in other historical writings. Indeed, she observed: "The drawing of political lines goes to the motivation behind impeachment; but impeachment must proceed within the confines of the constitutional term, 'high crime and misdemeanors.' "

As a Democrat considering the demise of a Republican president, Jordan reminded those assembled that Congress' agenda was too full with issues and problems of national importance to engage in the impeachment process "for petty reasons." Emphasizing the importance of the Committee's task, she decried the President's lack of cooperation in delivering evidentiary materials to the Committee. She reminded the audience that Nixon had been slow to obey a Supreme Court order to release tapes to the Watergate investigation's Special Prosecutor. She also criticized a suggestion to delay the Committee's proceedings on the assumption that the President might present new evidence for its consideration. As she curtly stated: "The committee subpoena is outstanding, and if the President wants to supply that material, the committee sits here."

Having reinforced a growing perception in Congress and throughout the country that Mr. Nixon indeed was "stonewalling" to prevent the release of information damaging to his credibility, Jordan began to recite presidential actions which appeared to justify a Committee vote in support of articles of impeachment. Concurrently, she offered a listing of impeachment criteria, juxtaposed with these actions.

As is mentioned earlier in this chapter, a speaker makes choices when developing a speech. Jordan presented the following evidence against the President in support of her thesis:

** The President had knowledge of money paid to Watergate defendants—money paid from his campaign funds.
** The President met with the Assistant Attorney General and others implicated in the Watergate cover-up.
** The President was involved with, or had knowledge of, other covert and illegal political activities.
** The President made statements to the press and public about Watergate which were false.

True to her nature as an attorney, Jordan had been researching impeachment criteria throughout the sessions of the House Judiciary Committee. She enumerated several of these criteria in her statement as they related to specific evidence germane to the charges of presidential misconduct. She quoted James Madison's remarks at the Constitutional Convention as well as the opinions he voiced at the ratification convention in Virginia. She also cited Justice Story and the South Carolina Ratification Convention impeachment criteria. In one succinct sentence she summarized the major offenses committed by the President which justified, in her analysis, a vote in favor of articles of impeachment:

The Constitution charges the President with the task of taking care that the laws be faithfully executed, and yet the President has counseled his aides to commit perjury, willfully disregarded the secrecy of grand jury proceedings, concealed surreptitious entry, attempted to compromise a federal judge while publicly displaying his cooperation with the processes of criminal justice.

A major strength of Jordan's statement is the logical proof she presents within it, which includes the recitation of authoritative sources and the condensation of documents and testimony she considers to be most important in the debate regarding presidential misconduct. These supporting materials were appropriate, considering the audience and occasion, because they focused on legal and Constitutional doctrine, not opinions of partisan politicians. Consequently, the conclusion to this statement was an appeal to rationality as the Committee proceeded with its deliberations, its debate, and its decision.

Jordan appealed to her audience's sense of logic and reasoning through the use of supporting materials. However, *language* is the tool a speaker uses to craft his or her message, to paint a verbal picture of one's ideas. Through vivid and forceful language and a commanding style of delivery, she also appealed to the audience's emotions—to a sense of patriotism as well as an appreciation of political ethics. To create this emotional appeal she eloquently declared her devotion to the Constitution and the structure of government established by the nation's founding fathers. Jordan used formal, elevated language which was appropriate to the audience, the setting, and the occasion.

Early in the statement she characterized her faith in the Constitution as being whole, complete, and total. In a strong and resonant voice, which seemed at times to punch consonants off the printed page, she vowed she would not be a party to the diminution, subversion, or destruction of the Constitution. In these examples and in other places in the statement, she used groups of three words or phrases for emphasis.

Midway in the speech, Jordan chose to illustrate her interest in keeping political self-interest out of the impeachment discussion. Using the stylistic device of repetition she stated: "Common sense would be revolted if we engaged upon this process for petty reasons." "Pettiness cannot be allowed to stand in the face of such overwhelming problems" (those Congress was facing at the time). "So today we are not being petty."

Jordan then began to present her evidence justifying a vote for Articles of Impeachment. The junior Congresswoman chastised the second-term President for his lack of cooperation in supplying evidence to the Committee. She used strong, terse words filled with consonants that projected rhetorical authority. "There has not even been an obfuscated indication that this committee would receive any additional materials from the President."

Effectively creating parallelism, or rhythm, by repeating phrases, she reminded the audience of the facts known by the Judiciary Committee. "We know the President met with Mr. Henry Peterson 27 times..." "We know about the Huston plan." (In Theodore White's words, this plan "spelled out a structure of super-police and super-espionage such as had never before been known in America."[11] It was approved by Nixon but ultimately revoked by direction of the Attorney General who informed the President of its illegality.) "We know about the break-in of the psychiatrist's office." (This break-in was arranged to obtain personal information about Daniel Ellsberg, a former Pentagon employee, who had stolen government files on the Vietnam war and given them, the "Pentagon Papers," to the New York *Times*.)

To summarize the major offenses committed by the President, Jordan used phrases filled with hard consonant sounds that reflected an accusatory tone. Such phrases included: "counseled his aides to commit perjury;" "concealed surreptitious entry;" and "attempted to compromise a Federal judge while publicly displaying his cooperation with the processes of criminal justice."

In the final sentences of her remarks, Jordan delivered a forceful conclusion. First, she presented the statement that left no doubt as to how she would vote on the impeachment question: "If the impeachment provision in the Constitution of the United States will not reach the offenses charged here, then perhaps that Eighteenth Century Constitution should be abandoned to a Twentieth Century paper shredder." Secondly, she asked a rhetorical question, believing her evidence and analysis had provided the answer. "Has the President committed offenses and planned and directed and acquiesced in a course of conduct which the Constitution will not tolerate?" Finally, she effectively used parallelism and alliteration to state that reason, not passion, must "guide our deliberations, guide our debate, and guide our decision."

The major strengths of Barbara Jordan's statement to the House Judiciary Committee were the organization and enumeration of her supporting materials, the vivid and forceful language she used to present her message, and her oratorical prowess. There are several components of effective delivery inherent in her rhetorical style. Like an opera singer or a concert pianist, she was an example of the rhetor as artist. Through vocal pitch and inflection, the rising and falling of her voice to provide emphasis, and a "rich" resonance that permeated and transmitted her words, she presented her observations and opinions on impeachment, and on Richard Nixon. Not only did she emphasize words and phrases through the use of vocal expression, she also spoke clearly and distinctly, carefully enunciating words and reflecting the oratorical skills she had been developing since her high school days in Houston. She understood the importance of varying her rate of speech and using pauses—short silences in her stream of facts, quotations and opinions which emphasized those points she deemed particularly important.

Perhaps the most significant component of Jordan's delivery on the evening of July 25, 1974, was her tone, her attitude toward the subject, which she portrayed in both the words she chose to use and the ways she spoke those words. Listening to Jordan gives her statement a dimension beyond that which one finds on the printed page. The way she speaks about the President and his actions conveys an accusatory tone which reflects more about her attitude toward the subject than the logic-based supporting materials communicated. One can hear anger throughout the speech, tempered by the use of logical proof. This tone gave power to her words and stature to her presence on the Committee. As *Newsweek* described the presentation: "Her anger was as stunning as her eloquence. Congresswoman Barbara Jordan of Texas sounded the most memorable indictment of Richard Nixon to emerge from the House impeachment hearings—and rocketed to national prominence on its echo." [12]

THE "AFTERMATH"

Two days after Barbara Jordan's statement was delivered, the House Judiciary Committee passed an article of impeachment against Richard Nixon. On Saturday, July 27th, the Committee decided that the President should stand trial in the Senate for obstruction of justice. On Monday, the 29th, the Committee approved impeachment Article II, citing the President's abuse of power; and on the following day a third article passed, charging Nixon with refusal to obey Congressional subpoenas for information needed in its inquiry. The hearings were then suspended.

Shortly thereafter the President and his advisers realized that one of the tapes released to the Special Prosecutor at the behest of the Supreme Court proved Nixon's knowledge of the Watergate break-in and his subsequent involvement in the "cover-up" that ensued. Nixon announced his resignation on Thursday evening, August 8, and officially left office the following day. Vice President Gerald R. Ford assumed the presidency. All these events occurred before the House Judiciary Committee submitted its articles of impeachment to the U.S. House of Representatives on August 20, 1974. On September 8, President Ford pardoned Richard Nixon for any crimes he might have committed during the Watergate scandal.

In his descriptive analysis of the people and events that became intertwined during the Watergate cover-up and the ensuing Congressional investigations, Theodore H. White called Barbara Jordan one of the "stars" of the House Judiciary Committee's hearings, "loosing a flow of Churchillian eloquence, of resonance, boom and grip so compelling as to make one forget to take notes—and remind oneself that here was a new force to be reckoned with in years to come." [13] Indeed, Jordan's oratory on the evening of July 25, 1974, earned her "overnight" public and press attention.

The day after her speech Jordan began receiving laudatory letters from citizens around the country, and one individual put up billboards around Houston which proclaimed: "THANK YOU, BARBARA JORDAN, FOR EXPLAINING THE CONSTITUTION TO US." [14] According to Newsweek: "Television interviewers suddenly queued up, congressmen…implored her to help their reelection bids, and President Gerald Ford abruptly invited the 38-year-old Democrat to join a delegation to the People's Republic of China." [15]

Due to her work in Congress, and the response to her televised statement in the Summer of 1974, Jordan was asked to give the keynote address at the National Democratic Convention in 1976. Later that year she was selected by Time magazine as one of its "Ten Women of the Year." She began to receive numerous honorary doctoral degrees, including one from Harvard, where she once yearned to go to law school.

Jordan served in Congress until 1978 and then retired from politics, convinced that, "I had reached a point where my words were going to be heard and attended to, whether I prefaced my name with Representative, Congresswoman, Senator, or whatever." [16] Consequently, she decided "to free my time in such a way that it could be structured by the country's needs as I perceived them. I decided to move in a new direction." [17] In 1979 she accepted a professorship in the Lyndon B. Johnson School of Public Affairs at the University of Texas at Austin and now holds the Lyndon B. Johnson Centennial Chair in National Policy.

Barbara Jordan's statement before the House Judiciary Committee on the impeachment of Richard M. Nixon was a turning point in her political career and professional life. It is most deserving of study, however, because it served as an eloquent reminder during a time of national crisis that the President of the United States is not above the law, and that those who understand and value the rights safeguarded by the Constitution are sometimes its strongest defenders.

Patricia D. Witherspoon is an associate dean at the University of Texas, Austin.

NOTES

1. Theodore H. White, *Breach of Faith* (New York: Atheneum Publishers, 1975), p. 5.
2. *Ibid*, p. 314.
3. Author's interview with Barbara C. Jordan, September 16, 1986, p. 5 of transcript.
4. *Ibid.*
5. *Ibid.*
6. Barbara Jordan and Shelby Hearon, *Barbara Jordan, A Self-Portrait* (Garden City, New York: Doubleday and Company, Inc., 1979), p. 184.
7. *Ibid.*
8. *Ibid*, p. 185.
9. *Ibid*, p. 186.
10. *Ibid*, p. 185.
11. White, p. 134.
12. *Newsweek*, November 4, 1974, p. 22.
13. White, p. 318.
14. Jordan and Hearon, p. 193.
15. *Newsweek*, p. 22.
16. Jordan and Hearon, pp. 249-250.
17. *Ibid*, p. 250.

PRESIDENTIAL RESIGNATION

Richard M. Nixon

White House, Washington, D.C., August 8, 1974 (Transcribed from the video, GREAT SPEECHES, VOLUME III)

Good evening. This is the 37th time I have spoken to you from this office where so many decisions have been made that shape the history of this nation. Each time I have done so to discuss with you some matter that I believe affected the national interest. In all the decisions I have made in my public life I have always tried to do what was best for the nation.

Throughout the long and difficult period of Watergate, I have felt it was my duty to persevere; to make every possible effort to complete the term of office to which you elected me. In the past few days, however, it has become evident to me that I no longer have a strong enough political base in the Congress to justify continuing that effort. As long as there was such a base, I felt strongly that it was necessary to see the constitutional process through to its conclusion; that to do otherwise would be unfaithful to the spirit of that deliberately difficult process, and a dangerously destabilizing precedent for the future. But with the disappearance of that base, I now believe that the constitutional purpose has been served. And there is no longer a need for the process to be prolonged.

I would have preferred to carry through to the finish whatever the personal agony it would have involved, and my family unanimously urged me to do so. But the interests of the nation must always come before any personal considerations. From the discussions I have had with Congressional and other leaders I have concluded that because of the Watergate matter I might not have the support of the Congress that I would consider necessary to back the very difficult decisions and carry out the duties of this office in the way the interests of the nation will require.

I have never been a quitter. To leave office before my term is completed is abhorrent to every instinct in my body. But as President I must put the interests of America first. America needs a full-time President and a full-time Congress, particularly at this time with problems we face at home and abroad. To continue to fight through the months ahead for my personal vindication would almost totally absorb the time and attention of both the President and the Congress in a period when our entire focus should be on the great issues of peace abroad and prosperity without inflation at home.

Therefore, I shall resign the Presidency effective at noon tomorrow. Vice President Ford will be sworn in as President at that hour in this office.

As I recall the high hopes for America with which we began this second term, I feel a great sadness that I will not be here in this office working on your behalf to achieve those hopes in the next two and a half years. But in turning over direction of the government to Vice President Ford I know, as I told the nation when I nominated him for that office 10 months ago, that the leadership of America will be in good hands. In passing this office to the Vice President I also do so with the profound sense of the weight of responsibility that will fall on his shoulders tomorrow, and therefore of the understanding, the patience, the cooperation he will need from all Americans. As he assumes that responsibility he will deserve the help and the support of all of us. As we look to the future, the first essential is to begin healing the wounds of this nation. To put the bitterness and divisions of the recent past behind us and to rediscover those shared ideals that lie at the heart of our strength and unity as a great and as a free people.

By taking this action, I hope that I will have hastened the start of that process of healing which is so desperately needed in America. I regret deeply any injuries that may have been done in the course of the events that led to this decision. I would say only that if some of my judgments were wrong—and some were wrong—they were made in what I believed at the time to be the best interests of the nation.

To those who have stood with me during these past difficult months, to my family, my friends, the many others who joined in supporting my cause because they believed it was right, I will be eternally grateful for your support. And to those who have not felt able to give me your support, let me say I leave with no bitterness toward those who have opposed me because all of us in the final analysis have been concerned with the good of the country however our judgments might differ. So let us all now join together in affirming that common commitment and in helping our new President succeed for the benefit of all Americans.

I shall leave this office with regret at not completing my term but with gratitude for the privilege of serving as your President for the past five and a half years. These years have been a momentous time in the history of our nation and the world. They have been a time of achievement in which we can all be proud—achievements that represent the shared efforts of the administration, the Congress and the people. But the challenges ahead are equally great. And they, too, will require the support and the efforts of a Congress and the people, working in cooperation with the new Administration.

We have ended America's longest war. But in the work of securing a lasting peace in the world, the goals ahead are even more far-reaching and more difficult. We must complete a structure of peace, so that it will be said of this generation—our generation of Americans—by the people of all nations, not only that we ended one war but that we prevented future wars.

We have unlocked the doors that for a quarter of a century stood between the United States and the People's Republic of China. We must now insure that the one-quarter of the world's people who live in the People's Republic of China will be and remain, not our enemies, but our friends.

In the Middle East, 100 million people in the Arab countries, many of whom have considered us their enemy for nearly 20 years, now look on us as their friends. We must continue to build on that friendship so that peace can settle at last over the Middle East and so that the cradle of civilization will not become its grave.

Together with the Soviet Union we have made the crucial breakthroughs that have begun the process of limiting nuclear arms. But we must set as our goal, not just limiting, but reducing and finally destroying these terrible weapons so that they cannot destroy civilization. And so that the threat of nuclear war will no longer hang over the world and the people, we have opened a new relation with the Soviet Union. We must continue to develop and expanded [sic] that new relationship so that the two strongest nations of the world will live together in cooperation rather than confrontation.

Around the world—in Asia, in Africa, in Latin America, in the Middle East—there are millions of people who live in terrible poverty, even starvation. We must keep as our goal turning away from production for war and expanding production for peace so that people everywhere on this earth can at last look forward, in their children's time if not in our own time, to having the necessities for a decent life.

Here in America we are fortunate that most of our people have not only the blessings of liberty but also the means to live full and good, and by the world's standards, even abundant lives. We must press on, however, toward a goal not only of more and better jobs but of full opportunity for every American, and of what we are striving so hard right now to achieve— prosperity without inflation.

For more than a quarter of a century in public life, I have shared in the turbulent history of this evening. I have fought for what I believed in. I have tried, to the best of my ability, to discharge those duties and meet those responsibilities that were entrusted to me. Sometimes I have succeeded, and sometimes I have failed. But always I have taken heart from what Theodore Roosevelt once said about the man in the arena whose face is marred by dust and sweat and blood, who strives valiantly, who errs and comes short again and again because there is not effort without error and shortcoming, but who does actually strive to do the deed, who knows the great enthusiasms, the great devotions, who spends himself in a worthy cause, who at the best knows in the end the triumphs of high achievements and with the worst, if he fails, at least fails while daring greatly. I pledge to you tonight that as long as I have a breath of life in my body I shall continue in that spirit. I shall continue to work for the great causes to which I have been dedicated throughout my years as a Congressman, a Senator, Vice President and President: the cause of peace—not just for America but among all nations—prosperity, justice and opportunity for all of our people.

There is one cause above all to which I have been devoted and to which I shall always be devoted for as long as I live. When I first took the oath of office as President five and a half years ago, I made this sacred commitment: to consecrate my office, my energies and all the wisdom I can summon to the cause of peace among nations. I've done my very best in all the days since to be true to that pledge. As a result of these efforts, I am confident that the world is a safer place today, not only for the people of America but for the people of all nations, and that all of our children have a better chance than before of living in peace rather than dying in war.

This, more than anything, is what I hoped to achieve when I sought the Presidency. This, more than anything, is what I hope will be my legacy to you, to our country, as I leave the Presidency.

To have served in this office is to have felt a very personal sense of kinship with each and every American. In leaving it, I do so with this prayer: May God's grace be with you in all the days ahead.

THE APOLOGY OF RICHARD M. NIXON

I must put the interests of America first.

CRITIC: Richard A. Katula

(This essay was originally published in Today's Speech, 23, No. 4, Fall, 1975, pp. 1-5. The author revised it for the express purpose of publication in this book.)

On August 8, 1974, President Richard M. Nixon delivered his final Presidential address to the American people. The scandal created by the 1972 break-in at the national headquarters of the Democratic Party in the Watergate apartment complex brought the Nixon administration to an end. Nixon's own release three days earlier of taped recordings which directly implicated him in the cover up of White House involvement in the affair and the subsequent loss of support by Republican leaders in Congress brought him to this hour of valediction. The man who had been President since January, 1969, and who had survived, by his own account, six crises in his twenty-eight years of public life faced two final challenges: resigning his office and saying farewell to the American people. Aside from its historical interest, Nixon's dual purpose of resigning and saying farewell makes this an interesting speech for critical examination. This essay examines Nixon's overall persuasive strategy of folding one event into a larger context of events and shifting the audience's attention to that larger context.

THEORETICAL BASIS FOR ANALYSIS

The critical approach taken in this analysis is *generic*; that is, the speech is analyzed as a type of speech that often occurs in public or political life and thus has certain features, both in substance and in style, that are common to the situation. By looking at Nixon's address as a specific instance of a larger class of speeches, we can see whether it meets the standards for speeches of its type or whether it fails to fulfill the expectations set for it by other speeches in the genre (Campbell and Jamieson, 1978, pp. 9-32).

Nixon's resignation speech fits predominantly into the class of speeches known as "apologies." Two communication scholars, B.L. Ware and Wil Linkugel, define the apology as a "public speech of self-defense," usually motivated by an attack upon a person's "moral nature, motives, or reputation" (1973, p. 274). Because this definition describes Nixon's situation on the night of August 8, it is helpful to apply the Ware-Linkugel classification of apologetic discourse to the Nixon address.

By using a theory of resolution of belief dilemmas developed by psychologist Robert Abelson, Ware and Linkugel discovered four persuasive strategies commonly used in apologetic discourse: (1) denial, (2) bolstering, (3) differentiation, and (4) transcendence (Abelson, 1959). In other words, when faced with having to change an audience's (or even one other person's) belief about one's behavior, a speaker has four available ways to defend himself or herself. A brief explanation of each strategy will clarify their meaning.

Denial is a strategy that consists of "the simple disavowal by the speaker of any participation in, relationship to, or positive sentiment toward, whatever it is that repels the audience" (Ware and Linkugel, p. 276). When a speaker denies, he or she simply says, "I had nothing to do with it and I condemn that kind of behavior in general."

Sometimes a speaker will deny by intent. That is, a speaker will say that he or she had no intention to do wrong or that if wrong was committed, he or she is innocent of it by lack of intent. In fact, a speaker will often defend wrongful behavior by arguing that is was not wrong because it was motivated by some greater objective.

Bolstering is the obverse of denial because it attempts to get the audience to identify with something they view favorably. When a speaker bolsters, she or he does not try to change the audience's view of the behavior under question; rather, the speaker tries to create a positive feeling in the audience, perhaps by drawing them into the situation. We have all heard someone rationalize his or her behavior; for instance, a shoplifter might condone his behavior by noting that the store is "ripping people off with its prices," thereby trying not to deny the shoplifting charge but to get the audience to see it as justifiable behavior. When a speaker tries to get the audience to identify favorably with him or her in some way, the speaker is bolstering.

Denial and bolstering are called *reformative* persuasive strategies because they involve admitting that something occurred, but they do not admit the accusation against the speaker with regard to the behavior. Denial tries to improve the speaker's position by denying involvement in and condemning the behavior itself. Bolstering tries to improve the speaker's position by identifying with something the listeners think of favorably. The purpose of reformative strategies, then, is to repair the negative view held by the audience toward the speaker as a result of the accusation.

The third strategy, *differentiation*, involves particularizing the charge at hand. When a speaker differentiates, he or she tries to actually change the meaning of an event by separating it from the larger, more homogeneous context (Ware and Linkugel, p. 278). We often hear people admit that they did something wrong, but they will add that it was an isolated incident and that, in general, they behave properly. "I am not a bad person," the speaker is saying, "I just made one mistake." Notice that the speaker is actually trying to change the nature of the event itself by minimizing it as a once-in-a-lifetime event in his or her life.

The final strategy, *transcendence*, is the obverse of differentiation in that the speaker tries to fold the behavior of which he or she is accused into the larger context. "Yes, a mistake was made," the speaker says, "but let's look at the bigger picture." Transcendence often involves a change of subject altogether so that the actual event gets lost in the portrayal of other events seen by the speaker as more important. Once again, transcendence involves actually changing the nature of the accusation by folding it into something else.

Differentiation and transcendence are considered to be *transformative* strategies because they attempt to change the audience's view of the accusation by asking them to see it differently, either as a minor event separate from the speaker's usual behavior (differentiation) or as a minor event when viewed in the context of the person's entire life (transcendence).

Having mapped the four strategies of apologetic discourse, Ware and Linkugel assert that, "Speakers usually assume one of four major rhetorical postures when speaking in defense of their characters: absolution, vindication, explanation, or justification (Ware and Linkugel, p. 282). Each one of these postures utilizes one reformative strategy and one transformative strategy. Thus, each may be viewed as a sub-genre of the apology. Put simply, when a public figure is accused of improper behavior and is forced to defend himself or herself in a speech of apology, he or she will usually choose to first address the charge and then change the subject to talk about something else. Let's see briefly how each posture does this.

Absolution is a posture used by a speaker to seek acquittal of the charges. The speaker uses *denial* to deny the charge at hand and *differentiation* to show that he or she is incapable of such behavior because it would be out of character for them. In other words, "I didn't do it, I couldn't do it."

Vindication as a rhetorical posture is a more generalized version of absolution involving the use of *denial* and *transcendence* strategies. When a speaker seeks to be vindicated of a charge, he or she will deny the charge and then move to a discussion of his or her entire life in order to bury the charge in the much larger context. The speaker is saying, in so many words, "I didn't do this bad thing, but I have done lots of good things."

Explanation postures involve the use of *bolstering* and *differentiation* strategies. The speaker assumes that if the audience understands his or her motives, actions, beliefs, or whatever, they will be unable to condemn the behavior (Ware and Linkugel, p. 284). In a sense, the speaker is saying that, "We have all been in similar situations. This one is no different, and we will overcome it."

Finally, *justification* as a rhetorical posture in apologetic discourse uses *bolstering* and *transcendence* strategies to persuade. The speaker attempts to say, "We are all human and subject to error, and when we sum up our lives, we need to look at the big picture we have painted through our lives." The speaker is justifying his or her behavior by casting the inevitability of error (a more positive view of wrongdoing) into the larger context of success.

Ware and Linkugel state that their classification scheme lacks an evaluative dimension. The value of the system is that it allows the critic to analyze the speech by mapping the strategies used by the speaker, seeing them coupled together to form overall rhetorical (persuasive) postures or defenses. The critic is still required to form a judgment following the analysis. Now that the theory has been clarified, we can move to the analysis and then form a judgment about Nixon's resignation address.

ANALYSIS OF THE SPEECH

Nixon's resignation speech fits into the vindicative mode of apologetic discourse. While strategies of denial and transcendence cannot be wholly separated, a vindicative pattern emerges during the speech. In the resignation portion of the address, Nixon attempted to deny guilt in the Watergate cover up by a "denial of intent" strategy. He denied that his resignation was prompted by guilt by arguing that the process of proving his innocence would be long and agonizing and would deprive the nation of a full-time President. Thus, he was resigning in the "best interests of the nation." Finally, in the farewell portion of the address, Nixon attempted transcendence by constructing a larger context, the "legacy of peace" which he felt should be the measure of his presidency.

Mr. Nixon recognized the futility of a strategy of pure denial. As Ware and Linkugel note, "Strategies of denial are obviously useful to the speaker only to the extent that such

negations do not constitute a known distortion of reality or to the point that they
conflict with other beliefs held by the audience (p. 276). In Nixon's case, his release of
tapes of conversations with H.R. Haldeman which showed that Nixon sought to use
the CIA to slow FBI investigations of Watergate, was conclusive proof to most
Americans of his guilt. Even prior to this, so much evidence had been developed during
the Congressional hearings on Watergate that two bills of impeachment had been
passed. Finally, Nixon's Gallup Poll ratings had fallen so low (27% acceptability in
November, 1973) that he could gain little by outright denial.

In view of such evidence, Nixon's defensive strategy became denial of intent.
Decisions made by him with reference to Watergate were based upon larger interests,
he asserted, and his intent was not to cover up wrongdoing in his administration, but
to serve the best interests of the nation. The actual statement of denial is quite brief,
and is, in fact, a restrictive clause in a "best interest of the nation" statement:

> I regret deeply any injuries that may have been done in the course of the events that led to
> this decision. I would say only that if some of my judgments were wrong—and some were
> wrong—they were made in what I believed at the time to be in the best interests of the
> nation.

Nixon placed his misguided judgments within a larger context: the national interest.
The "best interest of the nation" appeal appeared explicitly six times in the address and
implicitly was the theme which bound the first half of the speech together. For instance,
Nixon emphasized that his personal resolve to continue his term of office was
subordinated to the nation's need to have a full-time President:

> I have never been a quitter. To leave office before my term is completed is abhorrent to every
> instinct in my body. But as President I must put the interests of America first.

In another statement, Nixon notes that his "political base" had weakened and he
could not carry out the duties for which he had been elected, despite the fact that he
"...would have preferred to carry through the defense whatever the personal agony it
would have involved, and my family unanimously urged me to do so. But the interests
of the nation must always come before any personal considerations."

Through such emotional, pathetic appeals, Nixon presented himself as a victim of
the national interest, or at the least a servant to it. Having done so, he continued his
vindication in the farewell portion of the address by adopting transformative strategies.
His denial of intent in the Watergate affair and his resignation prompted by the
national interest became the materials for Mr. Nixon's construction of his own legacy.
Through transcendence to a "legacy of peace" strategy, Nixon subordinated the entire
Watergate affair and his resignation to the larger victories of his administration. It is
here that Nixon's decision to resign and say farewell in one address become clear as a
persuasive strategy.

First, there are Nixon's personal victories. Watergate is characterized as just one more
episode in the turbulent history of the past quarter century. It is simply one loss amidst
a greater number of wins. Most important is not the win or the loss but the personal
victory of having made the team, played in the game and given his all. Although this
strategy permeates the second half of the address, it is strikingly revealed in one
particularly emotional appeal:

Sometimes I have succeeded, sometimes I have failed, but always I have taken heart from what Theodore Roosevelt once said about the man in the arena whose face is marred by dust and sweat and blood. Who strives valiantly. Who errs and comes short again because there is not effort without error in shortcoming. But who actually does strive to do the deed. Who knows the great enthusiasms, the great devotions. Who spends himself in a worthy cause. Who at best knows in the end the triumphs of high achievement. And with the worst, he fails—at least fails while daring greatness.

The use of such strikingly emotional references is a familiar Nixon strategy. From his notorious "Checker's Address" when he adamantly refused to return a little puppy, "Checkers," given to his two little girls as a present to his press conference after losing the governor's race in California in 1962, when he noted that, "You won't have Nixon to kick around anymore…" listeners had come to expect a sometimes mawkish statement to slip into Nixon's rhetoric.

Along with his personal victory, Nixon reiterates the nation's victories during his administration; victories he would like us to view as transcending the minor setback at Watergate. In familiar tones, Nixon reminds the audience that, "We have ended the longest war [Vietnam]." Further, "We have unlocked the doors that for a quarter of a century stood between the United States and the People's Republic of China." We now have "friends" in the Middle East, and a "new relationship" with the Soviet Union. In short, Mr. Nixon's foreign policy is his legacy, and it is a legacy of peace. Nixon concludes:

As a result of these efforts, I am confident that the world is a safer place today, not only for the people of America, but for the people of all nations, and that all of our children have a better chance than before of living in peace, rather than dying in war.

Following this remark, Nixon said goodbye to the American people. Through his vindicative apology, he hoped to persuade the American public that he was not intentionally responsible for Watergate and that Watergate was really a minor affair blown out of proportion by political enemies and that his real legacy was one of peace.

As one looks at the television screen, one cannot help but notice Nixon's manner. His composure during his sixteen minutes before the camera is at once laudable and uncharacteristic. *Time* magazine noted that the speech was delivered with "remarkable restraint, given the circumstances…." (August 19, 1974, p. 14). Indeed, the following morning Nixon delivered an emotional tirade to the White House staff just prior to his departure for his home in California. What can account for the control exhibited on this night?

The look on Nixon's face is one of defeat. Having played every card, he now was forced to fold. He appears to us as a man who has already experienced the worst and is now simply telling us about it. The speech itself is an anti-climax, and it shows in no more telling way than the blank, exhausted facial expression and the tone of voice more characteristic of a eulogy than a personal defense.

Richard Nixon was never known as a "congenial," or "personal," communicator in the mold of, for instance, John F. Kennedy. And Nixon was at his worst when communicating with the public, the American people, especially when warmth and good humor were the requisite moods to capture. Therefore, when we notice little nonverbal communication, little enthusiasm in gesture or tone, we understand that this is an embattled orator, one who has already lost and is struggling for his dignity in this most humiliating moment.

EVALUATION

Audience reactions to the Nixon resignation speech were diverse and seemed to fall along party lines or one's predilection for tastefulness or content. Republicans appeared to be sad but relieved. Senator Barry Goldwater was quoted as saying to former Secretary of State William P. Rogers, "You would have been proud of him today." Rabbi Bernard Korff, Nixon's staunchest public supporter and chair of the National Citizens Committee for Fairness to the Presidency, said that Nixon "...made the supreme sacrifice." John O. Pastore, influential Democratic senator from Rhode Island observed that, "It is a tragic valedictory done with dignity" (Providence *Journal*, August 9, 1974, pp. 7-9).

On the opposite end of the spectrum, a *Nation* editorial noted, "Few confessions match Nixon's for moral squalor, irredeemable tackiness, poverty of imagination, and absence of authentic personal feeling" (August 17, 1974, p. 98). Others in the public sector felt that Nixon should still be prosecuted for Watergate connected crimes. For example, Helen Gahagan Douglas, who lost to Nixon in the 1950 California senatorial race and was the victim of Nixon tactics linking her to communist causes, felt that an impeachment hearing in the Senate, where Nixon would have been found guilty or not guilty, "...would have educated us as to what a President can do and cannot do; what Congress must do and must not give up...if we are to retain our freedom" (NBC interview, August 9, 1974). Noted historian Arthur Schlesinger was quoted in *Newsweek* magazine as saying, "In a way, Mr. Nixon was consistent to the finish. He showed himself as morally obtuse about Watergate at the end as at the beginning. To the very last he gave no evidence of recognizing that he had done anything really wrong" (August 19, 1974, p. 59).

Perhaps the spectrum of effects is best characterized by two CBS reporters, Dan Rather and Roger Mudd, who commented immediately after the speech. Rather noted that, despite our private opinions about Richard Nixon, "He gave to this moment a touch of class, a touch of majesty" (CBS commentary, August 8, 1974). Mudd, reacting less to tone and taste and more to content, observed:

> From a congressional point of view, it was not a satisfactory speech. It did not deal with the realities of why he was leaving. There was no accounting in the speech of how he got there, why he was leaving that oval room...in the absence of any explanation or any acknowledgment of the President's responsibility in the Watergate cover-up, the viewer is left to conclude that it was simply some craven politicians in the Congress who collapsed in their defense of the President, and solely, because of that was he having to leave the Presidency. I think it was from a congressional standpoint realistic to think that the President would make some bow toward the Hill to accept the blame that he admitted last week was his, but there was nothing like that tonight (CBS commentary, August 8, 1974).

From this diversity of responses an important fact emerges: no one, not even Nixon's most ardent supporters, speaks of his being vindicated. No commentary that this critic could locate referred to a changed or altered affect or relationship toward Nixon and his involvement in Watergate. Nor does Nixon appear to have succeeded in dissolving

Watergate into the homogeneous mass he called "the legacy of peace." On the basis of effects, then, it can be concluded that Nixon's speech was delivered tastefully, but that it failed in its basic purpose. It is no wonder, then, that a popular magazine such as *Time* would call the speech "...a peculiar performance" (August 19,1974, p. 9), while the equally popular *Newsweek* would note that, "There was grace but no contrition in his surrender...." (August 19, 1974, p. 16).

The purpose of an apology, as Ware and Linkugel note, is to offer a personal, direct refutation of charges made against a person's moral character:

> In life, an attack upon a person's character, upon his worth as a human being, does seem to demand a direct response. The questioning of a man's moral nature, motives, or reputation is qualitatively different from challenging his policies. Witnesses to such personal charges seem completely and most easily satisfied only by the most personal of responses by the accused (p. 274).

When a speaker defends himself or herself against an accusation, the audience needs to feel closure, the sense of completeness communicators feel when they sense that some reality has been shared. Until closure has occurred for a set of experiences, the Gestalt notion of "unfinished business" is present between the communicators. Thus, as critic Edwin Black suggests, an apology ought to be an engulfment of the controversy (1978, p. 155). Sound advice to be sure. Until an audience perceives that an apologist has made, "the most personal of responses" (Ware and Linkugel, p. 274) and until an audience perceives that the apologist has told the entire story, closure cannot occur.

Nixon attempted to secure closure by using the farewell portion of the address to absorb the resignation portion. The former aims to transcend and thus engulf the latter. But by failing to secure closure in the resignation part of the speech which actually addressed the charges made against Nixon's nature, motives and reputation, the audience resisted Nixon's efforts at transcendence. His attempt to vindicate himself failed, and Nixon's total effort is thus seen as transparent.

The major deterrent to closure in Nixon's resignation speech was his denial of intent strategy. Tapes released by Nixon himself and his own televised comments on August 5, 1974, clearly indicted him as chief conspirator in the Watergate cover-up affair. As the *Nation* put it, "Richard Nixon convicted Richard Nixon. The tapes and his own statements have been primarily responsible for his downfall" (August 17, 1974, p. 98). Nixon's admission on August 5 that he had monitored the "damaging" tapes in May, 1974, and that he had kept their contents from the House Judiciary Committee and his own attorneys negated the value of the denial of intent since this strategy flew in the face of audience perceptions of reality.

Compounding the problem, Nixon implicitly attempted to shift the burden of guilt to Congress and the exigencies of political life. Even casual observers were aware why Republican leaders had abandoned Mr. Nixon, and the record is clear that the final abandonment came only after the August 5th disclosure of personal involvement. Similarly, blaming national interest defeated any attempt at closure since Nixon offered no evidence that his cover-up of Watergate was related to foreign or domestic policy.

The vagueness of Nixon's address may cause a psychological scar as deep as that made by the break-in at Watergate itself. The public clangor over President Ford's pardon of Nixon clearly indicates that closure was not achieved and that closure was most needed. The *New Republic*, for instance, noted:

Who is there who does not want the wounds of Watergate to be healed? But they won't be healed by concealing the infection, its nature and cause; it will only fester.... Justice has not been done, and mercy has been shown for behavior that has not been identified or admitted (March 30, 1974, p. 6).

Richard Nixon simply chose the wrong strategy for his situation. And it is somewhat clear why he did. He chose a strategy that had worked for him during his other televised apology, the slush fund scandal of the 1952 Presidential campaign. In his "Checker's Address," (his response to the charges of having a slush fund) Mr. Nixon also presented a speech in two parts, the first a response to the charge and the second a rousing campaign speech for the Eisenhower-Nixon ticket. In the campaign speech portion of the address, Mr. Nixon shifted the question before the American people from whether he was guilty or not of misusing campaign funds for his own personal purposes to whether Eisenhower should be President and whether he, Richard Nixon, should remain on the ticket to help fight communism and corruption in government. In the instance of the "Checker's Address," Nixon was overwhelmingly successful in rousing public opinion—not on the question of his guilt or innocence, but on the question of which ticket should be elected. One must speculate that Nixon, caught in this moment of crisis, retreated to a strategy that had worked for him once, hoping that it would work for him again. But it did not.

In the final analysis, the Nixon resignation speech rates quite low as a standard or model and instead becomes one more symptom of decay in the art of apologizing. Closure did not occur simply because Nixon failed to address the questions that had forced the speech. Because he did not engulf the controversy centered on the Watergate affair, the speech did not improve the acrimonious political climate nor contribute to the development of a sense of well-being and peace within the body politic. Rather than being a vindication of Richard Nixon, the address beckons us to consider the moral state of public discourse in our country and the integrity of the nation's leaders in general.

Richard A. Katula is professor and chairperson of the Speech Communication Department at Northeastern University.

NOTES

Abelson, R. (1959). "Modes of Resolution of Belief Dilemmas," *Journal of Conflict Resolution*, 3, pp. 343-352.

Black, E. (1978). *Rhetorical Criticism*. Madison: University of Wisconsin Press.

Campbell, K.K. and Jamieson, K.H. (1978). *Form and Genre: Shaping Rhetorical Action*. Falls Church, VA: Speech Communication Association.

Douglas, H. (August 8, 1974). Commentary on NBC television.

Editorial (August 17, 1974). *Nation*. p. 98.

Mudd, R. (August 8, 1974). Commentary on CBS television.

Newsweek (August 19, 1974, entire issue).

Osborne, J. (March 30, 1975). "Unpardonable Offense, " *New Republic*, p. 6.

Rather, D. (August 8, 1974). Commentary on CBS television.

Sekeres, J.H. (August 9, 1974). "Republicans Sad But Relieved," *The Providence Journal*, p. 1

Time magazine, (August 19, 1974, p. 9).

Ware, B.L. and Linkugel, W. (October, 1973). "They Spoke in Defense of Themselves: On the Generic Criticism of Apologia," *Quarterly Journal of Speech*, 59, pp. 273-283.

STATEMENT ON THE KAL 007 DISASTER

Jeane Kirkpatrick

United Nations Security Council, New York City, September 6, 1983
(Transcribed from excerpts on the video, GREAT SPEECHES, VOLUME III)

Most of the world outside the Soviet Union has heard by now of the Korean flight 007 carrying 269 persons between New York and Seoul which strayed off course into Soviet air space, was tracked by Soviet radar, was targeted by a Soviet SU-15, whose pilot coolly, and after careful consideration, fired two air-launched missiles which destroyed the Korean airliner and apparently its 269 passengers and crew.

This calculated attack on a civilian airliner, unarmed, undefended, as civilian airliners always are, has shocked the world. Only the Soviet people have still not heard about this attack on the KAL 007 and the death of the passengers because the Soviet Government has not acknowledged firing on the Korean airliner. Indeed, not until September 5 did Soviet officials acknowledge publicly that KAL 007 had disappeared in its icy waters. The Soviet Government has not been silent about the plane, however. It has merely lied.

On September 1, Foreign Minister Gromyko announced, and I quote:

> Fighters of the anti-aircraft defense, which were sent aloft toward the intruder plane, tried to give it assistance in directing it to the nearest air field, but the intruder plane did not react to the signals and warnings from the Soviet fighters and continued its flight in the direction of the Sea of Japan.

End quotation.

The United States Government, in co-operation with the Government of Japan, has decided to spread the evidence before this Council and the world. It is available on the video tape which will be played. On this tape you will hear the voices of pilots of Soviet interceptors, which included three SU-15 Flagons and one MiG-23 Flogger, including the SU-15 pilot who pulled the trigger which released the missiles that destroyed the Korean Air Lines flight 007.

[The following is a transcript of the tapes as played aloud and displayed in the Security Council chamber and does not appear on the videotape.]

VOICE: Soviet radar began tracking the Korean airliner at 1551 GMT. At 1635 GMT, the Soviets noted the 747 actually was flying over their land mass. At 1728 GMT, a Korean airliner was flying over the Sea of Okhotsk the same time a US reconnaissance flight RC-135 was landing at a base on the Aleutian Islands. The RC-135 had been flying a routine mission in support of the SALT compliance agreements off the Kamchatka Peninsula. At 1826 GMT, a full hour after the US reconnaissance flight had landed, the Korean airliner was destroyed near the Soviet Sakhalin Islands 1,200 miles away.

The tape you are about to hear begins at 1756 GMT, one hour before the Korean airliner was shot down. The communication is from four Soviet fighter pilots talking to their ground controllers while tracking the Korean airliner.

(interpretation from Russian)
{"Course 100 in a climb to 8(000 metres).
I didn't understand. What course? My course is 100.
I am executing.
Course 50.
(Answer)
On course 240.
I see it.
Roger. Understood. I'm flying behind.
Course 30—8,000 (metres).
Executing course 100.
Roger. Distance to airfield?
Roger.
Altitude 4,900. I'm executing.
I didn't understand.
I am executing.
Fuel remainder, three metric tons.
Roger. Repeat the course.
To the left, probably. Not to the right.
Carry out course 260.
On course 260. Understood.
Course 220—7,500 (metres).
Roger.
Should I turn off the weapons system?
163 needs to drop his wing tanks.
Yes, it has turned. The target is 80 degrees to my left.
Executing 240.
Course 240. Roger.
Executing 220.
Executing.
Course 220.
I didn't understand.
(The target's strobe) light is blinking.
Course 245—7,500 (metres).
8,000 (metres). Roger.
Course 280.
4,500 (metres).
Course 280.
Executing.
I see it visually and on radar.
Roger.
Executing 10 (degrees) left.
I have dropped my tanks. I dropped them. Executing.
I see it. I'm locked on to the target.
Roger.

The target isn't responding to IFF.

The target's course is 240 degrees.

(The weapons system) is turned on.

Roger. It's still on the same course for now.

Roger.

Roger. I have (enough) speed. I don't need to turn on my after-burner.

My fuel remainder is 2,700.

I've dropped my tanks: one at 4,000, one at 3,800.

Course 230.

The target's course is still the same—240.

Executing.

I am in lock-on.

Course 240.

The target's course is 240.

Yes.

Repeat the azimuth.

Roger.

Deputat sees me (on radar).

Deputat is inquiring: Do you see the target or not?

Do you see (it)?

Are you calling 805?

Who's calling 805?

I see it.

Karnaval does not see (unspecified).

Repeat .

Executing.

The ANO (air navigational lights) are burning. The (strobe) light is flashing.

I'm at 7,500, course 230.

I am closing on the target.

Have I enough time.

Repeat .

Executing.

I am flying behind the target at a distance of 25. Do you see me?

(Call)

Fiddlesticks. I'm going, that is, my Z.O. (indicator) is lit. (The missile warhead is already locked on.)

Answering.

I answered.

I need to approach it (closer).

I'm turning lock-on off and I'm approaching the target.

163?

I have switched off lock-on.

(Right now) I can't see it.

Exactly. I have executed (unspecified).

Executing.

Yes, I'm approaching the target. I'm going in closer.

The target's (strobe) light is blinking. I have already approached the target to a distance of about two (kilometres).

The target is at 10,000 (metres).
I see both, distance 10 (and) 15 kilometres.
What are the instructions?
Roger.
The target is decreasing speed.
I am going round it. I'm already moving in front of the target.
I have increased speed.
No. It is decreasing speed.
It should have been earlier. How can I chase it? I'm already abeam of the target.
Now I have to fall back a bit from the target.
Repeat.
The target's altitude is 10,000 (metres).
It is located 70 degrees to the left of me.
I'm dropping back. Now I will try a rocket.
12 (kilometres) to the target. I see both.
I'm in a right turn on a course of 300.
Executing.
Roger. I am in lock-on.
I am turning to a course of 30.
Roger.
I am closing on the target. I am in lock-on. Distance to target is 8 (kilometres).
I have already switched it on.
On a course of 30.
ZG. Missile warheads locked on.
I have executed the launch.
The target is destroyed.
I am breaking off attack.
What are (my) instructions?
(Call)
(The indicator/s for) my wing tanks lit up. The fuel remainder differs by 600 litres for now.
Fuel remainder 1,600.
I am executing. What is the distance to the airfield?
Roger."}

[Mrs. Kirkpatrick's Statement continues:]

The transcript we have just heard, Mr. President, needs little explanation. Quite simply, it establishes that the Soviets decided to shoot down a civilian airliner, shot it down, murdering the 269 persons on board, and lied about it. The transcript of the pilot's cockpit conversations illuminates several key points. The interceptor which shot KAL 007 down had the airliner in sight for over 20 minutes before firing his missiles. Contrary to what the Soviets have repeatedly stated, the interceptor pilot saw the airliner's navigation lights and reported that fact to the ground on three occasions. Contrary to Soviet statements, the pilot makes no mention of firing any warning shots—only the firing of the missiles, which he said struck the target. Contrary to Soviet statements, there is no indication whatsoever that the interceptor pilot made any attempt either to communicate with the airliner or to signal it for it to land in accordance with accepted international practice. Indeed, the Soviet interceptor planes may be technically incapable of communicating by radio with civilian aircraft, presumably out of fear of Soviet pilot defections.

Perhaps the most shocking fact learned from the transcript is that at no point did the pilots raise the question of the identity of the target aircraft, nor at any time did the interceptor pilots refer to it as anything other than "the target." The only activity bearing on the…the identity of the aircraft was a statement by the pilot of the attacking interceptor that "the target isn't responding to IFF." This means the aircraft did not respond to the electronic interrogation by which military aircraft identify friends or foes. But of course the Korean airliner or any civilian airliner could not have responded to IFF, because commercial aircraft are not equipped to do so.

In the days following the destruction of KAL 007, Soviet leaders and the Soviet press have said repeatedly they do not understand what all the fuss is about. They began by accusing the United States of creating a hullabaloo about nothing, and more recently they have accused us of a provocation, implying, though never quite saying, that we provoked them into shooting down an airliner that strayed into their space, provoked them into violating the internationally agreed upon standards and practices of behavior.

Why did the Soviet Union violate these norms? Why have they lied about it? Two reasons most often advanced to explain why the Soviet pilot shot down the airliner are, first, that it was a mistake—the mistake of a trigger-happy pilot who, with his ground controller, followed a philosophy of shoot now, identify later. But if pilot error was responsible for this tragic mistake, why has the Soviet Government not said so? Why has it lied? And why is it complementing its murderous attack on KAL 007 with a lying attack on the United States for provocation and aggression?

As I considered this question, my mind returned to a debate that took place in this Security Council some 21 years ago, when my distinguished predecessor, Governor Adlai Stevenson of Illinois, called the attention of the Council to the unmistakable evidence that a series of facilities for launching offensive nuclear missiles were being installed in the Western hemisphere. Soviet representative Ambassador Zorin flatly denied those charges and, as Soviet representatives so often do, coupled his denial with a vicious attack on the United States. Calling our attention to threatening Soviet behavior, Zorin asserted, only masked the United States' own aggression and piracy. But Adlai Stevenson too had evidence to back up his charge, photographic evidence as irrefutable as the audio tapes we have heard today. The fact is that violence and lies are regular instruments of Soviet policy. Soviet officials regularly behave as though truth were only a function of force and will; as if the truth were only what they said it is; as if violence were an instrument of first resort in foreign affairs.

We are reminded once again that the Soviet Union is a State based on the dual principles of callousness and mendacity dedicated to the rule of force. Here is how Lenin described the dictatorship of the proletariat in 1920. He said, and I quote:

> The scientific concept of dictatorship means nothing more than unrestricted power, absolutely unimpeded by law or regulations and resting directly on force.

It is this principle of force, this mentality of force, that lies at the root of the Korean Air Line tragedy. This is the reality revealed to the world by the tragedy. It is a reality we must all ponder as we consider threats to peace and human rights that face us today.

The United States deeply believes that immediate steps should be taken, here in the United Nations, to decrease the likelihood of any repetition of the tragedy of KAL 007. We ask our colleagues to join with us in the coming days in the effort to wrest from this tragedy new clarity about the character of our world and new, constructive efforts to render us all more secure, in the air and on the ground.

Thank you, Mr. President.

CHAPTER 6:
Legislative Speeches: National Policy

Legislative speaking for national policy promotes domestic acceptance of a proposed course of action. This type of political communication ranges from advocacy for a general policy to proposing a specific piece of national legislation.

In his 1942 State-of-the-Union Address, Franklin Roosevelt faced a nation preparing for war after the Japanese attack on Pearl Harbor. The critical analysis by Kurt Ritter and Lloyd Rohler evaluates how Roosevelt defined the threat and provided direction to an imperiled nation. In another wartime State-of-the-Union Address, George Bush assesses Desert Storm. Lyndon Johnson displayed characteristic determination in his speech supporting the Voting Rights Act of 1965. As an example of a non-officeholder attempting to influence policy, Jerry Falwell's speech before the National Religious Broadcasters demonstrates why he, as a cleric, was also a potent political force during the '80's.

THE STATE-OF-THE-UNION, 1942

Franklin D. Roosevelt

Joint Session of Congress, Washington, D.C., January 8, 1942 (Transcribed from the video, GREAT SPEECHES, VOLUME I)

In fulfilling my duty to report upon the State of the Union, I am proud to say to you that the spirit of the American people was never higher than it is today—the Union was never more closely knit together and this country was never more deeply determined to face the solemn tasks before it. The response of the American people has been instantaneous, and it will be sustained until our security is assured.

Exactly one year ago today I said to this Congress: "When, the dictators...are ready to make war upon us, they will not wait for an act of war on our part.... They—not we—will choose the time and the place and the method of their attack."

We now know their choice of the time: a peaceful Sunday morning—December 7, 1941. We know their choice of the place: an outpost, an American outpost in the Pacific. We know their choice of the method: the method of Hitler himself.

Japan's scheme of conquest goes back half a century. It was not merely a policy of seeking living room: it was a plan which included the subjugation of all the peoples in the Far East and in the islands of the Pacific, and the domination of that ocean by Japanese military and naval control of the western coasts of North, Central, and South America. The development of this ambitious conspiracy was marked by the war against China in 1894; the subsequent occupation of Korea; the- war against Russia in 1904; the illegal fortification of the mandated Pacific islands following 1920; the seizure of Manchuria in 1931; and the invasion of China in 1937.

A similar policy of criminal conquest was adopted by Italy. The Fascists first revealed their imperial designs in Libya and Tripoli. In 1935 they seized Abyssinia. Their goal was the domination of all North Africa, Egypt, parts of France and the entire Mediterranean world.

But the dreams of empire of the Japanese and Fascist leaders was [sic] modest in comparison with the gargantuan aspirations of Hitler and his Nazis. Even before they came to power in 1933, their plans for that conquest had been drawn. They provided for ultimate domination, not of any one section of the world, but of the whole earth and all the oceans on it.

When Hitler organized his Berlin-Rome-Tokyo alliance, all these plans of conquest became a single plan. Under this, in addition to her own schemes of conquest, Japan's role was obviously to cut off our supply of weapons of war to Britain, and Russia and China—weapons which increasingly were speeding the day of Hitler's doom. The act of Japan at Pearl Harbor was intended to stun us—to terrify us to such an extent that we would divert our industrial and military strength to the Pacific area, or even to our own continental defense.

The plan has failed in its purpose. We have not been stunned. We have not been terrified or confused. This very reassembling of the Seventy-seventh Congress today is proof of that; for the mood of quiet, grim resolution which here prevails bodes ill for those who conspired and collaborated to murder world peace. And that mood is stronger than any mere desire for revenge. It expresses the will of the American people to make very certain that the world will never so suffer again.

Admittedly, we have been faced with hard choices. It was bitter, for example, not to be able to relieve the heroic and historic defenders of Wake Island. It was bitter for us not to be able to land a million men in a thousand ships in the Philippine Islands. But this adds only to our determination to see to it that the Stars and Stripes will fly again over Wake and Guam. Yes, see to it that the brave people of the Philippines will be rid of Japanese imperialism; and will live in freedom and security and independence.

Powerful and offensive actions must and will be taken in proper time. The consolidation of the United Nations' total war effort against our common enemies is being achieved. That was and is the purpose of conferences which have been held during the past two weeks in Washington, and Moscow and Chungking. That is the primary objective of the declaration of solidarity signed in Washington on January 1, 1942, by 26 nations against the Axis powers.

Difficult choices may have to be made in the months to come. We do not shrink from such decisions. We and those united with us will make those decisions with courage and determination. Plans have been laid here and in the other capitals for coordinated and cooperative action by all the United Nations—military action and economic action. Already we have established, as you know, unified command of land, sea, and air forces in the southwestern Pacific theater of war. There will be a continuation of conferences and consultations among military staffs, so that the plans and operations of each will fit into the general strategy designed to crush the enemy. We shall not fight isolated wars—each Nation going its own way. These 26 nations are united—not in spirit and determination alone, but in the broad conduct of the war in all its phases.

For the first time since the Japanese and the Fascists and the Nazis started along their blood-stained course of conquest they now face the fact that superior forces are assembling against them. Gone forever are the days when the aggressors could attack and destroy their victims one by one. Destroy them without unity of resistance. We of the United Nations will so dispose our forces that we can strike at the common enemy wherever the greatest damage can be done him. The militarists of Berlin and Tokyo started this war. But the massed, angered forces of common humanity will finish it.

Destruction...destruction of the material and spiritual centers of civilization—this has been and still is the purpose of Hitler and his Italian and Japanese chessmen. They would wreck the power of the British Commonwealth and of Russia and of China and of the Netherlands—and then combine all their forces to achieve their ultimate goal, the conquest of the United States. They know that victory for us means victory for freedom. They know that victory for us means victory for the institution of democracy—the ideal of the family, the simple principles of common decency and humanity. They know that victory for us means victory for religion. And they could not tolerate that. The world is too small to provide adequate "living room" for both Hitler and God. In proof of that, the Nazis have now announced their plan for enforcing their new German, pagan religion all over the world—a plan by which the Holy Bible and the Cross of Mercy would be displaced by Mein Kampf and the swastika and the naked sword.

Our own objectives are clear; the objective of smashing the militarism imposed by war lords upon their enslaved peoples—the objective of liberating the subjugated

Nations—the objective of establishing and securing freedom of speech, freedom of religion, freedom from want, and freedom from fear everywhere in the world.

We shall not stop short of these objectives—nor shall we be satisfied merely to gain them and then call it a day. I know that I speak for the American people—and I have good reason to believe that I speak also for all the other peoples who fight with us— when I say that this time we are determined not only to win the war, but also to maintain the security of the peace that will follow.

But we know that modern methods of warfare make it a task, not only of shooting and fighting, but an even more urgent one of working and producing. Victory requires the actual weapons of war and the means of transporting them to a dozen points of combat.

It will not be sufficient for us and the other United Nations to produce a slightly superior supply of munitions to that of Germany and Japan and Italy, and the stolen industries in the countries which they have overrun. The superiority of the United Nations in munitions and ships must be overwhelming—so overwhelming the Axis Nations can never hope to catch up with it. And so, in order to attain this overwhelming superiority the United States must build planes and tanks and guns and ships to the utmost limit of our national capacity. We have the ability and capacity to produce arms not only for our own forces, but also for the armies, navies, and air forces fighting on our side.

And our overwhelming superiority of armament must be adequate to put weapons of war at the proper time into the hands of those men in the conquered Nations who stand ready to seize the first opportunity to revolt against their German and Japanese oppressors, and against...against the traitors in their own ranks, known by the already infamous name of "Quislings." And I think that it is a fair prophecy to say that, as we get guns to the patriots in those lands, they too will fire shots heard 'round the world.

This production of ours in the United States must be raised far above present levels, even though it will mean the dislocation of the lives and occupations of millions of our own people. We must raise our sights all along the production line. Let no man say it cannot be done. It must be done—and we have undertaken to do it.

I have just sent a letter of directive to the appropriate departments and agencies of our Government, ordering that immediate steps be taken. First, to increase our production rate of airplanes so rapidly that in this year, 1942, we shall produce 60,000 planes, 10,000...10,000 by the way, more than the goal that we set a year and a half ago. This includes 45,000 combat planes—bombers, dive bombers, pursuit planes. The rate of increase will be maintained, continued so that next year, 1943, we shall produce 125,000 airplanes, including 100,000 combat planes. Second, to increase our production rate of tanks so rapidly that in this year, 1942, we shall produce 45,000 tanks, and to continue that increase so that next year, 1943, we shall produce 75,000 tanks. Third, to increase our production rate of anti-aircraft guns so rapidly that in this year, 1942, we shall produce 20,000 of them; and to continue that increase so that next year, 1943, we shall produce 35,000 anti-aircraft guns. And fourth, to increase our production rate of merchant ships so rapidly that in this year, 1942, we shall build 8,000,000 dead-weight tons as compared with a 1941 completed production of 1,100,000. And finally, we shall continue that increase so that next year, 1943, we shall build 10,000,000 tons of shipping.

These figures and similar figures for a multitude of other implements of war will give the Japanese and the Nazis a little idea of just what they accomplished in the attack at

Pearl Harbor. And I rather hope that all these figures which I have given will become common knowledge in Germany and Japan.

Our task is hard—our task is unprecedented—and the time is short. We must strain every existing armament-producing facility to the utmost. We must convert every available plant and tool to war production. That goes all the way from the greatest plants to the smallest—from the huge automobile industry to the village machine shop.

Production for war is based on men and women—the human hands and brains which collectively we call Labor. Our workers stand ready to work long hours; to turn out more in a day's work; to keep the wheels turning and the fires burning twenty-four hours a day, and seven days a week. They realize well that on the speed and efficiency of their work depend the lives of their sons and their brothers on the fighting fronts.

Production for war is based on metals and raw materials—steel, copper, rubber, aluminum, zinc, tin. Greater and greater quantities of them will have to be diverted to war purposes. Civilian use of them will have to be cut further and still further—and, in many cases, completely eliminated.

War costs money. So far, we've hardly even begun to pay for it. We've devoted only 15 percent of our national income to national defense. As will appear in my Budget Message tomorrow, our war program for the coming fiscal year will cost 56 billion dollars or, in other words, more than half of the estimated annual national income. That means taxes and bonds and bonds and taxes. It means cutting luxuries and other nonessentials. In a word, it means an "all-out" war by individual effort and family effort in a united country.

Only this all-out scale of production will hasten the ultimate all-out victory. Speed will count. Lost ground can always be regained—lost time never. Speed will save lives; speed will save this Nation which is in peril; speed will save our freedom and our civilization—and slowness: well it has never been an American characteristic.

As the United States goes into its full stride, we must always be on guard, on guard against misconceptions which will arise, some of them naturally, or which will be planted among us by our enemies.

We must guard against complacency. We must not underrate the enemy. He is powerful and cunning—and cruel and ruthless. He will stop at nothing that gives him a chance to kill and to destroy. He has trained his people to believe that their highest perfection is achieved by waging war. For many years he has prepared for this very conflict—planning and plotting and training and arming and fighting. We have already tasted defeat. We may suffer further setbacks. We must face the fact of a hard war, a long war, a bloody war, a costly war.

We must, on the other hand, guard against defeatism. That has been one of the chief weapons of Hitler's propaganda machine—used time and again with deadly results. It will not be used successfully on the American people.

We must guard against divisions among ourselves and among all the other United Nations. We must be particularly vigilant against racial discrimination in any of its ugly forms. Hitler will try again to breed mistrust and suspicion between one individual and another, one group and another, one race and another, one Government and another. He will try to use the same technique of falsehood and rumor-mongering with which he divided France from Britain. He is trying to do this even now. But he will find a unity, a unity of will and purpose against him, which will persevere until the destruction of all his black designs upon the freedom and people of the world are ended.

We cannot wage this war in a defensive spirit. As our power and our resources are fully mobilized, we shall carry the attack against the enemy—we shall hit him and hit him again wherever and whenever we can reach him. We must keep him far from our shores, for we intend to bring this battle to him on his own home grounds.

American armed forces must be used at any place in all the world where it seems advisable to engage the forces of the enemy. In some cases these operations will be defensive, in order to protect key positions. In other cases, these operations will be offensive, in order to strike at the common enemy, with a view to his complete encirclement and eventual total defeat.

American armed forces will operate at many points in the Far East. American armed forces will be on all the oceans—helping to guard the essential communications which are vital to the United Nations. American land and air and sea forces will take stations in the British Isles—which constitute an essential fortress in this great world struggle. American armed forces will help to protect this hemisphere—and help also to protect bases outside this hemisphere, which could be used for an attack on the Americas.

If any of our enemies, from Europe or from Asia, attempt long-range raids by "suicide" squadrons of bombing planes, they will do so only in the hope of terrorizing our people and disrupting our morale. Our people are not afraid of that. We know that we may have to pay a heavy price for freedom. We will pay this price with a will. Whatever the price, it is a thousand times worth it. No matter what our enemies, in their desperation, may attempt to do to us—we will say, as the people of London have said, "We can take it." And what's more…what's more we can give it back—and we will give it back—with compound interest.

When our enemies challenged our country to stand up and fight, they challenge each and every one of us. And each and every one of us has accepted the challenge—for himself and for his Nation. There are only some…there were only some 400 United States Marines who in the heroic and historic defense of Wake Island inflicted such great losses on the enemy. Some of those men were killed in action; and others are now prisoners of war. When the survivors of that great fight are liberated and restored to their homes, they will learn that a hundred and thirty million of their fellow citizens have been inspired to render their own full share of service and sacrifice. We can well say that our men on the fighting fronts have already proved that Americans today are just as rugged and just as tough as any of the heroes whose exploits we celebrate on the Fourth of July.

Many people ask, "When will this war end?" There's only one answer to that. It will end just as soon as we make it end, by our combined efforts, our combined strength, our combined determination to fight through and work through until the end—the end of militarism in Germany and Italy and Japan. Most certainly we shall not settle for less.

That is the spirit in which discussions have been conducted during the visit of the British Prime Minister to Washington. Mr. Churchill and I understand each other, our motives and our purposes. Together, during the past two weeks, we have faced squarely the major military and economic problems of this greatest world war. All in our Nation have been cheered by Mr. Churchill's visit. We have been deeply stirred by his great message to us. He is welcome in our midst, now and in days to come, and we unite in wishing him a safe return to his home. For we are fighting on the same side with the British people, who fought alone for long, terrible months, and withstood the enemy with fortitude and tenacity and skill.

We are fighting on the same side with the Russian people who have seen the Nazi hordes swarm up to the very gates of Moscow, and who with almost superhuman will and courage have forced the invaders back into retreat. We are fighting on the same side as the brave people of China—those millions who for four and a half long years have withstood bombs and starvation and have whipped the invaders time and again in spite of the superior Japanese equipment and arms. Yes, we are fighting on the same side as the indomitable Dutch. We are fighting on the same side as all the other Governments in exile, whom Hitler and all his armies and all his Gestapo have not been able to conquer.

But we of the United Nations are not making all this sacrifice of human effort and human lives to return to the kind of world we had after the last world war. We are fighting today for security, for progress, and for peace, not only for ourselves but for all men, not only for one generation but for all generations. We are fighting to cleanse the world of ancient evils, ancient ills.

Our enemies are guided by brutal cynicism, by unholy contempt for the human race. We are inspired by a faith that goes back through all the years to the first chapter of the Book of Genesis: "God created man in His own image." We on our side are striving to be true to that divine heritage. We are fighting, as our fathers have fought, to uphold the doctrine that all men are equal in the sight of God. Those on the other side are striving to destroy this deep belief and to create a world in their own image—a world of tyranny and cruelty and serfdom.

That is the conflict that day and night now pervades our lives. No compromise can end that conflict. There never has been—there never can be—successful compromise between good and evil. Only...only total victory can reward the champions of tolerance, and decency, and freedom, and faith.

GOOD GUYS AND BAD GUYS

Roosevelt Defines the War

The militarists of Berlin and Tokyo started this war. But the massed, angered forces of Common Humanity will finish it.

CRITICS: Kurt W. Ritter and Lloyd E. Rohler

Many critics rank Franklin Delano Roosevelt as one of the most effective speakers of the 20th Century. Elected to the Presidency four times, he dominated the political scene of his time leading the United States through the crisis of the Great Depression and the danger of World War II. If it can be said of anyone that he was destined to become a leader, Roosevelt is that man.

THE SPEAKER

Born January 30, 1882, and reared on the ancestral estate at Hyde Park, Franklin Delano Roosevelt had the benefit of an upper class education complete with private tutors, an exclusive preparatory school, and trips to Europe. Roosevelt graduated from Harvard with an undistinguished record in 1904. He attended Columbia University Law School and while studying law married Eleanor Roosevelt, a distant cousin, in a ceremony attended by their uncle, Theodore Roosevelt, President of the United States. Politics seemed a natural calling for a man of FDR's talent and family background; and following admission to the bar in 1907, he became active in opposing the Tammany Hall faction in the New York Democratic Party. His actions won him election to the New York Senate in 1910. An early supporter of Woodrow Wilson for the Presidency, Roosevelt was rewarded with the post of Assistant Secretary of the Navy following the Democratic victory in 1912. Recognition for his administrative talents and speaking ability gained him the Vice Presidential nomination on a ticket with Ohio Governor James Cox in 1920. Although the ticket lost, the campaign marked Roosevelt as a rising star in the Democratic Party.

Tragedy struck in the summer of 1921 when he was stricken with polio while vacationing with his family. Paralyzed from the waist down, Roosevelt determined on a course of strenuous exercise to overcome his handicap and resume his political career. From this dark period of frustration and despair came a new confidence and optimistic spirit. Roosevelt reclaimed his place in national politics with a rousing speech nominating New York Governor Al Smith for the Presidency in 1924 as "the Happy Warrior." He followed this with such extensive political campaigning for the Democratic Party that he easily won the nomination and the Governorship of New York in 1928.

His success in dealing with the problems created by the Great Depression in New York made him the leading candidate for the Democratic Presidential nomination in 1932. He won the nomination and the office with the campaign calling for a "New Deal." For the next eight years Roosevelt presided over a major transformation of the

American economy while in Europe and Asia growing international tensions presaged war. Following the Japanese attack of Pearl Harbor, Roosevelt devoted his energies to defeating the Axis Powers and establishing a permanent system of security under the United Nations. He died of a massive cerebral hemorrhage at his retreat in Warm Springs, Georgia, on April 12, 1945.[1]

THE OCCASION

The occasion for this speech is a traditional one. The Constitution mandates that the President "shall from time to time give to the Congress information of the State of the Union." From Thomas Jefferson until Woodrow Wilson, Presidents sent written messages to Congress. Roosevelt followed Wilson's example of appearing in person to deliver a spoken address to a joint session of Congress. On this occasion greater attention than usual focused on Roosevelt's message. This was his first major address to the nation following a fireside chat broadcast two days after the Declaration of War.

It may require some imagination for the contemporary student to understand the importance of this speech or the exceptionally positive reception given it. To many it may seem long and repetitive. However, if we put ourselves in the place of the audience who heard the speech in person or on the radio on January 6, 1942, we can appreciate more fully its impact.

Americans viewed with mixed feelings the growth of German and Italian militarism. Many were clearly moved by the plight of Ethiopia and the stirring speech of its Emperor Haile Selassie before the League of Nations appealing for aid. Many saw the rise of Hitler as a threat to American security. Another equally important segment of the American public thought the problems of Europe were none of our business. Many Americans, disillusioned with the peace settlement following World War I, drew the conclusion that the United States had been deceived into supporting the British and French through propaganda and the efforts of arms merchants seeking to insure payment for their goods. Legislation reflecting this mood restricted American business dealings with nations at war in an effort to maintain our neutrality. As Hitler demanded and got more territory—marching into the Rhineland in violation of the peace treaty, absorbing Austria, and annexing parts of Czechoslovakia—a major debate developed between those favoring neutrality and those supporting American aid to the democracies of Britain and France. This division among the American people seriously hampered an effective foreign policy and produced bitterness and rancor.

The Japanese attack on Pearl Harbor silenced the debate as Americans rallied to the defense of the country, but deep divisions still remained over war aims and strategy. Some Americans and certain military leaders believed that we should concentrate our efforts in the Pacific where American interests and forces were under immediate threat. Others favored a unified strategy coordinating our forces with the other nations fighting the Axis Powers. This would give priority in military planning to Europe to prevent the Nazis from invading Britain and from consolidating their hold on the continent. A serious challenge to the Japanese in the Pacific would have to wait.

Other questions troubled Americans. How much would the war cost? How should it be paid for? How much production should be shifted to war material and how much left for domestic needs? How were the social problems created by massive dislocations in the economy to be handled? These and other questions needed answers that only the President could give, and Roosevelt had not made a major policy speech discussing war aims or strategy in any detail. Thus, Americans eagerly awaited the State-of-the-Union Address anticipating that some of their questions would be answered by the President.[2]

THE SPEECH

Without explicitly acknowledging that some Americans believed the United States should fight primarily, or even exclusively, where they had been attacked in the Pacific; FDR used two important arguments for unlimited participation in the war. First, he identified the Japanese with the other Axis powers; and second, he stressed that the success of the United States' war effort depended upon the success of the other Allied powers, including Britain and Russia.

Facing an audience outraged at Japan's sneak-attack on Pearl Harbor, Roosevelt opened his speech with a carefully developed analysis of Japan's methods and motives in war. Their method, he noted, was "the method of Hitler himself." Reviewing half a century of Japanese intrusions in Asia, he noted that "similar policy of criminal conquest (in Africa and the Mediterranean world) was adopted by Italy." Calling attention to the "Berlin-Rome-Tokyo alliance," FDR argued that the real purpose of the attack on Pearl Harbor was to distract America from the European conflict and give Germany time to consolidate its conquests. From the vantage point of history, FDR's remarks seem obvious, but in the context of January, 1942, this speech helped channel Americans' wrath so that it applied to Germany and Italy as well as to Japan.

A closely related argument centered on the need for the United States to provide significant material and military support to the Allied powers. The British Isles were characterized as "an essential fortress in this great world struggle." FDR portrayed America's interests as identical to those of Russia and China. The field of American military action, he declared, must not be limited to the Pacific; U.S. forces must be deployed so "we can strike at the common enemy wherever the greatest damage can be done him." To those who wanted America to gather its forces on its own shores for a defensive war, FDR declared: "We cannot wage this war in a defensive spirit…. We shall carry the attack against the enemy…. We must keep him far from our shores, for we intend to bring this battle to him on his own home grounds."

To an extraordinary degree, Roosevelt relied on the power of his personal authority in asserting that America would succeed. Military success remained a hope. Even increased military production was more dream than reality. Reason could support his calls for sacrifice as the only course for survival. Only his own reputation as a man who had led America through the crisis of the depression supported his claim that the war would end with an Allied victory: "It will end just as soon as we make it end, by our combined efforts, our combined strength, our combined determination to fight through and work through until the end—the end of militarism in Germany and Italy and Japan. Most certainly we shall not settle for less."

Roosevelt called upon Americans to take their fate into their own hands by imitating the enormous sacrifices already made by the British, the Russians, the Chinese, and the Dutch. In the face of a protracted war that might even reach American shores, FDR declared: "No matter what our enemies, in their desperation, may attempt to do to us—

we will say, as the people of London have said, 'We can take it.' And what's more, what's more, we can give it back—and we will give it back—with compound interest."

Instead of presenting a long list of initiatives, as is typical of State-of-the-Union Addresses, Roosevelt organized the entire speech in the "problem-solving" pattern. He devoted the first portion to defining the nature of the problem that America faced, and stressing its global implications. After analyzing the problems created by the war, FDR presented his proposals for converting the domestic economy into a war economy and for launching American forces into the worldwide struggle. The third portion of the address was devoted to the problems the nation would face as it tried to carry out FDR's plans—the dangers of complacency, defeatism, and division within ranks.

FDR designed the speech to confront the American audience with the harsh realities of the nation's global enemy, and then to present an uncompromising statement of the personal sacrifices that would be required on the home front as America became the munitions factory and the bread basket for the entire Allied force. This would mean reducing civilian consumption of goods through rationing and taxes, and long working hours as factories operated twenty-four hours a day, seven days a week. In short it meant "the dislocation of the lives and occupations of millions of our own people." To this awesome prospect, FDR added: "Let no man say it cannot be done. It must be done— and we have undertaken to do it."

An essential aspect of speech organization is the marshalling of supporting material to develop the main points of the speech. As you watch Roosevelt's speech (Great Speeches, Volume I videotape), notice how he uses statistics. Once he began to list production goals for airplanes, tanks, anti-aircraft guns, merchant ships, and other arms, he ran the risk of confusing his audience with a sea of numbers. Notice that his points were most clear when he presented statistics in pairs (45,000 tanks this year and 75,000 tanks next year; 20,000 anti-aircraft guns this year and 35,000 next year). When he tried to compare three or more statistics, the resulting jumble of numbers seems to obscure his point:

> ... in this year, 1942, we shall produce 60,000 planes, 10,000 more than the goal we set a year and a half ago. This includes 45,000 combat planes, bombers, dive bombers, pursuit planes. The rate increase will be maintained and continued so that next year, 1943, we shall produce 125,000 planes, including 100,000 combat planes.

A little later these statistics serve a useful purpose. In contrast to such large and impressive figures, Roosevelt stressed the small number of men who had defended Wake Island against the Japanese: "There were only some 400 United States Marines who in the heroic and historic defense of Wake Island inflicted such great losses on the enemy. Some of those men were killed in action; others are now prisoners of war." By personifying the war as a small group of men with which the audience could easily identify, FDR could emotionally declare: "When the survivors of that great fight are liberated and restored to their homes, they will learn that a hundred and thirty million of their fellow citizens have been inspired to render their own full share of service and sacrifice." In one passage, Roosevelt painted the vivid picture of a small embattled band of soldiers and capitalized on the power of sharply contrasting two statistics: 400 fighting Marines and 130 million aroused citizens.

No matter how well arguments are supported with evidence, or how sound the persuasive strategy, a speech must be well written and delivered to succeed. In these areas

FDR excelled. First, he carefully selected language that served his strategy of re-directing Americans' wrath to include Germany and Italy, rather than merely Japan. Second, he consistently employed a structure of language and soothing style of delivery which gave the audience a sense of continuity and stability. Hence, he achieved linguistically what could not be done through argument alone—a sense of stability amid turmoil.

FDR and his speechwriters recognized the power of language to classify and combine diverse elements. Once he had named the nation's opponents—Germany, Italy and Japan—he reinforced his persuasive goal of depicting a global (rather than an Asian) war for America by unifying all three Axis powers into a simple and singular "enemy." If he spoke of one, he spoke of all ("the Japanese and the Fascists and the Nazis"), but most often he spoke merely of "the dictators" or "the enemy." During the first third of the speech he used the plural pronoun to refer to the Axis powers:

> They know that victory for us means victory for freedom. They know that victory for us means victory for...democracy.... They know that victory for us means victory for religion. And they could not tolerate that.

By the last third of the speech, Japan, Germany, and Italy, were unified into a singular pronoun:

> We must not underrate the enemy. He is powerful and cunning.... He will stop at nothing.... He has trained his people.... For many years, He has prepared for this conflict....

As a natural consequence of unifying Japan, Italy, and Germany into a single "enemy," FDR used language which unified all Americans. For every "they" and "he" used to refer to the enemy, Roosevelt used a "we" to refer to Americans. At times, it was difficult to determine when "we" referred to all Americans, or all peoples of the Allied nations— an ambiguity that further served FDR's persuasive goals.

As his address progressed, the stylistic contrast between "them" and "us" was transformed into a contrast between all evil and all good:

> "brutal cynicism" and "unholy contempt for the human race"
> versus
> "the doctrine that all men are equal in the sight of God";

> "a world of tyranny and cruelty and serfdom"
> versus
> "the champions of tolerance, and decency, and freedom, and faith."

Closely associated with the stylistic device of contrast was FDR's use of parallel structure. Time and again during the speech Roosevelt repeated the same linguistic structure from one sentence to the next, and to each succeeding sentence. Often this parallelism included the repetition of a key phrase or a key clause. During the first moments of his address he established the pattern:

> We now know their choice of the time....
> We now know their choice of the place....
> We now know their choice of the method....

With unrelenting repetition FDR continued this pattern to the very end of his speech, when he moved to his conclusion through a series of declarations:

> We are fighting on the same side with the British people....
> We are fighting on the same side with the Russian people....
> We are fighting on the same side as the brave people of China....
> Yes, we are fighting on the same side as the indomitable Dutch....
> We are fighting on the same side as all the other Governments in exile, whom Hitler and all his armies and all his Gestapo have not been able to conquer.

This constant use of parallel structure and repetition provided a sense of stability, even inevitability, in the speech. One phrase followed another by an almost irrepressible logic. At least for the moment, the speech created linguistically and emotionally the sense of certainty which the American audience so badly needed to feel.

Although paralyzed from the waist down, Roosevelt gave the appearance of a vigorous man. He radiated energy and physical vitality. Usually speakers use movements of the arm, the torso, and the hand to convey physical vitality to an audience. Roosevelt needed to support himself at the podium with one hand while using the other to turn the pages of his manuscript. Too great a movement of his torso or the other hand would cause him to lose his balance and fall. It is remarkable testimony to his spirit that under such difficult conditions he managed to convey such great enthusiasm and vitality to the audience that many did not notice his physical disability. Denied the opportunity to use hand and arm gestures, Roosevelt compensated with an expressive face and a magnificently modulated and inflected voice. Refer to any passage on the videotape of his speech and you will hear his voice rising and falling, pausing, and changing tone to convey the meaning and the emotions of the words to the audience. These techniques of emphasis were exactly right for the new mass medium of radio that became a dominant force when he ran for the Governorship of New York in 1928. During this campaign he discovered that the inability to stride back and forth across the platform waving his hands and arms was no handicap when seated before a microphone that detected meaning in slight variations in the voice and broadcasted those meanings to a mass audience. Roosevelt's mastery of the medium of radio enabled him to become an effective communicator and leader. Robert T. Oliver, a distinguished professor of speech, called his voice, "the best modulated radio voice in public life."[3] Listening to him on the radio, Americans felt that they were in the presence of a friend who was speaking directly to them in a relaxed and friendly manner. He spoke slowly— usually at about 100-150 words per minute—and employed frequent pauses.[4] He was superb at reading the lines of his speeches to emphasize their rhetorical effects. He liked to employ parallel structure in his sentences and phrases and utilized repetition of pattern so intonation and inflection could emphasize the underlying structure for his listeners. He rarely stumbled over a line but when unexpectedly interrupted by audience reaction he was always ready with an ad lib or a quip. He had a quick wit and used it with devastating effect in his campaigns, often demoralizing his opposition with a deft line followed by the famous Roosevelt smile.

EVALUATION

The speech was well received by the contemporary audience. *Time* practically gushed over it: "In Britain there was a wave of elation. In the Axis countries there was a stunned silence—and then an uneasy denial that the program...could be carried out. In the United States that same program brought good tidings of hope."[5] The *New Republic* under the heading "FDR Gives Marching Orders," proclaimed that "President Roosevelt's annual message to Congress on the State of the Nation will rank as one of the great utterances of a leader whose State papers are already the most impressive in the history of the Presidency." The editorial writer complimented FDR for articulating "not only the power politics and military strategy of total war, but also the vast gulf that today separates the two causes." As an example of the moral gulf between the allies and the enemy, the writer cited FDR's "capacity to speak of the enemy in terms of intensity...without indulging in the hysterical violence and hate mongering of Hitler's speeches." He concludes, "these are brave words, bold words, heartening words."[6]

Roosevelt's speech successfully combined the three forms of proof into an effective structure to create support for his strategy for defeating the enemy and to persuade Americans to make the sacrifices needed for a long and difficult struggle. If today we do not share *New Republic's* estimate that this "utterance" ranks among his best, it is precisely because the policy was so successful in destroying the enemy that we have forgotten the fear and confusion of those perilous days.

It is instructive to compare the careers of the last two speakers on the Volume I videotape, Hitler and Roosevelt. Each achieved power in the same year and each died in the same month that the war in Europe ended. As leaders, each faced the problems created by worldwide depression and war. One was the leader of a great democratic nation who used the means of mass communication at his disposal in an ethical and responsible way to persuade the audience to support his programs. The other played upon the fears and hatreds of his audience through hysterical emotional appeals reinforced by spectacle and terror. The results of their leadership were clearly visible to the entire world in April, 1945.

Kurt W. Ritter is an associate professor of speech at Texas A. & M. University.

NOTES

1. There are many good biographies of Roosevelt and studies of his policies. James MacGregor Burns, *Roosevelt: The Lion and the Fox* (New York: Harcourt, Brace, 1956) is useful for a study of Roosevelt's leadership.
2. Denis W. Brogan, *The Era of Franklin D. Roosevelt: A Chronicle of the New Deal and Global War* (New Haven: Yale University Press, 1950).
3. Robert T. Oliver, "The Speech that Established Roosevelt's Reputation," *Quarterly Journal of Speech 31* (October 1945), p. 274.
4. Ernest S. Brandenburg and Waldo W. Braden, "Franklin D. Roosevelt's Voice and Pronunciation," *Quarterly Journal of Speech 38* (February 1952), pp. 23-30.
5. *Time*, January 19, 1942.
6. *New Republic*, January 19, 1942, p. 70.

THE VOTING RIGHTS ACT OF 1965

Lyndon B. Johnson

Joint Session of Congress, Washington, D.C., March 15, 1965 (Transcribed from the video, GREAT SPEECHES, VOLUME V)

MR. SPEAKER, Mr. President, members of the Congress, I speak tonight for the dignity of man and the destiny of democracy. I urge every member of both parties, Americans of all religions and of all colors, from every section of this country, to join me in that cause.

At times, history and fate meet at a single time in a single place to shape a turning point in man's unending search for freedom.

So it was at Lexington and Concord. So it was a century ago at Appomattox. So it was last week in Selma, Alabama. There, long suffering men and women peacefully protested the denial of their rights as Americans. Many were brutally assaulted. One good man, a man of God, was killed. There is no cause for pride in what has happened in Selma. There is no cause for self-satisfaction in the long denial of equal rights of millions of Americans. But there is cause for hope and for faith in our democracy in what is happening here tonight. For the cries of pain and the hymns and protests of oppressed people have summoned into convocation all the majesty of this great Government—the Government of the greatest nation on earth.

Our mission is at once the oldest and the most basic of this country—to right wrong, to do justice, to serve man. In our time we have come to live with the moments of great crisis. Our lives have been marked with debate about great issues, issues of war and peace, issues of prosperity and depression. But rarely in any time does an issue lay bare the secret heart of America itself. Rarely are we met with a challenge, not to our growth or abundance, or our welfare or our security, but rather to the values and the purposes and the meaning of our beloved nation.

The issue of equal rights for American Negroes is such an issue. And should we defeat every enemy, and should we double our wealth and conquer the stars, and still be unequal to this issue, then we will have failed as a people and as a nation. For, with a country as with a person, "What is a man profited if he shall gain the whole world, and lose his own soul?"

There is no Negro problem. There is no Southern problem. There is no Northern problem. There is only an American problem. And we are met here tonight as Americans, not as Democrats or Republicans; we're met here as Americans to solve that problem.

This was the first nation in the history of the world to be founded with a purpose. The great phrases of that purpose still sound in every American heart, North and South: "All men are created equal." "Government by consent of the governed." "Give me liberty or give me death." And those are not just clever words, and those are not just empty theories. In their name Americans have fought and died for two centuries and tonight, around the world, they stand there as guardians of our liberty risking their lives. Those words are promised to every citizen that he shall share in the dignity of man. This dignity cannot be found in a man's possessions. It cannot be found in his power or in his position. It really rests on his right to be treated as a man equal in opportunity to all others.

It says that he shall share in freedom. He shall choose his leaders, educate his children, provide for his family according to his ability and his merits as a human being.

To apply any other test, to deny a man his hopes because of his color or race or his religion or the place of his birth is not only to do injustice, it is to deny America and to dishonor the dead who gave their lives for American freedom.

Our fathers believed that if this noble view of the rights of man was to flourish it must be rooted in democracy. The most basic right of all was the right to choose your own leaders. The history of this country in large measure is the history of expansion of that right to all of our people. Many of the issues of civil rights are very complex and most difficult. But about this there can and should be no argument: every American citizen must have an equal right to vote.

There is no reason which can excuse the denial of that right. There is no duty which weighs more heavily on us than the duty we have to insure that right. Yet the harsh fact is that in many places in this country men and women are kept from voting simply because they are Negroes.

Every device of which human ingenuity is capable has been used to deny this right. The Negro citizen may go to register only to be told that the day is wrong, or the hour is late, or the official in charge is absent. And if he persists and, if he manages to present himself to the registrar, he may be disqualified because he did not spell out his middle name, or because he abbreviated a word on the application. And if he manages to fill out an application, he is given a test.

The registrar is the sole judge of whether he passes this test. He may be asked to recite the entire Constitution, or explain the most complex provisions of state law. And even a college degree cannot be used to prove that he can read and write. For the fact is that the only way to pass these barriers is to show a white skin.

Experience has clearly shown that the existing process of law cannot overcome systematic and ingenious discrimination. No law that we now have on the books, and I have helped to put three of them there, can...can insure the right to vote when local officials are determined to deny it. In such a case, our duty must be clear to all of us.

The Constitution says that no person shall be kept from voting because of his race or his color. We have all sworn an oath before God to support and to defend that Constitution. We must now act in obedience to that oath.

Wednesday, I will send to Congress a law designed to eliminate illegal barriers to the right to vote. The broad principles of that bill will be in the hands of the Democratic and Republican leaders tomorrow. After they have reviewed it, it will come here formally as a bill.

I am grateful for this opportunity to come here tonight at the invitation of the leadership to reason with my friends, to give them my views and to visit with my former colleagues. I have had prepared a more comprehensive analysis of the legislation which I had intended to transmit to the clerk tomorrow, but which I will submit to the clerks tonight. But I want to really discuss with you know *[sic]* briefly the main proposals of this legislation. This bill will strike down restrictions to voting in all elections, Federal, state and local, which have been used to deny Negroes the right to vote. This bill will establish a simple, uniform standard which cannot be used, however ingenious the effort, to flout our Constitution. It will provide for citizens to be registered by officials of the United States Government, if the state officials refuse to register them.

It will eliminate tedious, unnecessary lawsuits which delay the right to vote. Finally, this legislation will insure that properly registered individuals are not prohibited from voting.

I will welcome the suggestions from all the members of Congress (I have no doubt that I will get some) on ways and means to strengthen this law and to make it effective. But experience has plainly shown that this is the only path to carry out the command of the Constitution. To those who seek to avoid action by their national Government in their home communities, who want to and who seek to maintain purely local control over elections, the answer is simple: Open your polling places to all your people. Allow men and women to register and vote whatever the color of their skin. Extend the rights of citizenship to every citizen of this land.

There is no constitutional issue here. The command of the Constitution is plain. There is no moral issue. It is wrong, deadly wrong, to deny any of your fellow Americans the right to vote in this country. There is no issue of state's rights or national rights. There is only the struggle for human rights.

I have not the slightest doubt what will be your answer. But the last time a President sent a civil rights bill to the Congress it contained a provision to protect voting rights in Federal elections. That civil rights bill was passed after eight long months of debate. And when that bill came to my desk from the Congress for my signature, the heart of the voting provision had been eliminated. This time, on this issue, there must be no delay, or no hesitation, or no compromise with our purpose. We cannot, we must not, refuse to protect the right of every American to vote in every election that he may desire to participate in. And we ought not, and we cannot, and we must not wait another eight months before we get a bill. We have already waited 100 years and more and the time for waiting is gone.

So I ask you to join me in working long hours and nights and weekends, if necessary, to pass this bill. And I don't make that request lightly, for from the window where I sit with the problems of our country I recognize that from outside this chamber is the outraged conscience of a nation, the grave concern of many nations and the harsh judgment of history on our acts.

But even if we pass this bill the battle will not be over. What happened in Selma is part of a far larger movement which reaches into every section and state of America. It is the effort of American Negroes to secure for themselves the full blessings of American life.

Their cause must be our cause too. Because it's not just Negroes, but really it's all of us, who must overcome the crippling legacy of bigotry and injustice. And we shall overcome.

As a man whose roots go deeply into Southern soil, I know how agonizing racial feelings are. I know how difficult it is to reshape the attitudes and the structure of our society. But a century has passed—more than 100 years—since the Negro was freed. And he is not fully free tonight. It was more than 100 years ago that Abraham Lincoln— a great President of another party—signed the Emancipation Proclamation. But emancipation is a proclamation and not a fact. A century has passed—more than 100 years—since equality was promised, and yet the Negro is not equal. A century has passed since the day of promise, and the promise is unkept. The time of justice has now come, and I tell you that I believe sincerely that no force can hold it back. It is right in the eyes of man and God that it should come, and when it does, I think that day will brighten the lives of every American.

For Negroes are not the only victims. How many white children have gone uneducated? How many white families have lived in stark poverty? How many white lives have been scarred by fear, because we wasted our energy and our substance to maintain the barriers of hatred and terror? And so I say to all of you here and to all in the nation tonight that those who appeal to you to hold on to the past do so at the cost of denying you your future. This great rich, restless country can offer opportunity and education and hope to all—all, black and white, all, North and South, sharecropper and city dweller. These are the enemies: poverty, ignorance, disease. They are our enemies, not our fellow man, not our neighbor. And these enemies too—poverty, disease and ignorance—we shall overcome.

Now let none of us in any section look with prideful righteousness on the troubles in another section or the problems of our neighbors. There is really no part of America where the promise of equality has been fully kept. In Buffalo as well as in Birmingham, in Philadelphia as well as Selma, Americans are struggling for the fruits of freedom. This is one nation. What happens in Selma or in Cincinnati is a matter of legitimate concern to every American. But let each of us look within our own hearts and our own communities and let each of us put our shoulder to the wheel to root out injustice wherever it exists.

As we meet here in this peaceful historic chamber tonight, men from the South, some of whom were at Iwo Jima, men from the North who have carried Old Glory to far corners of the world and who brought it back without a stain on it, men from the East and from the West are all fighting together without regard to religion or color or region in Vietnam. Men from every region fought for us across the world 20 years ago. And now in these common dangers, in these common sacrifices, the South made its contribution of honor and gallantry no less than any other region in the Great Republic. And in some instances, a great many of them, more. And I have not the slightest doubt that good men from everywhere in this country, from the Great Lakes to the Gulf of Mexico, from the Golden Gate to the harbors along the Atlantic, will rally now together in this cause to vindicate the freedom of all Americans.

For all of us owe this duty and I believe that all of us will respond to it. Your President makes that request of every American.

The real hero of this struggle is the American Negro. His actions and protests, his courage to risk safety, and even to risk his life, have awakened the conscience of this nation. His demonstrations have been designed to call attention to injustice, designed to provoke change; designed to stir reform. He has called upon us to make good the promise of America. And who among us can say that we would have made the same progress were it not for his persistent bravery and his faith in American democracy?

For at the real heart of battle for equality is a deep-seated belief in the democratic process. Equality depends, not on the force of arms or tear gas, but defends [sic] depends upon the force of moral right; not on recourse to violence, but on respect for law and order.

And there have been many pressures upon your President and there will be others as the days come and go. But I pledge you tonight that we intend to fight this battle where it should be fought—in the courts, and in the Congress, and in the hearts of men. We must preserve the right of free speech and the right of free assembly. But the right of free speech does not carry with it—as has been said—the right to holler fire in a crowded theatre. We must preserve the right to free assembly. But free assembly does not carry with it the right to block public thoroughfares to traffic. We do have a right to protest. And a right to march under conditions that do not infringe the constitutional rights of our neighbors. And I intend to protect all those rights as long as I am permitted to serve in this office.

We will guard against violence, knowing it strikes from our hands the very weapons which we seek: progress, obedience to law, and belief in American values. In Selma, as elsewhere, we seek and pray for peace. We seek order, we seek unity, but we will not accept the peace of stifled rights or the order imposed by fear, or the unity that stifles protest, for peace cannot be purchased at the cost of liberty.

In Selma tonight as in every (and we had a good day there) as in every city we are working for a just and peaceful settlement. We must all remember that after this speech I'm making tonight, after the police and the F.B.I. and the marshals have all gone, and after you have promptly passed this bill, the people of Selma and the other cities of the nation must still live and work together. And when the nat [sic] the attention of the nation has gone elsewhere they must try to heal the wounds and to build a new community. This cannot be easily done on a battleground of violence as the history of the South itself shows. It is in recognition of this that men of both races have shown such an outstandingly impressive responsibility in recent days—last Tuesday and again today.

The bill that I am presenting to you will be known as a civil rights bill.

But in a larger sense, most of the program I am recommending is a civil rights program. Its object is to open the city of hope to all people of all races, because all Americans just must have the right to vote, and we are going to give them that right. All Americans must have the privileges of citizenship, regardless of race, and they are going to have those privileges of citizenship regardless of race. But I would like to caution you and remind you that to exercise these privileges takes much more than just legal right. It requires a trained mind and a healthy body. It requires a decent home and the chance to find a job and the opportunity to escape from the clutches of poverty.

Of course people cannot contribute to the nation if they are never taught to read or write; if their bodies are stunted from hunger; if their sickness goes untended; if their life is spent in hopeless poverty, just drawing a welfare check. So we want to open the gates to opportunity. But we're also going to give all our people, black and white, the help that they need to walk through those gates.

My first job after college was as a teacher in Cotulla, Texas, in a small Mexican-American school. Few of them could speak English and I couldn't speak much Spanish. My students were poor and they often came to class without breakfast; hungry. And they knew even in their youth the pain of prejudice, they never seemed to know why people disliked them, but they knew it was so because I saw it in their eyes. I often walked home late in the afternoon after the classes were finished wishing there was more that I could do. But all I knew was to teach them the little that I knew, hoping that it might help them against the hardships that lay ahead.

And somehow you never forget what poverty and hatred can do when you see its scars on the hopeful face of a young child. I never thought then, in 1928, that I would be standing here in 1965. It never even occurred to me in my fondest dreams that I might have the chance to help the sons and daughters of those students, and to help people like them all over this country. But now I do have that chance. And I'll let you in on a secret—I mean to use it. And I hope that you will use it with me.

This is the richest and the most powerful country which ever occupied this globe. The might of past empires is little compared to ours. But I do not want to be the President who built empires, or sought grandeur, or extended dominion. I want to be the President who educated young children to the wonders of their world. I want to be the President who helped to feed the hungry and to prepare them to be taxpayers instead of tax eaters. I want to be the President who helped the poor to find their own way and who protected the right of every citizen to vote in every election. I want to be the President who helped to end hatred among his fellow men and who promoted love among the people of all races and all regions and all parties. I want to be the President who helped to end war among the brothers of this earth.

And so at the request of your beloved Speaker and the Senator from Montana, the majority leader, the Senator from Illinois, the minority leader, Mr. McCulloch, and other members of both parties, I came here tonight, not as President Roosevelt came down one time in person to veto a bonus bill; not as President Truman came down one time to urge the passage of a railroad bill, but I came down here to ask you to share this task with me. And to share it with the people that we both work for.

I want this to be the Congress, Republicans and Democrats alike, which did all these things for all these people. Beyond this great chamber—out yonder—in 50 states are the people that we serve. Who can tell what deep and unspoken hopes are in their hearts tonight as they sit there and listen?

We all can guess, from our own lives, how difficult they often find their own pursuit of happiness. How many problems each little family has. They look most of all to themselves for their future, but I think that they also look to each of us.

Above the pyramid on the great seal of the United States it says in Latin, "God has favored our undertaking." God will not favor everything that we do. It is rather our duty to divine his will. But I cannot help believing that He truly understands and that He really favors the undertaking that we begin here tonight.

THE STATE-OF-THE-UNION, 1991

George Bush

Joint Session of Congress, Washington, D.C., January 29, 1991 (These closing comments transcribed from the video, GREAT SPEECHES, VOLUME VII)

As Americans we know that there are times when we must step forward and accept our responsibility to lead the world away from the dark chaos of dictators toward the brighter promise of a better day. Almost fifty years ago we began a long struggle against aggressive totalitarianism. Now we face another defining hour for America and for the world. There is no one more devoted, more committed to the hard work of freedom than every soldier and sailor, every marine, airman and coastguardsman, every man and woman now serving in the Persian Gulf. What a wonderful, fitting tribute to them. Each of them has volunteered, volunteered to provide for this nation's defense, and now they bravely struggle to earn for America, for the world and for future generations, a just and lasting peace. Our commitment to them must be equal to their commitment to their country. They are truly American's finest and....

The war in the gulf is not a war we wanted. We worked hard to avoid war. For more than five months we, along with the Arab League, the European Community, the United Nations, tried every diplomatic avenue. U.N. Secretary General Perez de Cuellar; Presidents Gorbachev, Mitterand, Ozal, Mubarak and Bendjedid; Kings Fahd and Hassan; Prime Ministers Major and Andreotti—just to name a few—all worked for a solution. But time and again Saddam Hussein flatly rejected the path of diplomacy and peace.

The world well knows how this conflict began, and when: it began on August 2nd, when Saddam invaded and sacked a small, defenseless neighbor, and I am certain of how it will end. So that peace can prevail, we will prevail.

Thank you. Tonight...tonight I am pleased to report that we are on course. Iraq's capacity to sustain war is being destroyed. Our investment, our training, our planning—all are paying off. Time will not be Saddam's salvation. Our purpose in the Persian Gulf remains constant: to drive Iraq out of Kuwait, to restore Kuwait's legitimate government, and to insure the stability and security of this critical region.

Let me make clear what I mean by the region's stability and security. We do not seek the destruction of Iraq, its culture or its people. Rather, we seek an Iraq that uses its great resources not to destroy, not to serve the ambitions of a tyrant, but to build a better life for itself and its neighbors. We seek a Persian Gulf where conflict is no longer the rule, where the strong are neither tempted nor able to intimidate the weak.

Most Americans know instinctively why we are in the gulf. They know we had to stop Saddam now, not later. They know that this brutal dictator will do anything, will use any weapon, will commit any outrage, no matter how many innocents suffer. They know we must make sure that control of the world's oil resources does not fall into his hands only to finance further aggression. They know that we need to build a new, enduring peace—based not on arms races and confrontation, but on shared principles and the rule of law. And we all realize that our responsibility to be the catalyst for peace in the region does not end with the successful conclusion of this war.

Democracy brings the undeniable value of thoughtful dissent, and we have heard some dissenting voices here at home, some handful reckless, most responsible. But the fact that all voices have the right to speak out is one of the reasons we've been united in purpose and principle for 200 years. Our progress in this great struggle is the result of years of vigilance and a steadfast commitment to a strong defense. And now, with remarkable technological advances like the Patriot missile, we can defend against ballistic missile attacks aimed at innocent civilians.

Looking forward, I have directed that the S.D.I. program be refocused on providing protection from limited ballistic missile strikes, whatever their source. Let us pursue an S.D.I. program that can deal with any future threat to the United States, to our forces overseas and to our friends and allies.

The quality of American technology, thanks to the American worker, has enabled us to successfully deal with difficult military conditions, and help minimize precious loss of life. We have given our men and women the very best and they deserve it.

We all have a special place in our hearts for the families of our men and women serving in the gulf. They are represented here tonight, by Mrs. Norman Schwarzkopf. We are all very grateful to General Schwarzkopf, and to all those serving with him. And I, I might uh also recognize one who came with uh…with uh Mrs. Schwarzkopf, Alma Powell, the wife of the distinguished chairman of the Joint Chiefs, and uh, and to the families…and to the families, let me say, our forces in the gulf will not stay there one day longer than is necessary to complete their mission.

The courage and the success of the R.A.F. pilots—of the Kuwaiti, Saudi, French, the Canadians, the Italians, the pilots of Qatar and Bahrain—all are proof that for the first time since World War II, the international community is united. The leadership of the United Nations, once only a hoped-for ideal, is now confirming its founders' vision.

And I am heartened that we are not being asked to bear alone the financial burden of this struggle. Last year, our friends and allies provided the bulk of the economic costs of Desert Shield, and now having received commitments of over $40 billion for the first three months of 1991, I am confident they will do no less as we move through Desert Storm.

But the world has to wonder what the dictator of Iraq is thinking. If he thinks that by targeting innocent civilians in Israel and Saudi Arabia, that he will gain advantage— he is dead wrong. And if he thinks that he will advance his cause through tragic and despicable environmental terrorism—he is dead wrong. And…and if he thinks that by abusing the coalition Prisoners of War he will benefit—he is dead wrong.

We will succeed in the gulf, and when we do, the world community will have sent an enduring warning to any dictator or despot, present or future, who contemplates outlaw aggression. The world can therefore seize this opportunity to fulfill the long-held promise of a new world order—where brutality will go unrewarded, and aggression will meet collective resistance.

Yes, the United States bears a major share of leadership in this effort. Among the nations of the world, only the United States of America has both the moral standing, and the means to back it up. We are the only nation on this earth that could assemble the forces of peace. This is the burden of leadership—and the strength that has made America the beacon of freedom in a searching world. This nation has never found glory in war. Our people have never wanted to abandon the blessings of home and work, for distant lands and deadly conflict. If we fight in anger, it is only because we have to fight at all. And all of us yearn for a world where we will never have to fight again. Each of us will measure, within ourselves, the value of this great struggle. Any cost in lives, any cost, is beyond our power to measure. But the cost of closing our eyes to aggression is beyond mankind's power to imagine. This we do know: Our cause is just. Our cause in moral. Our cause is right.

Let...let future generations understand the burden and blessings of freedom. Let them say, we stood where duty required us to stand. Let them know that together, we affirmed America, and the world as a community of conscience.

The winds of change are with us now. The forces of freedom are together united. We move toward the next century, more confident than ever, that we have the will at home and abroad, to do what must be done—the hard work of freedom.

May God bless the United States of America. Thank you very, very much.

AMERICA'S POLICY TOWARD SOUTH AFRICA

Jerry Falwell

National Religious Broadcaster's Association, Washington, D.C., February 5, 1985 (Transcribed from the video, GREAT SPEECHES, VOLUME VII)

Last night the regional chapter of the Moral Majority met at Senator Kennedy's home and uh...appointed and anointed him as local chairman. And uh...we...we had the advantage of the fact that he...his mother is a fundamentalist in a lot of ways...in a lot of ways. So he had a little experience with this. You know I was in this room just the other night when the Senator's name was taken in vain. I was here when the Washington Press Club was honoring the Congress and as John Riggins slept. And I uh...John D. Rockefeller IV was, as a freshman senator from West Virginia being roasted and he came to the plat...platform telling about the terrible experience of moving here looking for property. And he said, "You wouldn't believe the prices, that only a Kennedy could afford this kind of land." And finally he said, "You know you'd never believe what they want for The Ellipse." And his wife had decided never to let him run for president because she didn't want to move into a smaller house.

We uh...I know the Senator had to feel walking into this group, much like Daniel did walking into the lion's den and much like I did walking into Harvard. But I agree, I concur with what the Senator has said here this morning that we have one very basic common denominator that equates every one of us and that is we are free born Americans and we are charged with the responsibility of keeping this the bastion of freedom at any price for our children's and children's children's sake. And, Senator, thank you for coming here today, very, very much.

America enters the second half of the 1980's, a period some have properly called a "Decade of Destiny," faced with some very crucial and complicated issues—problems that we no longer can ignore or allow to go unsolved. We have an overwhelming and spiralling deficit caused by fifty years of new deals, bad deals, and great societies, and sick societies and a prevailing philosophy within both major political parties that we can eventually spend ourselves out of debt. And if Ronald Reagan and Tip O'Neill are successful in solving this dilemma, it is very good that neither of them is planning to run again for public office because neither of them would be re-electable. Some very unpopular things must be done by necessity.

The nuclear arms race is about to finish its last lap in what has been, in the opinion of many, a forty year marathon towards universal annihilation. Fortunately, because of the strong leadership of President Reagan during the past four years, the Soviets have now come back to the negotiating table and we have hope that at least the beginnings of meaningful and verifiable arms reductions may be achieved in the near future. And also fortunately in my opinion thanks again to Ronald Reagan, we will be dealing with the Soviets from a possession of strength—the only position, the only language the Soviets seem to respect and understand.

Central America poses another serious problem for this country. Nicaragua is gone. And regardless what you think of the Marxist/Leninist they do very well at keeping what they steal. El Salvador is tottering. And if many members of the Congress who are refusing to support President Reagan's efforts to help our neighbors in the South to defend themselves, if they're successful all of Central America may possibly go down: Guatemala, Honduras, Costa Rica, Belize, Panama, and, I think the plum of Latin America, Mexico with its gas and oil fields—all of these may very well fall into the malignant grip of Soviet/Cuban expansionism. It is something we cannot ignore and we must understand that we can no longer in this real world be isolationists and uh...have one little island of freedom here within our own borders.

And if the "Boat People" of Southeast Asia presented and have...are continuing to present a major problem—socially, economically, politically for the international community it is my opinion, that if Central America falls, the problem of "Boat People" will be a minuscule one compared to the "Feet People," multi-millions of Latin Americans will be crossing our southern borders into the United States. And for that reason I think we should be supporting unswervingly the administration's efforts to provide military and economic aid to our friends south of the border. Our...our American boys are not needed; our resources are needed.

And then we are facing moral and social issues which, in my opinion as a bible-believing and born again Christian, pose even greater danger for our beloved homeland than the deficit, the nuclear arms race, or the Central America problem. It is my conviction that we have far more as a nation to fear from the wrath of an Almighty God who is angry with us for the destruction of fifteen million innocent, unborn children during the past twelve years than we have to fear from the Soviet Union. And while we, as Christians, deplore all acts of violence and particularly clinic bombings as criminal activities as...and as detrimental to the cause of the liberation of the unborn, we must not allow these bombings to divert attention away from the violence and the ultimate acts of child abuse now being performed inside those clinics 4,000 times a day, every day. And we must continue pressing the battle for judicial and legislative reform. We must continue to curse the darkness, but along with cursing the darkness, we must also light some candle [sic]. We must put our money where our mouths are. The pro-life movement has not always been good at that. We've been famous for what we are against. We have not provided the alternatives and the time has come when we must establish enough Save-A-Baby centers and full service uh...maternity residence centers and homes and adoption agencies and crisis pregnancy centers in this country to accommodate the one and a half million women who are now having legal abortions in this country, who, when the court finally rules—and I feel they will—no longer will be able to have legal abortions.

We should give thanks to God that the momentum is finally moving to our favor. Judy Goldsmith agrees to that. President Reagan has said that and so has *Newsweek* magazine and ABC 20/20. In recent days we have become aware that public opinion, for example in *Newsweek* for the first time—a majority, fifty-eight percent of Americans—indicated that they want some kind of legislation to at least curb convenience abortions. I think that's encouraging. I think education is the answer–patient and persistent presentation of the facts. Men like Dr. Bernard Nathenson and others who are, from a scientific perspective, producing films like "The Silent Scream"—this is our hope for the future and we must press on and on and on. Along with that developing all of the...of the necessary mechanics and the structure in this country to account for and to accommodate the women who will need a loving alternative. And also the next four years we have high hopes that our president will be appointing several more persons to the Supreme Court. And if, like Sandra Day O'Connor they are as philosophical...philosophically compatible with the position of the president on the life issue, we can expect a pro-life court by 1988. And I...and to clear up the President...the Vice President's comment yesterday with the press, it will be President Reagan, not Jerry Falwell who will be doing that.

I, in addition, believe that before we can convince the Supreme Court that our position is valid, we must be ready when they ask us the question on that day when Roe v. Wade is either being reversed or modified—when they ask the question, "Who is going to prevent the development of an underground, underworld abortion industry, back alley, kitchen table abortions;" we must be able to say loud and clear, "Your Honors, now in place in this country because of the Church of the Lord Jesus Christ are adequate facilities, proper facilities without charge to every person who needs an alternative to abortion." And when we have done that we will earn the right to pick up our newspaper wherever we live and read that wonderful headline "Abortion outlawed in the United States."

I was criticized for a statement I made on ABC's 20/20 program with Barbara Walters two weeks ago when I...when I said I'm willing to accept legislation or judicial action that will allow for abortions in the case of rape, incest and where the life of the mother is threatened. I want to explain that position. I do not theologically believe that rape and incest are viable exceptions for abortion. I shall always preach and reach out for those girls who are victims thusly. But I also do not believe we'll ever have legislation that does not allow for those exceptions and since over 99 percent of all abortions are convenience abortions and are not as a result of rape and incest then I am willing to save 1.4 million of those who are being destroyed in this country now, and then through our loving Christian ministry reach out to do everything we can to save...save the other one percent. I often use the analogy of the hijacker who has commandeered a...an airliner filled with men, women and children. A negotiate...a negotiator achieves or...or procures from that hijacker an agreement to release the women and children. If he's wise he will not say, "No, all or nothing." He'll take those women and children and then work to get the men off later. And that is I think...that has got to be the reasonable position of...of those of us in the pro-life movement as we move towards putting to an end this biological holocaust in our country.

Last year there were five million families who expressed a desire to adopt a child. If all one and one half million children who had...who were aborted had, in fact, been offered the option life and been put up for adoption we would still have had a deficit of 3.5 million babies. So there is no lack of homes and love and money. And by the way, it is not a minority problem as some try to paint it. Seventy-one percent of all abortions are children who are white and so the problem is universal sin and the cure and the hope is the Church of the Lord Jesus Christ. And may we join hands together these next few years to put an end to it.

Senator Kennedy spent some time discussing his trip to Africa, the Republic of South Africa, the Region of East Africa which includes Ethiopia, Sudan, Kenya, and other impoverished nations. Last night my wife and I commented after going to bed—we were so moved as young Teddy, who is one of the finest skiers on one leg in the country, led the prayer in the Kennedy home and told of his own experience of physically involving himself in volunteer help. And he said, "You know the thing, Reverend, that so impressed me was that one person can make a difference." And uh...I wish all of you could have heard the prayer and I...we just left there...we fell in love with young

Teddy. Not that we don't love you, Senator, but uh...that young man, Teddy Kennedy, is something special.

First, let me comment on South Africa. Like Senator Kennedy, I too have been there only briefly and I've been there twice—less than a week in the region. So I'm, therefore, not an expert and I'm sure the Senator doesn't consider himself to be one, but we have both been observers from a distance. I have also observed those politicians and civil rights workers who have demonstrated outside the South African Embassy. I have heard the orchestrated comments all over the nation and the world that have been given to the media regarding this horrible and terrible South Africa. I have heard the demands that the business community disinvest South Africa and even some have gone so far as to recommend a break of diplomatic relations with that republic.

I too believe, and I suspect that everyone in this room agrees with the Senator, that Apartheid is abominable. The word Apartheid means...the word Apartheid means in English "apartness." That's our ugly word, segregation. This is wrong; must be repealed, it must be changed. But it is important to note that in the past few years, some major changes have occurred in South Africa. They haven't come far enough, nor have we, but today restaurants, shops, general commerce have been open to blacks. Coloreds and Asians were given the right to vote last year. And although blacks cannot vote in general elections in the Republic of South Africa they do vote in their own particular homelands.

Less than 25 million persons live in that country. Five million are white. The white are composed of...of English or British, Dutch or Afrikaaners plus Greeks, French, Jews and Portuguese. And then there are one and one half coloreds. The coloreds are the mixed black and white. They live mainly in Cape Province and they are mostly Christian. And then there are two million Asian. These include Indians, from the nation of India, who are primarily Hindus; Malays, who are Moslems; and Chinese, who are Buddhists. And then there are 15 million blacks. And among these blacks are many tribes, probably over 80 tribes and with all different...each having different languages. The Zulu tribe is the largest and then there are the Sotho, the Venda, the Xosha, the Swana, the Swazi, etc., so many of them and further, there are two black homelands within South Africa, namely Swaziland and Lesothu which have been recognized by the U.N. Others that have not been recognized such as Zululand, Transkie, Venda, and others.

The whites first arrived there in 1652 that's more than 300 hundred years. And they no more intend to give up their country than we plan to give ours back to the Indians. The British eventually took Cape Province and Nepal. The Dutch took Transvaal and Orange Free State. The Union of South Africa was formed in 1610 (the speaker meant to say in 1910) but the modern Republic of South Africa was formed in 1961, meaning that the current government, the current Republic of South Africa is less than 25 years old. A very young nation indeed.

Now it's important, if we're going to be fair and point the finger of blame at South Africa for their bad civil rights record, to remember that from 1776, the year that our country was born, to 1861, when we fought a war—an internal war over slavery—85 years transpired. And now, since that war a hundred years later, our generation continues to fight for the civil rights of minorities in this country.

And what I am saying is this: while South Africa has a long way to go, they have progressed and done far better than the United States of America has done with her problem. And they don't need our hypocritical condemnation. They need our coercive and patient encouragement to clean up their act while at the same time not passing them over to the Soviets.

It very much is possible to go into certain areas of South Africa and take photographs of poverty and squalor. This is indefensible. It is necessary to say that you can go into every nation in Africa and find even worse scenes. You can go into inner cities in the United States and find similar and pitiful conditions. This is unacceptable.

But there are some very good things to be said about South Africa as well and very few are saying them. One, in South Africa today the literacy rate is above 80 percent. In the rest of Africa; less than 10 percent. Presently thousands of blacks are immigrating into South Africa. Some have estimated as many as three quarters of a million a year, while none are leaving and they have permission to do so. So the problem in South Africa is not quite so simple a black and white issue as we Americans like to frame it. I believe that President Reagan is very wise in suggesting constructive engagement, which simply means that to continue working patiently with the South African government is the best policy for all persons in South Africa. He does not believe that force or disinvestment are the answers. And those who are suggesting disinvestment are ignoring the fact that this would immediately unemploy 150,000 blacks in that country who work for American companies and this would help no one.

One man-one vote, of course, is the ideal. We believe in that in this country—it works for us. Most of us has said…have said that if one hundred per cent of all eligible votes ever voted—and they don't—in a national election, every one of us could live with what 51 percent decided. That doesn't happen, unfortunately. But one man-one vote in Africa often means, almost always means "one man, one vote, one time!" And all one need do is look across the borders of the Republic of South Africa to her neighbors, to prove that point. Mozambique is now a communist country. It was formerly Portuguese. And the Mozambican government recently closed every church in the land. They are now bankrupt. Electricity and food supplies are low. And so out of necessity they recently signed peace accords with South Africa in order to get the food and supplies to survive. Angola is another neighbor of South Africa. It is also communistic—controlled by the Russians and the beloved Cubans. There are very hostile to South Africa. Why, because South Africa is the only reason that they cannot take over Southwest Africa, or Namibia as we know it, and thus confiscate all her diamonds, uranium, and minerals that the whole free world needs so badly. And then there's South Africa's immediate neighbor to the north—Zimbabwe, formerly Rhodesia. Communist leader Robert Mugabe rules that country. He is from the Shona tribe. His government persecutes all minority tribes and especially N'Debele Tribe of Joshua Nkomo his competitor for the throne there. Half the whites have left since 1981. They're in terrible economic condition and obviously they have no relations with South Africa. And in none of these communist countries do they have free elections. And in none of these communist countries do they have civil rights for any of their citizens black, white or otherwise. A key point then at this moment would be to ask if the black tribes in South Africa voted today and took control of that nation, which tribe would ultimately rule? Because at the moment the tribes are hostile towards each other. South African government troops must prevent constant civil war between those tribes. And if the Zulu tribe, the largest, should, as the Shona tribe in Zimbabwe, take control of the country, not only would the Asians, the coloreds and the whites be in serious trouble but so would all of the minority black tribes. This is a matter of fact and anyone who has studied history in that area knows that to be true.

I repeat that the ultimate goal in South Africa must be absolute equality. But we must not, like the moral policeman of the world, attempt to force South Africa into a position that would do nothing more than hand this very strategic and friendly nation over to the Soviet Union. We seem to have a talent in doing that. We…we've been hurting our friends for a long time. And I would like to ask the question of some of those who demonstrate outside the South African embassy, why don't you demonstrate against Zimbabwe? Why not outside the Soviet embassy where we have a repressive regime that is persecuting Christians and Jews today? And not only persecuting Christians and Jews but…but harassing and persecuting the Poles and the Afghans in the East Europeans. As a matter of fact, all 275 million citizens inside the Soviet Union are really inmates in one mammoth concentration camp unable to move from city to city without permission from the government. Unable to work where they please without governmental permission. That is slavery and I would suggest to those in the orchestrated demonstrations move up to the Soviet embassy. What about the Cuban embassy because of their intervention in Angola and Latin America? What about…what about Red China where they go into villages and gather up the pregnant women and give them forced abortions? And on and on the list goes.

What I'm saying is we have so many problems of our own and we look at the American Indian and what we've done to them. When we look at our own difficulties in the, you know, in the state of Virginia. We have about as many black representatives in the Congress as there are in Massachusetts. And the judiciary has the same problem and all across this country. And while we must coerce and use our influence to help South Africa to get in line we don't need to be hypocrites about it and ignore the fact that the worst crimes against civil rights are occurring in communist lands, Ethiopia, East Africa.

We can certainly blame the drought and the expanding desert for that horrible, horrible drought and…and uh…problem of starvation. But we can also place some blame on Marxist governments in the region like that one in Addis Ababa that will not allow food to be taken to those northern tribes because they consider them to be rebels while warehouses are filled. You know socialism is nothing but mutually shared poverty. And wherever socialism has gotten its grips on a land and Marxism is its philosophy starvation usually follows.

The Soviet Union is the pride and joy of the Marxist movement. Yet it's bankrupt, their people are hungry. A large percentage of their people are farmers and cannot feed themselves. Five percent of the American people in free enterprise are farmers and are feeding much of the world.

In summary we…we must sincerely and patiently use all of our leverage to help South Africa come to where we are as far as civil rights are concerned but at the same time attempt to improve our own blemished record. And we must remember that South Africa is a friend, like Israel is a friend and lately we've been kicking both of them in the teeth. If it were not for Israel in the Mideast and…and South Africa on that continent right now the oil fields and minerals of both areas would belong to the Soviet Union and what a mess we would be in indeed. All we need do is look at some recent trades we've made to see how foolish we've been. We traded our friend, the Shah, for that sweet loving amicable Ayatollah. We traded our friend Somoza for the Marxist Sandanistas. And if some persons in America had their way we would trade the government in Jerusalem, a democracy, for Khadafy. And the government in Pretoria for the Kremlin. Now admittedly the Shah and Somoza and some of these fellows with whom we've had good relations are far but desirable fellows. We, as a matter of fact, might admit that some of them have been skunks. But if we must do business with skunks and sometimes we must, I prefer the one who is spraying in the other direction. And we in the hills of Virginia, we call that common sense.

In summary, the...the world is in turmoil and we who believe in the gospel of our Lord and Savior Jesus Christ and who have accepted the claims of his death, burial and resurrection as the full atonement for our salvation we have an obligation. We are our brothers keeper. We must build mercy camps and bases as Liberty Baptist College is planning to do right now in northeast Sudan. Joining with great movements like World Vision and Food for the Hungry and hundreds like them but at the same time we must realize there are no quick fixes and no simple solutions. It is a long, long road and the real and permanent answer, while we work and plan for the benefit of the next generation; the real hope we have in our breast is that there's a God in heaven who loves us more than we love ourselves and who rules in the affairs of man as Ben Franklin said. And as we look to Him, trust in Him, pray and work to negotiate for peace I believe that we can be optimistic about America, about the world, about our children and very frankly, I fully expect that we'll pass on to our children a greater America and a greater free world than our parents passed on to us. God bless you.

CHAPTER 7:
Legislative Speeches: International Policy

World leaders frequently address an international audience urging support for policies which affect the well-being of all societies. They may cloak their parochial objectives in a statesmanlike concern for all peoples. They seek to shed the narrow image of national leadership and adorn their proposals with the aspirations of the international community.

In 1953, Dwight Eisenhower spoke to the United Nations urging international cooperation in the containment of nuclear power for peaceful purposes only. The detailed construction of what was known as his Atoms for Peace Speech is the subject of Martin Medhurst's critical essay. Golda Meir exerted ethical appeal to urge action by all nations to insure peace in the Middle East.

ATOMS FOR PEACE

Dwight D. Eisenhower

United Nations General Assembly, New York City, December 8, 1953
(Transcribed from the video, GREAT SPEECHES, VOLUME III)

Madam President, Members of the General Assembly:
When Secretary General Hammerskjold's invitation to address this General Assembly reached me in Bermuda, I was just beginning a series of conferences with the Prime Ministers and Foreign Ministers of Great Britain and of France. Our subject was some of the problems that beset our world. During the remainder of the Bermuda Conference, I had constantly in mind that ahead of me lay a great honor. That honor is mine today as I stand here, privileged to address the General Assembly of the United Nations. At the same time that I appreciate the distinction of addressing you, I have a sense of exhilaration as I look upon this assembly. Never before in history has so much hope for so many people been gathered together in a single organization. Your deliberations and decisions during these somber years have already realized part of those hopes. But the great test and the great accomplishments still lie ahead. And in the confident expectation of those accomplishments, I would use the office which, for the time being, I hold, to assure you that the Government of the United States will remain steadfast in its support of this body. This we shall do in the conviction that you will provide a great share of the wisdom, of the courage and the faith which can bring to this world lasting peace for all nations and happiness and well-being for all men.

Clearly, it would not be fitting for me to take this occasion to present to you a unilateral American report on Bermuda. Nevertheless, I assure you that in our deliberations on that lovely island we sought to invoke those same great concepts of universal peace and human dignity which are so cleanly etched in your Charter. Neither would it be a measure of this great opportunity merely to recite, however hopefully, pious platitudes. I therefore decided that this occasion warranted my saying to you some of the things that have been on the minds and hearts of my legislative and executive associates and on mine for a great many months; thoughts I had originally planned to say primarily to the American people.

I know that the American people share my deep belief that if a danger exists in the world, it is a danger shared by all and equally, that if hope exists in the mind of one nation, that hope should be shared by all. Finally, if there is to be advanced any proposal designed to ease, even by the smallest measure, the tensions of today's world, what more appropriate audience could there be than the members of the General Assembly of the United Nations.

I feel impelled to speak today in a language that, in a sense, is new—one, which I, who has spent so much of my life in the military profession, would have preferred never to use. That new language is the language of atomic warfare. The atomic age has moved forward at such a pace that every citizen of the world should have some comprehension, at least in comparative terms, of the extent of this development, of the utmost significance to every one of us. Clearly, if the peoples of the world are to conduct an intelligent search for peace, they must be armed with the significant facts of today's existence.

My recital of atomic danger and power is necessarily stated in United States terms, for these are the only incontrovertible facts that I know. I need hardly point out to this assembly, however, that this subject is global, not a [sic] merely national in character. On July 16, 1945, the United States set off the world's first atomic explosion. Since that date in 1945, the United States of America has conducted forty-two test explosions. Atomic bombs today are more than twenty-five times as powerful as the weapons with which the atomic age dawned while hydrogen weapons are in the ranges of millions of tons of TNT equivalent. Today, the United States' stockpile of atomic weapons, which, of course, increases daily, exceeds by many times the total equivalent of the total of all bombs and all shells that came from every plane and every gun in every theatre of war in all the years of World War II. A single air group, whether afloat or land based, can now deliver to any reachable target a destructive cargo exceeding in power all the bombs that fell on Britain in all of World War II.

In size and variety the development of atomic weapons has been no less remarkable. The development has been such that atomic weapons have virtually achieved conventional status within our armed services. In the United States, the Army, the Navy, the Air Force and the Marine Corps are all capable of putting this weapon to military use. But the dread secret and the fearful engines of atomic might are not ours alone. In the first place, the secret is possessed by our friends and Allies, Great Britain and Canada, whose scientific genius made a tremendous contribution to our original discoveries and the designs of atomic bombs. The secret is also known by the Soviet Union. The Soviet Union has informed us that, over recent years, it had devoted extensive resources to atomic weapons. During this period, the Soviet Union has exploded a series of atomic advices [sic], devices, including at least one involving thermonuclear reactions.

If at one time the United States possessed what might have been called a monopoly of atomic power, that monopoly ceased to exist several years ago. Therefore, although our earlier start has permitted us to accumulate what is today a great quantitative advantage, the atomic realities of today comprehend two facts of even greater significance. First, the knowledge now possessed by several nations will eventually be shared by others, possibly all others. Second, even a vast superiority in numbers of weapons, and a consequent capability of devastating retaliation, is no preventive of itself, against the fearful material damage and toll of human lives that would be inflicted by surprise aggression. The free world, at least dimly aware of these facts, has naturally embarked on a large program of warning and defense systems. That program will be accelerated and expanded. But let no one think that the expenditure of vast sums for weapons and systems of defense can guarantee absolute safety for the cities and the citizens of any nation. The awful arithmetic of the atomic bomb does not permit of any such easy solution. Even against the most powerful defense, an aggressor in possession of the effective minimum number of atomic bombs for a surprise attack could probably place a sufficient number of his bombs on the chosen targets to cause hideous damage. Should such an atomic attack be launched against the United States, our reactions would be swift and resolute. But for me to say that the defense capabilities of the United States are such that they could inflict terrible losses upon an aggressor—for me to say that the retaliation capabilities of the United States are so great that such an aggressor's land would be laid waste; all this, while fact, is not the true expression of the purpose and the hope of the United States. To pause there would be to confirm the hopeless finality of a belief that two atomic colossi are doomed malevolently to eye each other indefinitely across a trembling world. To stop there would be to accept helplessly the probability of civilization destroyed, the annihilation of the irreplaceable heritage of mankind handed down to us generation from generation—and the condemnation of mankind to begin all over again the age-old struggle upward from savagery toward decency and right and justice.

Surely no sane member of the human race could discover victory in such desolation. Could anyone wish his name to be coupled by history with such human degradation and destruction? Occasional pages of history do record the faces of the "Great Destroyers" but the whole book of history reveals mankind's never-ending quest for peace and mankind's God-given capacity to build. It is with the book of history, and not with isolated pages, that the United States will ever wish to be identified. My country wants to be constructive, not destructive. It wants agreements, not wars, among nations. It wants, itself, to live in freedom and in the confidence that the people of every other nation enjoy equally the right of choosing their own way of life.

So my country's purpose is to help us move out of the dark chamber of horrors into the light, to find a way by which the minds of men, the hopes of men, the souls of men everywhere, can move forward toward peace and happiness and well-being. In this quest, I know that we must not lack patience. I know that in a world divided, such as ours today, salvation cannot be attained by one dramatic act. I know that many steps will have to be taken over many months before the world can look at itself one day and truly realize that a new climate of mutually peaceful confidence is abroad in the world. But I know, above all else, that we must start to take these steps—now. The United States and its Allies, Great Britain and France, have, over the past months, tried to take some of these steps. Let no one say that we shun the conference table. On the record has long stood the request of the United States, Great Britain and France, to negotiate with the Soviet Union the problems of a divided Germany. On that record has long stood the request of the same three nations to negotiate an Austrian peace treaty. On the same record still stands the request of the United Nations to negotiate the problems of Korea.

Most recently, we have received from the Soviet Union what is in effect an expression of willingness to hold a four-power meeting. Along with our Allies, Great Britain and France, we were pleased to see that this note did not contain the unacceptable preconditions previously put forward. As you already know from our joint Bermuda communique, the United States, Great Britain and France have agreed promptly to meet with the Soviet Union. The Government of the United States approaches this conference with hopeful sincerity. We will bend every effort of our minds to the single purpose of emerging from that conference with tangible results toward peace, the only true way of lessening international tension. We never have, we never will, propose or suggest that the Soviet Union surrender what is rightfully theirs. We will never say that the people of Russia are an enemy with whom we have no desire ever to deal or mingle in friendly and fruitful relationship. On the contrary, we hope that this coming conference may initiate a relationship with the Soviet Union which will eventually bring about a free intermingling of the peoples of the East and of the West, the one sure, human way of developing the understanding required for confident and peaceful relations.

Instead of the discontent which is now settling upon Eastern Germany, occupied Austria and the countries of Eastern Europe, we seek a harmonious family of free

European nations, with none a threat to the other, and least of all a threat to the peoples of Russia. Beyond the turmoil and strife and misery of Asia, we seek peaceful opportunity for these peoples to develop their natural resources and to elevate their lot.

These are not idle words or shallow vision. Behind them lies a story of nations lately came to independence, not as a result of war but through free grant or peaceful negotiation. There is a record already written of assistance gladly given by nations of the West to needy peoples and to those suffering the temporary effects of famine, drought and natural disaster. These are deeds of peace. They speak more loudly than promises or protestations of peaceful intent. But I do not wish to rest either upon the reiteration of past proposals or the restatement of past deeds. The gravity of the time is such that every new avenue of peace, no matter how dimly discernible, should be explored.

There is at least one new avenue of peace which has not yet been well explored—an avenue now laid out by the General Assembly of the United Nations. In its resolution of November 18, 1953, this General Assembly suggested—and I quote—"that the Disarmament Commission study the desirability of establishing a subcommittee consisting of representatives of the powers principally involved, which should seek, in private, an acceptable solution—and report such a solution to the general assembly and to the security council not later than September 1, 1954."

The United States, heeding the suggestion of the General Assembly of the United Nations is instantly prepared to meet privately with such other countries as may be "principally involved" to seek "an acceptable solution" to the atomic armaments race which overshadows not only the peace but the very life of the world. We shall carry into these private or diplomatic talks a new conception. The United States would seek more than the mere reduction or elimination of atomic materials for military purposes. It is not enough to take this weapon out of the hands of the soldiers. It must be put into the hands of those who will know how to strip its military casing and adapt it to the arts of peace.

The United States knows that if the fearful trend of atomic military build-up can be reversed, this greatest of destructive forces can be developed into a great boon for the benefit of all mankind.

The United States knows that peaceful power from atomic energy is no dream of the future. That capability already proved, is here now—today. Who can doubt, if the entire body of the world's scientists and engineers had adequate amounts of fissionable material with which to test and develop their ideas, that this capability would rapidly be transformed into universal efficient and economic usage?

To hasten the day when fear of the atom will begin to disappear from the minds of people and the governments of the East and West there are certain steps that can be taken now. I therefore make the following proposals: the governments principally involved to the extent permitted by elementary prudence to begin now and continue to make joint contributions from their stockpiles of normal uranium and fissionable materials to an international atomic energy agency. We would expect that such an agency would be set up under the aegis of the United Nations. The ratios of contributions, the procedures and other details would properly be within the scope of the "private conversations" I have referred to earlier.

The United States is prepared to undertake these explorations in good faith. Any partner of the United States acting in the same good faith will find the United States a not unreasonable or ungenerous associate. Undoubtedly initial and early contributions to this plan would be small in quantity. However, the proposal has a great virtue that it can be undertaken without the irritations and mutual suspicions incident to any attempt to set up a completely acceptable system of worldwide inspection and control. The Atomic Energy Agency could be made responsible for the impounding, storage and protection of the contributed fissionable and other materials. The ingenuity of our scientists will provide special, safe conditions under which such a bank of fissionable material can be made essentially immune to surprise seizure. The more important responsibility of this atomic energy agency would be to devise methods whereby this fissionable material would be allocated to serve the peaceful pursuits of mankind. Experts would be mobilized to apply atomic energy to the needs of agriculture, medicine and other peaceful activities. A special purpose would be to provide abundant electrical energy in the power-starved areas of the world. Thus the contributing powers would be dedicating some of their strength to serve the needs rather than the fears of mankind.

The United States would be more than willing, it would be proud, to take up with others "principally involved" the development of plans whereby such peaceful use of atomic energy would be expedited. Of those "principally involved" the Soviet Union must, of course, be one.

I would be prepared to submit to the Congress of the United States, and with every expectation of approval any such plan that would:

First, encourage worldwide investigation into the most effective peacetime uses of fissionable material; and with the certainty that they had all the material needed for the conduct of all experiments that were appropriate.

Second, begin to diminish the potential destructive power of the world's atomic stockpiles.

Third, allow all peoples of all nations to see that, in this enlightened age, the great powers of the earth, both of the East and the West, are interested in human aspirations first rather than in building up the armaments of war.

Fourth, open up a new channel for peaceful discussion and initiate at least a new approach to the many difficult problems that must be solved in both private and public conversations if the world is to shake off the inertia imposed by fear and is to make positive progress toward peace.

Against the dark background of the atomic bomb, the United States does not wish merely to present strength, but also the desire and the hope for peace. The coming months will be fraught with fateful decisions. In this Assembly, in the capitals and military headquarters of the world; in the hearts of men everywhere, be they governed or governs *[sic]* governors, may they be the decisions which will lead this world out of fear and into peace.

To the making of these fateful decisions, the United States pledges before you—and therefore before the world—its determination to help solve the fearful atomic di-lemma—to devote its entire heart and mind to find the way by which the miraculous inventiveness of man shall not be dedicated to his death, but consecrated to his life.

I again thank the delegates for the great honor they have done me in inviting me to appear before them and in listening me *[sic]* to me so courteously. Thank you.

EISENHOWER'S ATOMS FOR PEACE SPEECH

A Case Study in the Strategic Use of Language

The miraculous inventiveness of man shall not be dedicated to his death, but consecrated to his life.

CRITIC: Martin J. Medhurst

(This essay was reprinted by permission of the Speech Communication Association and originally appeared in *Communication Monographs*, Vol. 54, June 1987.)

> "Personally, I think this [speech] will be a 'sleeper' as far as this country is concerned—but one of these days when the deserts do bloom, and atomic reactors are turning out electricity where there was no fuel before, and when millions of people are eating who never really ate before...the President's December 1953 speech and proposal will be remembered as the starting point of it all."[1]
>
> > C. D. Jackson, Special Assistant to the
> > President for Psychological Warfare
> > February 5, 1955.

More than thirty years later the deserts have not bloomed, famine is still a reality, and the nuclear reactor, once the hopeful sign of a better tomorrow, stands as a technological indictment of humanity's inability to see beyond the visions of the moment.

Dwight Eisenhower was not the first president to speak of the peaceful uses of atomic energy, yet it was his "Atoms for Peace" speech, delivered in front of the United Nations' General Assembly on December 8, 1953, that marked the public commencement of a persuasive campaign the dimensions of which stagger the imagination. Planned at the highest levels of government, shrouded in secrecy, aided by the military-industrial complex, and executed over the course of two decades, the campaign to promote the "peaceful" use of the atom was conceived in pragmatism, dedicated in realism, and promoted in the spirit of idealism. At each stage of the campaign rhetorical purposes, some lofty, some base, motivated both words and deeds.

Space does not permit a complete explication of this persuasive effort nor even a perfunctory glance at each of its component parts. That must await some future forum. In this essay the pragmatic atmosphere that prompted Eisenhower to deliver a speech advertised as a step away from the nuclear precipice will be described. At the same time, the realist assumptions and motives that reveal Eisenhower's true purposes for delivering his "Atoms for Peace" speech on December 8, 1953 will be explicated.

The argument has three parts. First, that despite American protestations to the contrary, Eisenhower's "Atoms for Peace" speech was, in fact, a carefully-crafted piece of cold war rhetoric specifically designed to gain a "psychological" victory over the Soviet Union. It was part of an American peace offensive launched, in part, as a response to an ongoing Soviet peace offensive.

Second, that the speech creates one audience on the level of explicit argument, but a much different audience when the implicit arguments are examined. Explicitly, the speech is addressed to the world at large, particularly those non-aligned nations in the midst of industrialization. It is aimed at that amorphous animal called world opinion. Implicitly, it is addressed to the Soviet Union, partly as warning, partly as challenge.

Third, that the speech is intentionally structured to invite the world at large to understand "Atoms for Peace" as a step toward nuclear disarmament. In addition to the internal structure, the persuasive campaign carried on immediately before and after the speech was designed explicitly to portray "Atoms for Peace" as part of the free world's (read America's) commitment to nuclear arms control. That the speech was not, in fact, related to disarmament talks but was, rather, an attempt to gain a psychological, cold war victory will be demonstrated.

CONCEIVED IN PRAGMATISM

To understand fully how "Atoms for Peace" evolved to the form in which it was delivered, one must return to the opening weeks of the Eisenhower administration, specifically the events of February, March, and April of 1953. Three events are particularly worthy of note.

In February, a top secret report commissioned by President Truman was delivered to the new Secretary of State, John Foster Dulles. Known internally as the Oppenheimer Report, the document "declared that a renewed search must be made for a way to avert the catastrophe of modern war" (Donovan, 1956, p. 184). Essential to this goal, the report held, was "wider public discussion based upon wider understanding of the meaning of a nuclear holocaust" (Donovan, 1956, p. 184).

As discussion of the policy implications of the Oppenheimer Report ensued, a new factor changed the complexion of American foreign policy: Stalin died. Announced to the world on March 6, 1953, the death of Stalin was viewed as a unique opportunity for advancing the cause of freedom, both in the occupied countries of Europe and within the Soviet Union itself. As historian Louis Halle puts it, the hope was "widespread throughout the West, that the Soviet state, unable to resolve the problem of the succession, would fall into the confusion and helplessness upon Stalin's removal from the scene" (Halle, 1967, p. 312). Nowhere was this hope more evident than within Eisenhower's inner circle.

C. D. Jackson, Special Assistant to the President for cold war strategy (also known as psychological warfare), and the man who would later be primarily responsible for the drafting of "Atoms for Peace," viewed the death of Stalin with both elation and alarm. On March 4, 1953, Jackson wrote to General Robert Cutler, head of the National Security Council:

> This morning's developments, both in Moscow and in Washington point up both a great need and a great opportunity. As to the need, it is hardly an exaggeration to say that no agency of this government had in its files anything resembling a plan, or even a sense-making guidance, to cover the circumstances arising out of the fatal illness or death of Stalin.... It is both fair and safe to say that, left to itself, the existing machinery will be incapable of assuming the initiative and moving on the first really great opportunity that has been presented to us.

Conversely—and this is the opportunity—if we do not take the initiative and capitalize on the dismay, confusion, fear, and selfish hopes brought about by this opportunity, we will be giving the enemy the time to pull himself together, get his wind back, and present us with a new monolithic structure which we will spend years attempting to analyze....

In other words, shouldn't we do everything possible to overload the enemy at the precise moment when he is least capable of bearing even his normal load.... During the present moment of confusion, the chances of the Soviets launching World War III are reduced virtually to zero, and will remain in the low numbers so long as the confusion continues to exist. Our task, therefore, is to perpetuate the confusion as long as possible, and to stave off as long as possible any new crystallization.

It is not inconceivable that out of such a program might come further opportunities which, skillfully exploited, might advance the real disintegration of the Soviet Empire (Jackson, 1953a).

Thus was set in motion a systematic plan to "exploit" the weakness perceived to accompany a Soviet transfer of power. Within the week plans were being laid, amidst much internal dissension, to take advantage of the historical moment. Against the wishes of John Foster Dulles, Jackson convinced the President to launch an American peace offensive and, with the assistance of Walt Rostow and Emmet Hughes, began to draft a major foreign policy address designed, in Rostow's words, "to hold up a vision of the specific long-range objectives of American diplomacy but to make the negotiations designed to achieve that vision contingent upon a prior Korean settlement" (Rostow, 1982, p. 7).

After "some fourteen drafts" (Rostow, 1982, p. 7) the "Age of Peril" speech was delivered before the American Society of Newspaper Editors on April 16, 1953. It was the opening shot in the psychological warfare advocated by Jackson as a means "to preempt a possible Soviet peace offensive" (Rostow, 1982, p. 4). The speech laid out American objectives: settlement in Korea, peace in Indochina, unification of Germany, an Austrian peace treaty, and, in one line, the peaceful use of atomic energy. The atom for peace, long sought after by scientists and visionaries, had now joined the cold war effort.

Having launched the offensive, Jackson, at Eisenhower's direction, continued to probe for opportunities to exploit the situation. In an effort to line up the American public behind the offensive and to prepare them for the twilight struggle that lay ahead, Jackson and Hughes were charged with producing drafts of what came to be known as Operation Candor—a straightforward report to the American people on the destructive capacity of nuclear weapons.

Both Eisenhower and Jackson agreed with the findings of the Oppenheimer Report: that the public must come to understand the full implications of nuclear war. Moreover, the Soviet peace offensive and public weariness with the Korean War made incorporation of the American audience behind the U.S. effort an absolute necessity lest Americans, in the words of Konrad Adenauer, be tempted "to succumb to the blandishments of a detente which for the time being was nothing but a pipedream [sic]" (Adenauer, cited in Rostow, p. 50). It was time to be completely candid with the American public concerning the possibility of mutual destruction, a possibility that now defined the very nature of superpower politics.

Numerous drafts of the Operation Candor speech were produced from late April to early October of 1953. None proved adequate to the task at hand. Furthermore, in the intervening months the situation had changed radically once again. On July 26 a Korean truce had been signed; the war was over. Two weeks later, on August 12, 1953, the Soviet Union tested their first hydrogen bomb. Unbeknownst to the American public, the type of thermonuclear weapon tested by the Soviet Union indicated that they were much closer to the capacity for delivering a hydrogen bomb than anyone imagined.[2] The need for "Candor" was now greater than ever. The public must be prepared for the worst, but there were problems.

On September 2, Jackson wrote to Gordon Arneson at the State Department: "I am afraid that the Candor speech is slowly dying from a severe attack of Committee-itis" (Jackson, 1953b). Though Jackson tried to establish new guidelines for production of the speech, the difficulty of the concepts involved along with a well-publicized leak to *Washington Post* columnist Stewart Alsop (1953, p. 23), resulted in the death of Operation Candor. On September 28, 1953, James Lambie distributed the following memo to the twenty people who were by then involved in the Candor question: "C. D. Jackson asks me to use this outworn method (rather than the more expeditious one of going directly to Stewart Alsop) to make sure you are apprised of the following: Subject Operation, *as a series* of connected and integrated weekly talks is canceled. The President may deliver a single speech of his own in the general area to have been covered by subject series. As of now, however, no final decision has been taken as to such a speech by the President—what, when or whether." [3]

Though no "final decision" had been made, Eisenhower wanted to continue the search for an appropriate speech, though with a different emphasis. Consulting with Jackson, Cutler, and Admiral Lewis L. Strauss, Chairman of the Atomic Energy Commission, Eisenhower proposed, in a very general sort of way, an international pool of fissionable material that could be used strictly for peaceful purposes. It was this idea, first shared with his three top advisors on September 10, that eventually matured into "Atoms for Peace." [4]

The story of the evolution of Project Wheaties, the code name given to the newly-resurrected "Atoms for Peace" speech, is an essay unto itself and must not detain us here. Suffice it to note that starting with the first complete draft on November 3, 1953, "Atoms for Peace" went through eleven major revisions before its presentation on December 8. The last four drafts were completed at the Big Three conference at Bermuda from December 4-7, with the final draft being edited on the flight from Bermuda to New York City on the afternoon of December 8. There is much to be learned from examination of the eleven drafts of the speech, but that, too, is a separate essay. I turn now to the speech delivered by Eisenhower at 4:30 p.m., December 8, 1953, in front of 3500 delegates, guests, and media representatives at the United Nations building in New York City.

DEDICATED IN REALISM

The address was a masterpiece of "realpolitik," long before the term became fashionable. Every line was included (or excluded) for a purpose, and that purpose was strategic advantage, whether defined in terms of placing the Soviet Union at a psychological disadvantage, or in terms of preparing the American audience for an "age" of peril, or in terms of ingratiating the foreign audience.

From the outset, the public posture of the U.S. was that this was *not* a propaganda speech, but a serious proposal that could, if accepted by the Soviets, lead to a climate more conducive to nuclear disarmament. As Eisenhower himself would later maintain in his memoirs, "if we were successful in making even a start, it was possible that gradually negotiation and cooperation might expand into something broader" (Eisenhower, 1963, p. 254). Possible, yes, but not probable. Indeed, given the relative strengths of each side's nuclear forces, the relative scarcity of mineable uranium within the U.S.S.R., and the diplomatic tradition which held that serious proposals were made through private, not public channels, it seems clear that any public offer would have had a propaganda *effect* by placing the Russians on the spot in front of a worldwide audience. Even if the American offer was sincere, it placed the U.S.S.R. in a position of either accepting the offer (and thereby implicitly testifying to America's long-professed desire for peace) or rejecting the offer (and thereby appearing to the world at large as an aggressor unwilling to explore a plan that, as presented by Eisenhower, would benefit directly the underdeveloped nations as well as the cause of international peace).

The beauty of "Atoms for Peace," as conceived by Jackson and Strauss, its primary authors, was precisely that it would place Russia in an awkward position and allow America to gain a psychological advantage on the stage of world opinion. As Jackson wrote to Eisenhower on October 2, 1953: "It must be of such a nature that its rejection by the Russians, or even prolonged foot-dragging on their part, will make it clear to the people of the world...that the moral blame for the armaments race, and possibly war, is clearly on the Russians" (Jackson, 1953c).

ANALYSIS OF THE TEXT

Eisenhower's speech follows a three-part pattern progressing from the present danger, to past efforts toward reconciliation, to a vision for the future. Each section features an America striving after "peace," a term that occurs twenty-four times in the address.[5] One might logically expect a deliberative speech structured chronologically to proceed from past to present to future. Why does Eisenhower violate expectations by starting with the present? There are several reasons.

First, the primary purpose of the speech is psychological advantage rather than historical narration. The story is important only insofar as it provides the context for the perceived psychological gains. Four such gains are paramount: to warn the Russians against nuclear attack on the United States; to alert Americans to the potential destructiveness of a nuclear exchange; to position the United States as a peacemaker and friend in the eyes of the developing nations; and to place the Soviet Union in a policy dilemma by issuing to them a public challenge.

Second, had Eisenhower started with the past he would have encountered two disadvantages: he would have been forced to start with a recitation of failure that would have set the wrong tone for the speech by drawing immediate attention to Russian intransigence, thereby establishing an atmosphere of confrontation, precisely the opposite of what needed to be done if the psychological advantage were to be obtained. Further, by elevating the past to the position of primacy, the president would have been forced to bury the present in the middle portion of the speech. This, too, would have been disadvantageous inasmuch as one of the primary purposes of the address was to issue an implicit warning to the Russians who, it was held widely in military circles, would soon possess the requisite number of nuclear weapons to launch a preemptive strike against the United States. Eisenhower wants to feature the warning, not bury it in the midst of an historical narrative.

Finally, by holding the past efforts at reconciliation until the middle portion of the speech, Eisenhower is able dramatically to juxtapose the failures of the past with his visionary plan for the future. The rhetorical disposition adopted adds argumentative force to the atoms-for-peace proposal by highlighting the significant departure from past plans represented by the new proposal for an international pool of fissionable materials dedicated to peaceful purposes. If the past was characterized by suspicions leading to fear, the future is presented as an opportunity leading to hope.

Atomic Strength of the United States. In the introductory paragraphs the term "hope" or its derivative occurs five times. "Never before in history," claims Eisenhower, "has so much hope for so many people been gathered together in a single organization. Your deliberations and decisions during these somber years have already realized part of those hopes." [6] After paying homage to the organization, Eisenhower asserts that it would not be "a measure of this great opportunity merely to recite, however hopefully, pious platitudes." He realizes, he says, "that if a danger exists in the world, it is a danger shared by all—and equally, that if hope exists in the mind of one nation, that hope should be shared by all."

Thus, in his opening statement, Eisenhower prepares the audience for a speech about the way out of the atomic dilemma that confronts humanity. At this point it would be easy to slip into a chronological pattern, starting with past efforts to solve the dilemma, the state of present negotiations, and, finally, his new plan for the future. A second alternative might be to review, in summary fashion, the hopes of the past and then to continue without pause into discussions of his plan. Eisenhower chooses a third way.

He begins by speaking of the present. "I feel impelled to speak today in a language that in a sense is new—one which I, who have spent so much of my life in the military profession, would have preferred never to use. That new language is the language of atomic warfare." Thus does Eisenhower launch the first part of the body, a section that might well be labeled "The Nuclear Capability of the United States of America," by confronting the audience with the paradox of a warrior who hates to speak of war, thereby distinguishing the persona of the General from that of the statesman. The General spoke the language of war; the President speaks the language of peace.

Though ostensibly a recitation of the extent to which nuclear weapons have proliferated both in size and number since 1945, the opening section is, in reality, a series of veiled warnings to the Soviet Union. Though ostensibly informative in intent, the opening section is really an exhortation whose central message is that the Soviet Union should reconsider any plans it might have for launching a preemptive strike against the United States.

The entire section is a series of warnings under the guise of a dispassionate report as demonstrated in the following chart:

1. *Explicit Argument.* Today, the United States' stockpile of atomic weapons, which, of course, increases daily, exceeds by many times the explosive equivalent of the total of all bombs and all shells that came from every plane and every gun in every theatre of war in all of the years of World War II.	*Implicit Argument.* Be assured that we are not reducing our weapons program despite reported cutbacks in the defense budget. We are building more nuclear weapons every day and will continue to do so as long as we must.

2. *Explicit Argument.* The development has been such that atomic weapons have virtually achieved conventional status within our armed services. In the United States, the Army, the Navy, the Air Force, and the Marine Corps are all capable of putting this weapon to military use.

Implicit Argument. If you think you can hope to prevail over us merely by knocking out our Air Force bases and missile silos, you are woefully mistaken. We are capable of launching a retaliatory nuclear strike against you with any branch of our services.

3. *Explicit Argument.* Our earlier start has permitted us to accumulate what is today a great quantitative advantage.

Implicit Argument. You may have enough nuclear devices to hurt us, but we have a lot more and can outlast you in any nuclear exchange.

4. *Explicit Argument.* The free world...has naturally embarked on a large program of warning and defense systems. That program will be accelerated and expanded.

Implicit Argument. Don't think for a moment that we are letting down our guard. We are prepared both militarily and psychologically.

5. *Explicit Argument.* But for me to say that the defense capabilities of the United States are such that they could inflict terrible losses upon an aggressor—for me to say that the retaliation capabilities of the United States are so great that such an aggressor's land would be laid waste—all this, while fact, is not the true expression of the purpose and the hope of the United States.

Implicit Argument. Think not that the land of Mother Russia will remain inviolate. It will not. We will inflict damage so great that it will make your losses in WW II seem like child's play.

That the movement from explicit to implicit argument was a conscious and intentional strategy is clear from the documentary history. On October 23, 1953, for example, Secretary of State John Foster Dulles sent a "personal and private" memorandum to Eisenhower in which he advises that the speech should "make clear our determination, so long as this danger exists, to take the necessary steps to deter attack, through possession of retaliatory power and the development of continental defense" (Dulles, 1953).

The speech drafts leading up to the December 8 address make it abundantly clear that the writers, principally Jackson and Strauss, are attempting to retain the threat of retaliation while, at the same moment, couching that threat in language that becomes successively less confrontative. In other words, the rhetoric of the drafts proceeds from bold, outright threats to implied warnings couched in the language of peaceful intentions. By comparing the last "Operation Candor" draft completed on or about October 1, 1953, by presidential speechwriter Emmet Hughes, with the final draft delivered by President Eisenhower on December 8, 1953, the movement from explicit to implicit argument can be clearly observed.

The evolution of the speech drafts from early October to early December evidences a shift away from straightforward assertion to implicative argumentation. That the implications are, in most cases, similar or identical to the authorial intentions of the original Candor draft can be seen by comparing the October 1, 1953 draft with the implicit arguments found in the December 8 address.

Candor Draft 10/1/53

We are today armed with bombs a single *one* of which—with an explosive equivalent of more than 500,000 tons of TNT—exceeds by more than *30 times* the power of the first atomic bombs that fell in 1945.... Each *year* sees this mass increase with a power that is many times greater than that of *all* explosives dropped by the aircraft of *all* the Allied nations in World War II.

Candor Draft 10/1/53

Any single *one* of the many air wings of our Strategic Air Command could deliver—in *one* operation—atomic bombs with an explosive equivalent greater than *all* the bombs that fell on Germany through *all* the *years* of World War II.

Any *one* of the aircraft carriers of our Navy could deliver *in one day* atomic bombs exceeding the explosive equivalent of *all* bombs and rockets dropped by Germany upon the United Kingdom through *all* the years of World War II.

We have certain knowledge that we can not only increase greatly the power of our weapons but also perfect their methods of delivery and their tactical use.

These, then, are measures of the fantastic strength we possess.

Candor Draft 10/1/53

We possess detailed evidence of the progress, over the past four years, of the Soviet Union's development of atomic and thermo-nuclear weapons.

We know that in this period the Soviet Union has exploded six atomic devices—and quite recently, one involving thermo-nuclear reaction.

We know, too, how the amassing of these weapons can be speeded by the implacable methods of police state and slave labor.

We know—above all else—this fact: Despite our own swift perfection of new weapons, despite our vast advantage in their numbers—the very nature of these weapons is such that their desperate use against us could inflict terrible damage upon our cities, our industries and our population.

Wheaties Draft 12/8/53

Today, the United States' stockpile of atomic weapons, which, of course, increases daily, exceeds by many times the explosive equivalent of the total of all bombs and all shells that came from every plane and every gun in every theatre of war in all the years of World War II.

Wheaties Draft 12/8/53

The development has been such that atomic weapons have virtually achieved conventional status within our armed services. In the United States, the Army, the Navy, the Air Force, and the Marine Corps are all capable of putting this weapon to military use.

Wheaties Draft 12/8/53

Our earlier start has permitted us to accumulate what is today a great quantitative advantage.

Candor Draft 10/1/53

The second decision is to devise for America a defense system unmatched in the world. Such a system—entailing the most developed use of radar, interceptor aircraft, antiaircraft artillery and guided missiles—is in the making.

The building of this defense will be pressed with uncompromising vigor.... Our defenses will be built with vision, care, common sense: and a frank readiness to spend whatever money or energy such a logical program demands.

Candor Draft 10/1/53

...we declare clearly that if—and wherever—United States forces are involved in repelling aggression, these forces will feel free to use atomic weapons as military advantage dictates.

Any such use of atomic weapons would be strictly governed by a clear order of priority.

(1) They would be used immediately against military forces operating against us or our allies.

Wheaties Draft 12/8/53

The free world...has naturally embarked on a large program of warning and defense systems. The program will be accelerated and expanded.

Wheaties Draft 12/8/53

But for me to say that the defense capabilities of the United States are such that they could inflict terrible losses upon an aggressor—for me to say that the retaliation capabilities of the United States are so great that such an aggressor's land would be laid waste—all this, while fact, is not the true expression of the purpose and the hope of the United States.

That the Soviets are likely to have understood the argumentative implications in ways roughly similar to the reconstructions above is a function both of timing and of access. For four months prior to the December 8 address, the American media ran story after story about governmental, military, and scientific concerns about a possible nuclear confrontation. Not only were such concerns easily picked up through environmental cues, but the Soviets were also given advanced warning about the December 8 speech and instructed to pay close attention and to take seriously what the President said.

In a top secret cable sent from Chip Bohlen, U.S. Ambassador to the Soviet Union, to Secretary of State John Foster Dulles, Bohlen apprised the Secretary of his talk with Russian Foreign Minister Vyacheslav Molotov: "The purpose of my visit to him," cabled Bohlen, "was to draw the attention of Soviet Government in advance to great importance which my Government attached to this speech...I concluded by saying there was no need to stress to him (Molotov) the immense importance of whole question of atomic weapons and repeated the hope that Soviet Government would receive this suggestion as seriously as it was made" (Bohlen, 1953).

In addition to the special visit of Bohlen to Molotov, the Soviet Union's representative to the United Nations, Andrei Vishinsky, was provided an advance copy of the entire address. Vishinsky, as one reporter noted, "appeared to be the only delegate with a copy of the speech" (James, 1953, p. 3). Thus, through both public and private sources, the Soviets were encouraged to listen closely to "Atoms for Peace."

The dichotomy between the arguments as explicitly stated and those same arguments' implications is matched by the dichotomous audiences created by each argumentative level. The audience created by the explicit argument is the world-at-large, the non-nuclear powers who, as spectators in the deadly game of superpower politics, have a legitimate interest in the state-of-the-standoff as perceived by the U.S. President.

A secondary audience for this explicitly argued content is the American public. Operation Candor was originally planned as a series of addresses to the domestic audience, and Eisenhower explicitly states at the outset of the address that these are "thoughts I had originally planned to say primarily to the American people." Though no longer the primary target audience, the American public will still be informed of the terrible destructive capacity of the U.S. arsenal, and thus Eisenhower is able to accomplish multiple goals simultaneously.

But while the audience for the explicit content is clearly the world at large, the target for the implicitly argued content can be none other than the Soviet Union. Why, in a speech ostensibly devoted to "peace," should Eisenhower spend fully twenty percent of his time issuing veiled warnings to the U.S.S.R.? The reasons are many.

According to C.I.A. estimates the Russians would, within a matter of months, have enough nuclear weapons to launch a preemptive strike against the United States. Knowledgeable sources within the scientific, political, and military establishments believed such an attack to be likely (Herken, 1980, p. 325; Menken, cited in "Briton Warns U.S.," 1953, p. 15; Urey, cited in Strauss, 1962, p. 228). Furthermore, the U.S.S.R. had exploded their first thermonuclear weapon and had immediately followed that test with a series of atomic tests lasting well into September. In the space of ninety days the Soviets had tested as many nuclear weapons as in the previous four years combined. Doubtless the sudden spate of activity could be read as a prelude to an all-out attack.

Hence, Eisenhower conceives his task not only to be the articulation of the atomic pool idea, but also the conveying of a strong warning, implicit though it is, that a "surprise attack" by an "aggressor in possession of the effective minimum number of atomic bombs" would be met with "swift and resolute" action. Though he informs the world of the terrible atomic might of the United States of America, he also exhorts the U.S.S.R. to behave itself or suffer the consequences.

Western Deeds and Desires. Having given his "report" on the present state of United States atomic strength, Eisenhower then makes a long, almost Churchillian, transition into the second major section of the speech—the past record of the Western Alliance in both word and deed. To stop with the recitation of the atomic dilemma, says Eisenhower, "would be to accept helplessly the probability of civilization destroyed— the annihilation of the irreplaceable heritage of mankind handed down to us generation from generation—and the condemnation of mankind to begin all over again the age-old struggle upward from savagery toward decency, and right, and justice.... So my country's purpose is to help us move out of the dark chamber of horrors into the light."

But again, it is not the light of the future to which Eisenhower moves, not to the atoms-for-peace plan. Instead, the President turns to the recent past and a recitation of the actions undertaken by the United States and her allies in an effort, he claims, to restore peace and justice to the world. While the explicitly argued content again functions as a report to the world, the implications of the report, the "conclusions" to be drawn by the world audience, are that the Soviet Union has been intransigent.

"Let no one say that we shun the conference table," says Eisenhower. "On the record has long stood the request of the United States, Great Britain, and France to negotiate with the Soviet Union the problems of a divided Germany. On that record has long stood the request of the same three nations to negotiate an Austrian Peace Treaty. On the same record still stands the request of the United Nations to negotiate the problems of Korea."

Eisenhower's method is clear. He seeks to establish the willingness of the Western powers to negotiate, and thereby implies the intransigence and bad faith of the U.S.S.R. Moreover, by positioning the Soviets in the role of spoilers in the recent past, he increases the pressure on them to respond favorably to future entreaties, specifically the plan he is about to announce, a plan no peace-loving nation could reasonably refuse.

Eisenhower seeks to leave no route of escape as he concludes the second section by observing: "There is a record, already written, of assistance gladly given by nations of the West to needy peoples, and to those suffering the temporary effects of famine, drought, and natural disaster. These are deeds of peace. They speak more loudly than promises or protestations of peaceful intent." Once again, Eisenhower seeks to back the Russians into a corner. In effect, he is saying to them, as the whole world watches, "put up or shut up." In the final section of the speech he gives them their chance.

An International Atomic Energy Agency. Eisenhower introduces his atoms-for-peace proposal by quoting a portion of the United Nations resolution passed by the General Assembly only three weeks earlier: "that the Disarmament Commission study the desirability of establishing a subcommittee consisting of representatives of the Powers principally-involved, which should seek in private an acceptable solution...and report on such a solution to the General Assembly and to the Security Council not later than 1 September 1954."

By opening his final section with a quote from the United Nations, itself, Eisenhower accomplishes two goals: first, he establishes a frame of reference with which all delegates are familiar and, ostensibly, with which the vast majority agree; second, he invites the audience to understand his comments within the context of *disarmament*. This fact becomes particularly salient as one seeks to understand precisely what Eisenhower meant by his atoms-for-peace proposal. At the very least, it is clear that the President immediately invites his ostensible audience, the world at large, to believe that what he is about to say has something to do with nuclear disarmament, the subject of both the U.S. resolution and of the first section of the President's own speech.

That such an interpretation could not have been missed by the delegates is assured by the sentence immediately following: "The United States, heeding the suggestion of the General Assembly of the United Nations, is instantly prepared to meet privately with such other countries as may be 'principally involved,' to seek 'an acceptable solution' to the atomic armaments race."

Having committed himself to the exploration of arms control, Eisenhower makes a crucial transition that both shifts the ground from which he originally opened his final section of the speech and commences his challenge to the Soviet Union, a challenge which, whether accepted or rejected by the U.S.S.R., will, it is believed, result in a great psychological victory for the United States: "It is not enough to take this weapon out of the hands of the soldiers. It must be put into the hands of those who will know how to strip its military casing and adapt it to the arts of peace." Thus begins Eisenhower's argument for the development of atomic energy for peaceful purposes.

After proclaiming that "peaceful power from atomic energy is no dream of the future," but rather is "here—now—today," Eisenhower launches into the heart of the atoms-for-peace proposal: "The Governments principally involved, to the extent permitted by elementary prudence, to begin now and continue to make joint contributions from their stockpiles of normal uranium and fissionable materials to an International Atomic Energy." This Agency, said Eisenhower, "could be made responsible for the impounding, storage, and protections of the contributed fissionable and other materials."

"The more important responsibility of this Atomic Energy Agency," he continues, "would be to devise methods whereby this fissionable material would be allocated to serve the peaceful pursuits of mankind. Experts would be mobilized to apply atomic energy to the needs of agriculture, medicine, and other peaceful activities. A special purpose would be to provide abundant electrical energy in the power-starved areas of the world."

The appeal is clearly to those non-nuclear nations represented in the U.N. audience, particularly those to whom power, and agriculture, and medicine are pressing needs. To the world audience of 1953 this would have included the vast majority of member states. The pledge is equally clear: to share of our abundance, in this case our nuclear know-how, with those nations less fortunate. But there is one condition attached.

"The United States would be more than willing," Eisenhower continues, "to take up with others 'principally involved' the development of plans whereby such peaceful use of atomic energy would be expedited. Of those 'principally involved' the Soviet Union must, of course, be one." The proposition could hardly have been put in a more explicit manner. Eisenhower challenges the Soviets to join in an international effort to aid U.N. member nations, and he does so right in front of them so there may be no mistake about his offer. The challenge shifts the burden of proof squarely onto the shoulders of the Soviets. If they really are interested in peace, then here, says Eisenhower, is the perfect chance to demonstrate their commitment .

The International Agency, Eisenhower pledged, would have four tasks:

1. To "encourage worldwide investigation into the most effective peacetime uses of fissionable material;"
2. To "begin to diminish the potential destructive power of the world's atomic stockpiles;"
3. To "allow all peoples of all nations to see that...the great powers of the earth...are interested in human aspirations first, rather than in building up the armaments of war;"
4. To "open up a new channel for peaceful discussion, and initiate at least a new approach to the many difficult problems that must be solved...."

"Against the dark background of the atomic bomb," he concludes, "the United States does not wish merely to present strength, but also the desire and the hope for peace.... To the making of these fateful decisions, the United States pledges before you—and therefore before the world—its determination to help solve the fearful atomic dilemma." The section ends, as it had begun, with allusions to atomic disarmament. Indeed, the implicit message to the assembled delegates is that atoms-for-peace, in addition to helping non-nuclear nations reap the benefits of nuclear energy, is a step toward and a mechanism for converting the means of war into instruments of peace. It is a different approach to the whole disarmament problem and the "awful arithmetic" to which Eisenhower had earlier referred.

The implied content of this final section is directed exclusively toward world opinion. The implications to be drawn by the world-wide audience are roughly as follows:

1. The United States is making a serious offer to share its nuclear materials and expertise with the international community.
2. The United States is doing this because it wants to reduce the risks of war and increase international cooperation.
3. If the "principally-involved" parties all cooperate, then there will be an advance in the quality of life all over the globe.
4. The powers of nuclear energy are near-miraculous and the cures mentioned by Eisenhower are immediately available if only the Soviets will cooperate.

The explicit message directed to the Soviet Union is this: Here's the plan; it will benefit the entire world community whose eyes now rest on you. Will you cooperate? Eisenhower places a challenge squarely before the Soviets and dares them—in front of the whole world—to accept the challenge or suffer the consequences that will be wrought, not by the military might of the United States, but by the psychological weight of world opinion turned sour.

EXTERNAL REACTION

As Eisenhower finished his speech there was a "burst of applause" (Hamilton, 1953, p. 2) that swelled to a crescendo. Even Soviet representative Andrei Vishinsky joined in the chorus. The next day Eisenhower's proposal was bannered across the nation's leading newspapers, and the effort to decipher precisely what he meant began.

Thomas Hamilton, writing on the front page of the New York *Times,* observed that "implicit in the President's speech was the realization that the United Nations would have to make a new start if the seven-year-old deadlock on international atomic control was ever to be broken" (Hamilton, 1953, p. 1). Hamilton recalled the failure of the Baruch Plan in 1946, and linked Eisenhower's atoms-for-peace proposal to that earlier effort. In Hamilton's opinion the speech clearly was aimed at moving disarmament talks off dead center.

The editorial page of the Washington *Post* also viewed Eisenhower's proposals as precursors to disarmament: "If the nations of the world—meaning Russia and the Western Allies—could cooperate on the diversion of nuclear materials for peaceful purposes, the groundwork might be laid for cooperation on genuine disarmament" ("The Choice," 1953, p. 10). The proposal was viewed as being part of the long-term process of disarmament .

Reaction on Capitol Hill was, if anything, even more infused with apocalyptic visions of peace. Representative James E. Van Zandt (R-PA) claimed that Eisenhower had "sounded the clarion call to all nations to beat the atomic sword of destruction into plowshares by harnessing the power of the atom for peaceful pursuits" ("Ike's Speech Praised," 1953, p. 16). Similar reactions were voiced throughout the corridors of official Washington .

Such reactions, in themselves, should not be surprising in light of the fact that the "correct" interpretation of the speech was carefully orchestrated and planted in the various media organs by none other than C. D. Jackson. It was Jackson who provided advance copies of the speech, then classified top-secret, to Ernest K. Lindley of *Newsweek,* Roscoe Drummond of the New York *Herald Tribune,* and James Shepley of *Time* magazine (McCrum, 1975, pp. 45-46). It was Jackson, who, in his capacity as a member of the Operations Coordinating Board, designed the campaign to "exploit" the speech, a campaign that included use of "leaders of opposition parties," the Voice of America, Radio Free Europe, the C.I.A., and other "non-attributable instrumentalities" (Jackson, 1954). The message, regardless of medium, was the same: "Atoms for Peace" is a serious peace proposal that could lead to control of the atomic armaments race.

Despite Jackson's best efforts, not all opinion leaders bought into the official "line" on the speech. One such group was the leadership of the Canadian government. Reporting from Ottawa, a correspondent for the New York *Times* noted that "as the speech was interpreted here, President Eisenhower's proposal for an international body and a common stockpool *[sic]* of fissionable material was limited to peaceful uses of atomic energy and could not have any decisive effect on the question of the use of atomic weapons in war" ("Canadians Await Details," 1953, p. 3).

Here was the crucial point. Was the atoms-for-peace proposal a serious effort to take the first step toward disarmament or was it not? If it was not intended as a step toward disarmament why was it given in the first place and, why was it placed within the general context of nuclear destruction and within the specific context of the ongoing disarmament debate at the U.N.? Clearly, the structuring of the speech invites the listeners to associate atoms-for-peace with the general disarmament debate.

INTERNAL DEBATE

If Eisenhower's precise meaning was, despite Jackson's best efforts, a matter of some speculation on the international scene, it was no less obscure within the administration's own inner circles. The debate over what the president meant to say started even before the speech was delivered. As early as mid-October there was fierce disagreement between Jackson and the State Department over the advisability of making any speech at all. As Candor evolved into Wheaties, early in November, the disagreements within the administration began to crystallize.

Jackson chronicled the struggle in his personal log. On November 17, 1953, he wrote: "Meeting in Foster Dulles' office with Lewis Strauss. Unfortunately Bob Bowie invited in. Subject—Wheaties, and UN appearance on December 8. Dulles went into reverse, ably needled by Bowie—he didn't like UN idea; he didn't like Strauss' proposal; he didn't like anything. Bowie kept repeating that this was not the way to do things—quiet, unpublicized negotiations were the only thing that would get anywhere with Ruskies" (Jackson, 1953d).

But quiet diplomacy was anything but what Jackson had in mind. On November 21, 1953, Jackson wrote to Sherman Adams concerning "what we have in mind for December 8," and warning that "if this is *not* properly orchestrated, and these things are dribbled out without organized impact, we will fritter away what is probably the greatest opportunity we have yet had" (Jackson, 1953e). Jackson suggested six specific steps to Adams for insuring proper orchestration. One of these was that "every single one of the Departmental and Agency PR heads should be constantly worked with to see that they keep the news coming out of their departments beamed on a pre-determined frequency" (Jackson, 1953e). Jackson's concern was the psychological victory to be gained and the supposed benefits flowing therefrom. But the State Department had not yet rested its case.

On November 23, 1953, Bob Bowie sent his criticisms of the latest Wheaties draft (draft #4) to Secretary Dulles: "I question whether the proposal on atomic contributions by the United States and the Soviets will have its intended effect. Many people, and probably the Soviets, will treat it as a propaganda tactic rather than a serious proposal if it is made in this way. If serious results were hoped for, many would expect us to attempt private discussions with the Soviets as a beginning" (Bowie, 1953a).

Bowie's reservations came to fruition two days later at a "big meeting in Foster Dulles' office." According to Jackson's log, "red lights started blinking all over the place. Joint Chiefs and Defense have laid their ears back" (Jackson, 1953f). After a one-day Thanksgiving break, the group met again in Dulles' office. The "real problem," as Jackson recorded in his log,

> is basic philosophy—are we or are we not prepared to embark on a course which may in fact lead to atomic disarmament? Soldier boys and their civilian governesses say no. Foster Dulles doesn't say yes or no, but says any atomic offer which does not recognize ultimate possibility is a phoney and should not be made. Strauss and I say we won't be out of the trenches by Christmas, or next Christmas or the next one, but let's try to make a start and see what happens. Foster considers this mentally dishonest (he should talk!) (Jackson, 1953g).

Dulles was not the only one with reservations. His Policy Planning Staff head, Robert Bowie, was also deeply disturbed. As he wrote to Dulles on November 30, 1953: "The only serious point of substance is the one about which we have talked: whether the United States wishes to achieve full-scale atomic disarmament if that should prove possible. My own view is that we definitely should. But unless this is our view I do not think this speech should be made" (Bowie, 1953b). Bowie's opinion was not heeded. Eisenhower made the speech with no consensus among his inner circle as to precisely what, if anything, the United States would do if confronted with the possibility of disarmament.

CONCLUSION

The speech, as delivered, reflected the Jackson-Strauss position which held that disarmament, while desirable, was not an immediately realizable goal. The purpose for giving the speech was, therefore, not to establish a framework for talks about control of nuclear weapons, but instead was an effort to position the United States with respect to the peaceful uses of atomic energy and to bid the Soviets in a public forum to adopt that position, thereby gaining a psychological victory whatever the Russian response might be.

Jackson's memo to the Operations Coordinating Board on December 9, the day following the speech, is instructive: "It will be particularly important to impress upon world opinion the sincerity with which the United States seeks international security through the reduction of the arms burden, while at the same time avoiding any premature stimulation of false optimism regarding immediately realizable disarmament, which cannot be fulfilled under present conditions of international tensions" (Jackson, 1953h). From Jackson's point of view there was no doubt that the speech, though clothed in the language of disarmament, was not, itself, a vehicle for such disarmament, at least not at the present time.

That Eisenhower's speech raised the hope of turning weapons into plowshares can hardly be denied. That the majority of those in the inner circle who crafted the speech intended that nothing *more* than hope be offered can also hardly be denied. Though the public "exploitation" of the speech emphasized peace and negotiation, the backroom decision was that the United States would not "be drawn into separate negotiations with the Soviets on the elimination or control of nuclear weapons alone. For our part," says a summary of a top secret meeting held on January 16, 1954, "we intend to discuss only the peaceful uses of atomic energy" (O.C.B., 1954).

The summary of the January 16, 1954 meeting goes on to note that "Secretary Dulles reiterated that we should try through these discussions to get across to friendly nations the idea that the disagreement over the control of the atomic weapons was not a bilateral difference of opinion between the United States and the U.S.S.R., but rather was a split between the U.S.S.R. and the remainder of the free world" (O.C.B., 1954). If this could be accomplished, if the Soviet Union could be isolated as the foe who refused to cooperate with the rest of the world, then the psychological victory would be won. This was the great, and arguably the primary, purpose for the "Atoms for Peace" speech of December 8, 1953.

By employing both implicit and explicit argumentative techniques, Eisenhower was able to accomplish his goals. He warned the Soviet Union against a preemptive strike; he portrayed the United States as the friend and benefactor of the developing world; and, most importantly, he placed the Soviet Union in a policy dilemma by challenging the U.S.S.R. to accept his atoms-for-peace proposal. Throughout the speech and the subsequent campaign to "exploit" it, the administration portrayed the December 8 speech as a serious offer to negotiate the problems of the nuclear age with any potential adversary. That the speech was, in reality, not such an offer at all testifies to the ease with which human agents can shape language and guide perception in accordance with their own purposes .

Language is not self-explanatory. It is a reflection of the goals, motives, and values of those who choose to use it as an instrument by which to realize their ends. This study demonstrates how a particular group of rhetors used language to address multiple audiences for divergent purposes while, at the same moment, maintaining that the audience was one and the purpose straightforward. Criticism, at this level, is the study of how language is used by humans to channel response, and is, in the case examined, a paradigm both of linguistic deception and strategic posturing at the highest levels of government.

Martin J. Medhurst, Ph.D., is professor of Speech Communication at Texas A. & M. University.

NOTES

1. Letter from C. D. Jackson to Merlo Pusey, 5 February, 1955. C. D. Jackson Papers, Box 24, Dwight D. Eisenhower Library.

2. According to Robert A. Devine, "on August 12, 1953, American officials detected the first Soviet hydrogen explosion.... What neither Eisenhower nor Strauss revealed, however, was that the Russian device had used dry hydrogen isotopes that did not require unwieldy refrigeration. The Soviets now appeared not only to have caught up with American nuclear technology but to have moved closer than the United States to a deliverable hydrogen bomb." See Devine (1978), *Blowing on the Wind: The Nuclear Test Ban Debate 1954-1960.* New York: Oxford University Press, pp. 16-17.

3. Memo from James M. Lambie to R. Gordon Arneson, Edmond Gullion, Brig. Gen. P. T. Carroll, Emmet J. Hughes, Abbott Washburn, Roy McNair, William V. Watts, Ralph Clark, Ray Snapp, W. B. McCool, Jack DeChant, George "Pete" Hotchkiss, Edward Lyman, Maj. Gen. A. R. Luedecke, George Wyeth, Lt. Col. Edwin F. Block, William H. Godel, Fred Blachly, Mrs. Jeanne Singer, William Rogers, 28 September 1953, White House Central Files (WHCF), Box 12, Dwight D. Eisenhower Library.

4. Given the chronology of development of the *idea* for atoms-for-peace, it seems likely that Eisenhower picked up the general concept from a series of articles appearing in the New York *Times* from August 12-14, 1953. The three-part series written by William L. Laurence included the following lines: "The first international conference on atomic energy for industrial power voted unanimously at its closing session today in favor of establishing an international nuclear energy association, open to nuclear scientists of all the nations of the world, including the Soviet Union and other countries behind the Iron Curtain.... The purpose of the association would be to promote the peaceful uses of atomic energy through the exchange of knowledge by the various participating countries on subjects not related to military applications." See Laurence (1953, August 14). Atom scientists favor world pool of ideas, New York *Times*, p. 1.

5. The total count of twenty-four includes "peace" and its derivatives "peaceful" and "peacetime ."

6. All quotations from Eisenhower's "Atoms for Peace" address are from the text as printed in *Public Papers of the President of the United States, 1953*. Washington, D.C.: Government Printing Office, pp. 813-822.

REFERENCES

Alsop, S. (1953, September 18). Candor is not enough. Washington *Post,* p. 23.

Bohlen, C. (1953). Unpublished cablegram from Chip Bohlen to J. F. Dulles. John Foster Dulles Papers, Box 1, Dwight D. Eisenhower Library.

Bowie, R. R. (1953a, November 23). Unpublished memo from Robert R. Bowie to Secretary Dulles, John Foster Dulles Papers, Box 1, Dwight D. Eisenhower Library.

Bowie, R. R. (1953b, November 30). Unpublished memo from Robert R. Bowie to Secretary Dulles, John Foster Dulles Papers, Box 1, Dwight D. Eisenhower Library.

Canadians await details. (1953, December 9). New York *Times,* p. 3.

Donovan, R. J. (1956). *Eisenhower. The Inside Story.* New York: Harper and Brothers .

Dulles, J. F. (1953). Unpublished memo from J. F. Dulles to Eisenhower. John Foster Dulles Papers, Box 1, Dwight D. Eisenhower Library.

Eisenhower, D. D. (1963). *Mandate for a Change.* Garden City: Doubleday.

Halle, L. J. (1967). *The Cold War as History.* New York: Harper and Row.

Hamilton, T. J. (1953, December 9). Eisenhower bids Soviets join United States in atomic stockpile for peace. New York *Times,* pp. 1-2.

Herken, G. (1980). The winning weapon: The atomic bomb in the cold war 1945-1950. New York: Alfred A. Knopf.

Ike's speech praised generally on "Hill." (1953, December 9). Washington *Post,* p. 16.

Jackson, C. D. (1953a, March 4). Unpublished memo from C. D. Jackson to Gordon Arneson. White House Central Files, Confidential File, Box 12, Dwight D. Eisenhower Library.

Jackson, C. D. (1953c, October 2). Unpublished memo from C. D. Jackson to the President. C. D. Jackson Papers, Box 24, Dwight D. Eisenhower Library.

Jackson, C. D. (1953d, November 17). Unpublished log entry. C. D. Jackson Papers, Box 56, Dwight D. Eisenhower Library.

Jackson, C. D. (1953e, November 21). Unpublished memo from C. D. Jackson to Sherman Adams. C. D. Jackson Papers, Box 23, Dwight D. Eisenhower Library.

Jackson, C. D. (1953f, November 25). Unpublished log entry. C. D. Jackson Papers, Box 56, Dwight D. Eisenhower Library.

Jackson, C. D. (1953g, November 27). Unpublished log entry. C. D. Jackson Papers, Box 56, Dwight D. Eisenhower Library.

Jackson, C. D. (1953h), December 9). Unpublished memo from C. D. Jackson to members of the Operations Coordinating Board. Box 1, Dwight D. Eisenhower Library.

Jackson, C. D. (1954, February 16). Unpublished memo from C. D. Jackson to members of the Operations Coordinating Board. White House Central Files, Confidential File, Box 13, Dwight D. Eisenhower Library.

James, M. (1953, December 9). President's plan stirs doubts in U.N. New York *Times*, p. 3.

McCrum, M. (1975, May 15). Unpublished oral history interview, Dwight D. Eisenhower Library.

Operations Coordinating Board. (1954, January 16). Summary of O.C.B. Meeting, White House Central Files, Confidential File, Box 12, Dwight D. Eisenhower Library.

Rostow, W. W. (1982). *Europe After Stalin: Eisenhower's Three Decisions of March 11, 1953.* Austin: University of Texas Press.

Strauss, L. L. (1962). *Men and Decisions.* Garden City: Doubleday.

The choice on the atom. (1953, December 9). Washington *Post*, p. 10.

PEACE IN THE MIDDLE EAST

Golda Meir

United Nations General Assembly, New York City, October 7, 1957
(Transcribed from excerpts on the video, GREAT SPEECHES, VOLUME II)

Mr. President, it is my privilege at the outset of my remarks to express to you the deep pleasure and satisfaction evoked in my country by your election to the highest office and the gift of the United Nations. Your integrity of purpose, your clarity of thought and expression, your judicial temperament are an example here to us all and we feel fortunate indeed in the choice of our presiding officer. I wish also to convey to the Secretary-General the sincere congratulations of my government and his unanimous reelection to the honorous [sic] and distinguished office which he occupies.

In the course of the debate, the distinguished Prime Minister of Canada expressed the wish that this the 12th Assembly might be known as the assembly of disarmament. Many other speakers have echoed this wish and this hope. But Mr. President, is it not tragic that the 12th Assembly should still be talking of hopes for disarmament 12 years after a war that was characterized by horrors which no human mind could comprehend or envisage; is it not tragic that forty years after the First World War which was fought under the slogan of "The War To End All Wars," we of this generation, many of whom witnessed the ravages of both, are still engaged in debating the need and desirability of disarmament?

All employ almost the identical terminology. All speak of peace. But this is accompanied by such lack of confidence, by such lack of friendship that one often stops and wonders whether words have retained their original connotation. Whether the same word spoken by different representatives really has the same meaning.

We—all of the new sovereign States—should be permitted and encouraged to concentrate all our energy, all of our resources in manpower and economic resources in fighting poverty, illiteracy, disease and desolation. But, Mr. President, are these the realities of the world in which we live? No. The sad and cruel fact is that these new countries are born into a world bitterly divided and preoccupied by a headlong race to increase destructive power and distressed by a global tension which moves from one region to another without losing its acuteness or peril. The burden under which we, the young and small nations, begin our new life is that of armaments and before we can cope with the problems of development, we are driven by necessity to prepare to defend what was just gained—our freedom and our very being.

Israel fully agrees that problems of disarmament, both global and regional, should have a primary place in the work of this session. It is vital that we should break the cycle of failure which has for so long characterized this central problem. While it is true that effective progress is dependent upon the action and agreement of a very few of our membership it is the duty of all of us not to remain merely passive onlookers. We must express our opinion that it is inconceivable that these talks be discontinued. They must go on until an understanding is reached. If all those who call for peace mean it, then an agreement will be reached, has to be reached. Israel, together with all other members of this Assembly, will follow most closely and anxiously the disarmament negotiations.

Mr. President, ten years ago on November 29,1947, the General Assembly passed an historic resolution providing for the establishment of a Jewish State. In May 1948 the Arab League States launched against Israel a war intended to destroy the new State. They failed in their attempt and a few months later Israel was admitted to the United Nations; and yet to this day these same States, despite their membership of the United Nations refuse to accept the Charter as the basis of their relations with Israel—a fellow member.

This long-standing violation of the Charter is a basic factor in the unrest and tension in our area. It has expressed itself in the illegal continuance by these Arab countries of a declared state of war, of belligerency, blockade and organized acts of hostility. It was directly responsible for the crisis of last winter which in turn led to United Nations intervention. It continues unabated to this very day.

It is true that the United Nations, which initiated Israel's withdrawal last spring has itself assumed active responsibility for preventing belligerent acts at the two points where the United Nations Emergency Force is deployed. No Government of peaceful intent or aspiration would wish in any way to disturb the *status quo* which now prevails in these two sectors. But in the Suez Canal not even this limited degree of progress has been achieved. Its international character in fact has been subordinated and obscured and the Canal is being operated under an illegal system of discrimination. Israeli ships are not permitted to pass through the Canal and even ships of other flags bound for Israel are detained—cargo and crew are examined—and if an Israeli is among the crew, he is taken off the vessel, interrogated and mishandled and kept under arrest for weeks.

The distinguished delegate from New Zealand has accurately evaluated the situation as follows:

Shipping is once more passing through the Suez Canal, but the conditions of passage are by no means satisfactory. As long as Israel shipping is prevented from using the Canal, the provisions of the 1888 Convention will not be fully carried out, and the international character of the waterway will be infringed.

The apparent passivity of the United Nations in the face of Arab political terrorism and obstruction is unfortunately reflected also in the regional activities of the United Nations. The ramified boycott operations of the Arab League against Israel extend into the fields of health, of education, of agriculture, science and economics. In this tireless campaign the Arab States seek even to involve the United Nations and its Specialized Agencies despite the fact that their constitutions expressly or implicitly outlaw every form of discrimination. As a result, on the economic side, for example, the Middle East is today the only one of the world's regions without a United Nations Economic Commission. The regional office of the World Health Organization in Alexandria is inaccessible to one of the members of the region. The International Civil Aviation Organization, the United Nations Educational, Scientific and Cultural Organization and the Food and Agricultural Organization are other examples of bodies whose work has likewise been detrimentally affected. One is driven to ask whether the United Nations really has to accommodate itself to Arab tactics so that even its regional agencies are paralyzed or severely handicapped in their efforts to secure higher standards of economic and social progress, of health and education for all.

The distinguished Foreign Minister of the Soviet Union in his speech to the

Assembly last week placed much emphasis on "the need for and advantage of peaceful co-existence between States." That is an objective to which Israel stands committed with all its heart and soul. But, is the massive and uninterrupted flow of weapons of destruction into our region, to States that deny the right of existence to a neighbor State, remotely likely to bring about that desirable end? We believe that this is a question which answers itself and we feel entitled to ask Mr. Gromyko whether the principle which he has adumbrated for all, does not apply also to our part of the world.

In fact a deadly spiral is being created with these consequences:

(1) The danger of destructive war is increased;

(2) The tensions within the region make it the focus for even greater tensions from outside—to the detriment of the hard-won independence of Middle Eastern States;

(3) A pathetically large proportion of the region's own resources, and of the resources available to the region from outside, must be devoted to weapons of destruction, while the population and economics of the region languish in sterile hardship and backwardness.

The Middle East is one of the underdeveloped areas of the world. National income per capita in the Arab countries of the region is on the average estimated at a little above $100 per year, barely ten percent of that of some of the countries of Europe.

All this expresses itself in such very real things as insufficient food consumption, unhealthy and congested housing, primitive sanitary conditions, a high incidence of disease and especially of those chronic diseases which weaken the body, sap the energies and shorten life, a high infant mortality rate and a high rate of illiteracy. Most of the amenities of life are virtually absent in the vast rural areas of the region. At the same time while in Jordan, Syria, Iraq and Egypt—expenditures on health and education have amounted to between 8 and 21% of the total budget, defense expenditures have ranged from 19 to 60% of their budgets.

The combined defense expenditures in these four countries during the last three years amount according to their published budgets to some 930 million dollars. But this figure includes in part arms shipments by foreign powers at nominal value only, while the real value of these shipments is in some instances estimated to be several times as high. Some of the latest arms shipments are not included at all in this figure. The real value therefore of the resources used for armaments and the maintenance of armies in these countries, during three years up to now may be estimated at the figure, huge for our area, of one and a half to two billion dollars.

Imagine what such amounts, used for investment in irrigation works, farm implements, factory plants, transport facilities could have meant in economic development and in the expansion of health and education.

In Israel too the burden of armaments presses hard. For its part it would wish nothing better than to use all the resources available to it for development and the fruitful economic absorption of its growing population. But in the contexts of its neighbors' threats and menaces it has no alternative. Nevertheless despite this tragic diversion of manpower and resources to the needs of defense, Israel's record in the economic and social fields is one of no mean order.

Since 1948 it has received nearly one million immigrants, the great majority of whom are refugees, hailing from over 70 countries and from all corners of the world, including nearly 400,000 of them from the Arab-speaking lands.

But of all…above all we are proud of what has been done with people. The great majority of those who came to Israel during these ten years came either from the post-war camps in Germany and Italy or from Arab-speaking countries.

Practically each one from the camps reflected in his loneliness the destruction of all who were dear and close. These were the remnants of the six million—the Hitler slaughter of the Jews of Europe. Broken in body and spirit they came to a country of hardship, and yet at the meeting of desolate desert with victims of horror and destruction both the land and the people have come to life. The desert has given way to cotton and wheat; forest and vineyards are covering barren hills, and with a new dignity and hope the settlers themselves bear witness to the unconquerable spirit of free man.

Its policy is well known. It is the establishment of Israel is based on this very principle—that the doors of Israel remain open forever to any and every Jew who wishes or must come to its shores. We are convinced, not only is there no danger, no threat from this immigration to Israel to any one of our neighbors, on the contrary, as it has been proven in the last ten years the incoming of these people have helped in the development of the country and I'm convinced, eventually will serve as an example for the development also of our neighboring countries.

Within the area, the question is whether the Arab States are ready to change their outlook and policy and to bring them into conformity with Charter principles—especially those which concern the independence and integrity of each Member State.

Israel has, through the Secretary-General, addressed to Egypt and to Syria within the past 6 months the question as to whether they were prepared to renounce their claim to the maintenance of a state of war with Israel—surely a legitimate question when addressed to a United Nations Member State. The Secretary-General has received no reply from either country.

The position of Israel has been stated on many previous occasions and remains unchanged. It seeks peace above all. It remains ever ready to defend itself, if attacked, but it has never had and has not now any aggressive intentions or designs against the independence or integrity of any of its neighbors. The obvious and essential need for our area is the conclusion of peace treaties placing the relationship between neighboring States on a permanently normal footing.

However, if the Arabs are not ready for this, I reiterate what was stated by the Israel representative at the Ninth Session of the General Assembly, and I quote:

> …as a preliminary of transitory stage towards this end, towards a peace settlement, it might be useful to conclude agreements committing the parties to policies of non-aggression and pacific settlement. Such agreements would include undertakings to respect each other's territorial integrity and political independence, to refrain from all hostile acts of a military, economic or political character, and to settle all existing and future differences by pacific means.

Unquote.

Mr. President, I should like from this rostrum to address to the Arab States of the Middle East a solemn appeal: Israel is approaching her tenth anniversary. You did not want it to be born. You fought against the decision in the United Nations. You then attacked us by military force. We have all been witnesses to sorrow, destruction and the spilling of blood and tears. Yet Israel is here, growing, developing, progressing. It has gained many friends and their number is steadily increasing. We are an old tenacious people and, as our history has proved, not easily destroyed. Like you, the Arab countries, we have regained our national independence, and as with you, so with us, nothing will cause us to give it up. We are here to stay. History has decreed that the Middle East consists of an independent Israel and independent Arab States. This verdict will never be reversed.

In the light of these facts, what is the use or realism or the justice of policies and attitudes based on the fiction that Israel is not there, or will somehow disappear? Would it not be better for all to build a future for the Middle East based on cooperation? Israel will exist and flourish even without peace, but surely a future of peace would be better both for Israel and for her neighbors. The Arab world with its 10 sovereignties and over three million square miles can well afford to accommodate itself to peaceful cooperation with Israel. Does hate for Israel and the aspiration for its destruction make one child in your countries happier? Does it convert one hovel into a house? Does culture thrive on the soil of hatred? We have not the slightest doubt that eventually there will be peace and cooperation between us. This is an historic necessity for both people. We are prepared; we are anxious to bring it about now.

And Mr. President, I should like to address myself to all delegates in this Assembly and especially to the Powers directly involved in the problems of the Middle East. The deserts of the Middle East are in need of water, not bombers. The tens of millions of its inhabitants are craving for the means to live and not for the implements of death. I ask all of you, old members of the United Nations and the new, use your influence not to deepen the abyss of misunderstanding, but to bridge it.

And I wish to conclude with a word of the deepest appreciation to those countries, Member States of the United Nations, who just ten years ago helped to lay the foundations for Israel's statehood and whose continued understanding, assistance and friendship has enabled us to weather the storms which have beset our path.

In celebrating the tenth anniversary of Israel's independence we look back on a decade of struggle, of achievement in some areas, of failure in others. But by and large it has justified a thousandfold the vision of those who saw in the re-establishment of Israel's nationhood an historic act of reparation and of statesmanship. Our greatest grief has been the lack of progress towards peace with our Arab neighbors. It is our profoundest hope that the coming period we make a decisive forward step in this regard, to the inestimable benefit of all the people of the Middle East and perhaps of the entire world.

PART III: CEREMONIAL SPEECHES

CHAPTER 8:
Inaugural Addresses

In a country deprived of the ceremony associated with royalty, the Inaugural ceremony provides an important link between generations of Americans. The traditional Address honors the past and signals renewal of the American ideals. In recent times, two such addresses stand out as historic and noteworthy.

In 1932, facing the worst economic crisis in generations, Franklin Roosevelt used the stability of the Inaugural tradition to ease the fears of his countrymen. John F. Kennedy's Inaugural Address alerted his audience to the new agenda of his youthful leadership. Nicholas Cripe assesses Kennedy's presentation which has become one of the most frequently quoted speeches in American history.

FIRST INAUGURAL ADDRESS

Franklin D. Roosevelt

Washington, D.C., March 4, 1933 (Transcribed from the video, GREAT SPEECHES, VOLUME V)

President Hoover, Mr. Chief Justice, my friends. This is a day of national consecration, and I am certain that on this day my fellow Americans expect that on my induction into the Presidency I will address them with a candor and a decision which the present situation of our people impels. This is preeminently the time to speak the truth, {frankly} and boldly. Nor need we shrink from honestly facing conditions in our country today. This great nation will endure as it has endured, will revive, and will prosper. So, first of all, let me assert my firm belief that the only thing we have to fear is fear itself—nameless, unreasoning, unjustified terror which paralyzes needed efforts to convert retreat into advance.

In every dark hour of our national life, a leadership of frankness and of vigor has met with that understanding and support of the people themselves which is essential to victory, and I am convinced that you will again give that support to leadership in these critical days.

In such a spirit on my part and on yours we face our common difficulties. They concern, thank God, only material things. Values have shrunk to fantastic levels, taxes have risen, our ability to pay has fallen, government of all kinds is faced by serious curtailment of income, the means of exchange are frozen in the currents of trade, the withered leaves of industrial enterprise lie on every side, farmers find no markets for their produce, and the savings of many years in thousands of families are gone. More important, a host of unemployed citizens face the grim problem of existence, and an equally great number toil with little return. Only a foolish optimist can deny the dark realities of the moment.

And yet our distress comes from no failure of substance. We are stricken by no plague of locusts. Compared with the perils which our forefathers conquered, because they believed and were not afraid, we have still much to be thankful for. Nature still offers her bounty, and human efforts have multiplied it. Plenty is at our doorstep, but a generous use of it languishes in the very sight of the supply. Primarily, this is because the rulers of the exchange of mankind's goods have failed through their own stubbornness and their own incompetence, have admitted their failure, and have abdicated. Practices of the unscrupulous money-changers stand indicted in the court of public opinion, rejected by the hearts and minds of men.

True, they have tried, but their efforts have been cast in the pattern of an outworn tradition. Faced by failure of credit, they have proposed only the lending of more money. Stripped of the lure of profit by which to induce our people to follow their false leadership, they have resorted to exhortations, pleading tearfully for restored confidence. They only know the rules of a generation of self-seekers. They have no vision, and when there is no vision the people perish. Yes, the money-changers have fled from their high seats in the temple of our civilization. We may now restore that temple to the ancient truths. The measure of that restoration lies in the extent to which we apply social values more noble than mere monetary profit. Happiness lies not in the mere possession of money; it lies in the joy of achievement, in the thrill of creative effort. The joy, the moral stimulation, of work no longer must be forgotten in the mad chase of evanescent profits. These dark days, my friends, will be worth all they cost us if they teach us that our true destiny is not to be ministered unto but to minister to ourselves, to our fellow men.

Recognition of that falsity of material wealth as the standard of success goes hand in hand with the abandonment of the false belief that public office and high political position are to be valued only by the standards of pride of place and personal profit. And there must be an end to a conduct in banking and in business which too often has given to a sacred trust the likeness of callous and selfish wrongdoing. Small wonder that confidence languishes, for it thrives only on honesty, on honor, on the sacredness of obligations, on faithful protection, and on unselfish performance. Without them, it cannot live.

Restoration calls, however, not for changes in ethics alone. This nation is asking for action, and action now.

Our greatest primary task is to put people to work. This is no unsolvable problem if we face it wisely and courageously. It can be accomplished in part by direct recruiting by the government itself, treating the task as we would treat the emergency of a war but at the same time, through this employment, accomplishing great [sic] greatly needed projects to stimulate and reorganize the use of our great natural resources.

Hand in hand with that we must frankly recognize the overbalance of population in our industrial centers and by engaging on a national scale in a redistribution endeavor to provide a better use of the land for those best fitted for the land. Yes, the task can be helped by definite efforts to raise the values of agricultural products and with this the power to purchase the output of our cities. It can be helped by preventing realistically the tragedy of the growing loss through foreclosure of our small homes and our farms. It can be helped by insistence that the Federal, the state, and the local governments act forthwith on the demand that their cost be drastically reduced. It can be helped by the unifying of relief activities which today are often scattered, uneconomical, unequal. It can be helped by national planning for and supervision of all forms of transportation and of communications and other utilities that have a definitely public character. There are many ways in which it can be helped, but it can never be helped by merely talking about it.

We must act, we must act quickly.

And finally, in our progress towards a resumption of work we require two safeguards against a return of the evils of the old order. There must be a strict supervision of all banking and credits and investments. There must be an end to speculation with other people's money. And there must be provision for an adequate but sound currency.

These, my friends, are the lines of attack. I shall presently urge upon a new Congress, in special session, detailed measures for their fulfillment, and I shall seek the immediate assistance of the forty-eight states.

Through this program of action we address ourselves to putting our own national house in order and making income balance outgo. Our international trade relations, though vastly important, are in point of time and necessity secondary to the establishment of a sound national economy. I favor as a practical policy the putting of first things first. I shall spare no effort to restore world trade by international economic readjustment, but the emergency at home cannot wait on that accomplishment. The basic thought that guides these specific means of national recovery is not nationally *[sic]* narrowly nationalistic. It is the insistence, as a first consideration, upon the interdependence of the various elements in and parts of the United States of America, a recognition of the old and permanently important manifestation of the American spirit of the pioneer. It is the way to recovery. It is the immediate way. It is the strongest assurance that recovery will endure.

In the field of world policy I would dedicate this nation to the policy of the "good neighbor"—the neighbor who resolutely respects himself and, because he does so, respects the rights of others—the neighbor who respects his obligations and respects the sanctity of his agreements in and with a world of neighbors.

If I read the temper of our people correctly, we now realize as we have never realized before our interdependence on each other, that we cannot merely take but we must give as well, that if we are to go forward, we must move as a trained and loyal army, willing to sacrifice for the good of a common discipline, because without such discipline no progress can be made, no leadership becomes effective. We are, I know, ready and willing to submit our lives and our property to such discipline because it makes possible a leadership which aims at the larger good. This I propose to offer, pledging that the larger purposes will bind upon us, bind upon us all as a sacred obligation, with a unity of duty hitherto evoked only in times of armed strife. With this pledge taken, I assume unhesitatingly the leadership of this great army of our people dedicated to a disciplined attack upon our common problems.

Action in this image, action to this end, is feasible under the form of government which we have inherited from our ancestors. Our constitution is so simple, so practical, that it is possible always to meet extraordinary needs by changes in emphasis and arrangement without loss of essential form. That is why our constitutional system has proved itself the most superbly enduring political mechanism the modern world has ever seen. It has met every stress of vast expansion of territory, of foreign wars, of bitter internal strife, of world relations. And it is to be hoped that the normal balance of executive and legislative authority may be wholly equal, wholly adequate, to meet the unprecedented task before us. But it may be that an unprecedented demand and need for undelayed action may call for temporary departure from that normal balance of public procedure. I am prepared under my constitutional duty to recommend the measures that a stricken nation in the midst of a stricken world may require. These measures, or such other measures as the Congress may build out of its experience and wisdom, I shall seek within my constitutional authority to bring to speedy adoption. But in the event that the Congress shall fail to take one of these two courses, in the event that the national emergency is still critical, I shall not evade the clear course of duty that will then confront me. I shall ask the Congress for the one remaining instrument to meet the crisis: broad executive power to wage a war against the emergency, as great as the power that would be given to me if we were in fact invaded by a foreign foe.

For the trust reposed in me I will return the courage and the devotion that befit the time. I can do no less.

We face the arduous days that lie before us in the warm courage of national unity, with the clear consciousness of seeking old and precious moral values, with the clean satisfaction that comes from the stern performance of duty by old and young alike. We aim at the assurance of a rounded, a permanent national life. We do not distrust the uh, the future of essential democracy. The people of the United States have not failed. In their need they have registered a mandate that they want direct, vigorous action. They have asked for discipline and direction under leadership. They have made me the present instrument of their wishes. In the spirit of the gift, I take it.

In this dedication, of a nation, we humbly ask the blessing of God. May he protect each and every one of us. May he guide me in the days to come.

INAUGURAL ADDRESS

John F. Kennedy

Washington, D.C., January 20, 1961 (Transcribed from the video, GREAT SPEECHES, VOLUME I)

Vice President Johnson, Mr. Speaker, Mr. Chief Justice, President Eisenhower, Vice President Nixon, President Truman, Reverend Clergy, Fellow Citizens:

We observe today not a victory of party but a celebration of freedom—symbolizing an end as well as a beginning—signifying renewal as well as change. For I have sworn before you and Almighty God the same solemn oath our forebears prescribed nearly a century and three quarters ago.

The world is very different now. For man holds in his mortal hands the power to abolish all forms of human poverty and all forms of human life. And yet the same revolutionary beliefs for which our forebears fought are still at issue around the globe—the belief that the rights of man come not from the generosity of the state but from the hand of God.

We dare not forget today that we are the heirs of that first revolution. Let the word go forth from this time and place, to friend and foe alike, that the torch has been passed to a new generation of Americans—born in this century, tempered by war, disciplined by a hard and bitter peace, proud of our ancient heritage—and unwilling to witness or permit the slow undoing of those human rights to which this nation has always been committed, and to which we are committed today, at home and around the world.

Let every nation know, whether it wishes us well or ill, that we shall pay any price, bear any burden, meet any hardship, support any friend, oppose any foe to assure the survival and the success of liberty. This much we pledge—and more.

To those old allies whose cultural and spiritual origins we share, we pledge the loyalty of faithful friends. United, there is little we cannot do in a host of cooperative ventures. Divided, there is little we can do—for we dare not meet a powerful challenge at odds and split asunder.

To those new states who we welcome to the ranks of the free, we pledge our word that one form of colonial control shall not have passed away merely to be replaced by a far more iron tyranny. We shall not always expect to find them supporting our view. But we shall always hope to find them strongly supporting their own freedom—and to remember that, in the past, those who foolishly sought power by riding the back of the tiger ended up inside.

To those people in the huts and villages of half the globe struggling to break the bonds of mass misery, we pledge our best efforts to help them help themselves, for whatever period is required—not because the Communists may be doing it, not because we seek their votes, but because it is right. If a free society cannot help the many who are poor, it cannot save the few who are rich.

To our sister republics south of our border, we offer a special pledge—to convert our good words into good deeds—in a new alliance for progress—to assist free men and free governments in casting off the chains of poverty. But this peaceful revolution of hope cannot become the prey of hostile powers. Let all our neighbors know that we shall join with them to oppose aggression or subversion anywhere in the Americas. And let every other power know that this hemisphere intends to remain the master of its own house.

To that world assembly of sovereign states, the United Nations, our last best hope in an age where the instruments of war have far outpaced the instruments of peace, we renew our pledge of support—to prevent it from becoming merely a forum for invective—to strengthen its shield of the new and the weak—and to enlarge the area in which its writ may run.

Finally, to those nations who would make themselves our adversary, we offer not a pledge but a request: That both sides begin anew the quest for peace, before the dark powers of destruction unleashed by science engulf all humanity in planned or accidental self-destruction. We dare not tempt them with weakness. For only when our arms are sufficient beyond doubt can we be certain beyond doubt that they will never be employed. But neither can two great and powerful groups of nations take comfort from our present course—both sides overburdened by the cost of modern weapons, both rightly alarmed by the steady spread of the deadly atom, yet both racing to alter that uncertain balance of terror that stays the hand of mankind's final war.

So let us begin anew—remembering on both sides that civility is not a sign of weakness, and sincerity is always subject to proof. Let us never negotiate out of fear. But let us never fear to negotiate. Let both sides explore what problems unite us instead of belaboring those problems which divide us. Let both sides, for the first time, formulate serious and precise proposals for the inspection and control of arms—and bring the absolute power to destroy other nations under the absolute control of all nations. Let both sides seek to invoke the wonders of science instead of its terrors. Together let us explore the stars, conquer the deserts, eradicate disease, tap the ocean depths and encourage the arts and commerce. Let both sides unite to heed in all corners of the earth the command of Isaiah—to "undo the heavy burdens (and) let the oppressed go free."

And if a beachhead of cooperation may push back the jungle of suspicion, let both sides join in creating a new endeavor: not a new balance of power, but a new world of law, where the strong are just and the weak secure and the peace preserved.

All this will not be finished in the first one hundred days. Nor will it be finished in the first one thousand days, nor in the life of this administration, nor even perhaps in our lifetime on this planet. But let us begin.

In your hands, my fellow citizens, more than mine, will rest the final success or failure of our course. Since this country was founded, each generation of Americans has been summoned to give testimony to its national loyalty. The graves of young Americans who answered the call to service surround the globe.

Now the trumpet summons us again—not as a call to bear arms, though arms we need; not as a call to battle, though embattled we are—but a call to bear the burden of a long twilight struggle, year in and year out; "rejoicing in hope, patient in tribulation"—a struggle against the common enemies of man: Tyranny, poverty, disease and war itself. Can we forge against these enemies a grand and global alliance, North and South, East and West, that can assure a more fruitful life for all mankind? Will you join in that historic effort?

In the long history of the world, only a few generations have been granted the role of defending freedom in its hour of maximum danger. I do not shrink from this responsibility—I welcome it. I do not believe that any of us would exchange places with any other people or any other generation. The energy, the faith, the devotion which we bring to this endeavor will light our country and all who serve it—and the glow from that fire can truly light the world.

And so, my fellow Americans: Ask not what your country can do for you—ask what you can do for your country.

My fellow citizens of the world: Ask not what America will do for you, but what together we can do for the freedom of man.

Finally, whether you are citizens of America or citizens of the world, ask of us here the same high standards of strength and sacrifice which we ask of you. With a good conscience our only sure reward, with history the final judge of our deeds, let us go forth to lead the land we love, asking His blessing and His help, but knowing that here on earth God's work must truly be our own.

"ASK NOT..."

A Critical Analysis of Kennedy's Inaugural

Ask not what your country can do for you, ask what you can do for your country.

CRITIC: Nicholas M. Cripe

THE SPEAKER

John Fitzgerald Kennedy's Inaugural Address, ranked by critics among the great inaugural addresses, launched in memorable fashion a Presidency that was to last but a dramatically short thousand days. Kennedy, forty-six years old when assassinated in Dallas, Texas, November 22, 1963, was the youngest man ever elected to the Presidency and the youngest to die in that office.

The first Catholic to be elected President, Kennedy inherited his religious and political party affiliations. His parents were the grandchildren of Irish Catholic immigrants. Joseph Kennedy, his father, graduated from Harvard and became one of the wealthiest men in the United States. An active Democrat, he held several important political appointments including that of Ambassador to Great Britain during FDR's administration. Rose Kennedy was the daughter of John F. (Honey Fitz) Fitzgerald, a wealthy and legendary Boston Democrat politician. John Fitzgerald Kennedy grew up in a family where politics was considered an honorable profession and going to Mass on Sunday morning was an act of faith.

When elected to Congress from a Boston district in 1946, John Kennedy was a cum laude graduate of Harvard and an authentic hero of World War II but, at best, only a fair public speaker. For many years, the reporters covering his speeches saw a man who did not enjoy public speaking and was not very good at it. But over the years, and particularly during the 1960 primaries and the Presidential campaign, he successfully worked at improving his delivery. His speaking changed. Theodore Sorensen, Kennedy's principal speech collaborator, tells us:

> The Congressman and freshman Senator whose private conversations were always in-formed and articulate but whose public speeches were rarely inspired or inspiring became the candidate and President whose addresses stirred the hearts of the world.... He became less shy and more poised in his public appearances...became in time the President who welcomed every opportunity to get away from his desk and get back to the people.[1]

From his first campaign for Congress, Kennedy's speeches had been "so uttered as to make him worthy of belief." He was elected to the House of Representatives in three consecutive elections, and in 1952 defeated Senator Henry Cabot Lodge in one of the political upsets of the day. The popular Lodge lost by 70,000 votes in a year when Eisenhower carried the state by an overwhelming majority; Kennedy became only the third Democrat to be elected to the Senate from Massachusetts.

Although reporters may have been critical of Kennedy's delivery, audiences liked him. They responded to the warmth of his smile, his directness, and "his sincerity." Audiences believed him. *Time* magazine's election edition gave an excellent description of the Kennedy appeal:

> In appearance he is a slender man with a boyish face, an uncontrollable shock of hair, a dazzling smile. In manner he is alert, incisive, speaking in short, terse, sentences in a chowderish New England accent that he somehow makes attractive...reaching with no apparent effort into a first class mind for historical anecdotes or classical allusions...he projects a kind of conviction and vigor even when talking of commonplace things in a commonplace way.[2]

Kennedy's *ethos* as a speaker played a major role in his becoming President. Through his speaking he gained the public support that led to his election. Kennedy's successful race for the Presidency began with his nominating speech for Adlai Stevenson at the 1956 Democratic National Convention.[3] Kennedy came to the convention interested, available, and frequently mentioned for the vice presidential nomination, but did not consider himself to be a serious candidate. The night before the Presidential nominations began, Stevenson invited Kennedy to deliver the principal nominating speech. Kennedy accepted and the resulting speech was a success with the convention delegates and the national TV audience. Upon being nominated Stevenson dramatically announced he would leave it to an open convention to select his running mate. The positive response to the nominating speech inspired Kennedy to try for the vice presidential spot. In the ensuing TV drama played out in the living rooms of America, Kennedy lost the nomination to Estes Kefauver by a handful of votes. In losing he gained more than in winning. Had he won the nomination and been defeated with Stevenson, some political leaders would have blamed the loss on Kennedy's Catholicism, thus possibly ending any hope for a future nomination. As it was, his prominent role in the convention, his speech for Stevenson, his close race with Kefauver, and his graceful acceptance of defeat made him a nationally acclaimed figure. Clearly it was this 1956 convention that first made John Kennedy a leading contender for the 1960 Democratic nomination for President.

Several things combined to make John Kennedy, the candidate and the President, the successful speaker he was. One was his deep confident belief in himself and his abilities to do the job. It was not arrogance but a quiet self-confidence that his audience sensed. When Kennedy declared his intention to seek the Presidency, no one in the upper echelons of the party was for him. Truman and other national party leaders thought he had the wrong religion, the wrong age, the wrong job, and the wrong home state to be nominated and elected President. Many did, however, favor him for the vice presidency; both to avoid charges of anti-Catholicism, and to bring back to the party the many Catholic Democrats who had voted for Eisenhower. Kennedy did not ignore party leaders nor did he follow their advice. During the three years prior to 1960 he spoke at political meetings around the country, established contacts, gained good will, and cultivated support in those states which held primaries to choose delegates. Consequently, this confident young man went into the primaries with more support among rank and file Democrats than any other candidate.[4]

Another strong *ethos* factor for Kennedy was his intelligence. Audiences sensed that he knew what he was talking about. Sorensen describes his speeches: "They were generally factual, direct and specific.... They conveyed a sense of concern and conviction, a vast command of information, a disdain for demagoguery and a mood of cool, decisive leadership." [5] Kennedy trained himself to read rapidly and to retain what he read. He maintained notebooks of quotations, poems, articles. He utilized these to construct speeches filled with statistics, historical references, and quotations. Audiences perceived him as a well-informed, intelligent speaker.

Kennedy's temperament contributed to his *ethos*. He had an ability to keep his temper and coolness of mind even when provoked. He seldom lost sight of other people's motives and problems. He seemed to instinctively possess the ability to see the situation from their point of view and to react accordingly.

Schlesinger recounts an incident during the 1960 campaign when Kennedy and a group of friends went to a famous New York City restaurant for dinner. At a neighboring table, a man who obviously had been drinking, began to direct unprintable comments to Kennedy. Kennedy's friends raised their own voices hoping to keep him from hearing the comments, but without success. One of his friends started to call the headwaiter; but Kennedy stopped him, saying, "No, don't bother. Think how the fellow's wife must be feeling." His friends looked and saw her flushed with embarrassment. [6]

Not the least of his charm was his wit and sense of humor. Spontaneous and sharp, his wit could silence a heckler while bringing a laugh. During a parade a high school boy yelled at him, "How did you become a hero?" Kennedy's reply brought a cheer, "It was involuntary. They sank my boat." At the Los Angeles Convention a reporter asked Kennedy, "Do you feel, objectively, that a Protestant could be elected President?" Amid general laughter, a straight-faced Kennedy replied, "If he is prepared to answer questions about the separation of church and state, I see no reason to discriminate against him." The 420 attending reporters gave him a standing ovation. [7]

His confidence, his intelligence, his self-control, his wit, and his sense of humor all combined during those long months of campaigning to create a favorable image in millions of minds. Salinger described the Kennedy *ethos*:

> Eloquence depends not only on the words but on the man, the subject, and the situation. Kennedy was still no orator. Others could be more forceful in voice gestures, emphasis and pauses. But as Lord Rosebery said of the impassioned oratory of Pitt, it was "the character which breathes through the sentences" that was so impressive. Kennedy's character could be felt in every word.... [8]

On November 8, 1960, Kennedy won one of the closest Presidential races in our history. In an election in which 64.5% of the eligible voters voted and 68,832,818 Americans cast their ballot for a President, Kennedy carried the Electoral College 303 votes to 219 for Nixon but won the popular vote by only 112,881 votes. In winning Kennedy had the same Electoral College total as Truman in 1948, but got 11 million more votes than Stevenson did in 1956. Kennedy's *ethos*, the confidence he inspired in his listeners, won him the Presidency. Theodore White in his book, *The Making of the President 1960*, summarizes the election this way: "...the election of 1960 was a personal victory for John F. Kennedy, not for his Party." [9]

INAUGURATION DAY: THE OCCASION

January 20, 1961, Inauguration Day, brought sunny, windy, bitter cold weather.

Thousands of servicemen worked the previous night and into the morning clearing away eight inches of snow that virtually immobilized Washington. The temperature officially reached 22 degrees when the swearing-in ceremony began. *Time* magazine recounting the occasion said, "Foul weather and a fine speech provided the most memorable moments of a historic week.... A blizzard threatened to turn the whole momentous occasion into a farce—but President John Kennedy delivering his inaugural address more than saved the day."[10]

Inauguration Day in the United States is the equivalent of an English Coronation, only happening with more frequency and somewhat less pomp. John Kennedy began the day by attending mass. Then he and his wife drove to the White House for coffee with the Eisenhowers, the Lyndon Johnsons, the Richard Nixons and several congressional leaders. Following this congenial social period, President Dwight Eisenhower and President-elect John Kennedy emerged from the White House smiling and in the top hats Kennedy mandated for the platform dignitaries. They stepped into the long black bubble-topped presidential limousine, and drove down Pennsylvania Avenue to Capitol Hill. Along the wide avenues thousands of cheering onlookers greeted them. The bitter cold did not diminish the size nor dim the enthusiasm of the crowds. The fur coats, bright colored stocking caps and blankets added even more color to the occasion.

The ceremony ran behind schedule and John Kennedy's term as President of the United States had run for thirteen minutes according to the Constitution when he stepped out onto the wind swept platform and took his seat next to Eisenhower. The platform was filled with the political elite of Washington and the nation: Justices of the Supreme Court, members of the Senate and House of Representatives, new Cabinet members, Joint Chiefs of Staff, the diplomatic corps, and families and friends of the chief participants. The plaza in front of the platform was packed with the party faithful anxious to celebrate the change of administrations and to cheer their new leader.

The Marine Band struck up "America the Beautiful" and the ceremonies were underway. Marian Anderson sang "The Star Spangled Banner." As Boston's Cardinal Cushing began what was to be an unduly long invocation smoke started wafting from the lectern. The Cardinal prayed on and on ignoring the plume of smoke. When he finally closed, Vice President Nixon and several others rushed to the lectern, located the fire in a short-circuited electric motor, and pulled the connecting plug. The smoke quickly drifted away.

Lyndon Johnson took his oath as Vice President and clearly muffed a line. Next came one of the most emotional moments of the program. Kennedy had invited Robert Frost to read a poem as part of the ceremony. Frost attempted to read a newly written dedication to his famous poem, "The Gift Outright." Blinded by the bright sun, the wind whipping the paper in his hands, the 86 year old poet faltered, started over, and faltered again. Lyndon Johnson tried to shade the paper with his hat, but it did not help. Frost tried again, stopped, then turned to the microphones and said, "This was supposed to be a preface to a poem that I can say to you without seeing it. The poem goes this way...." The nervous titters of the embarrassed crowd stopped as Frost recited from memory in a clear, strong, almost young voice the poem he had chosen for this President.

Despite the biting wind snapping the flags on the platform and surrounding buildings, John Kennedy left his top hat and coat on his chair when he stepped forward to join Chief Justice Earl Warren at the lectern. He took the oath of office which every

Chief Executive has sworn to uphold since that April day in 1789 when George Washington became the first President of the United States. Perhaps taking off his top coat was a conscious gesture, perhaps it was not, but it clearly indicated Kennedy's sense of the solemnity of this special occasion. As his opening words quickly indicated, he was quite conscious of the historical significance of this ceremony.

Having been duly sworn in as President, he turned to face the bank of microphones and the waiting crowd before him. The speech he delivered made this inaugural memorable.

THE SPEECH

A Presidential Inaugural Address is a unique form of public speech which falls under the broad definition of ceremonial speaking. Ceremonial speeches have a variety of forms but a centrality of purpose. Whether the speech is a commencement address, a eulogy, the presentation of an award, or an acceptance speech, it shares the common function of reaffirming and intensifying social values. Scholars identify these speeches this way:

> At moments like these, speakers address audiences about the values that both share as members of a common group. The speeches given in such moments are thus noncontroversial for a specific audience. They do not urge adoption of new values or rejection of old values. Rather they seek to reinforce and revitalize the existing audience values. The speaker seeks unity of spirit or re-energizing of effort or commitment; he tries to inspire, to kindle enthusiasm, or to deepen feelings of awe, respect, and devotion.[11]

Whether it was Lincoln asserting "With malice toward none, with charity for all...;" or Franklin Roosevelt telling the American people, "We have nothing to fear, but fear itself;" or John Kennedy asking his fellow citizens to "Ask not what your country can do for you—ask what you can do for your country;" American Presidents have used the inaugural address to appeal to their countrymen to take pride in their country, to cherish her long held traditions, and to put behind them the divisiveness of the past campaign and unite for the common good. From George Washington to the present, presidents have delivered inaugural addresses which range in distinction from the mundane to the sublime in extolling these values, but few have achieved either the immediate or lasting favorable response to their efforts that John F. Kennedy did for the speech he delivered on January 20, 1961.

Every President hopes his inaugural address will be a memorable one, and John Kennedy was no exception. As the New York *Times* reported, "President-elect John Kennedy worked today on an inauguration address he obviously wants to make one of the lasting documents of American history.... Mr. Kennedy has already worked over several drafts of it, it was understood." Kennedy started thinking about the inaugural address in November, for it was shortly after the election that he solicited suggestions from Adlai Stevenson, John Kenneth Galbraith, and others; and suggested to Sorensen he read previous inaugural speeches plus Lincoln's Gettysburg Address. But as Salinger points out, Kennedy was determined from the outset that the speech "would be his and his alone."[12] And it was. Salinger, Sorensen, and scholars agree that this speech was Kennedy's own.

From the organization, wording, and content of the speech it is clear that Kennedy knew that he would be addressing a wide and varied audience. While the speech was clearly intended for the American public, it was also adapted to a worldwide audience.

From the beginning of the preparation of this speech, Kennedy wanted it to be brief. In fact, until he became aware of the extreme brevity of Roosevelt's Fourth Inaugural Address, he aspired to make his the briefest on record. This concern plus his desire to appeal to more than the domestic audience contributed to his decision to concentrate on foreign policy—a topic in which all his listeners were vitally interested.

The organization of this speech is clear and simple—an introduction that focuses attention and clarifies the topic, a three segment body, and a conclusion that ends the speech on a note of inspiration.

Kennedy opens the speech with the classical techniques of a direct reference to the speaker, the audience, and the occasion. Having established the relation of the present ceremony to the long, solemn tradition of the past, he then quickly brings the traditional meanings to the present, "that the torch has been passed to a new generation of Americans," a generation of Americans believing strongly in their Revolutionary heritage.

Kennedy concludes the introduction by stating the premise of his speech: "Let every nation know, whether it wishes us well or ill, that we shall pay any price, bear any burden, meet any hardship, support any friend, or oppose any foe to assure the survival and the success of liberty. This much we pledge—and more."

The body is divided into three sections, Kennedy first directs his pledges to the various foreign segments of his audience. He begins with "those old allies whose cultural and spiritual origins we share," moves to various other segments of the world, then to the United Nations, "our last best hope." This section has obviously been directed to the friendly and neutral members of his foreign audience.

The second section is directed "to those nations who would make themselves our adversary." A good example of the attention given to wording in this speech is that the word adversary replaced enemy in the final draft because it had a less hostile connotation. The USSR and her allies are not mentioned by name, but the audience knew to whom the message was addressed. In these two sections the relationship of the ideas is made clear by the parallel structure of the sentences.

In the final section of the body, Kennedy comes back to his American audience, appealing to them to join him in a "struggle against the common enemies of men: tyranny, poverty, disease, and war itself." Only five short paragraphs, this section's clarity comes not from any organizational pattern, but rather from the careful structuring of the language.

Kennedy's conclusion is a textbook example of what a speech conclusion should do. It is short and focuses the audience's thinking on the response desired, while at the same time ending the speech on a note of completeness and finality. The conclusion begins with the unforgettable, "And so my fellow Americans: Ask not what your country can do for you—ask what you can do for your country." He quickly challenges his other audience, the citizens of the world, and then puts the responsibility on both as he ends his speech with words that left no doubt the speech was concluded: "With good conscience our only sure reward, with history the final judge of our deeds, let us go forth to lead the land we love, asking His blessing and His help, but knowing that here on earth God's work must truly be our own."

The simplicity of the organization lies in the fact that the listener is never made aware that there is a pattern. Each succeeding sentence unobtrusively links to the one preceding it. Each paragraph leads naturally into the one following it. Not the least of the values for students of his speech is the recognition of the seemingly artless fashion in which this speech was so artfully formed. This is a speech that literally flows from the opening words to the closing sentence.

In this day of "ghostwriting," two questions students of public address studying a speech must answer are, "How much of this speech is the speaker's?" and "Whose ideas are these; whose language?" In this case the evidence is overwhelming, the language, the ideas, and the speeches he gave were Kennedy's. Of course he had help in the preparation, because no person running for President of the United States or serving as President can find the time to prepare by himself all the various speeches demanded. The time has long passed when a Herbert Hoover could literally shut down the Oval Office while he spent days writing a speech. Sorensen and others have frequently pointed out, Kennedy was the architect of the speeches he gave, extemporaneous or manuscript. He was the chief contributor to the planning of strategy and to the securing of supporting materials. Sorensen or some others would frequently then write a first draft, but the final product was Kennedy's.

Salinger tells us: "Actually, speeches were not written for the President but with him. He knew what he wanted to say and how he wanted to say it. The role of the speech writer was to organize JFK's thoughts into a rough draft, on which he himself would put the final touches. His versions would often change it dramatically." [13]

Golden tells us: "When time permitted and the occasion challenged him Kennedy moved from his typical role of outliner, editor, and collaborator to that of creator. Here he selected his own topic and emphasis, gathered much of his supporting material, then organized and expressed the ideas in hand written manuscripts…it was the mode of preparation which Kennedy used in…(his) Inaugural Address." [14]

As with Lincoln's Gettysburg Address, it was not so much the ideas as the working of those ideas that made Kennedy's Inaugural Address memorable. The ideas had been expressed by others before, but never before had they been expressed in such a memorable manner.

One of the distinctive attributes that Lincoln, Roosevelt, Churchill, and Kennedy shared was a sense of style. That is why, when time permitted, their speeches frequently went through so many drafts prior to delivery. Sorensen says of the Inaugural Address, "No Kennedy speech ever underwent so many drafts. Each paragraph was reworded, reworked, and reduced." [15] For example:

First Draft
We celebrate today not a victory of party but a sacrament of democracy.

Next-to-Last Draft
We celebrate today not a victory of party but a convention of freedom.

Last Draft
We observe today not a victory of party but a celebration of freedom.

First Draft
Each of us, whether we hold office or not, shares the responsibility for guiding the most difficult of all societies along the path of self-discipline and self-government.

Next-to-Last Draft
In your hands, my fellow citizens, more than mine, will be determined the success or failure of our course.

Last Draft
In your hands, my fellow citizens, more than mine, will rest the final success or failure of our course.[16]

Nor, apparently, did Kennedy quit reworking the speech even after the supposed final draft had been released to reporters on the evening of January 19, with the stipulation that it should not be published until after the actual presentation. Reporters had learned to pay attention to such stipulations for a Kennedy speech; many referred to him as, "That well known text deviant." They found 30 differences in word choice, sentence structure, and grammatical form in the speech they heard and the copy they had been given. For instance, the reporters' copy read, "Those who foolishly sought to find power by riding on the tiger's back inevitably end up inside." They heard the President say, "Those who foolishly sought power by riding the back of the tiger ended up inside."[17]
Even the antithetical sentence by which this speech is most frequently identified changed. In the reporters' copy, "Ask not what your country will do for you…" in the speech became "Ask not what your country can do for you…."[18]
Kennedy used the "Ask not…" expression in prior speeches, but seldom has the importance of wording to the impact of an idea ever been more vividly demonstrated than in this speech. In his Acceptance Speech at the National Democratic Convention, July 15, 1960, Kennedy said, "…the New Frontier of which I speak is not a set of promises—it is a set of challenges. It sums up not what I intend to offer the American people, but what I intend to ask of them." At a Labor Day Rally in Detroit, the phrasing became more audience directed, "The New Frontier is not what I promise I am going to do for you. The New Frontier is what I ask you to do for our country." Finally, in the Inaugural Address, he had in one dramatic sentence focused the attention of the American public on its challenging role in his administration.
Kennedy was no ordinary wordsmith, he was an artisan in working with words. To discuss his craftsmanship in detail would be a long essay in itself, but let us notice a few examples. In this speech, Kennedy uses many abstract words, but abstractions to which his audience would respond favorably.
Probably the most notable stylistic quality of this speech is the sentence structure. It is with the structuring of the sentences—the variety of length, the various stylistic devices, the rhythm—that he achieved the emphasis and the impact of this speech.
Kennedy was familiar with many of Lincoln's speeches, particularly his Gettysburg Address. It is quite possible Lincoln's affinity for short sentences and short words influenced the Kennedy style, for these characteristics are to be found frequently in this speech. For example, asyndeton, the stylistic device of omitting the conjunctions between co-ordinate sentence elements, is an effective tool to cut out words and at the same time gain a forceful effect. Kennedy used this device when he said, "…we shall pay any price, bear any burden, meet any hardship, support any friend or oppose any foe to assure the survival and the success of liberty." His use of antithesis, repetition in successive clauses in reverse grammatical order, for brevity and emphasis appears in his

"Ask not what your country can do for you—ask what you can do for your country," and "Let us never negotiate out of fear. But let us never fear to negotiate."

Kennedy's use of parallelism to give emphasis and forcefulness to his ideas has been mentioned previously. Add the use of contrast, comparison, metaphor, and the rhythm that pervades the entire speech and it becomes evident why this speech has long been recommended to speech students as an excellent example of "wording the speech." This is a speech that has achieved historical significance not so much because of what Kennedy said, but because of the language with which he said it.

It was only late in the Presidential campaign that Kennedy's voice became a dependable and effective instrument that strengthened rather than weakened response to what he said. As a speaker he was always knowledgeable, sometimes witty, but he possessed a voice that lacked depth and variety, and frequently became high pitched. On several occasions the strain on his throat from constant campaigning left him voiceless and others had to substitute for him. His voice had a definite Harvard-Boston accent. He had a tendency to interject "ers" and "ahs" rather than pauses while speaking at a very rapid rate. At the beginning of the 1960 Presidential campaign, speech teachers who heard him and the reporters who were with him at every speech agreed that he was a poor public speaker.

Kennedy consistently abused his voice during the primaries, losing it entirely for a time in West Virginia, Indiana, and Oregon. He strained it again speaking at the numerous caucuses at the Los Angeles convention so that even a few weeks of rest in the Cape Cod sun did not ease all the soreness. At this time Kennedy, aware of how Wendell Willkie lost his voice in the crucial last days of the 1940 campaign, decided to do something about his vocal delivery.

The New York *Times* for August 22, 1960 reported: "Senator John F. Kennedy... has disclosed to close friends that his occasional loss of voice results from the faulty speech habit of talking from his throat. So, when he can find a free moment from politicking, the Democratic candidate from Massachusetts is taking lessons on speaking from the diaphragm." A reporter for *Time* who followed his California swing in middle September, said, "Under the direction of Voice Coach Blair McCloskey, the Kennedy voice was usually well modulated, right from the diaphragm. But occasionally it launched into uncontrolled stridency."

As the campaign was drawing to a close Douglas Cater writing in *The Reporter*, October 27, 1960, observed:

> Kennedy has come a long way since he first began his relentless drive for the Presidency. For one thing, with help of coaches he is beginning to master the art of projecting his voice so it has lost some of its shrill, grating quality.... There is still an unfinished quality about his oratory. But for brief moments, mainly during the gigantic outside rallies, he has achieved an eloquence that is distinctively his own.

During the fall Presidential campaign Kennedy's vocal delivery noticeably improved. His voice grew less nasal, less harsh and developed more cadence. His Harvard-Boston accent became less pronounced though still noticeable at times. He was learning to pace rather than rush his sentences, thus giving his audiences the opportunity to applaud, to laugh, and to follow and appreciate what he was saying. As his Inaugural Address demonstrates so vividly, Kennedy learned to adapt his delivery as well as his ideas and language to the audience and occasion. His speaking changed for the better because he was willing to recognize weaknesses and take the time and effort to learn how to correct them. Like so many things in life, speaking well in public can be an acquired ability. Kennedy acquired this ability.

However, one aspect of Kennedy's delivery never did change, his limited variety of gestures. Kennedy had two—the pointed index finger long jab, and the short jab, usually with the right hand.

The Kennedy Inaugural Address was a well delivered speech, read from a manuscript with excellent eye contact. The overall delivery rate and cadence of the speech adapted well to the solemnity of the occasion. For a speaker notorious for rushing his response lines, this speech more closely resembles his later efforts rather than his earlier speeches. While there was a place or two where a longer pause or more emphasis on a question might have evoked a greater response, the overall use of timing in this speech cannot be seriously faulted.

To listen to Kennedy delivering this speech is to be caught by the beauty of its language, and the challenge of the speaker. One is not aware of the delivery, at least not consciously. That is the true mark of the well delivered speech, when the delivery adds meaning and color to what is being said, but the listener is not aware that the delivery is doing so.

John F. Kennedy was an intelligent, responsible, effective speaker who, January 20, 1961, gave a memorable speech which is still considered one of the best inaugural speeches ever given as well as one of the finest examples of the beauty a speaker can achieve with the English language. These are two very good reasons for studying this speech. There is a third. We should realize that this speech was created and delivered by a man who began his public career as a poor public speaker, who did not like the speaking experience, but who not only learned how to deliver a memorable speech, but even to enjoy doing so.

Nicholas M. Cripe, Ph.D., is a professor emeritus at Butler University, Indianapolis, Indiana.

NOTES

1. Theodore C. Sorensen, *Kennedy*, (New York Harper and Row, Publishers, 1965), p. 24.
2. *Time*, November 7, 1960. p. 27.
3. Robert N. Bostrom, "'I Give You A Man'—Kennedy's Speech for Adlai Stevenson," *Speech Monographs*, June 1968, p. 129.
4. See Sorensen, pp. 122-126 for an interesting account of this period.
5. Sorensen, p. 178.
6. Arthur M. Schlesinger, Jr., *A Thousand Days*, (Boston: Houghton Mifflin Company, 1965), p. 110.
7. Ralph G. Martin, *A Hero For Our Time*, (New York: Macmillan Publishing Co., 1983), p. 164.
8. Pierre Salinger, *With Kennedy*, (New York: Doubleday & Co., Inc., 1966), p. 331.
9. White, p. 364.
10. *Time*, January 27, 1961, p. 7.
11. Linkugal, Allen, Johannesen, *Contemporary American Speeches*, 2nd. Ed., (Belmont, California: Wadsworth Publishing Co., Inc. 1969), p. 278.
12. Salinger, p. 109.

13. Salinger, p. 66.
14. James L. Golden, "John F. Kennedy and the 'Ghosts,' " *Quarterly Journal of Speech*, December 1966, p. 353.
15. Sorensen, p. 241.
16. *Ibid.*
17. Golden, p. 354.
18. *Ibid.*

CHAPTER 9:
Eulogies

The death of a prominent member of society provides the setting for one of the oldest forms of oratory—the eulogy. The speaker not only offers solace but finds meaning in the event. Ultimately, that meaning provides significance beyond any individual tragedy.

Robert Kennedy's impromptu eulogy of Martin Luther King, Jr. provides a model for this genre of speaking. Roger Cook uses ancient rhetorical theory to explain the unusual nature and impact of Kennedy's eulogy. The nationally witnessed tragedy of the explosion of the *Challenger* space shuttle prompted Ronald Reagan's Tribute to the *Challenger* Astronauts.

EULOGY OF MARTIN LUTHER KING, JR.

Robert F. Kennedy

Indianapolis, Indiana, April 4, 1968 (Transcribed from the video, GREAT SPEECHES, VOLUME V—additional material drawn from various sources)

{Ladies and gentlemen, I am only going to talk to you for just a minute or so this evening, because I have some very sad news for all of you. Would you lower those signs please?} I have some very sad news for all of you, and I think—sad news for all of our fellow citizens and people who love peace all over the world. And that is—that Martin Luther King was shot and was killed tonight.

Martin Luther King dedicated his life to love and to justice between fellow human beings. He died in the cause of that effort. In this difficult day, in this difficult time for the United States, it is perhaps well to ask what kind of a nation we are and what direction we want to move in. For those of you who are black, considering the evidence there evidently is that there were white people who were responsible, you can be filled with bitterness, and with hatred, and a desire for revenge. We can move in that direction as a country, in greater polarization—black people amongst blacks, and white amongst whites, filled with hatred toward one another. Or we can make an effort, as Martin Luther King did, to understand and to comprehend, and replace that violence, that stain of bloodshed that has spread across our land, with an effort to understand; compassion and love.

For those of you who are black and are tempted to fill with [sic] be filled with hatred and distrust of the injustice of such an act, against all white people, I would only say that I can also feel in my own heart the same kind of feeling. I had a member of my family killed, but he was killed by a white man. But we have to make an effort in the United States, we have to make an effort to understand, to get beyond or go beyond these rather difficult times.

My favorite poem, my favorite poet was Aeschylus. And he once wrote: "Even in our sleep, pain which cannot forget falls drop by drop upon the heart until, in our own despair, against our will, comes wisdom through the awful grace of God."

What we need in the United States is not division; what we need in the United States is not hatred; what we need in the United States is not violence and lawlessness, but is love and wisdom, and compassion toward one another, feeling of justice towards those who still suffer within our country, whether they be white or whether they be black. {We've had difficult times in the past. We will have difficult times in the future.} It is not the end of violence; it is not the end of lawlessness and is not the end of disorder. But the vast majority of white people and the vast majority of black people in this country want to live together, want to improve the quality of our life, and want justice for all human beings that abide in our land.

{Let us} dedicate ourselves to what the Greeks wrote so many years ago: to tame the savageness of man and make gentle the life of this world. {Let us dedicate ourselves to that, and say a prayer for our country and for our people.}

"TO TAME THE SAVAGENESS OF MAN"

Robert Kennedy's Eulogy of Martin Luther King, Jr.

Replace that violence; that stain of bloodshed that has spread across our land.

CRITIC: Roger Cook

While the violence of the era may mar our recollections of the sixties, two men, with separate paths but parallel philosophies, challenged us to follow the dictates of our highest ideals. Their rhetoric appealed to what was noble in a society which harbored much that was ignoble. Their words offered direction for a country adrift in an unpopular war overseas and violent racial strife at home. Ironically their voices were silenced by the very violence they so eloquently opposed. Martin Luther King, Jr.'s tragic assassination preceded Robert Kennedy's by weeks, leaving the latter to search for meaning in a mindless act, and for the words to quiet the voices of retaliation. On April 4, 1968, against the advice of some of his staff and the warnings of local law enforcement officials, Kennedy, shaken by the news of King's death, gathered his composure, walked into a black ghetto and relayed the tragic events to a crowd of about 2500. He then delivered an extemporaneous eulogy which many feel stands as one of his most eloquent speeches. It also exemplifies the importance of *ethos* as a persuasive tool. Theodore Sorensen summarized the impact of this remarkable eulogy not only on the black audience that heard it but on others who cautiously followed the events of those terrible days. "Many whites, frightened by the terror and turmoil that followed the murder of Martin Luther King were impressed that only Robert Kennedy could walk unafraid into the ghettos at the time, to urge angry blacks to cool it, and to tell them that violence was self-destructive."[1]

BIOGRAPHY

Robert F. Kennedy walking amidst angry blacks became a familiar sight for those who knew him. His close friend, Charles Evers noted, "He was the only politician with the courage to walk into the toughest ghettos and talk to the black militants... not a boo or a rock [would be] thrown."[2] These frequent forays into the stark, tough, impoverished side of society belied the genteel, comfortable environment into which Kennedy was born.

Robert was the seventh of nine children of millionaire Joseph P. Kennedy and his wife Rose. More significantly he was the third male child in a family which bequeathed the family's political future to the oldest male child. As he once explained, "I was the seventh of nine children and when you come from that far down you have to struggle to survive."[3] Those who met him, even in later years, mistakenly thought him frail. A strong physically active man, he pursued dangerous and challenging activities: mountain climbing, running rapids, skiing, etc. If his physical prowess contradicted his appearance, so too was his personality fraught with contradictions.

He began his political career as counsel to Senator Joseph McCarthy's investigative committee where he served aggressively for six months before becoming disenchanted with the committee's careless investigative measures. His later role as chief counsel for the Select Committee on Improper Activities in the Labor or Management Field cultivated for him an image as a relentless and vindictive "prosecutor, judge and jury, all consolidated into his one efficient person."[4] Robert Kennedy spent years trying to dispel his early image. Contributing to this "ruthless" facade was his successful role as the hard-nosed campaign director for his brother John. When John won the Presidency, he appointed Robert to the post of Attorney General of the United States.

While the Kennedy Administration has been heralded for advancing a host of legislative and executive actions that improved the conditions of blacks in America, much of the credit goes to Robert's active role in the Justice Department. Upon discovering that only 10 of 955 Department lawyers were black, he moved to attract black attorneys from around the nation. Less symbolically, the new Attorney General insisted upon strict enforcement of voting rights statutes. Under his leadership, the Justice Department brought 57 suits; 30 in Mississippi to ensure black franchise rights.[5] His speeches in the South made clear his intentions to strongly enforce Federal laws, while in the North he chided listeners for their racial hypocrisy. It was Robert Kennedy who impressed upon his brother the importance of taking clear, dramatic steps for new civil rights legislation thereby helping to maintain black leadership in the less radical hands of Martin Luther King, Jr.

Once again, Robert faced accusations of ruthlessness. This time from Southern conservatives who identified him as the motivating force behind the Administration's civil right's initiatives. Undaunted, he continued to use the powers of the Justice Department to safeguard the rights of black Americans and began the Administration's push for a sweeping federal Civil Rights Law. Then, on November 22, 1963, Lee Harvey Oswald climbed the stairs of the School Book Depository and abruptly ended the 1000 days of the Kennedy Presidency.

Robert Kennedy retreated into a personal world where he sought solace in the Ancient Greeks and their sense of the Tragic to explain what had happened. Finding comfort in their philosophy of fatalism, he rejected what for many would be its twin sister, pessimism. Life, he concluded was a matter of destiny but also a struggle against the Gods. His literary romance with the ancient Greeks greatly influenced his political decisions and his rhetoric.

Resuming his duties as Attorney General in the new Johnson Administration, he redoubled his efforts to secure eventual passage of the Civil Rights Act of 1964. He also harbored thoughts of running for Vice President with Lyndon Johnson. The personal differences between the two men do not merit elaboration here but to those close to both, thoughts of such a political marriage must have been amusing. Ending any such speculation, Johnson announced that he would consider no member of his cabinet as a running mate. A disappointed Kennedy publicly joked that his greatest regret about Johnson's decision was that he, Kennedy, had taken so many good men down with him. Eventually, Kennedy resigned his cabinet post.

In 1964, he decided to seek elective office. Since his younger brother Ted was serving as Senator from Massachusetts, Robert risked carpetbagging accusations by opposing and eventually defeating Republican Kenneth Keating for the New York Senatorial seat. Though he sponsored some significant legislation he longed for the executive authority he once had.

He began staking positions to the left of the Johnson Administration. In his eyes the Great Society fell short of what was needed in civil rights, job creation, housing and ghetto programs. When he toured the ghettos he saw the poverty, saw the rats scurrying across the floor of a child's room, and was sickened.

He also began criticizing Johnson's conduct of foreign affairs. In 1965 he attacked the administration for its military excursion in the Dominican Republic. Finally, he spoke out on the issue that would crystallize his opposition to the Johnson administration: the advisability of America's continuing role in the war in Vietnam.

Early in '68 Eugene McCarthy entered the Presidential race and made impressive showings in the primaries against Johnson. On March 16, Kennedy announced for the Presidency. Two weeks later, with polls casting doubts on his ability to secure renomination, Lyndon Johnson surprised a national television audience and announced that he would not seek nor accept his party's nomination for President.

Denied the clear issues inherent in a run against Johnson, the Kennedy campaign floundered. Kennedy entered the Indiana primary knowing that a victory in a conservative Midwestern state could insure his nomination. Just days after Johnson's withdrawal, with Kennedy on his way to a campaign rally in a black ghetto in Indianapolis, Martin Luther King, Jr. was assassinated by a white man in Memphis, Tennessee.

THE AUDIENCE

General

Before Robert Kennedy announced for President, Stokeley Carmichael, the young but influential black militant claimed, "I would not like to see [Kennedy] run for President because he can get the votes of my people without coming to me. With the other candidates, I'll have bargaining power." [6] John Kennedy enjoyed considerable support from black Americans, but Robert's popularity did not arise entirely from his familial connections with John. In many instances the younger Kennedy enjoyed stronger ties with the black community.

Robert Kennedy simply could not tolerate any injustice perpetrated against a black citizen. When Martin Luther King, Jr. was jailed in Georgia, a saddened John Kennedy called Mrs. King. An incensed Robert called authorities demanding King's release. At the funeral of Medgar Evers, Robert sat with Medgar's brother, Charles who later noted, "He said I could call him any time day or night, if Negroes were being harassed and intimidated.... Whenever I had the need to call him, I never found it too late or too early."

It was Evers who encouraged his tour of the Mississippi Delta. Visiting shacks which smelled of mildew and urine, walking on crude wooden floors teaming with rats and bugs, seeing a starving child with a distended belly, all in his own country, shocked and nauseated him. On one occasion he sat crying on a filthy bed holding a small child. When the mother realized who he was, she reached for his hand proclaiming, "Thank God." [7]

Kennedy wanted to see through the eyes of those less fortunate; understand their plight and their reactions to the crushing knowledge that chance had dealt them out of so much that life had to offer. In the following years, Kennedy met often with black activists, occasionally subjecting himself to humiliating personal attacks. In Oakland,

California he met in-person with black militants and remained to listen to grievances despite encountering extensive personal denunciation. Charles Evers claims Robert Kennedy changed because he listened.[8]

The education of Robert Kennedy in black politics was evidenced by his rhetoric. Though he consistently abhorred violence, he both understood its causes and defended the rights of militants to be heard. When Eisenhower asserted that Watts was part of a "trend" toward lack of respect for the law, Kennedy attacked the premise as an oversimplification: "There is no point in telling Negroes to obey the law. To many Negroes the law is the enemy. [They must be allowed] to acquire and wisely exercise power in the community...[and] establish meaningful communication with a society from which they have been excluded."[9] Two weeks after extensive black rioting in Detroit and Newark, Kennedy addressed a political banquet in San Francisco. Above the contemporary backlash crying for a "get tough" response, the audience heard Kennedy's plea for understanding:

> Every day, as the years pass, and he becomes aware that there is nothing at the end of the road, he watches the rest of us go from peak to new peak of comfort. A few blocks away or on his television set, the young Negro of the slums sees the multiplying marvels of white America: more new cars and more summer vacations, more air-conditioned homes and neatly kept lawns. Every day he is told, by the television commercials we broadcast, that life is impossible without the latest products of our consumer society. But he cannot buy them.[10]

He also counseled on the importance of re-establishing black pride damaged by ages of slavery and segregation, claiming blackness should be a badge to be worn with honor and pride.

By his words and by his deeds he earned the esteem of the black community. When he campaigned in California, his body guard consisted of, "The Sons of Watts." Throughout his African tour black leaders received him in a style usually reserved for heads of state.[11] What might have honored Kennedy more was an observation by a ghetto youth, "Kennedy...is on our side. We know it. He doesn't have to say a word."[12]

April 4, 1968

At 9:30 on the evening of April 4, 1968 a predominately black crowd of approximately 2,500 gathered in a near northside inner city ghetto in Indianapolis. They filled an outdoor basketball court and much of the rest of the block. One witness reported, "they were packed in like sardines." The driving wind and thirty-nine degree temperature combined to cut through the shivering crowd. A chilling mist reduced visibility and dimmed the soft glow from the old outdoor lighting system. It was cold and miserable but the crowd had been growing since 7:30 for a scheduled 9:00 p.m. speech. The chance to see and hear Robert Kennedy compelled them to brave the elements. Some had brought campaign placards urging voters to choose Kennedy in the May primary and most were in a festive mood. Just after 8:30, those on the outskirts of the crowd began to receive word of King's assassination. Transistor radios began popping up and a few heated exchanges caused some of the whites to leave. One black lady cried, "Dr. King is dead and a white man did it, why does he [Kennedy] have to come here?" A local black gang began searching the neighborhood for militants who would support their quest for violence. The local group who had arranged the rally met hurriedly to determine the advisability of announcing King's death to the crowd. It was decided that those closest to the speaker's stand might be endangered by any violent crowd reaction. Many in the crowd had not heard of the events. Estimates were that the crowd included about 200 black militants. Fear for Kennedy's life prompted them to quietly begin checking for possible assassins.[13]

Suddenly the flashing lights from the police cars heralded the arrival of their candidate. Jockeying for position, they began to cheer as a pale looking Robert Kennedy climbed onto a flatbed truck under some oak trees in the adjacent parking lot. The mist swirled through the gleam of the spotlights and in a few anguish-filled minutes he addressed his audience.

THE SPEAKER

Style and Delivery

Inevitably any examination of Robert Kennedy draws comparisons to his brother John. Indeed, in some respects Robert invited these comparisons. He looked upon his older brother as a hero, frequently quoting him. He copied John's phrasing, use of statistics, and self-deprecating humor. There were, of course significant differences. Of the Kennedy brothers, Robert was the least poised, the least articulate. While John was extroverted, Robert was shy. John was intellectual, logical, and frequently aloof. Robert was tough, physical, and emotional. Robert was prone to interact with a crowd. His informality was evidenced by his jacketless, loosened-tie appearance. Such informality was rare from the more sophisticated John.

The critic, however, can find one other similarity. As John before him, Robert began his political career as an ineffective speaker. Robert Kennedy hid behind his manuscript reading it in a dull, flat monotone. Unlike John he never found comfort behind the lectern. His nervousness as a speaker did not subside over the years. Several who knew him have commented on the most prominent manifestation of this nervousness, a severe shaking of his hands. He could never control this palsy-like problem. He did learn to hide his hands just out of sight below the lectern. As TV correspondent Charles Quinn noted, "He stood up there, and looked very serene and cool as he spoke. But his hands were just shaking like leaves in a full wind."[14] His delivery suffered from a high pitched voice which at times shrieked. Kennedy worked on this problem by slowing his rate, lowering his tone, and softening his volume particularly for the television cameras.

While Robert Kennedy never mastered many of the techniques required of an outstanding speaker, he compensated for his inadequacies with his sincerity, conviction, and message. David Brinkley once remarked, "People liked him for what he was and what he had been and what they hoped he would be, and what he said. Not so much in the way he said it."[15]

It would, however, be misleading to conclude that Kennedy never significantly improved his technique. During his campaign for the Senate he began departing from his manuscript in favor of a more personal extemporaneous style. He employed more wit and revealed more of his passionate nature. Audiences could see his moods change. The more moved or angered he became, the more effective he was. Some of his most memorable speeches occurred during these moments. He would then employ his higher-pitched voice to his favor as it rose to great emotional heights.

Content

Obviously the compelling element of Robert Kennedy's speaking was not his delivery. It was, as David Brinkley mentioned, the *what* of his messages. Kennedy, especially after John's death, embraced a modified form of fatalism—a fatalism of suffering. His favorite quotation came from the *Agamemnon* of Aeschylus, "He who learns must suffer. And even in our sleep pain that cannot forget, falls drop by drop upon the heart, and in our own despair, against our will, comes wisdom to us by the awful grace of God." Suffering was redemptive, but he also felt that man's destiny was to try to reduce the suffering of others. Next to the Greeks, he most frequently quoted Camus. "Perhaps we cannot prevent the world from being a world in which children are tortured. But we can reduce the number of tortured children. And if you believers don't help us, who else in the world can help us do this?" [16]

Kennedy's speeches called for action while employing a pedagogical pattern: (1) locate a problem (i.e. an area of intolerable suffering), (2) substantiate the extent of the suffering with a flood of statistics, (3) discuss what little relief is now available, and (4) judge its ineffectiveness inevitably concluding, "I say that is not acceptable," and plead for action from his audience. In step four he generally paraphrased George Bernard Shaw with the line most commonly associated with Kennedy: "Some men see things as they are and say, 'Why?' I dream things that never were and say, 'Why not?' "

Kennedy's appeal can be explained by examining his creation of *ethos*. Most important to Aristotle was moral character—is the speaker believable? Initial *ethos* predisposes the audience for later appeals. Nowhere did he enjoy stronger initial credibility than with the poor, the minorities, and the powerless. Examples of Kennedy's expressions of concern for these audiences abound. Sorensen capsulized this concern:

> Gripping the hand of a dying woman in a nursing home until she was gone, talking with a little retarded girl in an institution, sharing the indignation of a Mexican-American migrant farm couple while their children huddled outside a filthy hovel, throwing a football around with teenage boys in a ghetto—not for affect or even self-gratification, but out of human kindness—such acts were characteristic of Robert F. Kennedy.[17]

A speaker's real challenge according to Aristotle is to maintain *ethos* throughout the speech. For the politician, this is a primary objective. To do so, political speakers employ image consultants, speech writers and coaches, and a whole array of communication experts. Slick commercials, well-rehearsed speeches, choreographed rallies, all assault the voters' sensibilities and challenge their judgments. Was Robert Kennedy well packaged? Probably he was. Does that explain his success? Probably it does not. Socrates in the *Apology* discusses a form of *ethos* frequently overlooked by today's Madison Avenue campaigns, a form difficult to "engineer," yet a form Kennedy displayed: a speaker unskilled in speaking but honest and deserving. Some thought that his weaknesses as a speaker may, in reality, have been one of his strengths. His nervous, self-deprecating jokes, his trembling hands, the uneven staccato pace of his speech, all may have conveyed the human, believable side of the politician. Lysias, the famous ancient Greek speech writer, stressed the importance of the concept of *ethopoiia*: i.e., a speaker building character by revealing some trivial human weakness and thereby establishing rapport with the audience by convincing them of his human virtue.[18] As if aware of this technique, Stewart Alsop wrote of Kennedy: "The style is neither elegant nor polished, the statements are made staccato and there are frequent repetitions; yet what comes through most strongly is a sense of deep and true concern, a feeling that this man cares very greatly." [19]

He employed logos in typical fashion through statistics and the almost syllogistic structure of his arguments. As mentioned earlier, the flood of statistics served to stress the severity of the suffering: "14,000 American children are treated for rat bites every year." Statistics also supported the fourth point of his organizational pattern (the "This is not acceptable" step): "Our citizens this year will spend three billion dollars on their dogs and less than two billion dollars for the War on Poverty."[20] Kennedy showed a fondness for arguments which were both stylistic and syllogistic: "To be an American means to have been an outcast and a stranger, to have come to the exiles' country, and know that he who denies the outcast and stranger among us at that moment also denies America."[21]

Cicero viewed effective *pathos* as nearly merging with *ethos.* A speaker must feel the emotions he seeks to awaken in his audience.[22] Sorensen claims Kennedy inspired his listeners primarily through his unusual gift of empathy, particularly when addressing the poor and disadvantaged.[23] Dr. Robert Coles theorized that Kennedy came across as a man with a great deal of emotion going on inside but, like the poor who identified with him, he was not always glib enough to express it.[24] Schlesinger concluded that more than just deploring poverty and injustice, Kennedy really felt it.[25]

April 4, 1968

Kennedy had just completed a foreign policy address at Ball State University in Muncie, Indiana. Before leaving he answered some questions, the last from a student who questioned Kennedy's belief that the feelings of whites toward minorities had improved. Kennedy reaffirmed his belief. Boarding the plane for Indianapolis, he received a call from Pierre Salinger. Martin Luther King had been shot. Salinger counseled against Kennedy's upcoming speech in the Indianapolis ghetto. On the plane, Kennedy told John J. Lindsay of *Newsweek*, "You know it grieves me...that I just told that kid this and then walk out and find that some white man has just shot their spiritual leader." As the plane landed in Indianapolis, Kennedy was informed of King's death. He "seemed to shrink back, as though struck physically." Dropping his face in his hands he cried, "Oh God. When is this violence going to stop?"[26] Journalist David Murray, seated opposite Kennedy described the reaction: "He just broke down. It was unbearable to watch him, to know that he was thinking about his brother getting it the same way. I don't want to go through that again." [27]

The plane sat for ten minutes before Kennedy emerged. To the small crowd at the airport, he spoke briefly of the tragedy. He ignored the warning of the chief of police not to go into the ghetto and without hesitation climbed into the car. During the next half hour Kennedy reduced his philosophy of suffering, the events of the day, and his personal tragedies to a few notes on the back of a white envelope. As the car approached the Broadway Christian Center, the site of the rally, the police escort pulled away. He heard the crowd cheer and saw the television lights and cameramen. He asked the crowd to lower their posters. When he opened with the news of King's death the crowd gasped so loudly that it was heard by a motorist two blocks away.[28]

THE SPEECH

His speech writer, his chief strategist and his press aide all agreed that Robert Kennedy's Indianapolis eulogy of Martin Luther King was his best speech. One of the few speeches that was not ghost written, it was entirely his own. One of his biographers, Jack Newfield, called it a speech, "that his skilled speech writers working together could not have surpassed." [29]

A man, who at one time depended on reading from manuscript, on this occasion with no help from his staff, with only a few scribbled notes on an envelope, and with little preparation time, delivered what critics agree was an outstanding speech. An artistic success, it followed the traditional epideitic structure prescribed since the times of Pericles. A pragmatic success, it accomplished the speaker's primary objective: "to tame the savageness of man."

Classical rhetorical theory recommends a simple three part structure for the funeral oration: (1) praise, (2) lament, and (3) consolation with reference to the greatness of the country. Kennedy begins his speech praising the ideals to which King dedicated his life: love and justice—two important themes which he employees throughout the remainder of the speech. He laments the loss for the United States and what would be a greater loss, his ideals—the loss of justice which leads to "violence," the loss of love which leads to "bitterness," "hatred," "revenge" and "polarization." The bulk of his speech is devoted to consolation. He uses the Aeschylus quotation to emphasize the redemption of suffering through greater wisdom. More importantly, he asks that they pray for "our country" which is ultimately "a prayer for understanding and...compassion."

Plato in the *Gorgias* cautions that the techniques of the funeral orator should de-emphasize the expedient and exalt courage, forgiveness and virtue. Kennedy's speech provides a model for addressing these concerns. Kennedy fears King's death will lead to the *expedient*, the polarization which sets, "black people amongst black, and white amongst whites, filled with hatred toward one another." He refers to the temptation to "be filled with hatred and distrust of the injustice of such an act." To help his audience resist this temptation he employees the three qualities extolled by Plato. King had the *courage* to oppose violence and bloodshed, a courage so strong that he dedicated his life to and ultimately died for that effort. Kennedy defines courage for his listeners. It is the courage of their fallen leader, "to understand and to comprehend, and to replace that violence, that stain of bloodshed that has spread across our land, with an effort to understand with compassion and love." Courage is *forgiveness*. Forgiveness yields the ultimate *virtue*, "justice for all human beings who abide in our land."

In the *Menexenus*, Plato's Socrates urges the speaker to present, "the world as it ought to be rather than as it is, and [make] the ignoble seem noble so public morality may thus be improved." George Kennedy in *The Art of Persuasion in Greece* explains Plato's assessment of a great funeral orator:

> As an educator who may influence the conduct of future generations the orator must present the state as good, as engaged in good causes, whether in fact it is or not. In blotting out the errors of the past the orator educates his citizen audience to a new future virtue. [30]

Once again we see Kennedy, the teacher, employing the same common pattern used throughout his campaign speaking. This time he need spend but little time locating and substantiating the suffering. He does discuss expedient measures for relief, hatred, distrust and revenge—all leading to increased violence. Tacitly, Robert Kennedy once again concludes, "I say that is not acceptable." The acceptable course of action is for each listener to raise the public morality and thereby the nobility of the country. Note the frequency of his references to "the United States." The suffering is transferred from the individual to the entire country. "Say a prayer for the family of Martin Luther King, that's true, but more importantly...say a prayer for our country." The only way to reduce the suffering is to determine what is good for the country. "What we need in the United States is not division," hatred violence or lawlessness, "but love and wisdom, and compassion, and a feeling of justice." He closes with another reference to the ancient Greeks asking his listeners to dedicate themselves, "to tame the savageness of man and to make gentle the life of this world," and once more imploring them to, "say a prayer for our country." Obviously Kennedy employed the structure and strategy of the ancients. However, this foundation does not totally explain the speaker's success.

Those who followed Kennedy closely point out that the Indianapolis speech was the first time he spoke publicly about his brother's assassination. That passage became the most frequently quoted segment of the speech by those who were present and its impact was electrifying. "I can also feel in my own heart the same kind of feeling." His brother too, he notes, died at the hands of a white man. This section recalls once more Cicero's teachings. Effective *pathos* is secured when the speaker convinces his audience that he sincerely feels the emotions to which he is appealing in his audience. In this situation it is critical lest Kennedy, a white man, appear self serving when he recommends calm and forgiveness. An elderly black gentleman who witnessed the speech later reported Kennedy, "had tears in his eyes, I saw it, he felt it man, he cried." One of the organizers, Reverend Deer commented, "They were in common grief together; they share a common experience; he reminded them of that; he communicated." [31]

Lysias touches on one other *ethos* building technique. He stresses the importance of not changing diction to suit various audiences. Literally he refers to the necessity for flawless speech regardless of the educational level of the audience. The principle expanded suggests the importance of a speaker not "talking down" to his audience. Kennedy seeks to elevate the concerns of his audience with a similarly exalted content. Few would gamble on the prospects of a wealthy white man going into a black ghetto, announcing the murder of a beloved black leader, addressing their suffering, and easing their hostilities by quoting the ancient Greeks. Kennedy's ability to do so verifies the strength of his *ethos* and supports Lysias' teachings.

The content of his speech and his general familiarity with the ancient Greeks suggest Kennedy's familiarity with their rhetorical prescriptions, particularly for the funeral oration; all of which he applied to his eulogy of Martin Luther King, Jr.

AFTERMATH

Impact

One week after King's death, *Newsweek* magazine reported, "From Washington to Oakland, Tallahassee to Denver, the murder of Martin Luther King, Jr. in Memphis last week touched off a black rampage that subjected the U.S. to the most widespread spasms of racial disorder in its violent history." [32] Riots were recorded in 110 cities.

GREAT SPEECHES

Over 25,000 people were injured and thirty-nine, mostly blacks, were killed. Throughout the country 75,000 National Guardsmen and federal troops patrolled city streets.[33]

At approximately 9:45 on the evening of King's death a saddened crowd of 2,500, mostly inner city blacks, disbanded from the Broadway Christian Center in an orderly manner and returned to their homes. Reverend Deer claimed he had, "never seen anything like it." One member of a local black gang remembered, "Man there was going to be trouble. They kill Martin Luther and we was [sic] ready to move." Another member commented, "We went there for trouble, after he spoke we couldn't get nowhere, I don't understand why, I don't understand." [34] In fact for the following week, Indianapolis unlike almost all other large cities in the country avoided racial violence. While we cannot quantify Kennedy's contribution to this nearly unique reaction, we can conclude that his eulogy contributed to the calm conditions. Word of mouth, radio and television, and newspaper reports spread Kennedy's eloquent message beyond the confines of that basketball court.

The Kennedy campaign found renewed purpose. His strategists had sought to enlarge the issues beyond Vietnam. Observers claimed that King's assassination proved a turning point for Kennedy and his campaign. He saw deeper into America's real problem—its insensitive treatment of minorities and the poor. Support from these groups for Kennedy intensified. For those "in the ghetto, Kennedy was now the last friend left." [35]

Epilogue

Kennedy surprised even his strategists and won the Indiana primary. On Tuesday, June 4, 1968 he captured the significant California primary to all but secure the Democratic nomination for President. Some polls suggested that if nominated he would defeat Nixon and become the thirty-seventh President. After his California victory statement a last minute decision changed his route from the ballroom. Minutes later, Robert F. Kennedy, lay dying from a gunshot wound to the head.

In the forward of Schlesinger's biography of Kennedy appears the following epitaph: "He lived in a time of unusual turbulence in American history, and he responded to that turbulence more directly and sensitively than any other political leader of the era." During his trip to South Africa the *Cape Times* explained Kennedy's effectiveness; his ability to stress the common bond of humanity as superior to the superficial differences of race and culture.[36] It was a bond of common suffering which he eloquently addressed in his Eulogy of Martin Luther King.

Roger Cook is president of The Educational Video Group.

NOTES

1. Theodore C. Sorensen, *The Kennedy Legacy* (New York Macmillan Co., 1969), p. 145.
2. William A. McWhirter, "The Kennedys", *Life Special Edition* (1968), p. 53.
3. Sorensen, p. 34.
4. Jack Newfield, *Robert Kennedy, A Memoir* (New York Dulton & Co., Inc., 1969), p. 68.
5. Arthur M. Schlesinger, *Robert Kennedy and His Times* (Boston: Houghton Mifflin Co., 1978), p. 343.

6. Sorensen, pp. 227-28.
7. Schlesinger, pp. 794-95.
8. Charles Evers in interview, *The Journey of Robert F. Kennedy* (A David Wolper Film Documentary, 1978).
9. Schlesinger, p. 780.
10. Newfield, p. 76.
11. Schlesinger, p. 749.
12. Schlesinger, p. 799.
13. Karl W. Anatol and John R. Bittner, "Kennedy on King The Rhetoric of Control," *Today's Speech* 16 (1968), p. 31.
14. George Plimpton and Jean Stein, *American Journey The Times of Robert Kennedy* (New York: Harcourt Brace Javanovich, Inc., 1970), p. 316.
15. Plimpton, p. 248.
16. Schlesinger, p. 619.
17. Sorensen, pp. 33-34.
18. George Kennedy, *The Art of Persuasion in Greece* (Princeton, New Jersey Princeton University Press, 1963), p. 136.
19. Schlesinger, p. 886.
20. Sorensen, p. 160.
21. *Robert F. Kennedy: Promises to Keep* (Kansas City: Hallmark, Inc., 1969), p. 31.
22. G. Kennedy, p. 292.
23. Sorensen, p. 160.
24. Plimpton, p. 278.
25. Schlesinger, pp. 276-77.
26. Schlesinger, p. 874.
27. Newfield, p. 57.
28. Anatol and Bittner, p. 32.
29. Newfield, pp. 246-47.
30. G. Kennedy, pp. 160-64.
31. Anatol and Bittner, pp. 32-33.
32. *Newsweek*, April 15, 1968, p. 31.
33. Schlesinger, p. 877.
34 Anatol & Bittner, pp. 32-33.
35. Newfield, p. 251.
36. Schlesinger, p. 748.

TRIBUTE TO THE *CHALLENGER* ASTRONAUTS

Ronald Reagan

White House, Washington D.C., January 28, 1986 (Transcribed from the video, GREAT SPEECHES, VOLUME V)

Ladies and gentlemen, I'd planned to speak to you tonight to report on the State of the Union but the events of earlier today have led me to change those plans. Today is a day for mourning and remembering. Nancy and I are pained to the core by the tragedy of the shuttle *Challenger*. We know we share this pain with all of the people of our country. This is truly a national loss.

Nineteen years ago, almost to the day, we lost three astronauts in a terrible accident on the ground. But we've never lost an astronaut in flight; we've never had a tragedy like this. And perhaps we've forgotten the courage it took for the crew of the shuttle; but they, the *Challenger* Seven, were aware of the dangers, but overcame them and did their jobs brilliantly. We mourn seven heroes: Michael Smith, Dick Scobee, Judith Resnik, Ronald McNair, Ellison Onizuka, Gregory Jarvis, and Christa McAuliffe. We mourn their loss as a nation together.

{For} the families of the seven, we cannot bear, as you do, the full impact of this tragedy, but we feel the loss, and we're thinking about you so very much. Your loved ones were daring and brave, and they had that special grace, that special spirit that says, "Give me a challenge and I'll meet it with joy." They had a hunger to explore the universe and discover its truths. They wished to serve, and they did. They served all of us.

We've grown used to wonders in this century. It's hard to dazzle us, but for 25 years the United States space program has been doing just that. We've grown used to the idea of space, and perhaps we forget that we've only just begun. We're still pioneers. They, the members of the *Challenger* crew, were pioneers.

And I want to say something to the schoolchildren of America who were watching the live coverage of the shuttle's takeoff. I know it is hard to understand, but sometimes painful things like this happen. It's all part of the process of exploration and discovery. It's all part of taking a chance and expanding man's horizons. The future doesn't belong to the fainthearted; it belongs to the brave. The *Challenger* crew was pulling us into the future, and we'll continue to follow them.

I've always had great faith in and respect for our space program, and what happened today does nothing to diminish it. We don't hide our space program. We don't keep secrets and cover things up. We do it all up front and in public. That's the way freedom is, and we wouldn't change it for a minute. We'll continue our quest in space. There will be more shuttle flights and more shuttle crews and, yes, more volunteers, more civilians, more teachers in space. Nothing ends here; our hopes and our journeys continue.

I want to add that I wish I could talk to every man and woman who works for NASA or who worked on this mission and tell them: "Your dedication and professionalism have moved and impressed us for decades. And we know of your anguish. We share it."

There's a coincidence today. On this day 390 years ago, the great explorer Sir Francis Drake died aboard ship off the coast of Panama. In his lifetime the great frontiers were the oceans, and an historian later said, "He lived by the sea, died on it, and was buried in it." Well, today we can say of the *Challenger* crew: Their dedication was, like Drake's, complete. The crew of the space shuttle *Challenger* honored us by the manner in which they lived their lives. We will never forget them, nor the last time we saw them, this morning, as they prepared for their journey and waved good-bye and "slipped the surly bonds of earth" to "touch the face of God." Thank you.

CHAPTER 10:
Celebration of Values

Occasionally a speaker pays tribute to his country, its citizens and its principles. He or she addresses the nobility in man, directing his audience to fulfill the promise of its highest ideals. Responding to a specific event, the speech, if successful, transcends the occasion by providing a lasting tribute to a central value of society.

We begin this final section with two excerpts from Eleanor Roosevelt speaking in favor of the United Nation's Universal Declaration of Human Rights. A program from Bishop Fulton J. Sheen's "Life is Worth Living" program is followed by an article by Dorman Picklesimer on the rhetorical and media techniques of this early television pioneer. We then offer John Kennedy's "I Am a Berliner" address and Lech Walesa's keynote address at the RFK Foundation Awards. Martin Luther King, Jr.'s, "I Have a Dream" speech pays tribute to the ideals of freedom and equality. Lloyd Rohler places this historic address in the context of this remarkable American's life and explores the richness of his eloquence in the concluding critical essay. We end with King's last speech, "I've Been to the Mountaintop."

TWO SPEECHES ON HUMAN RIGHTS

Eleanor Roosevelt

(Transcribed from excerpts on the video, GREAT SPEECHES, VOLUME VI)

PROPOSING PASSAGE OF THE INTERNATIONAL DECLARATION OF HUMAN RIGHTS
(United Nations General Assembly, Paris, France, December 9, 1948)

Mr. President, fellow delegates. The long and meticulous study and debate of which this universal declaration of human rights is the product means that it reflects the competent views of the many men and governments who have contributed to its formulation. Not every man or every government can have what he wants in a document of this kind. There are, of course, particular provisions in the declaration before us with which we are not fully satisfied. I have no doubt this is true of other delegations and it would still be true if we continued our labors over many years.

Taken as a whole the delegation of the United States believes that this is a good document, even a great document, and we propose to give it our full support.

SECOND ANNIVERSARY OF DECLARATION OF HUMAN RIGHTS
(Carnegie Hall, New York City, December 10, 1950)

The tenth of December is now being celebrated in many countries as human rights day. One hopes that this observance will spread to all countries because the more the day is celebrated, the more people throughout the world will be brought to think about the observance of human rights and freedoms within their own lands. Human rights must be applied to all human beings regardless of race or creed or color. When they are applied it will mean a growing understanding among the peoples of the world.

One of the fundamental human rights is freedom for the individual. Freedom can never be absolute because it must be consistent with the freedom of others but the more observance there is of human rights, the more freedom the individual will have.

We are fortunate in this country and particularly in the city of New York to have the United Nations established in our midst. It brings close to us an opportunity to meet and to know the nationals of fifty-nine other nations. As we grow to know these representatives of the various nations, we come to realize that human beings are much the same wherever they may be situated geographically. Their basic needs are similar and love and life and death are the same everywhere.

One wonders sometimes why hate plays such an important part in human affairs. Then one comes to realize that the reason lies in the lack of understanding of the meaning of human rights. Men have struggled for these rights of individual and even of nations for centuries and now at last in an organization of sixty nations they are struggling together to achieve the actual implementation of human rights through law as well as through the power of public opinion.

The Universal Declaration of Human Rights was an expression of the aspirations of peoples. It set standards toward which peoples throughout the world must strive. Now we are embarked on the effort to translate some of the rights and freedoms set forth in Universal Declaration of Human Rights into a covenant or covenants which may someday become law in the world as a whole. Whether this is accomplished soon or whether it takes a long time, the process will be educational and progress is bound to be made.

I have seen in my lifetime a great change come over the social conscience of governments, of economic systems and even of individuals. Fifty years ago it probably would have been impossible to get the representatives of so many nations to vote for the acceptance of the Universal Declaration of Human Rights. When it was accepted in Paris two years ago, no nation voted against it and only eight nations abstained.

I have no way of judging what the acceptance will be of the First Covenant of Human Rights until I know what the Covenant is actually going to contain. I had hoped that the First Covenant would be rather simple so that a great number of countries might have acceded to it and we might have gone forward then with what...with that first acceptance behind us to the formulation of the newer and more difficult rights. That it has been recommended that the First Covenant include all these rights and until the work is actually undertaken it is hard to foresee what the results will be. I can only say that I feel sure that the conscience of the world is stirred and that human rights and freedoms are going to move forward. How fast is still a question which we cannot foresee because there are forces in the world which have no regard for human rights and freedoms and those forces will have to be neutralized before progress for the peoples under their domination will be possible in this field.

We must continue to strive for improvement and I feel when human rights and freedoms and a consciousness that the United Nations means that reaches down into the hearts of the people we have accomplished a great deal.

THE ROLE OF COMMUNISM AND THE ROLE OF AMERICA

Bishop Fulton J. Sheen

From the "Life is Worth Living" television series telecast on May 12, 1953, over the DuMont network. (Transcribed from the video, GREAT SPEECHES, VOLUME VIII)

Friends. This telecast concludes our series of 26 weeks. We are very happy to announce we will be back again in the fall over the DuMont network and with the Admiral Corporation

I received a letter from someone the other day who said, "Why are you leaving the air? You really look good on television, you do not need a vacation." Listen to me, I tell you, I'm not leaving the air because I'm going to get a vacation. Telecasting is purely incidental in my life. My life is dedicated to the missions, I have to work for 100,000 missionaries throughout the world; help keep their 44,000 schools. Last year they cared for about 60 million aged, sick and orphans and lepers. That's my job. Now that I do not have this half hour with you I will be able to give this half hour to them. But we'll be back in the fall and you will see us much better on Admiral over DuMont.

You know I have noticed that since I came out here that my angel has been at the board. (blackboard) I'm afraid he's up to tricks and maybe we'll have to go over and take a look at the board. This probably will be very humiliating for me. My angel will be back too again in the fall. I'm very happy...(looking at blackboard) say what has he got here? (reading) "What will you do for me until the fall?" What fall?

I tell you what I will do for him. He's been cleaning my blackboard all along. So I tell you what I will do this summer for my angel until we come back again in the fall. This is what I will do for him. I will...(draws) use a long feather duster to clean his wings. He's been cleaning my blackboard so I clean his wings. Maybe he will like it. Yes he will like that—that pleases the angel. I wonder if he will let me use his halo? For the summer. How would he look in a beanie? He looks alright in a beanie, I wonder how I look in a halo? You see, I'm not ready for a halo yet. I'll be back in the fall.

Now for the conclusion of the series, we thought maybe it might be interesting if we took a look at the world and summarized it. In order that we might carry these thoughts with us for the summer.

The whole world is sick, not just one part of the world. When a human organism is sick one cannot amputate an arm or a leg and feel that one has completely eradicated a poison—particularly when it is through the system. So it is with the world. We cannot...(noise off stage) My angel is getting rambunctious tonight, I see that.

It is impossible for us; just simply point our finger to one particular country and say that it is wrong. Our great problem, of course, is communism.

What is the role of communism? That will be our subject tonight. Or, perhaps, half of it. The role of communism in the world and also, in relation to it, the role of America. The role of communism we will discuss, first of all, before the conversion of Russia

319

because communism will never be defeated. Communism will be converted if the world is ever to have peace—be converted to God. Then we will talk of the role of communism after conversion.

First of all the role of communism before conversion. The role of communism now, in other words. What is it? The best answer to that question is given in the words of our divine Lord. He said, "Where the body is, there shall the eagles be gathered together." Where ever the carcass is, there shall come the vultures.

Very often in the desert an animal or a human dies; the moment of its death one can see nothing in the clear skies and then suddenly from out mass mountain fastnesses and rocky crags these vultures of the skies come down to this glittering rottenness in order to devour it. These winged creatures are a kind of an avenger and a punisher. They are a judgment upon death and corruption. Just as soon as corruption sets in, these winged monsters appear shrieking and croaking and winging their way to death itself. That indeed is a symbol of civilizations. For they die too. Just as well as animal and human life. And whenever a civilization begins to die, morally or spiritually, then there begin to appear vultures and that is the mission of communism in the world. Communism is the scavenger of decaying civilizations. It makes its way into a country and into a culture only when that culture begins to rot from the inside. Measure of the incipient death in any civilization is the progress that communism makes just as soon as this culture begins to die. Then this winged scavenger with the mechanical wings of hammer and sickles descend upon these decaying countries in order to devour them.

Toynbee says in his history that sixteen out of nineteen civilizations that have decayed from the beginning of the world until the present time have decayed from within. Lincoln always said that America would never be conquered from without. If it ever perished, please God it will not, it will come from only within.

The proper way, then, to look upon communism is to see in it the judgment of God. Communism is something that came out of our western civilization anyway. It came out of what was putrid and foul and dead in our thinking. There is not a single philosophical idea in communism that did not come from the West. Its philosophy came from Germany; sociology from France; its economics from England. What Russia gave it was an Asiatic soul and power and force. Communism, then, is coming back upon the Western world because something died in the Western world; namely, the strong faith of men in the God that made them. Before Russia's won back in the faith, therefore, regard Communism as a kind of a manure—a fertilizer. It is a death that is spread upon the civilizations of the world until the springtime of a newer and better world begins to come into being.

This is the role of communism from a divine point of view before conversion. And then, afterwards what will it be? When Russia receives the gift of faith, Russia will have a new role, and its role then will be to be an apostle to the rest of the world. It will help bring faith to the rest of the world. Why are we so hopeful about Russia? Why should it be the means of evangelizing nations of the earth? For one reason, Russia has fire; it has zeal. Communism has that. The great shame of the world is that we have the truth but we have no zeal; they have zeal but they have no truth. Communism is like a fire that is spreading itself over the world and this fire is already in their hearts. Someday, instead of burning downward, that fire will begin to burn upward in a Pentecostal fashion. And then it will bring light and peace and joy to men as today it's bringing hate and tyranny and destruction and death.

Our Western world lacks that fire. We lack it obviously. Where is the fire of patriotism today—the fire of men trying to kindle sparks of love in other men? We of the Western world are rather cold, dull and apathetic. That's one of the reasons why today in our Western world there are no longer any orators. We have only readers in the world. Why readers? Simply because they have not got enough in their own hearts to speak out. So something cold and dead inert has to be read to man. What girl is there, for example, that would ever take a man who wrote out a wedding proposal? Glory be to God, if he loves the woman he ought to be able to talk about her. We love God, we ought to be able to talk about Him. If we love our country, we ought to be able to talk about our country. If we love our sciences, talk about our sciences. Where are the fires?

An Episcopalian English minister in the first world war did a remarkable lot of good with the English soldiers; bore the name of Studdert Kennedy. He wrote a poem called, "Indifference," and in this poem he contrasted Our Lord coming to Calvary and coming to the modern city of Bethlehem, or Birmingham I mean. And he says about Golgotha:

> When Jesus came to Golgotha,
> They nailed Him on a tree,
> They crowned Him with a crown of thorns,
> Red were his wounds and deep,
> For those were crude and cruel days,
> And human flesh was cheap.
>
> When Jesus came to Birmingham,
> They only passed Him by,
> They would not hurt a hair of Him,
> They only let him die;
> For men had grown more tender,
> They would not give Him pain,
> They only just passed down the street
> And left Him in the rain.
>
> And so it rained,
> The winter rain
> That drenched him through and through;
> And when all the crowds had left the streets
> Without a soul to see
> Then Jesus crouched against a wall,
> And sighed for Calvary.

Their hate, their violence was more tolerable to Him than those who are neither hot nor cold. Scripture says God vomits out of his mouth, and this Russian fire has tremendous potentialities about it. They do not deny God; they merely challenge God. They are not like our sophomores in college who are dismissing Him without any zeal at all. They are fighting against Him because they know He exists. Some day they will love Him. And that will be the new role of Russia. Finally it comes back to now its God, it will help bring it (inintelligible) throughout the world.

As for ourselves, what is our role? Oh, we have a magnificent role—we in America. We are destined, under Providence, to be the secondary cause for the restoration of the freedom and liberties of the peoples of the world. The secondary cause; God is primary cause. Therefore, we will have to make ourselves worthy of it. And we will speak of that in a moment.

Our country has always had a great role. First of all it was a sanctuary—a sanctuary for the oppressed. Then it became an arsenal for democracy. And now it's a pantry for the world. Every American has given five dollars to Africa. That's a mark of beneficence and goodness.

America's role also is now to roll up the curtain on the Eastern world. I do not mean to say that the Western world is to perish, but rather America's to help give birth now to the Eastern world and prosperity and peace and fraternity with the other nations of the earth.

Our great country was hidden for centuries behind a veil as it were. And then the ships of Columbus pierced that veil one by one. And now, it is the destiny of America to pierce another veil, the veil of the Eastern peoples of the world, in whom we are so interested in our mission life, and to restore these people to some decency of living. Two thirds of the people of the world go to bed hungry every night.

But in order to do that America must make itself worthy. And it will make itself worthy by regenerating itself. That is why we ask you to write to our President to ask him for a day of reparation and penance and prayer and fasting for the peace in the world. Remember our blessed Lord said, "I came not to bring peace, but the sword." What did he mean by that? Peter thought that he meant an outward sword. For the night our Lord was arrested, Peter drew a sword, and as a swordsman he proved to be an excellent fisherman, for the best he could do was hack off the ear of the servant of the high priest. And our Lord said to him, "Peter, put thy sword back again into its scabbard. They who take the sword will perish by the sword." Our blessed Lord was telling Peter, "I do not mean when I say I came to bring the sword, that this is a sword that is thrust into the enemy, it's a sword that is thrust into yourself to rout out all of your selfishness and sin." That's the way that peace comes to the world and also to man.

America has a far nobler destiny, really, than it knows. And if there is any way of telling what that destiny is, I think that America's role at the present time is very much like that of Simon of Cyrene. You remember Simon of Cyrene was a stranger in the city on the day the Friday that was called Good. He stationed himself on the roadway in order to watch a man go to His death. He did not know who He was, he was just curious, as some men are about men going to death. And as he watched the procession, the Son of God carry His cross to Calgary, the long arm of the Roman law reached out to him and said to him, "Take up His cross! Bear it!" He did not want to do it, but he took it and followed in the footsteps; the yoke soon became sweet and the burden soon became light.

And America is at the crossroads too—crossroads of a suffering world. It is undergoing a crucifixion of communism. The long arm of Providence reaching out to America and is saying to America, "Take up that cross! That cross of all the starving people of the world. Take it up! Bear it!"

And America is presently carrying that cross. Our great country does not know whose cross it is carrying. Actually, we are carrying a nobler cross than we know. We are bearing a nobler cross than we deserve. We have already saved the world from the swastika, that would cross out the cross and make a double cross. Now we must save the world from the hammer and the sickle: the hammer that would re-crucify man and the sickle that would cut immature wheat in order that it would never be the Bread of Life.

And America's role is to change these symbols so that one day men will carry hammers erect and these hammers will look like crosses as they parade in the Name of God; and the sickle will look like the moon under the Lady's feet to whom these telecasts were dedicated. To bring you to God and to make Americans love one another unto the betterment of the world and the peace of human souls.

"I HATE COMMUNISM, BUT I LOVE THE COMMUNIST"

Bishop Fulton J. Sheen Views Communism

Communism is the scavenger of decaying civilizations.

CRITIC: Dorman Picklesimer, Jr.

For over three decades, beginning in 1930 with his weekly radio broadcast on "The Catholic Hour," Bishop Fulton J. Sheen ranked as the foremost apologist for the Catholic Church. His widely circulated views were considered by many to be an "unusual blend of eminent scholarship, high sanctity, and warm human friendliness," while others believed them to be "an effort to create a religious majority for the minority he represented."[1] Both interpretations are credible because his views, though presented in an intellectual style supported by frequent quotations from classical literature and widely respected historians, usually reflected the doctrines of the Catholic Church. In either case, there is no question that the secret to Bishop Sheen's success was his ability to view his audience as "people" and not "masses." According to Father John Doran, "[Sheen] liked people, not just people in general, but people in particular, people in the concrete."[2] Herein one also finds the key to understanding Sheen's attack on Communism. "The Constitution of the United States reads 'We the people,'" Sheen told the Executive Club of Chicago:

> [B]ut of what do the Communists speak? The masses. What is the difference between the two? The people have reason, self-determination, they have genuine liberty. The masses are people who have lost their own conscience, lost the power of self-determination, who are governed totally by alien influences outside themselves.[3]

Thus, Sheen did not consider the primary threat of Communism to be economic or political but moral because Communism threatens the very core of people's faith and their ability to worship in the religion of their choice. As early as 1948, Sheen preached that "Communism has lost the concept of man as a creature made to the image and likeness of God, and reduced him to either a component part of the universe, to an economic animal, or to a physiological bag filled with psychological libido."[4] His conclusion: The rise of Communism depended upon the people turning away from God. His solution: The world can be healed only by returning to God. Like most religious leaders, he classified Communism as a Godless dogma and a threat to religious freedom. This appeal, by its generic nature, provided a wider audience for Sheen and won for him a strong following among Catholics, Protestant and Jews.

BACKGROUND

Fulton J. Sheen was born in El Paso, Illinois, on May 8, 1895, the oldest child of Newton and Delia Fulton Sheen. The young Fulton and his three brothers were taught the values of hard work and education by their devoted and industrious parents.[5]

When Sheen reached school age his parents moved to Peoria, Illinois, so that he could enroll in St. Mary's Parochial School and receive a Catholic education. The aspiring scholar soon distinguished himself in the classroom and eventually graduated as valedictorian from Bishop John L. Spalding Institute. After graduating Sheen entered St. Viator College immersing himself in the study of the classics, philosophy and Shakespeare. When Sheen graduated, Bishop Edmund Dunne of Peoria sent him to St. Paul's seminary, St. Paul, Minnesota, to complete his studies for the priesthood. Following his ordination on September 20, 1919, Sheen enrolled in Catholic University to complete a doctorate in philosophy. After receiving his doctorate Sheen received an invitation from the University of Louvain to take a higher degree, known as Agrégé, which meant that one would be aggregated to the faculty. This required an extended period of extensive study, an eight-hour oral examination by faculty from other universities and the completion of a book. Sheen passed with Very Highest Distinction.[6]

In 1922, the well educated priest, responding to a letter from his bishop to "come home," received an appointment to be a curate in a parish located in the poorest section of Peoria, where the streets were not even paved. Still longing to teach, Sheen, nevertheless, honored his vow of obedience and went about his duties with a zeal. At the end of his first year in the parish, the Bishop told him that he could now go to join the faculty in the School of Theology at Catholic University.[7] Sheen later transferred to the faculty of the School of Philosophy and continued his teaching for nearly a quarter of a century.

Sheen proved to be a very popular teacher whose classes were filled with registered students and auditors. His love for teaching helped him formulate his speaking style, and subsequently he received numerous invitations to speak on special occasions for the Church. Sheen's strong reputation as a speaker attracted the attention of the Paulist Fathers of New York, who in 1928 invited him to give a series of sermons that were broadcast from their church over station WLWL. He delivered the first radio message from Radio City.

Two years after this first broadcast, the National Council of Catholic Men began its sponsorship of "The Catholic Hour" over the National Broadcasting Company, and Bishop Sheen became the first regular speaker on March 2, 1930. He continued his weekly messages until 1951, when he began his first regular television show, "Life Is Worth Living." The speech transcript included in this text is the closing program from the first of Sheen's five seasons as the sole speaker for "Life Is Worth Living." Sheen contrasted his work on radio with his work on television:

> When I began television nationally and on a commercial basis, the approach had to be different. I was no longer talking in the name of the Church and under the sponsorship of its bishops. The new method (using commercial sponsors) had to be more ecumenical and directed to Catholics, Protestants, Jews and all men of good will.[8]

THE AUDIENCE

Faithful to this analysis of his viewers, Sheen worked hard to build a common bond with his multidimensional audience. His strategy seldom varied, even though his subjects covered such diverse topics as science, art, war, peace, teenagers and character.

Sheen would search for common ground and move his audience to his interpretation of the subject. In Sheen's words:

> I would gradually proceed from the known to the unknown or to the moral and Christian philosophy.... This was the same method used by St. Paul at Athens when the only common denominator he could find between himself and those who had lined the streets of the Acropolis with their gods was an inscription on one of them "to the Unknown God." From there he went to the concept of the true God. That was the way I tried to reach the vast television audience of America.[9]

Who, then, constituted Sheen's "vast television audience?" Because television was a relatively young medium and the price of a television set did not fit into the budgets of many families, one might conclude that the estimated four million people who tuned in on Sunday evenings were the newly emerging middle class and the growing upper class. Sheen claimed that a sampling of his mail (estimated to be as many as 6,000 letters per day) revealed that "in proportion to the population, the greatest numbers of letters came to me from the Jews, the second largest amount from the Protestants, and the third from Catholics."[10]

What prompted so many people from diverse faiths to tune in Bishop Sheen instead of the comedy and variety "Milton Berle Show" that appeared opposite "Life Is Worth Living"? Perhaps they found in Sheen's strong message and commanding presence a person in whom they could believe. Although America was recovering well from the Second World War, there was a sense of uneasiness in people. Suburbs with new housing developments were mushrooming, employment was improving and people were beginning to attend college in greater numbers than at any time in American history. Yet most of the population remembered the deprivation of the Depression Years and the even greater struggle during World War II. Then, there was "The Bomb" and the growing awareness that Russia had begun producing an atomic bomb of its own. The enjoyment of a better life style was undermined by fear that all the gains could be taken away. Eric Goldman illustrated these anxieties well in an anecdote about a St. Louis reporter who interviewed a young mother about her expectations for the postwar era: "'Oh, things are going along just wonderfully,' she bubbled, 'Harry has a grand job, there's the baby.'...Then she frowned. 'Do you think it's really all going to last?'"[11] This feeling of dread became pervasive. Louis B. Seltzer captured it in his editorial for the Cleveland Press.

> What is wrong with us?...We have everything. We abound with all of the things that make us comfortable. We are, on the average, rich beyond the dreams of the kings of old. Yet...something is not there that should be—something we once had. Are we our own worst enemies? Should we fear what is happening among us more than what is happening elsewhere?[12]

Richard Hofstadter provides a partial answer in his essay, "The Paranoid Style in American Politics." Indeed, there was, as Hofstadter claimed, a certain paranoia rampant among people in America in 1952. With the cold war succeeding World War II, an uneasy peace had descended over the land; but just as there appeared to be strong evidence of recovery, the Korean conflict started. Many feared the loss of faith in God and country, the turning from previously unassailable values and a certain powerlessness should Russia drop "the Bomb." Fear of Communist infiltration into the very heart of government, religion and industry grew rapidly. Those alarmed about this menace found a messiah in the junior senator from Wisconsin, Joseph McCarthy, who told the Senate and the American people that the only way to account for the situation was that "a great conspiracy, a conspiracy on a scale so immense as to dwarf any previous such venture in the history of man," was underway. McCarthy claimed this conspiracy was propagated by "men high in the government [who] are concerting to deliver us to disaster."[13]

Hofstadter claimed that three elements have to exist in order to understand the right-wing thought of the time:

> First there had to be a sustained conspiracy, running over more than a generation,... second, that top government officialdom has been so infiltrated by Communists that American policy...has been dominated by sinister men who were shrewdly and consistently selling out American interests, and...third, the country is infused with a network of Communists agents...so that the whole apparatus of education, religion, the press, and the mass media are engaged in a common effort to paralyze the resistance of loyal Americans."[14]

Sheen's keen ability to apply his depth of knowledge of philosophy to contemporary thought no doubt led him to make Communism a recurring topic for his telecasts: seven of the 26 programs aired during his first year on "Life Is Worth Living" dealt with the subject of Communism.[15] He appealed especially to the emerging middle class who feared the loss of and the turning from values found in hard work, faith-directed actions and belief in God and country. Many of Sheen's viewers were newly educated and admired his intellect almost as much as they feared the loss of recent economic gains. Some of those who looked to Sheen for guidance were just getting a firm foothold on the American dream. They had purchased new homes and new cars and had started families. The ever-present fear that all this could change if Communism took control from the capitalist system brought many people to their newly purchased television sets to hear the uplifting message of Bishop Fulton J. Sheen.

THE MESSAGE

Sheen did not disappoint those who sought his guidance. He gently but dramatically assured his audience members that they had nothing to fear as long as they maintained their belief and faith in God. His most frequent argument advanced the notion that "Communism is the logical extension of a heart and mind that refuse to recognize a God above."[16] Sheen considered Communism a punishment from God for a civilization that neglects His teaching. "As Assyria was the 'rod and staff' of God in former days, so Soviet Russia is that scourge today."[17] He supported this analogy with quotations from the Bible and with historical references. A favorite quotation came from Arnold Toynbee, who determined that "sixteen of the nineteen civilizations that have decayed since the beginning of the world have decayed from within."[17] According to Sheen, the decay from within is more to be feared than external aggression: "[Because] Communism is active barbarism from without, it can make progress only when there is passive barbarism from within." Sheen strove to expose the dangers in the covert and not the overt actions of the Communists, and he equated the tactics of Communism with those of Lucifer. "The Devil is not coming as a cloven hoofed, arrowed tail apparition," he told his radio audience when he began his seventeenth season on "The Catholic Hour," "he will come disguised as the great humanitarian; he will talk peace, prosperity, and plenty, not as a means to lead us to God, but as ends in themselves."[18] To dispel any doubts concerning this comparison, Sheen pointed out that "Communism...has taken the whole content of Christianity and substituted the spirit of Satan for the Spirit of Christ."[19] He observed that "Communism is possessed of a complete dogma" and that it is not a "political or economic appeal to man, but a profoundly religious one." Accordingly he was able to conclude that "Communism is a religion and must therefore be combatted on religious grounds."[20]

Sheen believed that the failure to conquer Communism by means of religious tenets would drive men further from God. Relying again on comparison, his favorite rhetorical device, Sheen equated Communist slavery with the form of slavery existing before the American Civil War. "The slave owner of Civil War days did not care how the slave used his soul, or even if he had a soul. He was concerned only with his labor. The new slavery seizes not only what is human in man, but also what is divine."[21] The analogy is strengthened when Sheen proclaimed that "in Russia 160,000,000 of God's creatures, destined for eternal life, are dehumanized and reduced to the state of ants whose sole business in life is to build up the great ant hill of the classless class."[22]

To make his audience aware that the threat of Communism is primarily religious and at the same time demonstrate that Christianity can cope with Communist arguments to the contrary, Sheen offered the following points for refutation: "Why can't the modern mind see there is nothing new in Communism?" he asked the faithful at a Lenten service in St. Patrick's Cathedral. "It is the groan of despair, not the revolution that starts a new age. It is the logical development of civilization which for the last 400 years has been forgetting God." Refuting the economic argument, Sheen declared that "Communism...is the logic of the worst aspects of the spirit of capitalism; capitalism made economics the principal end of human life; Communism made it the unique end."[23] To the argument that Communism emphasizes the brotherhood of all people Sheen replied that "Communism fails to satisfy the hunger for brotherhood because it denies God. Materialism never can be the cause of unity among men, only division."[24]

Sheen viewed Communism and Christianity as absolutes. To Sheen there could be no "gray area" between the two. He predicted that "in the future there will be only two great capitals in the world, Rome and Moscow; only two temples, the Kremlin and St. Peter's; only two sanctuary lamps, the red flag and the red sentinel of the altar."[25] From now on, he concluded, "the conflict is between the absolute who is the God man and the absolute who is the man God."[26]

These arguments, refutations and conclusions were considered by Sheen and most of his listeners to be self-evident. Members of the Communist Party, for obvious reasons, were not content to remain silent. An attack on Earl Browder, Communist candidate for President of the United States in 1936, in which Sheen denounced Browder as "one who is offering the kiss of Judas when he says Communism is not an enemy of property, the family, and religion," brought a challenge for a debate between the two antagonists to be conducted at Catholic University.[27] In a letter to Sheen, Browder called attention to the tradition of primitive communism during the first three centuries of the history of the Catholic Church by stating, "for these traditions Christian martyrs were crucified by the wealthy Hearsts of that day."[28] Unable to deny the charge, Sheen weakly substituted questions for argument when he asked, "Will you kindly tell me why he [Browder] wishes to sing the praises of the history of the Catholic

Church if he believes in anti-religious education? Is it not inconsistent for a man who hates flowers to want to talk of their beauty?" [29] In most instances, Sheen was able to answer Browder's arguments with thoughtful, carefully researched and well-worded responses.[30] But when the argument focused attention on the actions of the Church and/or the Pope, Sheen often took refuge in answering arguments with questions.[31]

As Bishop Sheen's attack on Communism intensified—in print, in broadcasts, in sermons and in public appearances—a contradiction seemed to be developing. A reporter asked Sheen how he could reconcile the Christian ethic of "love thy fellow man" with his opposition to Communism. Sheen replied: "I hate Communism, but I love the Communist."[32]

RHETORICAL ANALYSIS

Invention: Bishop Sheen had devoted over two decades to denouncing Communist ideology when he closed his first season on "Life Is Worth Living." During this time, he had immersed himself in the study of Communism. He used the knowledge he acquired to prepare his sermons as well as to prepare for the many debates in which he faced some of the top Communist officials. Thus Sheen deemed it appropriate to again use the topic of Communism for his closing show, in order to keep the issue active and so that "we [he and his audience] might carry these thoughts with us for the summer." Because this speech represents a summary of previously delivered points on this familiar and recurring topic, there are few new ideas. Rather, Sheen re-articulates his strongest convictions so that those audience members who turned to his program for guidance could receive reinforcement for their beliefs and arguments. Sheen's invention, therefore, does not create an air of newness.

Sheen's *ethos* remained the strongest of his artistic proofs. He carried with him the attained *ethos* of a successful person who works hard, is devoted to a good cause and is trustworthy. His role as national director of the Society for the Propagation of the Faith, to which he was appointed in 1950, closely allied Sheen with the worldwide missionary movement, and many of the hundreds of converts he had brought into the Church could make-up a Who's Who in America.

One convert in particular had a great bearing on Sheen's *ethos*. In 1937, Louis Francis Budenz, managing editor of the *Daily Worker*, denounced Sheen's attack on Communism in an editorial. The article closed by asking Sheen eight questions. Sheen's reply, printed and widely circulated under the title *Communism Answers the Questions of a Communist*, answered each question by means of documentation from Communist sources. After the pamphlet appeared, Sheen invited Budenz to dinner and began his campaign to proselytize him back to Catholicism (Budenz was born a Catholic and had been baptized as an infant). The subsequent meetings between the two representatives of opposing dogmas were kept secret—so secret that on October 10, 1945, when Budenz renounced Communism by declaring "Communism and Catholicism are irreconcilable," his name still appeared on the masthead of the *Daily Worker*.[33] After baptizing Budenz's wife and three children, Sheen announced Budenz's return to the faith—a dramatic illustration for Sheen's frequent claim that Communism would end in conversion.

The impact of Budenz's conversion on Sheen's audience is best understood by applying Hofstadter's view of the renegade. "The renegade," according to Hofstadter, "derives special authority because he/she is the man or woman who has been in the secret world of the enemy and brings forth with him or her the final verification of suspicions which might have otherwise been doubted by a skeptical world."[34] The Budenz story received such wide circulation in the American press that Sheen made only scant reference to it in his speeches. Yet, his audience's knowledge of the event invested Sheen with an elevated *ethos.* He had demonstrated Hofstadter's claim that "the renegade is living proof that all the conversions are not made by the wrong side. He brings with him the promise of redemption and victory."[34]

Sheen's speeches fulfill the three qualities of *ethos*: character, sagacity and good will. His character stood strong even among his detractors. His sincerity, his genuine love for people and his courage to speak for causes in which he believed were often cited as reasons why many of Sheen's converts sought his counseling.[35] Moreover, Sheen strove for fairness in his criticism: "The Communists are right in their protest against social injustice, but wrong in advocating violence," he told 1,200 men of the Holy Name Society after a parade in New York City.[36] Never content merely to indict without offering an alternative; Sheen urged his listeners to "go down to the poor and the unemployed and build up as strong a Christian proletariat as they would a Communist proletariat."[37]

Sheen's education, keen mind and thorough preparation for his speeches strongly established his sagacity. Sheen claimed that he "would spend about thirty hours preparing every telecast...so that the knowledge [he] had on a certain subject would be far greater than that which is imparted."[38] Such careful preparation not only contributed to general perceptions of Sheen as an intellect, it also rescued him in the event of a memory lapse. "Though I would forget this or that point which I intended to deliver," Sheen confessed, " I could draw on the store of accumulated information to take its place."[38]

Above all, Sheen strove to create good will with his audience. He selected words and illustrations to which most people could relate and often used humor to make his points—usually in the opening and near the middle. Even his byplay with the imaginary angel became a device to relax and engage his audience in the message. In the opening of this season finale, Sheen drew a picture of a feather duster on his chalkboard—to keep the angel's wings clean over the summer. Clearly, Sheen was not an artist. Yet, his rudimentary attempt at drawing not only confirmed that he was not gifted in all things, it also, according to Sheen, "allowed the audience to enjoy a superiority over the speaker."[39]

Sheen employed inartistic proofs freely. His use of the quotation from Toynbee and the reference to President Abraham Lincoln offer historical perspectives. His love for and use of poetry, both in speeches and in letters, often constituted the *pathos* of his speech. In this speech, Sheen dramatically recited a poem by Studdert Kennedy titled "Indifference," which depicts a modern Christ who prefers the cruelty of Calvary to the apathy of the times.

Disposition: Because this speech comprises a summary of ideas from earlier programs, its organization is somewhat disconnected. Sheen began the speech in his usual fashion, combining techniques of teaching with methods of public address. Like any good teacher, he wrote his outline on the blackboard and let the two main points (the role of Communism and the role of America) guide his presentation. Although he adhered to these issues, his points lack the necessary directness. By viewing the videotape (Great Speeches, Volume VIII), one can determine by the almost imperceptible flicker in Sheen's eyes that he has lost his wording, but he quickly recovers and the speech proceeds fluently, if not sequentially. He maintained his device of inserting a point of humor in the middle of the speech. Here Sheen illustrates his reference to the scarcity of orators in our Western world by asking, "What girl is there, for example, would take a man who wrote out a wedding proposal?" Viewers will note that the audience does not immediately respond to this attempt at humor until Sheen pauses and smiles.

Sheen followed Cicero's teaching that speeches should build toward a climax. Thus, he always put his most important point last in the body, with all preceding ideas leading to the climactic point. This practice also helped Sheen complete his program (27 minutes, 20 seconds) on time without the aid of a floor director; instead, he had a huge clock installed in front of the stage. According to Sheen, "the trick to conclude on time without hurrying or without being cut off was to assign an exact time to the conclusion. If it were two minutes or three minutes long, I would break off from my regular theme and begin the conclusion so there was never any hurried cutoff." [40]

Style: Sheen employed a middle style in his speeches. He used carefully balanced sentences that created a rhythm. Note the building toward crescendo when Sheen states, "We love God, we ought to be able to talk about Him. If we love our country, we ought to be able to talk about our country. If we love our sciences, talk about our sciences." At times, he uses one syllable words: "The whole world is sick, not just one part of the world." When Sheen wanted to praise or challenge, he used the grand style: "Our country always had a great role. First of all it was a sanctuary...then it became an arsenal for democracy. And now it's a pantry for the world."

Sheen's favorite stylistic devices were metaphor, simile and comparison. Early in the speech he uses the disease metaphor: the "sick" world is equated with a sick human organism. Later, he employs simile in declaring that "Communism is like a fire." He uses comparison in declaring that just as the ships of Columbus pierced the veil of America, so America and Christianity are called upon to pierce the veil of Communism that had descended over Eastern Europe.

Throughout the speech, Sheen uses imagery to create word pictures that graphically illustrate his message. The audience can visualize metaphorical "vultures devouring carrion on the desert;" imagine themselves "carrying the Cross" in his challenge to them to bear witness to the truth; and observe a parade in which men "carry hammers erect and these hammers will look like crosses"—a celebration of Christianity's ultimate victory over Communism.

Delivery: Sheen's verbal and nonverbal delivery were, perhaps, his best remembered assets as a speaker. His strong, resonant voice commanded his audience's attention, and his inflection, vocal variety and precise enunciation added natural emphasis to each sentence. He combined piercing eye contact with appropriate gestures that were congruent with his dynamic verbal delivery. The effect was compelling.

Sheen preferred the extended conversation method of delivering his messages. But his extemporaneous style of delivery demanded the most extensive preparation. He would "research the subject to be discussed,...arrange it to a few clear points,...write from memory his recollection of the material,...and check his memory with the research." [41] The time devoted to preparation made it possible for Sheen to use his delivery to maximum effectiveness.

Sheen's style of delivery translated well to television. His director knew how to take full advantage of Sheen's assets as a speaker. First, a set depicting a well-appointed and comfortable study was designed by the award-winning Broadway designer, Jo Mielziner. The set was furnished with undersized furniture to give the appearance that Sheen was taller than his five feet, seven inches. Next, the cameras were positioned so that all shots would be angled up at Sheen. This, too, gave an impression of greater stature. To these technical preparations, Sheen added his own methods of looking at the camera as if it were a person and executing his gestures so as to add emphasis, yet not be too oratorical. The naturalness of Sheen's delivery set the style for evangelists who followed him to television. Few people today remember that Sheen originated these techniques. They are taken for granted in much the same way as the close-up, the product of the creative genius of D.W. Griffith.

CONCLUSION

Sheen's approach to dealing with the problem of Communism is an interesting study in the rhetoric of values. Beginning his attack in the midst of the Depression, Sheen surprisingly chose not to consider the problem as an economic or political issue, but as a religious challenge. To Sheen, the Communists' economic appeals, which promised more money and better working conditions, and their humanistic appeals to brotherhood were mere tactics used to propagate a hidden and sinister goal. He believed and preached that all the benefits promised by Communism could be obtained through Christianity, and the individual could keep his soul in the exchange.

Sheen offered more than emotional haranguing on the subject of Communism. His numerous speeches and writings testified to an enormous amount of research in what he often called the "dogma" of Communism. He countered each point of argument advanced by Communism with a point of Christian doctrine. To understand the points of summary appearing in his "The Role of Communism..." speech, one has to recount Sheen's fundamental views of Communism, which grew stronger with each speech, book, pamphlet and telecast.

Sheen's ultimate conclusion concerning Communism received enthusiastic support from clergy and lay people alike: "Communism is vulnerable in one spot—death. As long as men die, Christianity will have the advantage, for it promises men not death but life." [42] Using the "sifting of residues" method of measuring good and evil (a common technique used for proposition of value speeches), Sheen claims the final victory for Christianity.

When one evaluates the entire scope of Sheen's public speaking—his inventive mind; his thorough preparation; his attention to the needs, wants and desires of his audience; his careful attention to delivery; and his desire to elevate the thoughts and minds of his listeners—one must conclude that Bishop Fulton J. Sheen epitomized Quintilian's "good man speaking well."

Dorman Picklesimer, Jr., is a professor and department chairperson at Boston College.

NOTES

1. "Letters," *Time* (May 5, 1952), p. 11; and "Letters," *Time* (April 28, 1952), pp. 4-5.

2. "Bishop Fulton J. Sheen," *The Criterion*, January 27, 1967, p. 5.

3. Fulton J. Sheen, "The Changed Concept of Man," *Vital Speeches of the Day*, (November 15, 1953), p. 85.

4. Fulton J. Sheen, *Communism and the Conscience of the West* (Indianapolis: The Bobbs-Merrill Company, 1948), p. 1.

5. The accounts of Bishop Sheen's life come from his autobiography: Fulton J. Sheen, *Treasures in Clay* (Garden City, New York: Doubleday and Company, Inc., 1980). See especially Chapter Two, "The Molding of the Clay," and Chapter Three, "The Gift of the Treasure."

6. *Treasures in Clay*, pp. 27-28.

7. *Treasures in Clay*, p. 42.

8. *Treasures in Clay*, p. 72.

9. *Treasures in Clay*, pp. 72-73.

10. *Treasures in Clay*, p. 73.

11. Eric Goldman, *The Crucial Decade and After: America, 1945-1960* (New York: Alfred S. Knopf, 1966), p. 14.

12. Goldman, p. 218.

13. *Congressional Record*, 82nd Congress, 1st Session (June 14, 1951), p. 6602.

14. Richard Hofstadter, *The Paranoid Style in American Politics and Other Essays* (New York: Vintage Press, 1967), pp. 25-26.

15. See Fulton J. Sheen, *Life Is Worth Living* (New York: McGraw-Hill," 1953). This is the first of five volumes (one for each year of the "Life Is Worth Living" television program). It contains edited transcripts of each of the 26 sermons delivered by Sheen during the television season, 1951-1952.

16. "Bolshevism Traced to Atheism," New York *Times*, April 3, 1933, p. 18.

17. *Life Is Worth Living*, p. 264. This source is cited instead of the speech because the quotation is omitted from the television version.

18. Fulton J. Sheen, "Signs of the Times," *Time* (February 3, 1947), p. 65.

19. "Communist 'Faith' Defined by Sheen," New York *Times* (March 25, 1935), p. 18.

20. New York *Times* (March 25, 1935), p. 18.

21. "Neglect of God Held as Cause of Reds' Rise," New York *Times* (March 16, 1936), p. 15.

22. "Sheen Attacks Communism," New York *Times* (September 25, 1935), p. 10.

23. New York *Times* (March 16, 1936), p. 16.

24. "Ism Fails to Satisfy Hunger for Brotherhood," New York *Times* (October 7, 1947), P. 30.

25. New York *Times* (September 25, 1935), p. 10.

26. *Time* (February 3, 1947), p. 65.

27. "Mgr. Sheen Assails Browder at Dinner," New York *Times* (September 11, 1936), p. 26.

28. "Browder Requests Talk to Catholics," New York *Times* (September 27, 1936), Section II, p. 2.

29. "Sheen vs. Earl Browder," New York *Times* (September 27, 1936), Section II, p. 2.

30. For example: To the argument that Communism sought peaceful means of co-existence, Sheen quoted from the 1935 and 1936 International Congress of the Communist Party in Moscow to show that the Communists then decided to abandon the traditional tactics of violent revolution in favor of working from within labor bodies, peace societies, and anti-fascist organizations by a disguised approach. See: New York *Times* (September 11, 1936) p. 26.

31. When, in 1944, the Communists accused the Vatican of fascism because it maintained silence when Italy attacked France in June 1940, Sheen answered: "Does that make the

Vatican Communist because the Vatican was silent when Russia invaded Finland and Poland? And incidentally, what was Russia doing in France in 1940, particularly since it was bound to France by a treaty?" See: Fulton J. Sheen, "*Nova et Vetera,*" *Catholic World* (March 1944), p. 589.

32. "Sheen Tells How Editor Rejoined Church," New York *Times* (October 12, 1945), p. 15.
33. "Workers' Loss, Budenz Returns to Catholicism," *Newsweek* (October 22, 1945) p. 100.
34. Hofstadter, p. 45.
35. *Treasures in Clay.* See especially the chapter "Making Converts," pp. 251-80.
36. "Forced Religion," New York *Times* (December 21, 1936), p. 21.
37. "Mgr. Sheen Calls on Church to Rival Communism's Appeal to Poor and Jobless," New York *Times* (October 7, 1936), p. 29.
38. *Treasures in Clay,* p. 70.
39. *Treasures in Clay,* p. 69.
40. *Treasures in Clay,* pp. 69-70.
41. *Treasures in Clay,* p. 55.
42. New York *Times* (March 25, 1935), p. 18.

"I AM A BERLINER"

John F. Kennedy

West Berlin in the Federal Republic of Germany, June 24, 1963 (Transcribed from the video, GREAT SPEECHES, VOLUME VIII)

I am proud to come to this city as the guest of your distinguished mayor who has symbolized throughout the world the fighting spirit of West Berlin. And I am proud...and I am proud to visit the Federal Republic which your distinguished chancellor who for so many years has committed Germany to democracy and freedom and progress and to come here in the company of my fellow American, General Clay, who...who has been in this city during its great moments of crisis and will come again if ever needed.

Two thousand years ago...two thousand years ago the proudest boast was, "*Civis Romanus sum.*" Today, in the world of freedom the proudest boast is, "*Ich bin ein Berliner.*" I uh...I uh...I appreciate...I appreciate my interpreter translating my German.

There are many people in the world who really don't understand, or say they don't, what is the great issue between the free world and the communist world. Let them come to Berlin! There are some who say...there are some who say that communism is the wave of the future. Let them come to Berlin! And there are some who say in Europe and elsewhere, "We can work with the communists." Let them come to Berlin! And there are even a few who say that it's true that communism is an evil system but it permits us to make economic progress, *Lasst sie nach Belin en kommen!* Let them come to Berlin!

Freedom has many difficulties and democracy is not perfect but we have never had to put a wall up to keep our people in, to prevent them from leaving us.

I want to say on behalf of my countrymen who live many miles away on the other side of the Atlantic who are far distant from you that they take the greatest pride that they have been able to share with you even from a distance the story of the last eighteen years. I know of no town, no city that has been besieged for eighteen years that still lives with the vitality and the force and the hope and the determination of the city of West Berlin.

While the wall is the most obvious and vivid demonstration of the failures of the communist system for all the world to see, we take no satisfaction in it for it is, as your mayor has said, an offense not only against history but an offense against humanity—separating families, dividing husbands and wives and brothers and sisters and dividing a people who wish to be joined together. What is true of this city, is true of Germany. Real lasting peace in Europe can never be assured as long as one German out of four is denied the elementary right of free men, and that is to make a free choice. In eighteen years of peace and good faith this generation of Germans has earned the right to be free, including the right to unite their families and their nation in lasting peace with good will to all people.

You live in a defended island of freedom but your life is part of the main. So let me ask you as I close to lift your eyes beyond the dangers of today to the hopes of tomorrow.

Beyond the freedom merely of this city of Berlin or your country of Germany to the advance of freedom everywhere, beyond the wall to the day of peace with justice, beyond yourselves and ourselves, to all mankind, freedom is indivisible and when one man is enslaved, all are not fee. When all are free then we look and look forward to that day when this city will be joined as one, and this country and this great continent of Europe in a peaceful and hopeful glow. When that day finally comes, as it will, the people of West Berlin can take sober satisfaction in the fact that they were the front lines for almost two decades.

All...all free men, wherever they may live, are citizens of Berlin and therefore as a free man I take pride in the words, "*Ich bin ein Berliner.*"

TRUTH AND TOLERANCE IN AMERICA

Edward M. Kennedy

Liberty Baptist College, Lynchburg, Virginia, October 3, 1983 (Transcribed from the video, GREAT SPEECHES, VOLUME VI)

Thank you very much Professor Calmbey for that generous introduction. And let me say that I never expected to hear such kind words from Dr. Falwell. So, in return, I have an invitation of my own: On January 20, 1985, I hope Dr. Falwell will say a prayer—at the inauguration of the next Democratic president of the United States. Now, Dr. Falwell, I'm not sure exactly how you feel about that. You might not appreciate the president, but the Democrats certainly would appreciate the prayer.

Actually, a number of people in Washington were surprised that I was invited to speak here—and even more surprised when I accepted the invitation. They seem to think that it's easier for a camel to pass through the eye of a needle than for a Kennedy to come to the campus of Liberty Baptist College.

In honor of our meeting, I have asked Dr. Falwell, as your chancellor, to permit all the students an extra hour next Saturday night before curfew. And in return, I have promised to watch "The Old Time Gospel Hour" next Sunday morning.

I realize that my visit may be a little controversial, but as many of you have heard, Dr. Falwell recently sent me a membership in the Moral Majority—and I didn't even apply for it. And, I wonder if that means I am a member in good standing. Somewhat, he says huh.

This is, of course, a nonpolitical speech—which is probably best under the circumstances. Since I am not a candidate for president, it would certainly be inappropriate to ask for your support in this election—and probably inaccurate to thank you for it in the last one.

I have come here to discuss my beliefs about faith and country, tolerance and truth in America. I know we begin with certain disagreements, and I strongly suspect at the end of the evening some of our disagreements will remain. But I also hope that tonight and in the months and years ahead, we will always respect the right of others to differ, that we will never lose sight of our own fallibility, and that we will view ourselves with a sense of perspective and a sense of humor. After all, in the New Testament, even the disciples had to be taught to look first to the beam in their own eyes, and only then to the mote in their neighbor's eyes. I am mindful of that counsel. I am an American and a Catholic; I love my country and treasure my faith. But I do not assume that my conception of patriotism or policy is invariably correct—or that my convictions about religion should command any greater respect than any other faith in this pluralistic society. I believe there surely is such a thing as truth, but who among us can claim a monopoly on it?

There are those who do, and their own words testify to their intolerance. For example, because the Moral Majority has worked with members of different denomination, one fundamentalist group has denounced Dr. Falwell for hastening the ecumenical church and for "yoking together with Roman Catholics, Mormons, and others." I am relieved that Dr. Falwell does not regard that as a sin—and on this issue, he himself has become the target of narrow prejudice. When people agree on public policy, they ought to be able to work together, even while they worship in diverse ways. For truly, for truly we are all yoked together as Americans—and the yoke is the happy one of individual freedom and mutual respect.

But in saying that, we cannot and should not turn aside from a deeper and more pressing question—which is whether and how religion should influence government. A generation ago, a presidential candidate had to prove his independence of undue religious influence in public life, and he had to do so partly at the insistence of the evangelical Protestants. John Kennedy said at that time, "I believe in an America where there is no (religious) bloc voting of any kind." Only twenty years later, another candidate was appealing to a evangelical meeting as a religious bloc. Ronald Reagan said to fifteen thousand evangelicals *[sic]* at The Roundtable in Dallas, "I know that you can't endorse me. I want you to know I endorse you and what you are doing."

To many Americans, that pledge was a sign and a symbol of a dangerous breakdown in the separation of church and state. Yet this principle, as vital as it is, is not a simplistic and rigid command. Separation of church and state cannot mean an absolute separation between moral principles and political power. The challenge, the challenge today is to recall the origin of the principle, to define its purpose, and refine its application to the politics of the present. The founders of our nation had long and bitter experience with the state as both the agent and the adversary of particular religious views. In colonial Maryland, Catholics paid a double land tax and in Pennsylvania they had to list their names on a public roll—an ominous precursor of the first Nazi laws against the Jews. And Jews in turn faced discrimination in all of the thirteen original colonies. Massachusetts exiled Roger Williams and his congregation for contending that civil government had no right to enforce the Ten Commandments. Virginia harassed Baptist teachers and also established a religious test for public service, writing into the law that no "Popish followers" could hold any office.

But during the revolution, Catholics, Jews and nonconformists all rallied to the cause and fought valiantly for the American commonwealth—for John Winthrop's "city upon a hill." Afterwards, when the Constitution was ratified and then amended, the framers gave freedom for all religion and from any established religion the very first place in the Bill of Rights. Indeed the framers themselves professed very different faiths—Washington was an Episcopalian, Jefferson a deist, and Adams a Calvinist. And although he had earlier opposed toleration, John Adams later contributed to the building of Catholic churches—and so did George Washington. Thomas Jefferson said his proudest achievement was not the presidency, or the writing the Declaration of Independence, but drafting the Virginia Statute of Religious Freedom. He stated the vision of the first Americans and the First Amendment very clearly: "The God who gave us life gave us liberty at the same time."

The separation of church and state can sometimes be frustrating for women and men of religious faith. They may be tempted to misuse government in order to impose a value which they cannot persuade others to accept. But once we succumb to that temptation, we step onto a slippery slope where everyone's freedom is at risk. Those who favor censorship should recall that one of the first books ever burned was the first English translation of the Bible. As President Eisenhower warned in 1953, "Don't join the bookburners...the right to say ideas, the right to record them and the right to have them accessible to others is unquestioned—or this isn't America." And if that right is denied, at some future day the torch can be turned against any other book or any other belief. Let us never forget, today's Moral Majority could become tomorrow's persecuted minority.

The danger is as great now as when the founders of the nation first saw it. In 1789 their fear was of factional strife among dozens of denominations. Today there are hundreds and perhaps even thousands of faiths and millions of Americans who are outside any fold. Pluralism obviously does not and cannot mean that all of them are right; but it does mean that there are areas where government cannot and should not decide what it is wrong to believe, to think, to read, and to do. As Professor Larry Tribe, one of the nation's leading constitutional scholars has written, "Law is not theocratic, in a nontheocratic state, cannot measure religious truth"—nor can the state impose it.

The real transgression occurs when religion wants government to tell citizens how to live uniquely personal parts of their lives. The failure of Prohibition proves the futility of such an attempt when a majority or even a substantial minority happens to disagree. Some questions may be inherently individual ones or people may be sharply divided about whether they are. In such cases like Prohibition and abortion the proper role of religion is to appeal to the conscience of the individual, not the coercive power of the state.

But there are other...but there are other questions which are inherently public in nature, which we must decide together as a nation, and where religion and religious values can and should speak to our common conscience. The issue of nuclear war is a compelling example. It is a moral issue; it will be decided by government, not by each individual; and to give any effect to the moral values of their creed, people of faith must speak directly about public policy. The Catholic bishops and the Reverend Billy Graham have every right to stand for the nuclear freeze and Dr. Falwell has every right to stand against it. There must be standards for the exercise of such leadership, so that the obligations of belief will not be debased into an opportunity for mere political advantage. But to take a stand at all when a question is both properly public and truly moral is to stand in a long and honored tradition. Many of the great evangelists of the 1800's were in the forefront of the abolitionist movement. In our own time, the Reverend William Sloane Coffin challenged the morality of the war in Vietnam. Pope John XXIII renewed the Gospel's call to social justice. And Dr. Martin Luther King, Jr., who was the greatest prophet of this century, awakened our nation and its conscience to the evil of racial segregation. Their words have blessed our world. And who knew [sic]...now wishes that they had been silent? Who would bid Pope John Paul to quiet his voice against the oppression in eastern Europe; the violence in Central America; or the crying needs of the landless, the hungry, and those who are tortured in so many of the dark political prisons of our time?

President Kennedy, who said that "no religious body should seek to impose its will," also urged religious leaders to state their views and give their commitment when the public debate involved ethical issues. In drawing the line between imposed will and essential witness, we keep church and state separate and at the same time, we recognize that the city of God should speak to the civic duties of men and women.

There are four tests which draw that line and define the difference. First, we must respect the integrity of religion itself. People of conscience should be careful how they deal in the word of their Lord. In our own history, religion has been falsely invoked to sanction prejudice, even slavery, to condemn labor unions and public spending for the poor. I believe that the prophecy "the poor you always have with you" is an indictment, not a commandment and I respectfully suggest that God has taken no position on the Department of Education and that a balanced budget constitutional amendment is a matter of economic analysis and not heavenly appeals. Religious values cannot be excluded from every public issue but not every public issue involves religious values. And how ironic it is when those very values are denied in the name of religion. For example, we are sometimes told that it is wrong to feed the hungry, but that mission is an explicit mandate given to us in the twenty-fifth chapter of Matthew.

Second, we must respect the independent judgments of conscience. Those who proclaim moral and religious values can offer counsel, but they should not casually treat a position on a public issue as a test of fealty to faith. Just as I disagree with the Catholic bishops on tuition tax credits, which I oppose, so other Catholics can and do disagree with the hierarchy, on the basis of honest conviction, on the question of the nuclear freeze. Thus, the controversy about the Moral Majority arises not only from its views, but from its name, which in the minds of many seems to imply that only one set of public policies is moral and only one majority can possibly be right. Similarly, people are and should be perplexed when the religious lobbying group Christian Voice publishes a morality index of congressional voting records, which judges the morality of senators by their attitude toward Zimbabwe and Taiwan.

Let me offer another illustration. Dr. Falwell has written and I quote, "To stand against Israel is to stand against God." Now there is no one in the Senate who has stood more firmly for Israel than I have. Yet I do not doubt the faith of those on the other side. Their error is not one of religion, but of policy, and I hope to be able to persuade them that, that they are wrong in terms of both America's interest and the justice of Israel's cause.

Respect for conscience is most in jeopardy and the harmony of our diverse society is most at risk, when we reestablish, directly or indirectly, a religious test for public office. That relic of the colonial era, which is specifically prohi...prohibited in the Constitution, has reappeared in recent years. After the last election, the Reverend James Robison, Robison warned President Reagan not to surround himself, as presidents before him had, "with the counsel of the ungodly." I utterly reject any such standard for any position anywhere in public service. Two centuries ago, the victims were Catholics and Jews. In the 1980's, the victims could be atheists; in some other day or decade, they could be the members of the Thomas Road Baptist Church. Indeed, in 1976 I regarded it as unworthy and un-American when some people said or hinted that Jimmy Carter should not be president because he was a born again Christian. We must never judge the fitness of individuals to govern on the base of where they worship, whether they follow Christ or Moses or whether they are called "born again" or "ungodly." Where it is right to apply moral values to public life, let all of us avoid the temptation to be self-righteous and absolutely certain of ourselves. And if that temptation...and if that temptation ever comes, let us recall Winston Churchill's humbling description of an intolerant and inflexible colleague: "There but for the grace of God—goes God."

Third, in applying religious values, we must respect the integrity of public debate. In that debate, faith is no substitute for facts. Critics may oppose the nuclear freeze for what they regard as moral reasons. They have every right to argue that any negotiation with the Soviets is wrong, or that any accommodation with them sanctions their crimes, or that no agreement can be good enough and therefore all agreements only increase the chance of war. I do not believe that, but it surely does not violate the standard of fair public debate to say it. What does violate that standard, what the opponents of the nuclear freeze have no right to do, is to assume that they are infallible and so any argument against the freeze will do, whether it is false or true. The nuclear freeze proposal is not unilateral, but bilateral—with equal restraints on the United States and the Soviet Union. The nuclear freeze does not require that we trust the Russians, but demands full and effective verification. The nuclear freeze does not concede a Soviet lead in nuclear weapons, but recognizes that human beings in each great power already have in their fallible hands the overwhelming capacity to remake into a pile of radioactive rubble the Earth which God has made.

There is no morality...there is no morality in the mushroom cloud. The black rain of nuclear ashes will fall alike on the just and the unjust. And then it will be too late to wish that we had done the real work of this atomic age—which is to seek a world that is neither Red nor dead.

I am perfectly prepared to debate the nuclear freeze on policy grounds or moral ones. But we should not be forced to discuss phantom issues or false charges. They only deflect us from the urgent task of deciding how best to prevent a planet divided from becoming a planet destroyed. And it does not advance the debate to contend that the arms race is more divine punishment than human problem, or that in any event, the final days are near. As Pope John said two decades ago, at the opening of the Second Vatican Council, "We must beware of those who burn with zeal, but are not endowed with much sense...we must disagree with the prophets of doom, who are always forecasting disasters, as though the end of the Earth was at hand." The message which echoes across the years is very clear: The Earth is still here; and if we wish to keep it, a prophecy of doom is no alternative to a policy of arms control.

Fourth, and finally, we must respect the motives of those who exercise their right to disagree. We sorely test our ability to live together if we readily question each other's integrity. It may be harder to restrain our feelings when moral principles are at stake, for they go to the deepest wellsprings of our being. But the more our feelings diverge, the more deeply felt they are, the greater is our obligation to grant the sincerity and essential decency of our fellow citizens on the other side.

Those who favor E.R.A. are not "antifamily" or "blasphemers" and their purpose is not "an attack on the Bible." Rather we believe this is the best way to fix in our national firmament the ideal that not only all men, but all people, are created equal. Indeed, my mother who strongly favors E.R.A. would be surprised to hear that she is antifamily. For my part, I think of the amendment's opponents as wrong on the issue, but not lacking in moral character.

I could multiply the instances of name-calling, sometimes on both sides. Dr. Falwell is not a "warmonger" and "liberal Clergymen" are not, as the Moral Majority suggested in a recent letter, equivalent to "Soviet sympathizers." The critics of official prayer in public schools are not "Pharisees"; many of them are both civil libertarians and believers, who think that families should pray more at home with their children and attend church and synagogue more faithfully. And people are not "sexist" because they stand against abortion and they are not "murderers" because they believe in free choice. Nor does it help anyone...nor does it help anyone's cause to shout such epithets or to try and shout a speaker down, which is what happened last April when Dr. Falwell was hissed and heckled at Harvard. So I am doubly grateful for your courtesy here this evening. That was not Harvard's finest hour, but I am happy to say that the loudest applause from the Harvard audience came in defense of Dr. Falwell's right to speak.

In short, I hope for an America where neither fundamentalist nor humanist will be a dirty word, but a fair description of the different ways in which people of goodwill look at life and into their own souls. I hope for an America where no president, no public official, no individual will ever be deemed a greater or lesser American because of religious doubt or religious belief. I hope for an America where the power of faith will always burn brightly but where no modern inquisition of any kind will ever light the fires of fear, coercion or angry division. I hope for an America where we can all contend freely and vigorously, but where we will treasure and guard those standards of civility which alone make this nation safe for both democracy and diversity.

Twenty years ago this fall, in New York City, President Kennedy met for the last time with a Protestant assembly. The atmosphere had been transformed since his earlier address during the 1960 campaign to the Houston Ministerial Association. He had spoken there to allay suspicions about his Catholicism, and to answer those who claimed that on the day of his baptism, he was somehow disqualified from becoming president. His speech in Houston and then his election drove that prejudice from the center of our national life. Now, three years later, in November of 1963, he was appearing before the Protestant Council of New York City to reaffirm what he regarded as some fundamental truths. On that occasion, John Kennedy said, "The family of man is not limited to a single race or religion, to a single city or country.... The family of man is nearly three billion strong. Most of its members are not white and most of them are not Christians." And as President Kennedy reflected on that reality, he restated an ideal for which he had lived his life, that "the members of this family should be at peace with one another." That ideal shines across all the generations of our history and all the ages of our faith, carrying with it the most ancient dream. For as the apostle Paul wrote long ago in Romans, "If it be possible, as much as it lieth in you, live peaceably with all men."

I believe it is possible; the choice lies within us. As fellow citizens, let us live peaceably with each other; as fellow human beings, let us strive to live peaceably with men and women everywhere. Let that be our purpose and our prayer; yours and mine, for ourselves, for our country, and for all the world.

RFK HUMAN RIGHTS AWARD SPEECH

Lech Walesa

Georgetown University, Washington, D.C., November 16, 1989 (Transcribed from the video, GREAT SPEECHES, VOLUME VII)

I indeed am an electrician but please don't short circuit me now. I've got to read my statement here, my message. I do apologize not to listen to your song.

First of all, I'd, I'd like to thank you very much for inviting me and my colleagues to take part in today's ceremony. I know I am among good and tested friends. I will remember the visit Senator Kennedy, members of his family, as well as representatives of the Robert Kennedy Memorial paid to Poland in May of 1987. You came to my country to present the coveted Robert Kennedy Human Rights Award to two of my close friends, Zbignew Buyok and Adam Mitnick and to honor the memory of a young Polish priest, Father Yuri Popoyushski, who gave his life for the rights of each man to live in truth and freedom.

Your presence in Poland then meant a lot to us. It testified to the fact that we are not alone in our difficult struggle for freedom and justice. It testified to solidarity.

We meet today to honor a very exceptional man, a scholar, a teacher and a great fighter for human rights, Professor Fong Li Xing. Thinking today of Professor Fong Li Xing we remember the young people from Bejing, the students of the Square of Heavenly Peace. Many of them paid with their lifes [sic] for the natural right of every man to a life of dignity and truth. Others similar to their teacher, Professor Fong Li Xing, are being opposed and hunted down. Information reaching us from Bejing tell us that the authorities are sectionally ruthless in hunting down members of the first independent Chinese trade union. And their leaders being kept in total isolation.

We of people of solidarity well understand our Chinese brothers. Only recently we were very [sic] in very similar situation. And though all comparisons in this case can be dangerous or even tactless, permit me to say that our presence here today provides reason for hope for our Chinese friends. That hope about which Professor Fong Li Xing speaks in his message.

Invited to take part in today's ceremony I was wondering what links together people so seemingly apart as the young American senator from a well known Boston family, a Polish priest performing his religious duties during the difficult period of martial law in Poland and an astrophysicist from Bejing.

I recall an excerpt from a poem I heard some time ago and though I do not deal with poetry this particular piece I think I remember. I'll try to quote it. It went more or less like this:

Do not fear your enemies, in the worst case they will kill you. Do not fear your friends, in the worst case they will betray you. Beware of the indifferent ones, it is with their silent consent that murder, treason exist in the world.

What links Robert Kennedy, Father Popoyushski, Professor Fong Li Xing as well as other winners of your award is the fact that they decided not to be indifferent. They did not shrug their shoulders, they did not turn away, they did not cross the street when they saw another human being being harmed. Where others were complacent, they acted. They not only spoke about freedom, they made freedom.

The people we are honoring today actively resisted evil. They rallied others because they fought evil with good. And good has this wonderful ability of rallying people around.

Finally, finally I would like to address our young friends, the students of Georgetown University, and especially the Chinese students who I see among the guests. I would like to draw your attention to that part of Professor Fong's message in which he talks about the necessity of acquiring knowledge. Tyrants were always afraid of knowledge. That is why they falsified history, burned books and fought freedom of speech. Nothing brought more tragedy to the human kind than the alliance of mad tyrants with ignorance. In knowledge lies the one key to a better future.

Thank you very much.

"I HAVE A DREAM"

Martin Luther King, Jr.

Washington, D.C., August 28, 1963 (Transcribed from the video, GREAT SPEECHES, VOLUME I)

I am happy to join with you today in what will go down in history as the greatest demonstration for freedom in the history of our nation.

Five score years ago, a great American, in whose symbolic shadow we stand today, signed the Emancipation Proclamation. This momentous decree came as a great beacon light of hope for millions of Negro slaves who had been seared in the flames of withering injustice. It came as a joyous daybreak to end the long night of their captivity.

But one hundred years later, the Negro still is not free. One hundred years later, the life of the Negro is still sadly crippled by the manacles of segregation and the chains of discrimination. One hundred years later, the Negro lives on a lonely island of poverty in the midst of a vast ocean of material prosperity. One hundred years later, the Negro is still languished in the corners of American society and finds himself an exile in his own land. So we've come here today to dramatize a shameful condition.

In a sense we've come to our nation's capital to cash a check. When the architects of our republic wrote the magnificent words of the Constitution and the Declaration of Independence, they were signing a promissory note to which every American was to fall heir. This note was a promise that all men, yes, black men as well as white men, would be guaranteed the unalienable rights of life, liberty, and the pursuit of happiness.

It is obvious today that America has defaulted on this promissory note insofar as her citizens of color are concerned. Instead of honoring this sacred obligation, America has given the Negro people a bad check, a check which has come back marked "insufficient funds."

But we refuse to believe that the bank of justice is bankrupt. We refuse to believe that there are insufficient funds in the great vaults of opportunity of this nation. So we've come to cash this check, a check that will give us upon demand the riches of freedom and the security of justice.

We have also come to this hallowed spot to remind America of the fierce urgency of now. This is no time to engage in the luxury of cooling off or to take the tranquilizing drug of gradualism. Now is the time to make real the promises of democracy. Now is the time to rise from the dark and desolate valley of segregation to the sunlit path of racial justice. Now is the time to lift our nation from the quicksands of racial injustice to the solid rock of brotherhood. Now is the time to make justice a reality for all of God's children.

It would be fatal for the nation to overlook the urgency of the moment. This sweltering summer of the Negro's legitimate discontent will not pass until there is an invigorating autumn of freedom and equality. 1963 is not an end but a beginning. Those who hope that the Negro needed to blow off steam and will now be content will have a rude awakening if the nation returns to business as usual.

There will be neither rest nor tranquility in America until the Negro is granted his citizenship rights. The whirlwinds of revolt will continue to shake the foundations of our nation until the bright day of justice emerges.

But that is something that I must say to my people who stand on the warm threshold which leads into the palace of justice. In the process of gaining our rightful place we must not be guilty of wrongful deeds. Let us not seek to satisfy our thirst for freedom by drinking from the cup of bitterness and hatred. We must forever conduct our struggle on the high plane of dignity and discipline. We must not allow our creative protest to degenerate into physical violence. Again and again we must rise to the majestic heights of meeting physical force with soul force. The marvelous new militancy which has engulfed the Negro community must not lead us to a distrust of all white people, for many of our white brothers, as evidenced by their presence here today, have come to realize that their destiny is tied up with our destiny and they have come to realize that their freedom is inextricably bound to our freedom. We cannot walk alone.

And as we walk, we must make the pledge that we shall always march ahead. We cannot turn back. There are those who are asking the devotees of civil rights, "When will you be satisfied?" We can never be satisfied as long as the Negro is the victim of the unspeakable horrors of police brutality. We can never be satisfied as long as our bodies, heavy with the fatigue of travel, cannot gain lodging in the motels of the highways and the hotels of the cities. We cannot be satisfied as long as the Negro's basic mobility is from a smaller ghetto to a larger one.

We can never be satisfied as long as our children are stripped of their selfhood and robbed of their dignity by signs stating "for whites only." We cannot be satisfied as long as a Negro in Mississippi cannot vote and a Negro in New York believes he has nothing for which to vote. No, no we are not satisfied, and we will not be satisfied until justice rolls down like waters and righteousness like a mighty stream.

I am not unmindful that some of you have come here out of great trials and tribulation. Some of you have come fresh from narrow jail cells. Some of you have come from areas where your quest for freedom left you battered by the storms of persecution and staggered by the winds of police brutality. You have been the veterans of creative suffering. Continue to work with the faith that unearned suffering is redemptive.

Go back to Mississippi; go back to Alabama; go back to South Carolina; go back to Georgia; go back to Louisiana; go back to the slums and ghettos of our Northern cities, knowing that somehow this situation can, and will be changed. Let us not wallow in the valley of despair.

I say to you today, my friends, so even though we must face the difficulties of today and tomorrow, I still have a dream. It is a dream deeply rooted in the American dream. I have a dream that one day this nation will rise up and live out the true meaning of its creed—we hold these truths to be self evident, that all men are created equal. I have a dream that one day on the red hills of Georgia, sons of former slaves and the sons of former slave-owners will be able to sit down together at the table of brotherhood.

I have a dream that one day, even the state of Mississippi, a state sweltering with the heat of injustice, sweltering with the heat of oppression will be transformed into an oasis of freedom and justice. I have a dream that my four little children will one day live in a nation where they will not be judged by the color of their skin but by the content of their character. I have a dream today! I have a dream that one day, down in Alabama, with its vicious racists, with its governor having his lips dripping with the words of interposition and nullification, one day, right there in Alabama, little black boys and black girls will be able to join hands with little white boys and white girls as sisters and brothers. I have a dream today! I have a dream that one day every valley shall be exalted, every hill and mountain shall be made low, the rough places will be made plain, and the crooked places will be made straight and the glory of the Lord will be revealed and all flesh shall see it together.

This is our hope. This is the faith that I go back to the South with. With this faith we will be able to hew out of the mountain of despair, a stone of hope. With this faith we will be able to transform the jangling discords of our nation into a beautiful symphony of brotherhood. With this faith we will be able to work together, to pray together, to struggle together, to go to jail together, to stand up for freedom together, knowing that we will be free one day. This will be the day, this will be the day when all of God's children will be able to sing with new meaning—"my country 'tis of thee, sweet land of liberty, of thee I sing; land where my fathers died, land of the pilgrim's pride; from every mountain side, let freedom ring"—and if America is to be a great nation, this must become true.

So let freedom ring from the prodigious hilltops of New Hampshire. Let freedom ring from the mighty mountains of New York. Let freedom ring from the heightening Alleghenies of Pennsylvania. Let freedom ring from the snow-capped Rockies of Colorado. Let freedom ring from the curvaceous slopes of California. But not only that. Let freedom ring from Stone Mountain of Georgia. Let freedom ring from Lookout Mountain of Tennessee. Let freedom ring from every hill and molehill of Mississippi, from every mountain side, let freedom ring. And when this happens, and when we allow freedom [sic] ring, when we let it ring from every village and every hamlet, from every state and every city, we will be able to speed up that day when all of God's children— black men and white men, Jews and Gentiles, Protestants and Catholics—will be able to join hands and sing in the words of the old Negro spiritual, "Free at last, free at last; thank God Almighty, we are free at last."

MARTIN LUTHER KING'S
"I HAVE A DREAM"

From every hill and molehill . . . from every mountainside, let freedom ring.

CRITIC: Lloyd E. Rohler

To fully understand the significance of Martin Luther King's historic address, we must recall the position of blacks in American society in 1963. There was no national law forbidding discrimination in public places and only a few states and localities had statutes even approaching equality. black Americans faced the public humiliation of being refused service at any eating establishment from the most humble greasy spoon to the most expensive restaurant. Travel presented a special nightmare. With most hotels and motels closed to them, black Americans drove long distances with no guarantee of finding even minimal comforts along the way. Discrimination existed in all sections of the country. Even in the supposedly more tolerant Northern states, black Americans never knew when a restaurant owner, obeying his own or his customers' prejudices, might decide not to serve them. The situation in the Southern states was particularly demeaning. There, the aftermath of Reconstruction left a legacy of "Jim Crow" statutes that mandated segregation in all public facilities. Separate entrances and exits in public buildings and separate seating arrangements on buses and trains were accompanied by signs reading "whites only" and "colored." All these measures assaulted the spirit and reinforced the idea of second class citizenship. In Southern communities, public recreation areas such as ball parks, swimming pools, and tennis courts paid for with taxes collected in part from black citizens were forbidden to them. Discriminatory voting practices including excessively difficult literacy tests prevented most black Americans residing in Southern states from voting. Denied their rights, and denied the legal means to redress these wrongs, black Americans confronted a "shameful condition."

Many Americans joined with religious leaders, civil rights organizations and prominent black and white civic leaders in calling for an end to this demeaning system. The election of John F. Kennedy in 1960 brought hope to this coalition. Personally committed to equal rights for all Americans, Kennedy received crucial support from black voters particularly in Illinois in his narrow victory over Richard Nixon. Worried that a confrontation over civil rights legislation with the Southern Senators and Representatives who dominated the major committees in Congress would doom his legislative program, Kennedy temporized for two years. Finally forced by racial strife in the South to take action, Kennedy proposed legislation to outlaw discrimination in public accommodations in a nationally televised address on June 11, 1963. He told the nation:

> We are confronted with a moral issue. It is as old as the Scriptures and is as clear as the American Constitution. The heart of the question is whether all Americans are to be afforded equal rights and equal opportunities, whether we are going to treat our fellow Americans as we want to be treated.[1]

348

While the President may propose legislation; Congress enacts it into law. Although public opinion polls showed widespread support for the proposed legislation and a majority of both the House and the Senate favored it, passage was far from certain. A determined minority using Senate rules that permit unlimited debate had in the past and could again, "filibuster" or talk a civil rights bill to death. Southern Senators suddenly discovered a myriad of questions about the bill that—questions requiring extended examination and discussion. Civil rights leaders unwilling to see this excellent opportunity to pass a civil rights bill blocked by legislative maneuvers, decided on the counter strategy of staging a massive protest march to demonstrate the importance of the issue.

A massive march on Washington to demonstrate support for Civil rights legislation does not happen overnight. All through the summer of 1963, the organizers coped with the many details involved in such a vast undertaking. Working through sympathetic organizations such as the National Council of Churches and the United Automobile Workers Union, the leaders of the march assembled a coalition of over one hundred groups that not only supported the goals of the demonstration but contributed the necessary money and manpower to make it work. A staff or organizers chartered trains, buses and airplanes to bring people to Washington; arranged for food to feed them; established emergency medical facilities; provided for security; coordinated coverage by the mass media; and even installed a sound system so that the marchers could hear the speeches. Public response exceeded expectations. The organizers optimistically predicted a crowd of 100,000 people; over 200,000 actually came to Washington for the march.

The actual march was only a short walk down the mall from the Washington Monument to the steps of the Lincoln Memorial where entertainers and then speakers aroused the crowd. Peter, Paul, and Mary, Bob Dylan and Joan Baez sang folk songs; Mahalia Jackson sang hymns. A long list of speakers including Senator Hubert Humphrey, UAW leader Walter Reuther, NAACP President Roy Wilkins, Urban League President Whitney Young, and other notables addressed the crowd. Each was to speak for only five minutes but all of the speakers went overtime as the crowd basked in the sunshine, waded in the reflecting pool, and drifted away. It was almost 3:30 p.m. when A. Phillip Randolph introduced Martin Luther King as the "moral leader of our nation" and the crowd grown listless with the heat and the speeches came to life and gave King a rousing welcome.[2]

THE SPEAKER

It was no accident that Martin Luther King spoke in the position of honor at the March on Washington, for he had become to both black and white Americans the symbol of the movement for civil rights. Born on January 15, 1929, in Atlanta, Georgia, Martin Luther King, Jr. grew up in a comfortable middle class family. Religion and education were important influences in the life of a child with a Baptist minister for a father and a school teacher for a mother. A precocious child, Martin graduated from Morehouse College at the age of 19 determined to pursue a career as a minister. He entered Crozer Seminary in Chester, Pennsylvania, and in 1951 graduated at the head of his class, winning a fellowship for advanced study in theology. Graduate study in theology at Boston University profoundly changed his life by deepening his understanding of the thought of Mohandas Ghandi and introducing him to the person of

Coretta Scott whom he married in 1953. In 1954 he accepted the call of the Dexter Avenue Baptist Church in Montgomery, Alabama, to be their minister and served in that post until 1960. Shortly after his arrival in Montgomery, he became involved in the organization of the boycott against segregated buses. Elected President of the Montgomery Improvement Association, he became the chief spokesman for the black community during the boycott. He now discovered that he had been called to minister to more than the spiritual concerns of a single congregation and took the lead in organizing the Southern Christian Leadership Conference. The SCLC promoted direct non-violent action to desegregate public facilities throughout the South and to end discriminatory voting practices. Confrontations in Selma and Birmingham drew world wide attention to the racial situation in the South. King's life was threatened, his house was bombed, and he was often arrested and jailed. At the same time his eloquence and his commitment to non-violence won him numerous honors including *Time* magazines's designation as Man of the Year in 1963.

THE SPEECH

No speaker could wish for a more impressive setting for a speech. King spoke from the steps of the Lincoln Memorial facing a crowd of over 200,000 Americans that stretched before him around the reflecting pool and back toward the Washington Monument. In the distance he could see the dome of the Capitol Building; to his right, the Jefferson Monument; to his left, the approach to Key Bridge leading to Arlington National Cemetery.

King begins the speech with a reference to the magnificent setting and thus introduces the first major theme, the promise of the American Dream. He invokes the memory of Lincoln, the Great Emancipator, to contrast the historical promise of freedom with the present-day reality. The images that he uses, "a great beacon of light" and "joyous daybreak," underscore the bright promise of the dawn with the bleak reality of segregation, poverty, and exclusion from the mainstream of life. This theme is developed through the extended metaphor of a "check" or "promissory note" given to all Americans by the sacred symbols of our nation, the Founding Fathers, in the sacred texts of our land, the Declaration of Independence and the Constitution. These documents enshrine the promise of the American Dream of "life, liberty, and the pursuit of happiness." This promissory note which was given to all Americans has not been redeemed for citizens of color and thus it is necessary to remind white Americans of their sacred obligation to make it good.

King and his supporters have gathered at this "hallowed spot" to remind Americans not only of their obligation but of the "fierce urgency of now." In repeating the word "now" in the following sentences, he reminds the audience of how long the promise has awaited fulfillment. Again he uses images of movement and progress to indicate that the country should go "from the dark and desolate valley of segregation to the sunlit paths of racial justice" to make "justice a reality for all God's children." This phrase introduces a second theme that will be amplified throughout the rest of the speech— the brotherhood of man under the fatherhood of God. He does not directly develop that theme in this part of the speech but continues to discuss the "urgency of the moment" and to warn that "whirlwinds of revolt will continue to shake the foundation of our nation until the bright day of justice emerges." King is using the familiar carrot and stick strategy employed by many protest groups. He offers the carrot of "rest and tranquility" if the "Negro is granted his citizenship rights" but warns of renewed disturbance to "business as usual" if he is not. In keeping with his commitment to non-violence and peaceful protest, King warns his followers against violence and hatred of whites, but his praise of the "marvelous new militancy which has engulfed the Negro community" is an implicit warning that there are others, more militant than he, waiting to challenge his strategy and leadership if it is not successful. Again he appeals to unity, claiming that freedom is indivisible and reminding blacks and whites of their common destiny in a shared land.

The formal text of the speech released to the press before the March and representing King's prepared remarks ends with a catalogue of grievances and a reassurance that the situation will change. The grievances are specific examples of the general propositions asserted early in the speech. For example, police brutality is used to show that the lack of respect given to blacks as individuals makes them feel like exiles in their own land. King uses repetition of the word "satisfied" and parallel structure to build to a climactic conclusion using a quotation from one of his favorite Hebrew Prophets, Amos. On the videotape of the speech (Great Speeches, Volume I), the viewer can see King look up from the manuscript, accept the applause of the crowd, and seemingly inspired by the moment begin to extemporize using passages taken from previous speeches, commonplaces taken from the Declaration of Independence, passages from the Bible, patriotic songs, and old Negro spirituals. He weaves all this material into a mosaic of the American Dream with themes of peace and brotherhood and justice joining together to produce a "beautiful symphony of brotherhood" and national unity.

In this extemporized section of his speech, King is amplifying or expanding on the meaning of the American Dream using the traditional techniques of division, comparison, antithesis, progression, and accumulation. He begins by defining the American Dream as "all men are created equal" and dividing this basic concept into two parts; brotherhood and justice. He uses antithesis to compare the present with the promise of the future. He foresees the progression of Mississippi, a state "sweltering with the heat of injustice," into "an oasis of freedom and justice." He welcomes the day when his four little children will be judged not "by the color of their skin but by the content of their character." He further prophesies that even in the racially troubled state of Alabama, "little black boys and black girls will be able to join hands with little white boys and white girls as sisters and brothers."

He compares this dream of political and social change in America with a Biblical passage that uses antithetical phrasing to prophesy even greater change. He intimates that this is a logical progression of our common faith in the following passage which repeats the word "faith" four times in a series of antithetical sentences that contrast "a mountain of despair" with a "stone of hope," "jangling discords" with "a beautiful symphony," and ends in a series of phrases repeating and emphasizing the word "together." The repetition of the phrases and the rhythm of the words make a stirring refrain:

> With this faith we will be able to work together, to pray together, to struggle together, to go to jail together, to stand up for freedom together, knowing that we will be free one day.

Again, King turns to a commonplace—a memory that the entire audience shares as he repeats a stanza of "America." Now that he had divided the American Dream into its two components and expanded upon their meaning, he progresses to the last segment of his speech designed to promote absolute identification between the ideas and the audience. This last section is an excellent example of the use of "accumulation"—a heaping up of details as a means of expanding upon the meaning of the American Dream and achieving unity with all the diverse segments of the audience.

He repeats the closing line of the song, "Let Freedom Ring" and takes it as a refrain repeating it as he invokes the images of the American landscape from the East to the West; from the North to the South. The geographic unity of the land parallels the unity of the people in one vast brotherhood of humanity. In the climactic conclusion of his speech, he unites the themes of brotherhood and justice into a magnificent image of all Americans united in a free land. Utilizing emotional appeals, he brings his speech to a triumphant conclusion that proceeds from the idea of the American land—"every village and hamlet, every state and city," to the idea of brotherhood—"all of God's children, black, white, Jew, Gentile, Protestant, and Catholic"—to the idea of Freedom and the American Dream—"Free at last! Free at last! Thank God Almighty, we are free at last!"[3]

King's physical action is restrained throughout the speech. He relies on vocal inflections, pauses, and facial expressions to convey emphasis. Occasionally he turns his head from side to side or nods to emphasize a word or phrase. The voice is rather high pitched, sounding at times almost melancholy. During the first part of the speech he uses a text, and obviously looks to the text, to the audience and back to the text again. Throughout this process, he maintains good eye contact with the audience. When he comes to the "I have a dream" section, he is no longer reading from a text but extemporizing his lines. His manner becomes more animated and his gaze is more completely focused on the audience. His gestures are still somewhat restrained. Not until he denounces Governor George Wallace does he raise his hand above the lectern. From that movement on, he becomes totally involved in the speech. He casts his eyes to heaven when he recites the words to "America" as though looking up to God. When he calls for freedom to ring from the "curvaceous slopes of California" his eyes are looking skyward as if to see the very peaks themselves. As he gathers momentum for the final appeals for unity for all Americans, his face and body convey the energy and excitement of the ideas and his arms are raised in an inclusive gesture as though he is gathering all Americans into his grasp. When he reaches the climactic phrase "all of God's children," he dramatically throws his right hand upward and sweeps in an arc those gathered before him and symbolically all Americans who are included in his prayer for unity.

An experienced preacher, King knew the importance of preparing the audience for an emotional conclusion. Twice earlier in the speech, he aroused the emotions of the audience without permitting them the full satisfaction of releasing their pent up feelings. Very early in the speech, he used the repetition of the phrase, "now is the time," to bring the audience to an emotional plateau but he quickly shifted the mood to a somber discussion of the responsibilities of the protesters to avoid violence. After another passage using repetition and parallel structure to catalog the injustices suffered by black Americans, King aroused the audience by building to an emotional quotation from Amos, "we are not satisfied, and we will not be satisfied until justice rolls down like waters and righteousness like a mighty stream." In gradually engaging the emotions of the audience, King created the condition for a tremendous surge of feeling when he ended his speech with the climactic vision of all God's children joining together to celebrate the reality of the American Dream.

We see King frequently interrupted by applause. The tumultuous reaction of the crowd to his climatic plea to "Let freedom ring," stands today as one of the most electrifying rhetorical moments in recent history. When the leaders of the March met with President Kennedy afterward at the White House, the President greeted them warmly and, shaking hands with King, repeated the phrase, "I have a dream."[4]

The media reacted with universal praise. *Life* proclaimed King's speech, "the strongest of the day" and praised the March as "an astonishingly well executed product of leadership."[5] *Newsweek* said it was "the emotional crescendo of an emotional day."[6] *Time* proclaimed it as "triumph."[7] James Baldwin captured the overwhelming sentiment, "that day, for a moment, it almost seemed that we stood on a height and could see our inheritance."[8] Murray Kempton saw clearly the role that memory played in the speech when he wrote that, "the Negro moves us most when he touches our memory."[9]

Since that day, the speech has gradually been recognized as a classic American document—a statement of the vision of America shared by all her people. It has been widely reprinted in textbooks, reproduced on records, and often excerpted in televised documentaries. The words have become familiar to most Americans and many can recite a line from the "I have a dream," sequence.

The March passed into memory as one of the shining moments of the civil rights movement when black and white Americans stood together united in a vision of justice and brotherhood. It is difficult to assess the impact of either the speech or the March on the passage of the civil rights legislation. Shortly after that August day, President John F. Kennedy travelled to Dallas, Texas, where an assassin's bullet made him a martyr. President Johnson urged passage of the Civil Rights Bill as a tribute to the slain leader and signed the legislation into law on July 2, 1964. In King's words, the March on Washington "subpoenaed the conscience of a nation" and strengthened public sentiment favoring equal rights for all Americans.

EPILOGUE: "I'VE BEEN TO THE MOUNTAINTOP"

The March on Washington showed King's career approaching its zenith. The demonstration successfully captured public attention and King's speech masterfully interpreted the civil rights movement as an expression of American ideals. The following year would bring worldwide recognition with the awarding of the Nobel Prize, and immense satisfaction as first the Civil Rights Act of 1964 outlawing discrimination in public facilities and then the Voting Rights Act of 1965 giving federal protection to voting rights passed Congress. His tactic of non-violent protest dramatically changed a nation.

Unfortunately for King, the years from 1966 to 1968 were times of personal trials and public humiliation. The tactics that worked so well to desegregate public facilities in the South did not work as well against the more intractable problems of employment and housing in the Northern cities of Chicago and Detroit. His split with the Johnson administration over the Vietnam War cut him off from some of his oldest friends and allies and made an enemy of a vindictive President. Younger and more militant leaders such as Stokeley Carmichael, and H. Rap Brown shouted down his plea for non-violence and peaceful protest. When riots broke out in Los Angeles, Detroit, and Newark, King's anguish over the desperate situation in the urban areas grew apace with his recognition that he had little or no influence with the desperate people burning down their own neighborhoods. His own organization, the Southern Christian

Leadership Conference (SCLC), frequently could not pay its staff and he spent more and more of his time in endless fund raising activities shuttling back and forth across the country giving speeches and meeting with potential donors. The FBI increased its surveillance of him and his activities during this period, bugging his most intimate meetings and conversations and threatening to expose him for his numerous affairs. All of this took its toll on his personal life. He rarely saw his family, and he felt increasingly estranged from his wife. He was mentally and physically exhausted as he and the SCLC staff began planning for the Poor People's Campaign, an ambitious project to bring poor-people to Washington in an encampment to dramatize the desperate plight of the poor. If the March on Washington marks a time of triumph for King, his last days in Memphis represent a time of trial and testing. The passage of the Martin Luther King holiday with its glorification of King has almost obliterated from memory the despair of King's final days.[10]

In the midst of all the planning and fund raising for the Poor People's Campaign set to begin in the summer of 1968, King had no real reason to get involved in the Memphis sanitation workers' strike. He did so because of his inability to say no to a plea from an old friend, Reverend James Lawson, pastor of Centenary Methodist Church. King did not want to become involved, but agreed that during his upcoming visit to Mississippi to recruit for the Poor People's campaign he would stop off in Memphis for a speech and a rally for the strikers.

The strike began on February 12, 1968, when because of bad weather, a supervisor sent 22 black sanitation workers home without pay while white employees were kept at work with pay. The 1300 members of the American Federation of State, County, and Municipal Employees Local 173 walked out and vowed not to return until the city recognized the union. Mayor James Loeb not only refused to recognize the union but, charging the members with violating a no strike local ordinance, threatened to dismiss them unless they returned to work immediately. What began as a labor dispute turned into a confrontation between the white elected officials of Memphis and the almost entirely black union after police attacked a march by sanitation workers with clubs and tear gas.[11]

On March 18, 1968, King flew into a Memphis that had all the potential to explode into violence. He and Andy Young were met at the airport by Reverend James Lawson and taken to Mason Temple where he spoke to a crowd of 15,000. After King's speech, Lawson and Jerry Wurf, the National President of AFSCME, asked King if he would return to Memphis to lead a march to dramatize the strikers' demands. King agreed to return after his Mississippi tour. When King returned 10 days later, he and Rev. Lawson led a march from the Clayborn Temple AME Church to City Hall through the down town business district. The march started late, and was poorly organized with the parade marshals who were to maintain order grouped near the head of the line and a group of unruly teenagers bringing up the rear. As the marchers moved down Beale Street violence erupted at the rear of the line as some of the teenagers threw long wooden sticks that had been supporting placards through the windows of businesses. When police reinforcements arrived with orders to disperse the crowd, they attacked the peaceful marchers at the front as well as the hoodlums at the back. At the first sounds of violence, Ralph Abernathy and Rev. Lawson flagged down a car and hustled King away from the scene.

The violent end to the march deeply disturbed King. In the past whenever violence occurred during one of his demonstrations it was not the marchers who started it but hecklers or even the police themselves. King told Abernathy, "maybe we just have to admit that the day of violence is here...the nation won't listen to our voice—maybe it'll hear the voice of violence."[12] The media response to the march only depressed King more. The Memphis *Commercial Appeal* ridiculed King for taking "off at high speed" when the violence broke out "instead of trying...to stop it." Even the New York *Times* warned that the Memphis riot did not bode well for the success of the Poor People's Campaign.[13] When King who had retreated to Atlanta for the weekend held an SCLC staff meeting, he recommended that SCLC staffers personally organize a second march to show that a non-violent demonstration was possible. When his own staff argued against returning to Memphis, King's despair grew. Stomping out of the meeting he ordered the staff to proceed with the plans.

On Wednesday Morning, April 9, King flew back to Memphis only to learn that the City had obtained an injunction preventing any march during the next ten days. Most of King's day was spent in meetings with lawyers seeking to modify the injunction and with local leaders trying to plan for a successful march. A meeting was planned for the Mason Temple that night but rainy weather kept the crowd down. Ralph Abernathy volunteered to go in King's place so that he could get some much needed rest. When Abernathy arrived, he found only 2000 people present in the vast hall where King had two weeks before spoken to 15,000. Though small, the crowd seemed in high spirits. Abernathy decided to call King and urged him to come over and speak. King agreed. Thus the stage was set for his climatic "I've Been to the Mountaintop" speech, his last before he was assassinated the following day.[14] We conclude our book with the transcript of this emotional address.

NOTES

1. John F. Kennedy, "Television Address to the People, June 11, 1963" in Allan Nevins, ed. *The Burden and The Glory*, (New York: Harper & Row, 1964), p. 182.
2. Accounts of the March are contained in *Life*, August 23, 1963 and September 6, 1963; *Newsweek*, September 9, 1963; *Time*, August 30, 1963.
3. The complete text of the King speech appears in this book.
4. Oates, p. 262.
5. *Life*, September 6, 1963, p. 22.
6. *Newsweek*, September 9, 1963, p. 13.
7. *Time*, September 6, 1963, p. 13.
8. Oates, *Ibid.*, P. 262.
9. *New Republic*, September 11, 1963, p. 20.
10. David J. Garrow, Bearing the Cross, Martin Luther King, Jr., and the Southern Christian Leadership Conference, (New York: Morrow, 1986). I have used this as a source for most of the information on King's life and the Memphis strike.
11. *Ibid.*, p. 604ff.
12. *Ibid.*, p. 612.
13. *Ibid.*, p. 615.
14. *Ibid.*, p. 620.

"I'VE BEEN TO THE MOUNTAINTOP"

Martin Luther King, Jr.

Mason Temple, Memphis, Tennessee, April 3, 1968 (Transcribed from excerpts on the video, GREAT SPEECHES, VOLUME VI)

.... Something is happening in Memphis, something is happening in our world. And you know, if I were standing at the beginning of time with the possibility of taking a kind of general and panoramic view of the whole of human history up to now, and the Almighty said to me, "Martin Luther King, which age would you like to live in?" I would take my mental flight by Egypt, and I would watch God's children in their magnificent trek from the dark dungeons of Egypt through—or rather across—the Red Sea through the wilderness on toward the Promised Land, and in spite of its magnificence I wouldn't stop there. I would move on by Greece and take my mind to Mt. Olympus, and I would see Plato, Aristotle, Socrates, Euripides and Aristophanes assemble around the Parthenon, and I would watch them around the Parthenon as they discussed the great and eternal issues of reality, but I wouldn't stop there.... I would come on up even to 1863, and watch a vacillating President by the name of Abraham Lincoln finally come to the conclusion that he had to sign the Emancipation Proclamation, but I wouldn't stop there. I would even come up to the early 'thirties, and see a man grappling with the problems of the bankruptcy of his nation, and come with an eloquent cry that "We have nothing to fear but fear itself," but I wouldn't stop there. Strangely enough I would turn to the Almighty and say, "If you allow me to live just a few years in the second half of the Twentieth Century, I will be happy."

Now that's a strange statement to make because the world is all messed up, the nation is sick, trouble is in the land, confusion all around. That's a strange statement. But I know somehow that only when it is dark enough can you see the stars.... Something is happening in our world. The masses of people are rising up, and wherever they are assembled today, whether they are in Johannesburg, South Africa; Nairobi, Kenya; Accra, Ghana; New York City; Atlanta, Georgia; Jackson, Mississippi; or Memphis, Tennessee, the cry is always the same: "We want to be free!"

.... Men for years now have been talking about war and peace but now no longer can they just talk about it. It is no longer the choice between violence and nonviolence in this world, it's nonviolence or nonexistence. That is where we are today. {And} also in the human rights revolution, if something isn't done and done in a hurry to bring the colored peoples of the world out of their long years of poverty, their long years of hurt and neglect, the whole world is doomed. Now I'm just happy that God has allowed me to live in this period, to see what is unfolding, and I'm happy that He has allowed me to be in Memphis.

.... Now what does all of this mean in this great period of history? It means that we've got to stay together. We've got to stay together and maintain unity....

The issue is the refusal of Memphis to be fair and honest in its dealings with its public servants who happen to be sanitation workers. Now we've got to keep attention on that. That's always the problem with a little violence. You know what happened the other day, and the press dealt only with the window-breaking. I read the articles. They very seldom got around to mentioning the fact that one thousand three hundred sanitation workers are on strike, and that Memphis is not being fair to them, and that Mayor Loeb is in dire need of a doctor. They didn't get around to that.

Now we're gonna march again and we've gotta march again in order to put the issue where it is supposed to be, and force everybody to see that there are thirteen hundred of God's children here suffering, sometimes goin' hungry, going through dark and dreary nights wondering how this thing is gonna come out. That's the issue....

We aren't going to let any mace stop us. We are masters in our nonviolent movement in disarming police forces. They don't know what to do. I've seen them so often. I remember, in Birmingham, Alabama, when we were in that majestic struggle there, we would move out of the 16th Street Baptist Church day after day. By the hundreds we would move out, and Bull Connor would tell them to send the dogs forth, and they did come. But we just went before the dogs singing, "Ain't gonna let nobody turn me around."....

We are going on. We need all of you. ....

This is what we have to do.

Now the other thing we'll have to do is this: Always anchor our external direct action with the power of economic withdrawal. Now we are poor people. Individually, we are poor when you compare us with white society in America. We are poor. Never stop...forget that collectively, that means all of us together, collectively we are richer than all the nations in the world with the exception of nine....

We don't have to argue with anybody. We don't have to curse and go around acting bad with our words. We don't need any bricks and bottles. We don't need any Molotov cocktails. We just need to go around to these stores, and to these massive industries in our country and say, "God sent us by here to say to you that you're not treating His children right. And we come by here to ask you to make the first item on your agenda fair treatment where God's children are concerned. Now if you are not prepared to do that we do have an agenda that we must follow. And our agenda calls for withdrawing economic support from you."

So as the result of this we are asking you tonight to go out and tell your neighbors not to buy Coca Cola in Memphis. Go by and tell them not to buy Sealtest milk, tell them not to buy—what is the other bread?—Wonder bread. What is the other bread, Brother Jesse? Tell them not to buy Hart's bread. As Jesse Jackson has said, "Up to now only the garbage men have been feeling pain. Now we must kind of redistribute the pain." We are choosing these companies because they haven't been fair in their hiring policies, and we are choosing them because they can begin the process of saying they are going to support the needs and the rights of these men who are on strike, and then they can move on downtown and tell Mayor Loeb to do what is right. ....

Now these are some practical things that we can do. We begin the process of building a greater economic base, and at the same time we are putting pressure where it really hurts. And I ask you to follow through here.

Now let me say as I move to my conclusion that we've got to give ourselves to this struggle until the end. Nothing would be more tragic than to stop at this point in Memphis. We've got to see it through.... Let us develop a kind of dangerous unselfishness. ....

That's the question before you tonight. Not, "If I stop to help the sanitation workers, what will happen to my job?" Not, "If I stop to help the sanitation workers, what will happen to all of the hours that I usually spend in my office every day and every week as a pastor?" The question is not, "If I stop to help this man in need, what will happen to me?" The question is, "If I do *not* stop to help the sanitation workers, what will happen to them?" That's the question. ....

You know, several years ago I was in New York City, autographing the first book that I had written. And while sitting there autographing books, a demented black woman came up, and the only question I heard from her was, "Are you Martin Luther King?" And I was looking down writing, and I said, "Yes." The next minute I felt something beating on my chest. Before I knew it, I had been stabbed by this demented woman....It was a dark Saturday afternoon. And that blade had gone through, and the X-rays revealed that the tip of the blade was on the edge on my aorta, the main artery, and once that's punctured you drown in your own blood. That's the end of you. It came out in the New York *Times* the next morning that if I had merely sneezed, I would have died....

I want to say tonight...I want to say tonight that I too am happy that I didn't sneeze, because if I had sneezed I wouldn't have been around here in 1960 when students all over the South started siting in at lunch counters.... If I had sneezed I wouldn't have been around here in 1961 when we decided to take a ride for freedom and ended segregation in interstate travel. If I had sneezed I wouldn't have been around here in 1962 when Negroes in Albany, Georgia, decided to straighten their backs up. And whenever men and women straighten their backs up they are going somewhere because a man can't ride you back unless it is bent. If I had sneezed...if I had sneezed I wouldn't have been here in 1963, when the black people of Birmingham, Alabama, aroused the conscience of this nation and brought into being the civil rights bill. If I had sneezed, I wouldn't have had a chance later that year in August to try to tell America about a dream that I had had. If I had sneezed, I wouldn't have been down in Selma, Alabama, to see the great movement there. If I had sneezed, I wouldn't have been in Memphis to see a community rally around those brothers and sisters who are suffering. I'm so happy that I didn't sneeze.

And they were telling me, Now it doesn't matter now. It really doesn't matter what happens now. I left Atlanta this morning, and as we got started on the plane—there were six of us—the pilot said over the public address system, "We are sorry for the delay, but we have Dr. Martin Luther King on the plane, and to be sure that all of the bags were checked and to be sure that nothing would be wrong on the plane, we had to check out everything carefully, and we've had the plane protected and guarded all night."

And then I got into Memphis, and some began to say the threats, or talk about the threats that were out of what would happen to me from some of our sick white brothers. Well, I don't know what will happen now. We've got some difficult days ahead. But it really doesn't matter with me now because I've been to the mountaintop. And I don't mind. Like anybody I would like to live a long life. Longevity has its place, but I'm not concerned about that now. I just want to do God's will, and He's allowed me to go up to the mountain, and I've looked over and I've seen the Promised Land. I may not get there with you, but I want you to know tonight that we as a people will get to the Promised Land. So I'm happy tonight, I'm not worried about anything, I'm not fearing any man. Mine eyes have seen the glory of the coming of the Lord.